Geocriticism and Spatial Literary Studies

Series Editor
Robert T. Tally Jr.
Texas State University
San Marcos, TX, USA

Geocriticism and Spatial Literary Studies is a new book series focusing on the dynamic relations among space, place, and literature. The spatial turn in the humanities and social sciences has occasioned an explosion of innovative, multidisciplinary scholarship in recent years, and geocriticism, broadly conceived, has been among the more promising developments in spatially oriented literary studies. Whether focused on literary geography, cartography, geopoetics, or the spatial humanities more generally, geocritical approaches enable readers to reflect upon the representation of space and place, both in imaginary universes and in those zones where fiction meets reality. Titles in the series include both monographs and collections of essays devoted to literary criticism, theory, and history, often in association with other arts and sciences. Drawing on diverse critical and theoretical traditions, books in the Geocriticism and Spatial Literary Studies series disclose, analyze, and explore the significance of space, place, and mapping in literature and in the world.

More information about this series at
http://www.palgrave.com/gp/series/15002

Kristina Malmio • Kaisa Kurikka
Editors

Contemporary Nordic Literature and Spatiality

palgrave
macmillan

Editors
Kristina Malmio
University of Helsinki
Helsinki, Finland

Kaisa Kurikka
University of Turku
Turku, Finland

Geocriticism and Spatial Literary Studies
ISBN 978-3-030-23352-5   ISBN 978-3-030-23353-2   (eBook)
https://doi.org/10.1007/978-3-030-23353-2

© The Editor(s) (if applicable) and The Author(s) 2020. This book is an open access publication.
Open Access This book is licensed under the terms of the Creative Commons Attribution 4.0 International License (http://creativecommons.org/licenses/by/4.0/), which permits use, sharing, adaptation, distribution and reproduction in any medium or format, as long as you give appropriate credit to the original author(s) and the source, provide a link to the Creative Commons licence and indicate if changes were made.

The images or other third party material in this book are included in the book's Creative Commons licence, unless indicated otherwise in a credit line to the material. If material is not included in the book's Creative Commons licence and your intended use is not permitted by statutory regulation or exceeds the permitted use, you will need to obtain permission directly from the copyright holder.

The use of general descriptive names, registered names, trademarks, service marks, etc. in this publication does not imply, even in the absence of a specific statement, that such names are exempt from the relevant protective laws and regulations and therefore free for general use.
The publisher, the authors and the editors are safe to assume that the advice and information in this book are believed to be true and accurate at the date of publication. Neither the publisher nor the authors or the editors give a warranty, express or implied, with respect to the material contained herein or for any errors or omissions that may have been made. The publisher remains neutral with regard to jurisdictional claims in published maps and institutional affiliations.

Cover illustration: Piotr Krzeslak / shutterstock.com

This Palgrave Macmillan imprint is published by the registered company Springer Nature Switzerland AG
The registered company address is: Gewerbestrasse 11, 6330 Cham, Switzerland

Series Editor's Preface

The spatial turn in the humanities and social sciences has occasioned an explosion of innovative, multidisciplinary scholarship. Spatially oriented literary studies, whether operating under the banner of literary geography, literary cartography, geophilosophy, geopoetics, geocriticism, or the spatial humanities more generally, have helped to reframe or transform contemporary criticism by focusing attention, in various ways, on the dynamic relations among space, place, and literature. Reflecting upon the representation of space and place, whether in the real world, in imaginary universes or in those hybrid zones where fiction meets reality, scholars and critics working in spatial literary studies are helping to reorient literary criticism, history, and theory. *Geocriticism and Spatial Literary Studies* is a book series presenting new research in this burgeoning field of inquiry.

In exploring such matters as the representation of place in literary works, the relations between literature and geography, the historical transformation of literary and cartographic practices, and the role of space in critical theory, among many others, geocriticism and spatial literary studies have also developed interdisciplinary or transdisciplinary methods and practices, frequently making productive connections to architecture, art history, geography, history, philosophy, politics, social theory, and urban studies, to name but a few. Spatial criticism is not limited to the spaces of the so-called real world, and it sometimes calls into question any too facile a distinction between real and imaginary places, as it frequently investigates what Edward Soja has referred to as the "real-and-imagined" places we experience in literature as in life. Indeed, although a great deal of important research has been devoted to the literary representation of certain identifiable and well-known places (e.g., Dickens's London, Baudelaire's Paris, or Joyce's Dublin), spatial critics have also explored the otherworldly spaces of literature, such as those to be found in myth, fantasy, science fiction, video games, and cyberspace. Similarly, such criticism is interested in the relationship between spatiality and such different media or genres as film or television, music, comics, computer programs, and other forms that may supplement, compete with, and potentially problematize literary representation. Titles in the *Geocriticism and Spatial Literary Studies* series include both monographs and collections of essays devoted to literary criticism, theory, and history, often in association with other arts and sciences. Drawing on diverse critical and theoretical traditions, books in the series reveal, analyze, and explore the significance of space, place, and mapping in literature and in the world.

The concepts, practices, or theories implied by the title of this series are to be understood expansively. Although geocriticism and spatial literary studies represent a relatively new area of critical and scholarly investigation, the historical roots of spatial criticism extend well beyond the recent past, informing present and future work. Thanks to a growing critical awareness of spatiality, innovative research into the literary geography of real and imaginary places has helped to shape historical and cultural studies in ancient, medieval, early modern, and modernist literature, while a discourse of spatiality undergirds much of what is still understood as the postmodern condition. The suppression of distance by modern technology, transportation, and telecommunications has only enhanced the sense of place, and of displacement, in the age of globalization. Spatial criticism examines literary representations not only of places themselves but also of the experience of place and of displacement, while exploring the interrelations between lived experience and a more abstract or unrepresentable spatial network that subtly or directly shapes it. In sum, the work being done in geocriticism and spatial literary studies, broadly conceived, is diverse and far reaching. Each volume in this series takes seriously the mutually impressive effects of space or place and artistic representation, particularly as these effects manifest themselves in works of literature. By bringing the spatial and geographical concerns to bear on their scholarship, books in the *Geocriticism and Spatial Literary Studies* series seek to make possible different ways of seeing literary and cultural texts, to pose novel questions for criticism and theory, and to offer alternative approaches to literary and cultural studies. In short, the series aims to open up new spaces for critical inquiry.

San Marcos, TX, USA   Robert T. Tally Jr.

Preface and Acknowledgments

In this volume we study the storied spaces of contemporary Nordic literature. *Contemporary Nordic Literature and Spatiality* elaborates on the ways spaces become stories and strives to understand the spaces created by the profound and complex interconnectedness of all things. The North, interpreted as a special thickening of space, is the meeting point of all the stories told in it.

In *For Space* (2005), geographer Doreen Massey urges us to renew our spatial imagination in order to properly meet the challenge that the inherent spatiality of the world presents. This is the important task of our volume. Massey's suggestion includes geography as well as fiction, and they both involve moments of imagination, inventing and telling stories about space. Viewing contemporary Nordic literature from the perspective of spatiality, we ask "What kind of spaces and places does contemporary Nordic literature depict, create, invent, and deconstruct after the spatial turn?"

Even this book is a spatial story: one of its tracks leads back to the lecture hall of the Society of Swedish Literature in Finland situated in the Kronohagen area of downtown Helsinki. Here, up "North," the research project *Late Modern Spatiality in Finland-Swedish Prose 1990–2010* organized a two-day seminar in February 2016 with invited guests from various Nordic countries to discuss spatiality in contemporary Nordic literature.

We would like to express our gratitude to all the scholars who attended our seminar and all our contributors who joined us in this volume. Thanks to the Society of Swedish Literature in Finland, whose generous financial support gave us time to deepen our insights in spatial studies. Thanks also to the Faculty of Humanities at the University of Helsinki and the Department of Finnish, Finno-Ugrian, and Scandinavian Studies for the possibility to publish an Open Access volume. Thanks to the fourth floor in Metsätalo ("The Forest House") university building, called Nordica, for spaces and places of work and meeting with colleagues. We thank the other project members Julia Tidigs and Hanna Lahdenperä for invigorating discussions around spatiality and for hilarious company after working hours in the nearby restaurants. We would also like to express our gratitude to our publisher in New York, Palgrave Macmillan, for their assistance with this volume. Many volumes from the "Geocriticism and Spatial Literary Studies" series have been discussed at our meetings, and the chance to contribute to the series makes us thrilled.

We wish to dedicate this book to two Nordic places, Vangsö and Putikko, that are the spaces of many wonderful stories, intensive moments of presence, and a deep understanding of what "here" means. The happy and inspirational stories connected to these spaces about how my mother met my father, how my grand grandfather bought a villa, or how my grandfather won on lottery, how my father built the cottage and its sauna, all are interconnected to the story of this volume.

Helsinki, Finland Kristina Malmio
Turku, Finland Kaisa Kurikka

Contents

1 Introduction: Storied Spaces of Contemporary Nordic Literature 1
Kristina Malmio and Kaisa Kurikka

Part I Whose Place Is This Anyway? On the Social Uses of Space and Power 23

2 On the Commons: A Geocritical Reading of *Amager Fælled* 25
Elisabeth Friis

3 Mapping a Postmodern Dystopia: Hassan Loo Sattarvandi's Construction of a Swedish Suburb 55
Cristine Sarrimo

4 Living Side by Side in an Individualized Society: Home, Place, and Social Relations in Late Modern Swedish-Language Picturebooks 79
Kristina Hermansson

| Part II | Where Do You Feel? Spaces, Emotions, and Technology | 101 |

5 Love, Longing, and the Smartphone: Lena Andersson, Vigdis Hjorth, and Hanne Ørstavik   103
   Christian Refsum

6 "Never Give Up Hopelessness!?": Emotions and Spatiality in Contemporary Finnish Experimental Poetry   121
   Anna Helle

| Part III | Which Language Do You Use? Spaces of Language and Text | 147 |

7 Stavanger, Pre- and Postmodern: Øyvind Rimbereid's Poetry and the Tradition of Topographic Verse   149
   Hadle Oftedal Andersen

8 The Poetics of Blank Spaces and Intervals in Selected Works of Elisabeth Rynell   169
   Antje Wischmann

9 What Have They Done to My Song? Recycled Language in Monika Fagerholm's *The American Girl*   185
   Julia Tidigs

| Part IV | Is This a Possible Space? Potentialities of Space | 209 |

10 "A Geo-ontological Thump": Ontological Instability and the Folding City in Mikko Rimminen's Early Prose   211
    Lieven Ameel

11 Uncanny Spaces of Transformation: Fabulations of the Forest in Finland-Swedish Prose   231
    Kaisa Kurikka

12 "The World in a Small Rectangle": Spatialities in Monika Fagerholm's Novels 257
Hanna Lahdenperä

13 The Miracle of the Mesh: Global Imaginary and Ecological Thinking in Ralf Andtbacka's *Wunderkammer* 277
Kristina Malmio

Index 301

Notes on Contributors

Lieven Ameel is Turku Institute for Advanced Studies (TIAS) researcher at the University of Turku, Finland, with an affiliation in Comparative Literature. He holds a Ph.D. in Comparative Literature and Finnish Literature from Justus Liebig University (JLU) Giessen and the University of Helsinki and is a docent in urban studies and planning methods at the Tampere University of Technology. He is the co-editor of the Palgrave Series in Literary Urban Studies. Recent publications include *Helsinki in Early Twentieth-Century Literature* (2018) and the co-edited *Literature and the Peripheral City* (2015) and *Literary Second Cities* (2017).

Hadle Oftedal Andersen is an adjunct professor and University Lecturer in Norwegian Language at the University of Helsinki, Finland. Andersen is a reviewer in *Klassekampen*, Norway, and has written extensively on Nordic literature, especially poetry.

Elisabeth Friis is Associate Professor of Comparative Literature at Lund University, Sweden. She has written several articles and books on ancient and contemporary poetry. Research interests include multilingual poetry, ecopoetics, the theory of poetic tropes, and posthumanist reading strategies. Her latest book is *Narrating Life: Experiments with Human and Animal Bodies in Literature, Science and Art* (2016). She is a member of the executive board of European Society for Literature, Science and the Arts (SLSA) Europe and a former editor of the peer-reviewed journal *Kritik*. Her current research project (co-run with Karin Nykvist), funded by The Swedish Research Council, is "Multilingualism in Contemporary Nordic Literature."

Anna Helle holds the title of docent in Finnish Literature at the University of Helsinki, Finland. She works at the University of Turku, Finland, as a university teacher. She received her Ph.D. in Literature at the University of Jyväskylä in 2009. Helle specializes in contemporary Finnish literature (both prose and poetry), often from the viewpoint of emotions, affects, and affectivity. She is also interested in experimentalism in literature.

Kristina Hermansson is Senior Lecturer in Comparative Literature at the University of Gothenburg, Sweden, and specializes in children's fiction. Her latest research publications are focused on contemporary Scandinavian picture books and norm critical children's literature. She is also involved in a literary research project on Gothenburg.

Kaisa Kurikka is a researcher and an adjunct professor in the School of History, Culture, and Arts Studies at the University of Turku, Finland. She holds a Ph.D. in Finnish Literature and is a docent in Finnish Literature at the University of Turku. She has specialized in early twentieth-century literature and in contemporary prose written both in Finnish and in Swedish. Her areas of interest are authorship studies, experimental prose fiction, posthumanism, and Deleuzian new materialism. As a member of the research project "Late Modern Spatiality in Finland-Swedish Prose 1990–2010" (2014–2017), Kurikka has also specialized in spatial literary studies. She has edited and co-edited several volumes, and written widely on Finnish literature.

Hanna Lahdenperä is finishing her doctoral dissertation *"En fullt tillräcklig filosofisk kommentar till världen." Om Monika Fagerholms Diva och den filosofiska läsningen* ("A Fully Adequate Philosophical Comment on the World. On Monika Fagerholm's *Diva* and Philosophical Reading"). Her research interests include feminist theory, postmodernism, and literature and philosophy. She is part of the research project "Tove Jansson's Productions" based at University of Oulu and funded by the Kone Foundation, and she has previously worked on the research project "Late Modern Spatiality in Finland-Swedish Prose 1990–2010" funded by Society of Swedish Literature in Finland.

Kristina Malmio is University Lecturer in Nordic Literature at the Department of Finnish, Finno-Ugrian, and Scandinavian Studies at the University of Helsinki, Finland. She was the leader of the research project "Late Modern Spatiality in Finland-Swedish Prose 1990–2010" funded by Society of Swedish Literature in Finland (2014–2017). Malmio specializes in Finland-Swedish literature, modern and postmodern literature, literary spatiality, and sociology of literature. Recent publications include the co-edited volumes *Values of Literature* (2015) and *Novel Districts: Critical Readings on Monika Fagerholm* (2016). She is the former member of the Nordic Council Literary Prize Committee and has several positions of trust in research organizations in Finland and Sweden.

Christian Refsum is Professor of Comparative Literature at the Department of Literature, Area Studies and European Languages, Faculty of Humanities, University of Oslo, Norway. He has written articles and books on the lyric, film, and literary translation. His latest book is *Kjærlighet som religion. Lidenskap og lengsel i film og litteratur på 2000-tallet*, Universitetsforlaget 2016 ("Love as Religion: Passion and Longing in the Film and Literature of the 2000s"). He has co-edited and contributed to *Living Together—Roland Barthes, the Individual and the Community*, Transcript Verlag 2018. He is also a published author of fiction and poetry.

Cristine Sarrimo is Associate Professor of Literary Studies, and Head of Literary, Film and Theatre studies and Creative Writing at the Centre for Languages and Literature, Lund University, Sweden. She does research on migration and space in contemporary literature, life writing, cultural journalism, and literary public spheres. She is finishing a book on bestselling autobiographies.

Julia Tidigs specializes in Literary Multilingualism Studies at the University of Helsinki, Finland. After receiving her Ph.D. in 2014 with a dissertation where literary multilingualism is investigated theoretically and methodologically as well as in the context of late nineteenth-century and early twentieth-century Finland-Swedish prose, Tidigs has written extensively on literary multilingualism and linguistic heterogeneity in connection to, for example, spatiality, multimodality, and questions of readership. A member of the research projects "Late Modern Spatiality in Finland-Swedish Prose 1990–2010" (2014–2017) and "Multilingualism in Contemporary Literature in Finland" (2014–2016), Tidigs' current research focuses on accent and acoustics in contemporary Swedish-language poetry and fiction.

Antje Wischmann is Professor of Scandinavian Literature and Culture at Universität Wien, Austria, since 2014; an associate professor at Humboldt-Universität Berlin and Universität Tübingen, 2006–2014; and a senior researcher at Södertörn University in Stockholm, 1998–2006. She is the author of *Verdichtete Stadtwahrnehmung. Untersuchungen zum literarischen und urbanistichen Diskurs in Skandinavien 1955–95* (2003; "On the Perception of Scandinavian Cities"), and has written widely on contemporary Scandinavian literature.

List of Figures

Fig. 4.1	Linda Bondestam's illustration in *Milja och grannarna* (2006), by Annika Sandelin and Linda Bondestam	85
Fig. 4.2	Eva Lindström's illustration in *Sonja, Boris och tjuven* (2007)	88
Fig. 4.3	Emma Adbåge's illustration in *Tilly som trodde att...* (2014), by Eva Staaf and Emma Adbåge	95
Fig. 6.1	Eino Santanen's artwork "TUNNESETELI / X20602643123", part 1/2 in *Tekniikan maailmat* (Santanen 2014, 30)	135
Fig. 6.2	Eino Santanen's artwork "L24680445062 TUNNISTAA", part 1/2 in *Tekniikan maailmat* (Santanen 2014, 32)	136
Fig. 6.3	Eino Santanen's artwork "L24680445062 TUNNISTAA", part 2/2 in *Tekniikan maailmat* (Santanen 2014, 32)	137

CHAPTER 1

Introduction: Storied Spaces of Contemporary Nordic Literature

Kristina Malmio and Kaisa Kurikka

"Every story is a travel story—a spatial practice." This sentence by Michel de Certeau (1988, 115) states the starting point of this volume, which traces the spatial tracks and trails of contemporary Nordic literature in order to map the imaginative geographies of the region. Moving from Danish to Swedish fiction, from Finnish to Norwegian literature, *Contemporary Nordic Literature and Spatiality* invests both in describing the specific cartographies of recent Nordic fiction and in fabricating methodological and conceptual ways of studying its spatial practices.

The citation by de Certeau refers to his book, *The Practice of Everyday Life*, and especially its chapter titled "Spatial Stories." Like de Certeau and several advocates of literary spatial studies, this book also underlines the importance of spatial features relating to settings, locations, orientations, or textual spatiality. Literature is as much spatial as it is temporal. In addition to the idea of literature as a spatial story, we wish to suggest another

K. Malmio (✉)
University of Helsinki, Helsinki, Finland

K. Kurikka
University of Turku, Turku, Finland

© The Author(s) 2020
K. Malmio, K. Kurikka (eds.), *Contemporary Nordic Literature and Spatiality*, Geocriticism and Spatial Literary Studies,
https://doi.org/10.1007/978-3-030-23353-2_1

notion, namely *storied spaces*. Fiction does not merely narrate spatial stories nor offer poetic spatial dimensions, it also sets spatiality into motion by stratifying spaces and places in multiple layers of meanings: spaces become literally storied—and stored—in fiction. This volume argues that the storied spaces of contemporary Nordic literature are filled with complexities which also point to the interconnectedness of space.

To explain this argument we proceed by making a story of a space outside fiction. The travel story highlighting many aspects of spatiality begins on the highway leading toward the Finnish southwestern archipelago. The road marks the beginning of the Archipelago trail, a 250-kilometer circular route starting from the city of Turku, and leading to Baltic Sea sceneries. The route is a tourist attraction targeted to lure nature enthusiasts, cyclists, and motorists. Traveling along this road one cannot miss a roadside sign announcing in Swedish "Livet är lokalt," that is "Life is local." Whether traveling by car, cycling, or walking, one can stop at the billboard to ponder on its surprising presence in the middle of a sparsely populated rural area with houses and farms scattered here and there besides the flat cornfields or some groups of spruce. This spatial element made of wood and steel astonishes passers-by and causes a series of affects to arise in them, varying from anger to amusement. This is an example of the ways spaces become storied and how they carry many layers of meanings that point to the affective forces of spatiality, the ways in which spaces are perceived, as well as the means by which spaces enter into a dialogue with historical, cultural, economic, and ecological perspectives. The chapters of this volume deal with all these issues.

The billboard provokes the traveler to think about the ways a cultural artifact has entered natural surroundings as if it was an example of *nature-culture*, a term coined by Donna Haraway (e.g., 2008) to denote how things and creatures categorized either as "natural" or as "cultural" are indeed intertwined and mingled. The eyes of the traveler sharpen on the white letters announcing the "locality of life"; the text resembles handwritten text which is resting on the red background. Then the eyes move to the other side of the sign and focus on the yellow background with the letters ÅU, which make the traveler realize that the billboard is actually an advertisement for *Åbo Underrättelser* (Åbo News), the oldest Finnish newspaper still in print since its first issue dating back to January 3, 1824. This realization combines a historical layer to capitalist undertones; the logics and strategies of late modern capitalist consumer culture have entered the Finnish countryside through the backdoor with this billboard that refers both to harmonious lifestyles and to a plea to subscribe to the newspaper and pay for more information about local life. Advertising a local Swedish-language newspaper in this setting is a sign of the logics of capitalist marketing strategies to profit from ever-increasing environmental awareness. After all, the tourists, who have traveled here to enjoy the unique natural environment of the archipelago, might be disturbed by the billboard, while the inhabitants of the area either subscribe to the newspaper or are at least aware of its existence. To summarize, this single spatial element, the billboard and its surrounding milieu, bring together the emblematic features of recent Nordic literature in terms of spatiality: the stratification of historical layers with contemporary issues, such as consumer capitalism and ecological thinking, the relationships between rurality and urbanity, nature and culture, and various cognitive and affective stances toward them.

Bertrand Westphal argues in his *Geocriticism* that the new space-time is characterized by chaos and describes postmodern space as "labyrinthine" (Westphal 2011, 2). He even argues that some of the salient features of how spatiality was perceived during the time before the Renaissance have returned. Namely, "the coherence of a world under the sign of nonexclusion and coexistence of all things" is reappearing (Westphal 2011, 2). Westphal's observation can be linked to the billboard and its slogan, "Life is local." As the billboard raises so many different and ambivalent affects, it also relates to Westphal's idea of postmodern space being chaotic or labyrinthine. The slogan is based on an apprehension of the authenticity and "realness" of both the local and life, ideas which have been put under erasure in the postmodern condition. But instead of arguing that all our space-times are chaotic, Westphal's apprehension needs to be nuanced and developed. For example, we are surrounded by various spatialities (both real and fictional) of which some are chaotic, some labyrinthine, some neither the former nor the latter. To be characterized as chaotic differs from being labyrinthine. And surely, the "protomodern" features of the contemporary must, despite similarities, be in a profound sense different from those of earlier times. This leaves us, then, with "the coexistence of all things." Rather than stating that the spatiality of the postmodern is chaotic or labyrinthine, we argue that one has to start by asking "who or what is interconnected with what or with whom" (Morton 2010, 15). We might even need to track what is *not* interconnected to who or what. And "all things" means literally all things: not only humans, but also non-humans, objects, animals, the living, and non-living. In order to describe the new space-time of contemporary Nordic literature, we find Westphal's attribute of "the labyrinthine" too precise, and "chaotic" too fuzzy to be useful. *Polytopy*, "space understood in its plurality" (Westphal 2011, 43), meets the requirements of both coherence and heterogeneity needed to grasp both ancient and contemporary space-time better.

As it is, the billboard—a plural spatial form in itself—is situated in the middle of a border zone, in between urban areas and the Finnish countryside. The placement of the billboard tells the story of *in-betweenness*, of being situated in between different spaces. Eric Prieto (2012) has argued that *entre-deux*, "in-between," is typical of postmodern literary spatiality, referring to the fact that late modern literature seems to move between spaces or situate itself at their borders. The chapters of this volume deal with works of literature, which also highlight this fact by sometimes covering embedded spaces. Such spaces are both highly public and deeply personal at the same time, such as city streets, or an island which is nevertheless connected to the mainland by means of bridges. Indeed, it could even be argued that the whole notion of "the Nordic," and thus the topic of this volume, Nordic literature, refers to a state of in-betweenness.

In a recent volume of *Nordic Literature* (2017), Steven P. Sondrup and Mark B. Sandberg deliver a highly instructive overview of how the expressions "Norden," "the North," and "the Nordic" have been used historically (Sondrup and Sandberg 2017, 1–18). Sondrup and Sandberg point out that first of all "the North" and "the Nordic" are geographical and cultural terms, referring both to a region situated in the high Northern latitudes and to the cultural imagination. While "Scandinavia" has been the term used mainly by people outside the area to designate it, "North" has been the term used within the region (Sondrup and Sandberg 2017, 7–8). "Norden," the North, is an area consisting of nations, languages, historical developments, and geographical and topographical features. The areas have been economically, socially, politically, linguistically, and culturally in long-lasting contact with each other. This has resulted in an underlying sense of unity, despite the fact that the outer and inner borders of the North have been in flux for centuries. Secondly, the North has been seen as the topographic and climatic opposite of the South, and also a certain cultural evaluation in terms of liminality has historically been attached to the region. When perceived from a Central European perspective, the North has been identified "as 'on the edge of Europe' and only partially implicated in broader European cultural norms" (Sondrup and Sandberg 2017, 9).[1] Today, the "Nordic" designates language communities and cultural practices that might even occur outside the geographic region, but which at least partly go back to shared experiences of place. Sondrup and Sandberg conclude that the North and the Nordic stand for an imaginary construction, largely created outside the region, but they also stand for regional cooperation created, for example, by the statutes of the Nordic Council (Sondrup and Sandberg 2017, 10–11).

We argue that the distinct *mixture* of global and local spatial relations in a certain territory, and the *in-betweenness* of the region, is what constitutes Nordic literature. The focus on Nordic contemporary authors connects literary works to a certain geographical area and argues that authors approach the problematics of spatiality from a specific location on earth. This has naturally been the argument of national literatures, which have frequently made a connection between a district/territory, language, population, and culture. Here Doreen Massey's (see e.g., Massey 1992, 2005) views, according to which space is produced by simultaneous existence and mutual relations, offer a useful point of departure in order to discuss and define Nordic literature in a manner that goes beyond nationalisms but nevertheless is able to take into account its territorial specificity. "It is not that the interrelations between objects occur *in* space and time; it is these relationships themselves which *create/define* space and time," she writes (Massey 1992, 79). Thus, we maintain that the uniqueness of contemporary Nordic literature is the result of its special location in a complicated global network of relations that creates space and spatiality—the Nordic islands (Iceland, Faroe Islands, and Greenland) form a special case of spatiality inside the Nordic region, and therefore they are not included in our book. While Sondrup and Sandberg's *Nordic Literature* aims to cover all the literatures of the North, namely Denmark, Norway, Sweden, and Finland as well as Iceland, the Faroe Islands, and Greenland, our volume includes works of literature from an area which we call *the continental North*.[2]

Literature, whether we focus on the text itself, the reader's response to it, or the relation between the text and the reader, is thoroughly bound up in a network of relations with space (Tally 2017, 1). Speaking generally, contemporary Nordic literature poses the question of "what does it mean to be Nordic?" It can also be rephrased as a question that refers to locality—to be or not to be local or global or something in-between them is a constant theme in recent Nordic literature. The argument of the billboard, "Life is local," seems at least questionable in connection to contemporary

Nordic literature, which asks "How local is living in the Nordic countries?" or "How does one lead a local life in a contemporary situation which is penetrated by global worries, such as climate change and economic and sexual inequality?" Whether the claim of the advertisement still holds true or not, it is an example of affective usage of spatial forms; the slogan appears as a (nostalgic) plea in favor of local communities, thus raising up affects of authenticity actualized by the harmony of the local.

However, literature, especially popular fiction, also utilizes this nostalgic need for harmonious localities. Scandinavian crime fiction written in the twenty-first century, often referred to as Nordic Noir, has even been said to carry "neo-romantic tendencies." Certainly, at least some recent Swedish crime fiction focuses on nature and cultural heritage and places murders and crimes in rural local communities depicted as idyllic regions (Bergman 2011, 41). According to Kerstin Bergman (2014, 103), almost all traces of globalization are absent from these depictions. Andrew Nestingen (2008, 17) has also noticed the "melodramatic" drive in Nordic Noir. However, Nestingen connects this melodrama to political and national discourse by taking up Henning Mankell's famous character Kurt Wallander and his repeated question "What is happening in Sweden?" Writing about the locations of Nordic Noir, K.T. Hansen and A. M. Waade (2017b, 110–11) argue that the romanticization of the local setting in Scandinavian crime fiction may be an idyllic response to the confidence that such a place may once have existed, but at the same time the rhetorics of such production of place may also refer to local self-references and identity.

Hansen and Waade, moreover, acknowledge that present-day Nordic Noir constantly negotiates with real places, and shows a "straightforward and somewhat unproblematic relationship between fictional and actual places as locations," meaning the places where the Nordic Noir TV-productions take place (Hansen and Waade 2017a, 10). They have noticed that despite postmodern concerns about the blurring of the boundary between fictional and alleged real worlds, which postmodernist literature tackles, real places do not pose any real epistemological questions concerning the ontological status of place and location in Nordic Noir.

The discussions over literature's relation to postmodernism and reality do not take place only within Nordic Noir but have also been addressed in the wider context of contemporary Nordic literature. In the introduction to *Millennium: Nye retninger i nordisk litteratur* (2013; "Millennium: New Directions in Nordic Literature") Mads Bunch suggests that one common feature in contemporary literature of the Nordic countries is that it strives to come to terms with the postmodernism of the 1980s and 1990s. This has resulted in a strong current of realism turning toward the surrounding world, and focusing on the interaction between individuals and their environment and with other people in specific historical contexts. The rapid development of political and economic globalization, new communication media, and the gradual dismantling of the welfare state, which was replaced by a more individualized society focused on competition, have also given rise to a growing interest in the private and biographical, namely autofiction (as in Karl Ove Knausgård's work), and other forms of self-representation in Nordic literature. Even here Bunch finds a growing interest in the real and reality due to the new media like the internet, reality TV, Facebook, and so on, which manipulate reality in various ways (Bunch 2013, 16–18). Bunch concludes that the developments in contemporary Nordic literature show affinities with global literary tendencies, and note that many more features than those he has taken up may be found.

The chapters of this volume concentrate on fiction from the 1990s to the present, and they discuss prose fiction and poetry as well as children's picture books. Scandinavian crime fiction or other popular genres, such as chick-lit or speculative fiction, are not discussed in this volume. True, all of them are extremely spatial literary genres—but such volumes as *Locating Nordic Noir* (2017) have already looked at the genre in terms of spatiality and situated Scandinavian crime fiction within its national and transnational connections. *Contemporary Nordic Literature and Spatiality* aims at widening the understanding of Nordic literature by introducing new authorships outside the internationally canonized authors dating back to past centuries, such as Henrik Ibsen, August Strindberg, Selma Lagerlöf, Ludvig Holberg, and Karen Blixen. Because we wish to present new authors and works of literature, our volume does not include chapters on recent internationally appraised authors, such as Knausgård and his *Min kamp* series (*My Struggle*), or winners of the Nobel Prize in Literature, like Tomas Tranströmer. We have lately noticed an enhanced interest in Nordic literature. The authors and works discussed in this volume are all widely read in their home countries and many of these works have been translated into other Nordic languages, although not in all cases into English. Moreover, we consider that our book develops the perspectives put forward in earlier publications by scrutinizing literature that has not yet been thoroughly analyzed and by putting forth various aspects of spatial theory into use in the analyses. Our emphasis on late modernity and its impact on Nordic literature offers a perspective which has not yet been studied as widely as it is in our volume.

The chapters focus on works by Danish, Norwegian, Swedish, and Finnish authors who elaborate themes and motifs that depict the cracks in the Nordic welfare state and the alleged homogenized social nature of this particular geographical area. Social criticism is a prevailing theme in Nordic literatures, but what makes this volume special is that this criticism against the welfare state and different power hierarchies is expressed in spatial terms. The chapters cover various narrative worlds and spaces from urban surroundings to parks and forests, from streets to personal homes, from textual spaces to spatial thematics—all of these spatial features are studied in relation to the problematics of late modernity. The chapters show that in late modern Nordic literature life appears both as local and as connected to global imaginative geographies.

Seen from outside, the "North" is mainly connected to phenomena such as Nordic Noir, Scandinavian-style design, or a politics consisting of social equality, welfare state economics, and international peacekeeping (Sondrup and Sandberg 2017, 11). In this volume we show how taking a closer look at the spatialities in contemporary Nordic literature provokes a much more complex picture of the constructions of the North.[3] At the same time, this collection opens up new and important perspectives on spatialities and new storied spaces in all their multi-layered characters.

Nordic Literature and/after the Spatial Turn

Contemporary Nordic Literature and Spatiality explores how the dynamic relationships between spatiality and literature are expressed in contemporary Nordic literature. The volume elaborates on the ways spaces become stories. As important as it is to scrutinize what kinds of spaces and forms of spatiality Nordic authors create in their works of literature, it is equally important to study what kinds of social, cultural, geographical, and economic relations they provide, in which ways and what surroundings they are interconnected, or how they imagine their position in relation to the surrounding world. What is more, they also imagine a North-to-come in terms of space, since the analyzed fiction does not merely depict the spaces of our real world but they also imagine the spaces and tell the stories of fictional locations.

Some recent publications approach literary spatiality in a similar manner as we do in this volume. One example of this is the above-mentioned *Nordic Literature: A Comparative History*, vol. I: *Spatial Nodes* (2017). Being a literary history in three parts, it examines the region's shared processes of literary production and communication, and argues for the power of "region" as an explanatory space. The first volume of *Nordic Literature* offers a historical overview of spatiality within Nordic literatures. In their introduction, Dan Ringgaard and Thomas A. DuBois take Doreen Massey's views on place as condensations of space as their point of departure in their discussion of the characteristics of a global, "postnational concept of place." Being the opposite of a stable home, place is a space transected by global flows rather than a shared history and shared memories. Thus, it needs to be defined horizontally, rather than vertically (Ringgaard and DuBois 2017, 25). After this, Ringgaard and DuBois turn to the basic premise of the volume, that of the *node*, stating that

> [T]he nodal principle employed throughout this volume of literary history meshes well with this horizontal and global concept of place. Place itself becomes a node, a thickening of space created by what ever passes through it, but also, one must imagine, by a power of the place to attract people, money, goods, and so forth. (Ringgaard and DuBois 2017, 26)

Despite some similarities, our book differs from *Spatial Nodes* on specific points. First, our focus is on recent literature, and on the effects of late modernity on contemporary literature, while *Spatial Nodes* puts more emphasis on a historical perspective. Second, *Spatial Nodes* combines the concept of "place" with the term "node," defined as "important clusters in the practice of spatial representation, imaginative figural tropes of heightened significance, or resonant temporal turning points" (Sondrup and Sandberg 2017, 5). For Massey, space and place are inseparable, and created in mutual interaction (Massey 2005, 184, 194). Thus, we do not find the term "node" necessary for analysis of the spatial dimension of (contemporary) Nordic literature. Also, we maintain that the current theories of space and spatiality used in this volume are as such both complex and useful.

The aim of *Contemporary Nordic Literature and Spatiality* is to perceive the North as a special thickening of space and to regard "the region as something that not only grows from its own past, but also constantly recycles the surrounding world" (Ringgaard and DuBois 2017, 26). We expand the aspects offered in *Spatial Nodes* in many ways. Our volume includes authors, works, and spaces that are not analyzed in that volume, and we develop and enrich many of the approaches on spatiality offered in it. Our book also covers a wider-ranging spectrum of spatial theories than *Spatial Nodes*, centering around the concept of "node." And finally, some of our chapters broaden the definition of the interconnectedness that creates space and spatiality. In *For Space* (2005) Massey defines space as the "sphere of the possibility of the existence of multiplicity," of "co-existing heterogeneity" inherently connected to social and political issues; space, geography, and identity, are co-constitutive (Massey 2005, 10). Despite the emphasis on humans and social issues, her views open up various possible other interrelations (Massey 2005, 15, 195).

Contemporary Nordic Literature and Spatiality is strongly connected to the so-called spatial turn of cultural and literary studies. Some 50 years ago Michel Foucault gave a lecture (published as "Of Other Spaces"), in which he said, "[t]he present epoch will perhaps be above all the epoch of space. We are in the epoch of simultaneity: we are in the epoch of juxtaposition, the epoch of near and far, of the side-by-side, of the dispersed" (Foucault 1986, 22). The "epoch of space" Foucault describes in this chapter is connected to the emergence of postmodernism, understood both as an aesthetic movement and sensibility in art, literature, and architecture, and as a historical period—a new way of understanding human existence and the surrounding world. As Robert T. Tally, Jr. (2017, 2; 2013, 11–17) has observed, postmodern philosophers and geographers, such as Henri Lefebvre, Jean-François Lyotard, Gilles Deleuze, Jacques Derrida, Fredric Jameson, David Harvey, and Edward Soja, among others, contrasted the late twentieth century to the nineteenth and early twentieth century and named the postmodern era a "reassertion of space." Globalization, postcolonialism, and more advanced information technologies pushed space and spatiality to the foreground, whereas earlier critical theory was obsessed with matters of time and left space and geography in the background.

This era of increasing interest in space has been named "the spatial turn." Spatiality has also become a major concern in the fields of literary and cultural studies, with growing numbers of publications devoted to literary geographies, *geoaesthetics* and *geopoetics*. It has given birth to new ways of describing and understanding space, including a growing awareness of space and its complexity, and the problems attached to it: the globe has become crowded and threatened (Tygstrup 2015, 303). Although no exact date can be given to the beginning of the spatial turn, it is strongly linked to various notions and theories of the postmodern. Today, some 30–40 years after the beginning of the spatial turn, we are living in the midst of an era in which some concerns and innovations of postmodern thinking have lost their novelty but are nonetheless continuing and developing into new dimensions and developments in the realm of critical theory.

Although this book insists on putting space and spatiality to the fore, it also suggests that "the spatial turn" is connected to other "turns" in critical theory, such as "the material turn" and "the affective turn," which date back to the mid-1990s. Notions of (new) materialisms no longer push materiality to the margins; instead of privileging immaterial things, such as language, consciousness, subjectivity, agency, mind, and soul, (new) materialisms focus on thinking about immaterial and material features side-by-side or even foregrounding materiality rather than idealities. Materiality is widely understood as the material artifacts and natural materials that populate our environments, and as socioeconomic structures producing and reproducing our everyday lives (see Coole and Frost 2010, 1–5). The material turn also means stepping away from human-centered thinking; spaces are important and meaningful in themselves without the presence of a human subject. Spaces, of course, are meaningful for human subjects but they are also significant for non-human beings, such as animals. We also argue that spaces are always-already affective and emotional, since "affect marks a body's *belonging* to a world of encounters," as Gregory J. Seigworth and Melissa Gregg (2010, 2) have written. Bodies, whether human or non-human entities, are affected by their situatedness in space and vice versa. This reciprocal interaction between spaces and bodies gives birth to a sense of space. Many studies on literary spatiality concentrate on human perspectives, but our volume opens up an understanding of the interconnectedness of spatiality to include non-humans.

The theoretical, aesthetic, technological, economic, social, and political developments that have been seen as the reasons for the spatial turn continue to transform the world with both speed and intensity. Therefore, some scholars already argue for a time "after the spatial turn," and for a "planetary turn." Critical of theories of globalization that perceive the *globe* in terms of a financial-technocratic system, a turn toward the *planet* as world-ecology is suggested (Elias and Moraru 2015, xvi). In this re-orientation, the planet as a living organism and a shared ecology becomes the conceptual and political dimension in which twenty-first-century writers picture themselves and their work. Moreover, an emphasis on ethical questions and responsibility comes to the fore (Elias and Moraru 2015, xii). Consequently, also the position of humans in space has changed—

humans are no longer in the center, and they exist on the same level as all other living and non-living things they are interconnected to, as part of a shared ecology, and with an ethical responsibility for the planet and all its elements. Various strivings to map spatialities in their wider connections, for example, with ecological issues, are increasingly actualized in recent literature. This also means that contemporary literature is problematizing the place of human beings in the world.

In the chapters of this book the contributors discuss literature using several notions of space. These notions and theoreticians can be linked to the spatial turn, but many of them also have connections to the material and affective turns. Most theories and notions of spatiality are proposed by non-literary scholars, but the chapters adapt them to adjust to the ways of literary world-making and literary geographies. Despite the recent rapid development of spatial studies, certain central theoretical approaches and scholars have maintained their position of importance in the field. That is also obvious when one approaches the chapters in our collection.

CONTRIBUTIONS TO THIS VOLUME

As already mentioned, in the chapters of *Contemporary Nordic Literature and Spatiality* space does not act as a background or a setting for story lines developed in time frames. Instead, the main focus of the chapters lies on spatialities. The volume is divided into four sections according to the main theme of the chapters. The titles of the four parts begin with questions, since we see spatiality as an ongoing conceptual and theoretical process without final solutions or answers.

Rephrasing Franco Moretti (2000, 55), we argue that spatiality is not an object; it is a problem or an open question. Part I of the volume asks "Whose Place Is This Anyway? On the Social Uses of Space and Power." This section concentrates on the interconnectedness between spaces and different formations of social power, which take place both in private and public spaces. The main focus lies on characters who belong to such social groups which do not possess power over spaces they inhabit. The chapters ask the following questions: Who has command over the depicted spaces? How is it possible to use—or abuse—these spaces? Is it possible to dream new kinds of socially shared spaces? What about dystopic spaces? How do such spaces, which are planned to be socially safe or progressive, function in contemporary literature? The chapters also manifest the layered structure of spatial formations by mapping the routes and paths the characters move along.

Elisabeth Friis in Chap. 2 proposes a geocritical reading of a rather inconspicuous place in Copenhagen in Denmark, *Amager Common*, which nonetheless stands out by virtue of its strikingly insistent appearance in Danish literature over the past three years. Following Bertrand Westphal, Friis regards *Amager Common* as a place whose specificity engenders particular movements within the literature that interacts with it. Westphal's eclectic and interdisciplinary geocriticism forms the theoretical basis of Friis's chapter, and Deleuze's and Guattari's philosophy of spatial formations is combined with the political-theoretical discussion of both the historical and present importance of *The Commons* during the era of (late) capitalist modernity. Friis shows how this special environment provides the stuff of dreams for other communities and other ways of being in the world than the one that is offered to us by late capitalism.

Chapter 3 by Cristine Sarrimo studies a Swedish novel *Still* (2008) by Hassan Loo Sattarvandi, which portrays a Million Housing programme area called Hagalund located North of the city center of the Swedish capital Stockholm. The novel is mostly narrated in the present tense, which shows that spatiality is always connected to the experiences of time; in Sattarvandi's novel loss of memory, history as well as the future shape spatial formations. In order to map the novel's dystopian space, Sarrimo analyzes Sattarvandi's construction of Hagalund using a Westphalian theoretical framework, Eric Prieto's study on the postmodern poetics of place, and Fredric Jameson's concept of *cognitive mapping*. Space is viewed as an accumulation of different historical strata which necessitates a multi-focal approach. Sarrimo shows how the sensorial perceptions of place in Sattarvandi's novel consist of the auditive, olfactory, and tactile, and not just the visual. Literature and other art forms can thus contribute to diversifying our understanding of sensorial perceptions of space.

One of the most common narrative patterns in children's literature begins with the protagonist leaving home for an adventure and ends with homecoming. Home is a familiar, secure, and private space in contrast to the often more open public or semi-public spaces in which various adventures take place. In Chap. 4, Kristina Hermansson explores the written and visual constructions of characters and social relationships in relation to space in a selection of contemporary picture books published in Sweden and Finland between 2006 and 2014. What characterizes the interplay between space and social relations in these works? How is the basic home-away-home pattern negotiated and renegotiated? In her analysis, Hermansson primarily applies Doreen Massey's theories of space and place, especially her concept of *throwntogetherness*.

Part II locates emotions and feelings by asking "Where Do You Feel?" The subtitle of this section, "Spaces, Emotions, and Technology" refers to the impact of technology on human emotions and experiences of space and spatiality during the era of late modern capitalism. The emotions and "realities" of human beings are constructed in relation to their physical and material surroundings, their immediate milieus, which have in profound ways been transformed by economic and technological changes. Literature offers a particular form of knowledge about the new manifestations of subjectivity and spatiality effectuated by technological developments; these developments also mold our perceptions of spatial existence in the world, and our interconnectedness to other people and the world as a whole. The novels and poems studied in the chapters of this section open new views on how Nordic authors reflect upon late modern developments. Above all, they pose the questions of how emotions and space are linked, what is the impact of the changes that have taken place on people living in the Nordic countries. The chapters also show the role of new technologies in the dismantling of the Nordic welfare states and the myth of social equality.

The smartphone, arguably the most important of various technological devices restructuring not only the experience of space and time in late modernity but also emotions, is the focus of Chap. 5 by Christian Refsum. By taking Giorgio Agamben's concept of *dispositif* as his point of departure, Refsum relates smartphones to the processes of subjectification and desubjectification which take place in the interaction (or conflict) between "living beings" and various apparatuses. All the three novels analyzed, Danish, Swedish, and Norwegian, deal with the relationship between geographical and mental distance in modern relationships and in all of them the mobile phone plays an important role in negotiating distance. Refsum argues that in a Nordic culture with a high degree of sexual equality, several female writers describe a situation of longing and waiting that has deep roots in the Western male discourses of love. In addition, the works discuss how the temporality of love and longing changes as the conditions of communication and negotiations on space change.

In Chap. 6 "Never Give Up Hopelessness!?," Anna Helle analyzes contemporary Finnish experimental poetry that examines twenty-first-century issues, such as finance capitalism, social problems, and unsatisfactory subject positions. Moreover, the poems express, describe, and arouse different kinds of emotions, closely related to how it feels to live in today's Finland. Helle suggests that the poems convey a kind of "politics of emotion," by which she means the ways in which things are made political through emotions; in other words Helle studies various technologies of the self in Finnish experimental poetry. Spatiality in this chapter does refer not only to late modern Finland as a space and cultural area but also to Finnish literature (poetry, to be more precise) as a public space in which emotional and potentially political topics are experienced and dealt with. Helle finds affinities between Finnish experimental poetry and American postmodern poetry and for example, New Sentence. Applying the insights of Fredric Jameson on the characteristic features of postmodern culture, and Raymond Williams's concept of *the structure of feeling*, Helle argues that innovative and experimental ways of using (found) language and found material (e.g. bank notes) open up a playful space where language is used for both poetic and political purposes.

Part III poses the question of "Which Language Do You Use?" with the subtitle "Spaces of Language and Text." This section deals with the interconnections between text, language, and space. The chapters of this section focus on the specific material dimensions of the spatiality of a text, that is textual spatiality on the one hand, and on the ways in which language shapes our understanding of spatialities on the other. Traditionally, monolingualism has been assigned to characterize, or even unite, certain geographical territories and their inhabitants; this might still hold true, but the chapters also take up questions of multilingualism as a mode of building postmodern literary spatialities. The section elaborates on genre-specific forms of spatiality either by concentrating on a particular genre or by comparing different genres. In this way, the material nature of literary spatialities is foregrounded in the chapters of this section.

Part III opens with Chap. 7 by Hadle Oftedal Andersen on the Norwegian author Øyvind Rimbereid's poetry and the tradition of topographic verse. Andersen analyzes Rimbereid's two long poems, *Solaris korrigert* (2004; "Solaris Corrected") and *Jimmen* (2008), by linking them to the tradition of topographic verse predating romanticism, to shed light on the specific ways in which the concept of space is unveiled in the poems. He argues that if we are to understand how space is perceived in early literature, we must bear in mind that it is written before phenomenology and before the romantic or Kantian understanding of the sublime. Since topographic verse is older than romanticism, it has no concept of a hypersensitive poetic subjectivity, and hence no interest in describing the reception of sensory data of chosen surroundings, or the emotional response to these either. By pouring present day-Stavanger into the old tradition of topographic verse, in ways which make the presence of the latter clear, Rimbereid makes us see how a specific position in time and space affects us, and how we in turn affect the ways this space is understood.

Chapter 8 investigates the phenomenon of textual spatiality—the conceptual, material-medial, and typographical dimension—in selected works of Swedish author Elisabeth Rynell and her blank-space technique. Antje Wischmann studies the positioning of material text, blank spaces, and the space of response, and how these spatial entities relate to each other, and finally, asks how meaning is generated by these relational processes. While the textual spatiality of poetry differs from that of prose, Rynell's hybrid prose-poetical work is an instructive exception, she argues. Using the concepts *Schriftraum*, *text-as-building*, and the *transactive space of reader response* from narratology and reader-response criticism, Wischmann shows how Rynell's treatment of embodied text and layout, and her systematic switching between points of view, stimulate readers' awareness of both composition and metanarrative. Following the specific features of textual spatiality and its spatiotemporal boundaries, Wischmann scrutinizes the texts' "typographical landscape."

In Chap. 9, Julia Tidigs explores the questions of multilingualism, translation, and spatiality in Finland-Swedish author Monika Fagerholm's novel *The American Girl* (2004/2009), a novel consisting of borrowed and translated phrases, or recycled language. At a glance, it may seem that questions of language and translation are absent in spatially oriented literary studies. In literary multilingualism studies, however, the functions of multilingualism in the literary construction of different geographic spaces (and their inhabitants) have been investigated. These studies have shown that just as conceptions of space are historically situated, the manner in which language has been conceptualized in spatial terms as well as in relation to geographical places has altered historically. Using the perspectives offered by Bertrand Westphal, Jan Blommaert, and Rebecca L. Walkowitz, Tidigs contrasts the rather stationary conception of linguistic and emotional bindings with a conception of language that puts the focus on movement and the temporal instability of spatio-linguistic constellations. Tidigs argues that in its insistence on mobility and translation, Fagerholm's novel is distinctly late modern. The transatlantic language of the novel is on the move between people and spaces, not locked in a relationship to any certain space or to the body of any particular speaker.

Part IV asks "Is This a Possible Space?" and focuses on the intensive forces of literature to imagine and create new spaces, even future spaces. In the chapters of this section the potentialities of space are studied in connection with literary genres and modes, which situate themselves in future times or which include a future-oriented dimension in their narration; in this way utopian and dystopian spatialities come to the fore. All the works of literature, both prose and poetry, of this section also stress the interconnectedness of time and space by underlining that spatial formations are always taking shape at a specific point in time and thus acquire features characteristic of their time. The chapters discuss both urban spaces and *naturecultural* spaces; here also the relationships between humans, non-humans (such as artifacts and animals), and spaces as affective encounters are studied. The chapters of this section ask whether it is possible for literature to imagine new spatial encounters that might lead to another kind of future in the realm of our everyday lives. Imagining new geographies is at the same time highly critical of the present situation.

Lieven Ameel in Chap. 10 studies Finnish author Mikko Rimminen, and proposes a new reading of his early prose from the perspective of the texts' apocalyptic undercurrents. The focus is on how the relationship between the fictional city and its referential counterpart, Helsinki, is foregrounded in the novel as well as undermined in a way that destabilizes the ontological status of the storyworlds in question. Using Brian McHale's *flickering effect* and Bertrand Westphal's *heterotopic interference* as his key concepts, and Gilles Deleuze's *fold* as a heuristic concept to describe how the ontological instability of postmodern storyworlds is shaped, Ameel explores the literary space and storyworld of the novel. An examination of Rimminen's prose texts confirms the notion proposed by Brian McHale that postmodern literature displays a conspicuous ontological instability: what at first appears to be a recognizable storyworld in the texts, with a firm referential relationship to actual Helsinki, the capital of Finland, turns out to be increasingly undermined by intimations of ontological disturbances.

Chapter 11 by Kaisa Kurikka focuses on the ways the forest is depicted in three contemporary Finland-Swedish novels by Kaj Korkea-Aho, Johanna Holmström, and Henrika Ringbom. All the Nordic countries share the notion of the forest as an important part of defining their cultural identities; the forest is a significant space for being alone in nature. Kurikka, however, approaches the forest as a potential space where human and non-human beings, namely a wolf and a fictional monster, face each other in affective encounters. The three novels studied in this chapter all bring an "otherworldly" element to the Finnish forest, thus making it a space for *the uncanny*. The uncanny forests of the novels also enable various transformations or becomings in which the contours of human and non-human beings blur into one another; the forest itself becomes deterritorialized while offering material creatures chances of transformation. By drawing on the geophilosophical concepts of Gilles Deleuze and Félix Guattari, Kurikka pays attention to the ways literature fabulates new kinds of forests.

The Finland-Swedish author Monika Fagerholm has above all been seen as a portrayer of girlhood, gender, language, and agency. In Chap. 12 by Hanna Lahdenperä, Fagerholm is, however, studied as a writer of spatiality who frequently layers real geographical spaces and their fictional counterparts in intricate ways. Using the perspectives offered by Eric Prieto, Yi-Fu Tuan, and Bertrand Westphal, Lahdenperä offers a careful examination of space as a mental construct and a form of knowledge in Fagerholm's prose. Lahdenperä shows how Fagerholm's characters go further than merely being in or inhabiting a place; they take possession of a place and use it for their own purposes. The novels, she argues, create mental spatialities through naming and renaming, spatialities that combine the characteristics of both space and place, as well as defy the constraints of physical and geographical spaces and places.

In the last chapter (Chap. 13) of the book, Kristina Malmio studies a collection of poetry by Finland-Swedish author Ralf Andtbacka, a volume characterized by spatial excess on every level. *Wunderkammer* (2008) takes place in flea markets, where objects from various parts of the world gather, in similar ways as catalogues and lists of words, objects, and phenomena pile up in the poems. Taking her points of departure from art history, postmodern spatiality, and ecological thought, Malmio shows how the cabinet of curiosities and the Chinese box structure—two traditional, limited forms of spatiality prevalent in Andtbacka's collection—not only construct a postmodern space, but also envisage a global imaginative geography. By drawing parallels between Andtbacka's portrayal of spatiality, and *the mesh*—a concept put forward by Timothy Morton (2010)—she claims that *Wunderkammer* portrays the interconnectedness of all humans and non-humans throughout the globe and, finally, approaches the planetary turn.

The chapters of *Contemporary Nordic Literature and Spatiality* constitute a rich collection of conceptual and methodological approaches to the storied spaces of the continental North. Contemporary literature of the region appears to take stances toward many themes and problematics on a global, or rather a planetary scale. The stories, whether novels, poems, or picturebooks, of the locality of life in the Nordic countries, however, maintain an atmosphere of specificity born from the locations and depicted spaces of the storyworlds and poetic contexts.

Notes

1. Postcolonial theories and the ways in which postcolonial theories have problematized national literary history writing have inspired studies in which earlier national perspectives and methodological nationalism have been put under scrutiny. Nevertheless, postcolonial theories have also been used to question the peripherality of the North. See, for example, *Rethinking National Literatures and the Literary Canon in Scandinavia* (eds. Ann-Sofie Lönngren, Heidi Grönstrand, Dag Heede, and Anne Heith, 2015), which studies the role of literature in the construction of national identities and literary canons in the various Nordic literatures. "Nordic" includes literatures from Finland, Denmark, Norway, Sweden, the Sami people, and the Faroe Islands, and the timespan varies from old to contemporary with an overall emphasis on historical perspectives. Thus, the spatialities of late modernity and the interaction between literature, society, and late modernity are not the main focus. See also Oxfeldt 2012.
2. While *Nordic Literature* focuses on the area surrounding the Baltic Sea, *Centring on the Peripheries: Studies in Scandinavian, Scottish, Gaelic and Greenlandic Literature* (ed. Bjarne Thorup Thomsen, 2007) offers another view on the topic. Focusing on the North Sea, it studies how Scandinavian and Scottish literatures deal with islands, borderlands, and landscapes of the North and Baltic Seas. By focusing on community, history, and identity, and using mainly postcolonial and postnational theories, it aims to deconstruct a center-periphery dichotomy prevalent in the Nordic region. The study covers a large geographical area, and therefore, the analyses of Nordic literature become somewhat scattered. Also, the ways in which the chapters apprehend space go back to an earlier phase in spatial studies.
3. *New Dimensions of Diversity in Nordic Culture and Society* (eds. Jenny Björklund and Ursula Lindqvist, 2016) takes its departure in the concept *diversity* which is broadened from ethnicity and nation to encompass various other social and cultural categories as gender, sexuality, class, age, religion, and so on. The aim of the book is to grasp the new realities of the Nordic region, the novel forms of diversity they give rise to, and to bring together scholars interested in diversity, but separated by disciplinary borders. The volume offers intersectional readings of various forms of culture, including literature, new media, film, and popular culture. It includes some articles on contemporary Nordic literature, but focuses on other issues than those in this book.

References

Bergman, Kerstin. 2011. The Well-Adjusted Cops of the New Millennium: Neo-Romantic Tendencies in the Swedish Police Procedural. In *Scandinavian Crime Fiction*, ed. Andrew Nestingen and Paula Arvas, 34–45. Cardiff: University of Wales Press.

———. 2014. *Swedish Crime Fiction: The Making of Nordic Noir*. Milano and Udine: Mimesis.

Björklund, Jenny, and Ursula Lindqvist, eds. 2016. *New Dimensions of Diversity in Nordic Culture and Society*. Newcastle upon Tyne: Cambridge Scholars Publishing.

Bunch, Mads. 2013. Millennium. Nye retninger i nordisk litteratur. In *Millennium: Nye retninger i nordisk litteratur*, ed. Mads Bunch, 7–22. Hellerup: Forlaget Spring.

de Certeau, Michel. 1988 [1984]. *The Practice of Everyday Life*. Translated by Steven Rendall. First Paperback Printing. Berkeley, Los Angeles and London: University of California Press.

Coole, Diana, and Samantha Frost. 2010. Introducing New Materialisms. In *New Materialisms: Ontology, Agency, and Politics*, ed. Diana Coole and Samantha Frost, 1–43. Durham and London: Duke University Press.

Elias, Amy J., and Christian Moraru. 2015. Introduction: The Planetary Condition. In *The Planetary Turn: Relationality and Geoaesthetics in the Twenty-First Century*, ed. Amy J. Elias and Christian Moraru, xi–xxxvii. Evanston, IL: Northwestern University Press.

Foucault, Michel. 1986. Of Other Spaces. Translated by Jay Miskowiec. *Diacritics* 16 (Spring): 22–27.

Hansen, K.T., and A.M. Waade. 2017a. Introduction: Where Is Nordic Noir? In *Locating Nordic Noir: From Beck to the Bridge*, ed. Kim Toft Hansen and Anne Marit Waade, 1–23. New York: Palgrave Macmillan.

———. 2017b. Stieg Larsson and Scandinavian Crime Fiction as a Stepping Stone. In *Locating Nordic Noir: From Beck to the Bridge*, ed. Kim Toft Hansen and Anne Marit Waade, 105–125. New York: Palgrave Macmillan.

Haraway, Donna. 2008. *When Species Meet*. Minneapolis and London: University of Minnesota Press.

Lönngren, Ann-Sofie, Heidi Grönstrand, Dag Heede, and Anne Heith, eds. 2015. *Rethinking National Literatures and the Literary Canon in Scandinavia*. Newcastle upon Tyne: Cambridge Scholars Publishing.

Massey, Doreen. 1992. Politics and Space/Time. *New Left Review* 1 (196): 65–84.

———. 2005. *For Space*. London: Sage.

Moretti, Franco. 2000. Conjectures on World Literature. *New Left Review* 1 (January–February): 54–68.

Morton, Timothy. 2010. *The Ecological Thought*. Cambridge, MA: Harvard University Press.

Nestingen, Andrew. 2008. *Crime and Fantasy in Scandinavia: Fiction, Film, and Social Change*. Seattle and London: University of Washington Press and Copenhagen: Museum Tusculanum Press.

Oxfeldt, Elisabeth. 2012. *Romanen, nasjonen og verden. Nordisk litteratur i et postnasjonalt perspektiv*. Oslo: Universitetsforlaget.

Prieto, Eric. 2012. *Literature, Geography, and the Postmodern Poetics of Place*. New York: Palgrave Macmillan.

Ringgaard, Dan, and Thomas A. DuBois. 2017. The Framework: Spatial Nodes. In *Nordic Literature. A Comparative History, Vol. I: Spatial Nodes*, ed. Steven P. Sondrup, Mark B. Sandberg, Thomas A. DuBois, and Dan Ringgaard, 19–29. Amsterdam and Philadelphia: John Benjamins Publishing Company.

Seigworth, Gregory J., and Melissa Gregg. 2010. An Inventory of Shimmers. In *The Affect Theory Reader*, ed. Gregory J. Seigworth and Melissa Gregg, 1–25. Durham and London: Duke University Press.

Sondrup, Steven P., and Mark B. Sandberg. 2017. General Project Introduction. In *Nordic Literature: A Comparative History, Vol. I: Spatial Nodes*, ed. Steven P. Sondrup, Mark B. Sandberg, Thomas A. DuBois, and Dan Ringgaard, 1–18. Amsterdam and Philadelphia: John Benjamins Publishing Company.

Tally, Robert T., Jr. 2013. *Spatiality*. London and New York: Routledge.

———. 2017. Introduction: Reassertion of Space in Literary Studies. In *The Routledge Handbook of Literature and Space*, ed. Robert T. Tally Jr., 1–6. London and New York: Routledge.

Thomsen, Bjarne Thorup, ed. 2007. *Centring on the Peripheries: Studies in Scandinavian, Scottish, Gaelic and Greenlandic Literature*. Norwich: Norvik Press.

Tygstrup, Frederik. 2015. Plats. In *Litteratur: Introduktion till teori och analys*, ed. Lasse Horne Kjælgaard, Lis Møller, Dan Ringgaard, Lilian Munk Rösing, Peter Simonsen, and Mads Rosendahl Thomsen, 301–310. Lund: Studentlitteratur.

Westphal, Bertrand. 2011. *Geocriticism: Real and Fictional Spaces*. Translated by Robert T. Tally, Jr. New York: Palgrave Macmillan.

Open Access This chapter is licensed under the terms of the Creative Commons Attribution 4.0 International License (http://creativecommons.org/licenses/by/4.0/), which permits use, sharing, adaptation, distribution and reproduction in any medium or format, as long as you give appropriate credit to the original author(s) and the source, provide a link to the Creative Commons licence and indicate if changes were made.

The images or other third party material in this chapter are included in the chapter's Creative Commons licence, unless indicated otherwise in a credit line to the material. If material is not included in the chapter's Creative Commons licence and your intended use is not permitted by statutory regulation or exceeds the permitted use, you will need to obtain permission directly from the copyright holder.

PART I

Whose Place Is This Anyway? On the Social Uses of Space and Power

CHAPTER 2

On the Commons: A Geocritical Reading of *Amager Fælled*

Elisabeth Friis

This chapter proposes a geocritical reading of a rather inconspicuous place in Denmark, which nonetheless stands out by virtue of its strikingly insistent appearance in Danish literature during the past three years. To read geocritically means, in Bertrand Westphal's phrasing, to examine "the multifocalization of viewpoints on a given reference space"[1] (Westphal 2007, 188), and this is precisely what the place that I shall be examining makes possible, since quite a lot has actually been written about it recently. In order to practice Westphal's geocentric criticism (as opposed to what happens in what he calls *geo*centric or *imagological* criticism), it is moreover of decisive importance to take the referentiality of an actual place as a starting point: "geocritics confront a referent whose literary representation is no longer considered a deformation, but a foundation" (Westphal 2007, 186).

This means two things. First, that we take the geographical determination of specific places seriously. And second, that we don't consider literary representations as independent of this place or completely different from the specific location they represent.

E. Friis (✉)
Lund University, Lund, Sweden

© The Author(s) 2020
K. Malmio, K. Kurikka (eds.), *Contemporary Nordic Literature and Spatiality*, Geocriticism and Spatial Literary Studies,
https://doi.org/10.1007/978-3-030-23353-2_2

Place as "a given reference space" and place as "literary representation" are thus not mutually exclusive categories—far from it. The traffic between those perspectives is dense, and getting a grip on it is exactly what Westphal's geocritical method allows us to do.

Following Westphal, I shall regard the specific place that is of interest here, *Amager Fælled* (or in English, Amager Common) as a place whose specificity engenders specific movements within the literature that interacts with it. Westphal's theoretical basis is one that is both eclectic and interdisciplinary, but Gilles Deleuze and Félix Guattari's philosophy of spatial formations—territorialization, deterritorialization, reterritorialization, the parceling out of striated space, and the nomadic distribution of smooth space—is a constant point of reference, just as it is going to be an important point for the present analysis in combination, on and off, with the political-theoretical discussion of both the historical and present import of the commons in the era of (late) capitalist modernity.

It may also be noted that my reason for pointing to Westphal (and not just to Deleuze and Guattari) as a central reference here is a methodological one. Westphal connects virtual space with actual space in a way that is not really practiced by Deleuze and Guattari. Where, for example, does the (literary) line of flight begin? In what specific reference is it fixed? *A Thousand Plateaus* has no general answer to that, but I understand Westphal's geocriticism as a response to that very question: He engages in a distinct reflection upon how to approach the specificity of sites.

Amager: And Amager Common

Next to Copenhagen is Amager, an island of 96.29 km² connected to the center of the capital of Denmark by two bridges. To an outside observer, Copenhagen and Amager are by and large one and the same place—it takes five minutes to cross the bridges by foot, and no time at all on a bicycle. But it is not just water and bridges that separate Copenhagen from Amager. You move "out" into Amager and "into" the city—the "city" can never be Amager. Seen from Copenhagen, Amager has almost always been viewed as either a wasteland or a low-status area.

The famous Danish writer and actress Johanne Luise Heiberg's (1812–1890) description of Amager[2] in her memoirs *Et Liv gjenoplevet i Erindringen* ("A Life Recalled in Memory"), posthumously published in 1891–1892, is thus both symptomatic and atypical of the relationship of Copenhageners to the island—then and now:

> This poor, flat island, little noticed by Copenhageners, I had granted my particular favours. Here, one had not the pleasure of seeing a single dressed up Copenhageners; one was met only by Amager's peasant life. (…) I do believe that no one in the entire city of Copenhagen knows the beauty of Amager as I do; perhaps I have a peculiar taste for exactly this kind of beauty, the beauty of the plains, where the eye meets no obstacle, but reaches forward indefinitely, only to be stopped by the arch of heaven. (…)
>
> *My friends often laughed at my love for this flat, and as they dared say, foul Amager.* (Heiberg 1944, 192)

And "foul" Amager has not on the whole been made more attractive to "Copenhageners" by the past 150 years' urban development. In Morten Pape's autobiographical debut *Planen* (2015; "The Plan"), depicting the author's upbringing in the largest social housing project in the island, *Urbanplanen*, Amager is described in the following terms:

> Many years ago the capital's shit and waste were stored in these parts. The shitty island of Amager was the place to hide the ugliness. Today its waste dump symbolism cannot be overlooked. Now this is the place you don't want your children to go near. Pale potatoes like myself are outnumbered. There are more headscarves than tulle skirts, and more Arabic is sung in the corners than Halfdan Rasmussen at the hopscotch grid. The grown-ups say it is because our school lies in the middle of a ghetto. (Pape 2015, 4)

A popular name for Amager is "Shitty Island," with reference to the fact that a cleaning station for Copenhagen's latrines was long located there. From 1777 onward, the open, so-called chocolate wagons drove overfilled soil tubs out from the city to the great soil pit on Amager (Lindegaard 2001). And as far as the "waste dump symbolism" is concerned, great amounts of waste have continuously been deposited on the island—in many cases toxic waste, for instance from ØK's (*Det Østasiatiske Kompagni* or the East Asiatic Company, EAC) infamous soy bean cake factory.[3] In an even darker vein, from 1806 Amager hosted Copenhagen's execution site, just as it was the home of the "Slave Graveyard" (abolished 1857), where prisoners convicted to hard labor (known in those days as "slaves") found their last resting place; they were buried in layers—and needless to say, in the cheapest of coffins.

But Amager also, as we learn from Mrs. Heiberg's praise of the island's nature, of its "beauty of the plains," has been an ambiguous place, since "foul" Amager supplied Copenhagen with vegetables for centuries.

Whether these products were fertilized using excrement from the latrine pit is hard to tell, but the market gardeners have a history of their own, being Dutch immigrants who as early as the 1500s were invited to settle in Amager by Denmark's king, Christian II, supplying the country's capital with vegetables into the twentieth century, and gaining Amager not only the epithet of Shitty Island but also the title of "The Larder of Copenhagen."

If the status of historical Amager is certainly complex, its complexity has not diminished today.

On Amager lies Københavns Universitet Amager (KUA)—, the Faculty of Humanities of the University of Copenhagen—soon to be Campus South, with Law and Theology joining in. On Amager lies Copenhagen Airport—the largest airport in Scandinavia. On Amager lies Denmark's biggest shopping mall, *Fields*, built as a direct outcome of the very expensive construction of a new metro, in connection with urban development modeled on London's Docklands. And right in the midst of Amager we find our primary object of study: *Amager Fælled* or Amager Common—a natural area consisting partly of land that has been claimed from the sea and partly of a salt marsh whose flora and fauna has remained largely undisturbed for 5000 years.

Here grow rare plants like *Filipendula vulgaris* and *Selinum dubium*, and here one stands a chance of seeing the red-listed hoverfly *Xanthogramma festivum* and many other insects that do not thrive on cultivated land. Overall, the soil of Amager Common is poor, which is why it has been used for pasture, and later as a military terrain. Since the military abandoned its positions, the Common has been open to the public and put to multiple uses. People gather berries and herbs in the area. Romani trailers have come and gone. Nowadays, stranded refugees—and indeed the homeless of the world—sleep under tarpaulins. Asa worshippers gather and perform *blót*.[4] And gay people have sex in the bushes. There are "shelters" put up by authorities so that anybody can sleep out there for a night or two, and safely light their campfire. There is a shop for renting bicycles, students getting some fresh air—all of these activities accompanied by a tight chain of airplanes cutting through the air above people's heads, and above the livestock that still grazes here and there.

Without the least exaggeration, all sorts of biodiversity can be said to blossom on *Amager Fælled*, so that this *fælled* forms a distinct form of geographical *space*.

It is time to make a couple of space-theoretical categorizations.

What Is a *Fælled*?

Fælled originally designates an area where all the livestock (in Danish, *fæ*) are put to pasture. It is a *common* space (in Danish, *fælled* means "common"), a space of the *community* (the Danish word for "community" is *fællesskab*), meaning that the notion of both livestock and community or commonness is semantically implied by the word *fælled*. In Marx's (1867) classical analysis, the *enclosure of the commons*—the fencing-in of fields formerly used for grazing and cultivation in common[5]—heralds the advent of the type of control over production that forms the basis of *original accumulation* on which modern capitalism is founded.[6]

The debate over the historical significance of common (non-territorialized) areas is flourishing on a global level. For obvious reasons, the question of "enclosure" versus the maintenance of some kind of commons is pressing in many "less developed" regions—whereas in "overdeveloped" areas environmentalists are trying to stake a claim for alternative principles of common cultivation which would be both sustainable and community-strengthening (urban gardening is perhaps the most well-known example of this). How to conceptualize our "common ground" and how to put it to good use are of course burning questions of great environmental importance, as well as being equally important in connection with the problem of the distribution of income and wealth. To capitalize land that is actually the home of people who live on it ranks, for instance, among the specialties of the World Bank,[7] whose modus operandi raises the question of what may, in the broadest sense, be considered to be "common": water, air, plants, that which sustains us on the planet we inhabit together with approximately 8.7 million other living species, whose right to exist, as is well known, is not counted among the top priorities of human societies.

The curve of biodiversity both locally and globally moves downward. In overdeveloped Denmark (55.8% of the country's surface is cultivated, making Denmark the world's most intensely farmed nation), the *Xanthogramma festivum* on *Amager Fælled* is not the only species fighting for its life. As these lines are written, 2262 species of plants and animals are on the so-called red list—an inventory following the guidelines of the International Union for Conservation of Nature (IUCN), which covers the species that are threatened in Denmark.

But a specific area's degree of biodiversity is not only related to the diversity of its species (including its microbiological diversity).

Amager Common is by no means a pristine natural reserve—the area is constantly put to *use*, for anything from picking elderflowers to having anonymous sex. Being on the common, a shopping mall and the metro line are close at hand—as planes go over your head—the common indeed is a *place in use*, and if we think of it as an "environment,"[8] it is an environment that includes Kentucky Fried Chicken and whatever has lately rolled off the assembly line at Boeing.

At the same time this is a nomadic space—both in the tangible sense of its housing Romani trailers and homeless asylum seekers, and in Deleuze and Guattari's sense, that is to say it is a space which is not determined through parceling (an infrastructure based upon private property—the space as an *espace strié/striated space*), but is rather drawn up through the movements of the bodies that are in motion across it (the space as an *espace lisse/smooth space*).

We could simply say that the space *becomes* a space as a consequence of these movements—and it is my claim that this is exactly what also happens in the treatment of *Amager Fælled* in contemporary Danish literature. As Westphal puts it, "at the interface between world and text, events produce themselves that are otherwise complex and ambitious (for literature) than the mere rendering [la pure presentation] of a service" (Westphal 2007, 185), and as we shall see The Common is quite simply a space that stimulates a certain type of literary distribution.

Furthermore, the idea of The Common as a place that has not yet been capitalized, that is, a place in which capitalist exploitation is not (yet) active—in short a more straightforward Marxist interpretation of the meaning of this place—is also traceable. The poet Liv Sejrbo Lidegaard (born 1986), who published her first book *Fælleden* ("The Common") in 2015, at any rate has the following to say about the significance of Amager Common in an interview with the newspaper *Information* ("*Slaget om Fælleden*," "The Battle of the Common," October 8, 2016):

> The Common has the ability not to be put to much use. Especially when you live in a city, every place has great economic value. And if economic value governs, it can become impossible to be there. This is the opposite. There is no economic value—or there is, and this is why it may not survive. But it hasn't been put to use. The fact that it hasn't been put to much use actually does that you are able to be here. (Villesen 2016)

When Lidegaard states that *Amager Fælled* is not "put to much use," she is clearly aiming at the area's lack of territorialization by capital, meaning, as she says, "that you are able to be there." We shall return to Lidegaard's perspective and its poetic articulation in *Fælleden*, but first we shall encounter another young Danish poet, Asta Olivia Nordenhof (born 1988), whose poem about, among other things, Amager Common, from her volume of poetry, *det nemme og det ensomme* (2013; "the easiness and the loneliness"), has become an instant classic in Danish literature.[9]

Asta Olivia Nordenhof: The Tenderness of the Common

The titleless poem which takes place on The Common is the first long poem in the collection, and it begins with a hangover and the anxiety of death, after which the lyrical I and her partner go for a walk on *Amager Fælled*:

> varmen og tømmermændene
> jeg fjerner mig fra dem jeg elsker med hele kroppens underlige styrke
> fik indsigt i hvordan jeg vil dø
> jeg så eksplosionen indefra. fra blodets perspektiv.
> jeg var oprørt over det. min kæreste sagde: rolig olli
> nu ved jeg det ikke længere, om jeg fik mulighed for at opleve min død som den i paralleltid
> allerede er indtruffet
> det er ikke sikkert. så senere: vi plukkede vilde blommer og mirabeller på ydre amar
> ved solnedgang og metroen drev med sit lys, som et strengt, som et underligt vredt samfund
> frem og tilbage på himlen
> ingen i fields ingen på kentucky fried chicken
> to mennesker foran et parcelhus. sad med tæpper på, talte med hinanden
> "jeg er meget træt nu" "jeg er også meget træt"
> hvorfor er knoglerne ik mere skøre
> røde røde sol
> du så dejlig du så ligeglad om jeg kaster en blomme i dit navn
> og amar hvor ømt du at du gav mig en blomme at kaste
> må skrive til morten!
> må skrive til bjørn! jorden er øm og jeg er ik nok til at fat det!

hvordan kan vi blive mer forgæves, mer beskidte
mer forgæves, prøv at høre ordet:
tak
hvordan! (…) (Nordenhof 2013, 8–9)

heat and hangover
i distance myself from those i love with the strange strength of my whole body
got insight into how i will die
i saw the explosion from inside. from my bloods perspective.
i was upset about it. my boyfriend said "easy, olli"
now i don't know anymore if i got to experience my own death as it already happened, in parallel time
its not certain. then later: we picked wild plums and mirabelles way out in amager
at sunset and the metro swept with its lights, like a severe, like a strangely irascible society
back and forth across the sky
no one in fields no one in the kfc
two people in front of a tract house. sat wrapped in blankets and talked with each other
"im very tired now" "im very tired too"
why arent my bones more brittle
red red sun
you so lovely you so indifferent to whether i throw a plum in your name
and amager how tender that you gave me a plum to throw
must write to morten!
must write to bjørn! the earth is tender and im not enough to grasp it!
how can we be any more pointless, any more dirty
more pointless, listen to the word:
thanks
how! (…)[10]

The first thing to notice is the poem's highlighting of the distinctive geography of *Amager Fælled*. Yes, you can indeed pick wild plums and mirabelles in the Common. And yes, a metro line does in fact cut through the landscape. *Fields* is the name of the large shopping mall that opened as a result of the development of Ørestaden.[11] The name *Fields* itself refers phonetically to the toponomy *Fælleden* (although the precise English translation would have been "The Common"), and Kentucky Fried Chicken is located inside *Fields*—right next to Ørestad Metro Station.

Furthermore, *Fields* borders upon the detached houses of the suburban borough of Tårnby. In other words, the lyrical subject and her partner find themselves in a very real, albeit rather deserted place (it is Sunday), and in this utterly mundane but also stimulating location anxiety about death is replaced by an experience of interconnectedness and solidarity with the surroundings and all that is in them. Opposite to the sunset's democratic coloring of everything in red stands "the metro" (*"metroen"*), which "swept with its lights, like a severe, like a strangely irascible society/back and forth across the sky" ("drev med sit lys, som et strengt, som et underligt vredt samfund/frem og tilbage på himlen"). In a contemporary Danish context it is hard to find a clearer image of capitalism's territorializing movement—using the "public sector" ("society") as a legitimizing engine[12]—than the building of the Copenhagen Metro, and the development of Ørestaden that is connected to it. Project "Ørestad" and the construction of the metro were launched by the City of Copenhagen in 1992 in view of capitalizing the unused—but potentially profitable—areas of Amager. The "severe" and "irascible" society's desire for profit is vectorized in the poem by the train that shoots through the Common, but the presence of this movement does not prevent the poem's *Amager Fælled* from being experienced as a very generous place.

Nordenhof's poetry, as is clear from the quoted verse, is marked by the forms of spoken language. Words are spelled as they are pronounced, and as yet another characteristic trait of her texts, all words are in lower-case letters, likewise indicating spoken language—the English translation also marks this by its elimination of the apostrophes. At the same time, the poems are marked by classic devices of "high poetry": metaphor, personification, here in combination with apostrophe, as the Sun and Amager are both personified and apostrophized in the lines "red red sun/you so lovely you so indifferent to whether i throw a plum in your name/and amar [Amager] how tender that you gave me a plum to throw" ("røde røde sol/du så dejlig du så ligeglad om jeg kaster en blomme i dit navn/og amar hvor ømt at du gav mig en blomme at kaste").

As Jonathan Culler remarks in his seminal text on apostrophe, this trope is able to call forth a special form of temporal experience: "The 'now' of the apostrophe is not a moment in a temporal sequence, but a *now* of discourse—an immediacy. If it works it produces a fictive, discursive event" (Culler 1981, 152). And I wonder whether the apostrophe's independence of sequentiality—the fact that the trope triggers an *event*—does not give rather a precise expression to a certain kind of spatialization:

The lyrical I throws a plum. It lands *wherever it lands*, which is a distributive movement that is in clear contrast to the train's "back and forth." This "throwing of a plum in the name of the sun" creates a *now* within discourse, which is of course able to create, for a moment, a space in the real *Amager Fælled*, but which within the text's poetic, apostrophic discourse also turns into an intense now of perpetual becoming, enhancing the strong sentiment of interconnectedness with the environment which is addressed by the poem. The Sun is "lovely" (*"dejlig"*) because it is "indifferent" (*"ligeglad"*), a proposition that can be understood in line with an ontological fact: the sun is the only phenomenon known to us that only *gives* and never *takes*.

In any case, "amar" is "tender" (*"ømt"*) because it allows us to pick its fruits for free—just like the indifferent sun does. The sun's indifference is no resigned conclusion. It is society, and the will of society, as personified by the metro, that is "severe" and "irascible" (as from the Old Testament)—it is not the sun or the ripe plums on the Common.

Interestingly, nor are *Fields* and Kentucky Fried Chicken negative places because they are soulless (there is "nobody" inside). The empty consumption spaces seem just as much a part of the surroundings as the plums do. There does not seem to be any difference between the environment that is "natural" and the environment that is "unnatural," the environment that is "manmade" and the environment that is not "manmade" within the space brought forth by the poem, something which is a strong and dark ecological point.[13]

To become more "pointless," more "dirty," would be the wish that we become less obsessed with teleology—we might say with utilitarian thought—and less unmixed with the earth (more dirty), a wish that the poem's gesture of throwing the free plum of amar in the name of the sun will locally realize. The two people sitting outside their tract house are in fact seated *outside* their house—and thus included in the poem's tenderness toward the place. And without taking the argument too far, one might say that precisely the *tract house*, at least in a Danish context, is an emblematic figure of the bliss of private property; and how are the two people doing who are sitting under their blankets, looking at the commons? They are tired.

Lea Løppenthin: The Nomadic Common

Connecting *Amager Fælled* to Deleuze and Guattari's concept of *territorialization/deterritorialization* is an idea that is close at hand—not least since Lea Løppenthin's (born 1987) volume of poetry, *nervernes adresse* (2014, "the address of the nerves") contains a suite of poems which is simply called *digt om territorier* (poem about territories)—and in this poem we once more find ourselves in *Amager Fælled*:

> en nat var vi en gruppe der tog ud på fælleden
> vi ville bosætte os afsides i sommeren
> hjortene og asylansøgerne er de fastboende i området
> vores tøj var mættet af bålets lugt
> vi havde siddet ved det i mange timer og bagt vores mad hen over ilden
> vi cyklede langs havet, forbi hestene
> gennem skoven og over metalbroen, nu skulle vi sove
> alle shelters var optagede
> alle shelters var bookede af mere forudseende sommergæster
> så sov vi i fuglekiggertårnet ved Hejresøen
> sov inde i vores soveposer i en Tetris-formation på gulvet
> situationen minder om en vinterdag i en lejlighed, jeg boede i
> jeg så ned på fortovet, der var dækket af sne
> et barn i flyverdragt bar langsomt skovlfulde af sne fra en del af fortovet til en anden
> sneen blev fordelt i et mønster rundtomkring på fortovet
> den var forsat i vejen for fodgængerne
> det kunne jeg rigtig godt lide, ikke det mislykkede ved det
> (at vi ikke var forudseende på fælleden, at der ikke blev ryddet sne)
> det var ikke det mislykkede ved det der var godt
> det mislykkede ved det var højst en charme
> det var formationerne der optog mig
> det mønster vi lå i i tårnet og sneen på fortovet
> et mønster vil bruge os, ligesom det fremmede barn jeg så, ville bruge sneen
> og det lykkedes
> det var en succes (…) (Løppenthin 2014, 20)

> one night we were a group that went out to the common
> we wanted to settle in a remote place in summer
> the deer and the asylum seekers are residents there

our clothes were saturated with the smell of the campfire
we had been sitting by it for many hours baking our food across the fire
we rode our bikes alongside the ocean, past the horses
through the woods and over the metal bridge, now we were going to sleep
all shelters were taken
all shelters had been booked by better prepared summer guests

so we slept in the bird watching tower next to Heron Lake
we slept in our sleeping bags in a Tetris formation on the floor
the situation recalls a winter's day in an apartment I was living in
i looked down at the sidewalk, which was covered with snow
a child in a siren suit was slowly carrying shovelfuls of snow from one part of the sidewalk to another
the snow was distributed in a pattern across the sidewalk
it was still in the way for pedestrians

that I really liked, not the failure in it
(that we weren't prepared at the common, that the snow wasn't cleared)
it wasn't the failure in it that was nice
the failure in it was a charm at best

it was the formations that occupied me
the pattern we were lying in in the tower and the snow on the sidewalk
that pattern wanted to use us, like the strange child I saw wanted to use the snow
and it happened
it was a success (…).[14]

The actual surroundings at *Amager Fælled* (campfire, deer, refugees, Heron Lake/"Hejresøen", bird watching tower/"fuglekiggertårnet") become a catalyst for reflections upon how bodies (the group in their sleeping bags, the child in the snow) follow the invisible, that is to say the *virtual* patterns in space, which is quite another type of pattern-forming movement, or distribution, than the one that takes place in what Édouard Glissant in his *Poetics of Relation* has so strikingly called arrow-like territorialization.[15] Let us dwell first on the nomadic implications of the Tetris formation that the sleeping bags form in the bird watchers tower.

Deleuze speaks of nomadic distribution in the tenth series of the *Logique du sens*, called "Du jeu idéal"—On the Ideal Game. The game refers to Carroll's *Alice in Wonderland* which, as is well known, is a constant reference throughout the *Logique du sens*—and more specifically to the so-called *Caucus-race* which Alice attends, mystified. The Caucus-race is a running contest in which there are no precise rules for the race's beginning or end, which is why the game has neither winners nor losers. In ordinary games, pre-existing, categorical rules and distributive hypotheses are given in advance (probabilities can be calculated for the throwing of dice, for instance, if the game is continued for a certain while). Ordinary games (Ludo is an obvious example) follow a fixed and distinct numerical distribution—one walks the number of fields that are shown by the eyes of the dice, only to win or lose.

This game, says Deleuze, is a caricature of work and morality (Deleuze 2004, 84–5). World economy is governed by the logics of cause and effect, and thinks in terms of means and ends. On the contrary, the results of the Caucus-race are mobile—and they take place in an open space in which the logic of winners and losers is suspended and hypotheses about the outcome are impossible to make. The Caucus-race, then, to Deleuze, is the perfect image of nomadic distribution. And in Løppenthin's text, it is precisely the nomadic distribution of the game or the playing that brings about the experience which the text calls a "success." The sleeping bags "all by themselves" ("af sig selv") make a Tetris formation—that is, a formation which, like the aggregation of forms in the game Tetris, is unpredictable, and the child shuffles snow simply in order to make a pattern; it is being stressed that the action has no utilitarian value—the snow still "got in the pedestrians' way" ("var fortsat i vejen for fodgængerne").

Løppenthin's text also anchors its nomadic theme in the palpable environment of *Amager Fælled*. The group goes into the Common in order "to settle in a remote place in summer" ("at bosætte sig afsides *i sommeren*"), where the sedentary residents ("de fastboende") are asylum seekers or deer. There are "shelters," but they are occupied by the "summer guests of more foresight" ("better prepared summer guests").

The text deconstructs the difference between "sedentary residents" and "summer guests"—placing its own point of enunciation (the group spending the night in the bird watchers tower) at the center of the deconstructed difference. The equation looks more or less like this: deer and asylum seekers are obviously anything but "sedentary"—the animal has its territory but its boundaries are variable, and asylum seekers are the marginalized of this world; affirmative "nomadism" presupposes open boundaries, which is why one should not believe that the proponents of subjective nomadism are naively paying tribute to the marginalization of the migrant or indulging in some kind of privileged cosmopolitanism.[16]

To be true, the "sedentary" of the text are the opposite of just that, and the "shelters" of which it speaks certainly have not been built in order to house asylum seekers, but in order to give the city's residents an opportunity to spend a night surrounded by nature. The group that wants to "settle" in a temporary situation (i.e. "the summer") has not secured a "shelter" for themselves—in order to obtain such shelter it would be necessary to have foresight—and so the distinction between the sedentary and the non-sedentary dissolves as the text slides toward the non-identical. The group places itself in a place-between—the intermezzo of the bird watchers tower—something that corresponds to what Deleuze and Guattari have to say about the nomad:

> The nomad has a territory. He follows customary trajectories, he goes from one point to another, he does not ignore the points (water point, dwelling point, assembly point). But the question is what is principle or merely consequence in nomad life. In the first place even though the points determine the trajectories they are strictly subordinate to the trajectories they determine, conversely from what happens with the sedentary. (…) The life of the nomad is intermezzo. (Deleuze and Guattari 1980, 471–2)

The nomadic distribution is thus not the movement of parceling out or of capitalization—it does not parcel out *Amager Fælled* into entities from which someone or something might capitalize or profit—for instance by creating infrastructures (like a metro) to connect two parcels:

> The nomad trajectory may well follow customary paths or ways, it does not have the function of sedentary route which is to distribute a closed space to humans, assigning to each one his part, and regulating the communication of these parts. The nomad trajectory does the contrary, it distributes humans (or animals) in a space which is open, indefinite, non-communication. (Deleuze and Guattari 1980, 471–2)

The experiences depicted in both Nordenhof's and Løppenthin's poetry are inseparably intertwined with the specific geography of *Amager Fælled* ("A pattern wanted to use us," "Et monster ville bruge os"; see Løppenthin). The experiences triggered by precisely this *place* are experiences of freedom from "the distribution of closed spaces," that is, what we used to call private property. Private property, whose antithesis is the notion of an intrinsically *common* place: the commons.

An interesting historical trait of the commons, according to Silvia Federici, is the multiplicity of activities for which these grounds were used in late medieval Europe. The commons not only served as pasture, but also as rallying grounds and meeting places in which to celebrate festive occasions.[17] As already mentioned, *Amager Fælled* offers Asa believers a place in which to celebrate their rituals,[18] just as it is a well-known cruising area.[19]

In US LGBTQ (lesbian, gay, bisexual, transgender, queer/questioning) contexts, quite a lot has been written on cruising as well as on the consequences of gentrification for cruising possibilities. To my knowledge, this perspective does not come in a Danish/Scandinavian variety. First, we in Scandinavia lack representations of the implications of cruising space for (especially) homosexuals, and second we have been slow to acknowledge what the desertification that is prompted by gentrification means to our existence.[20]

Then, in 2016, Niels Henning Falk Jensby published his love story *TECHNO*, in which a central episode depicts a gangbang set in a famous cruising area in *Amager Fælled*.

Niels Henning Falk Jensby: The Sexual Politics of the Common

TECHNO's protagonist and his partner have gone on a trip to *Amager Fælled*. Theirs is a very loving relationship, their sexual life marked by the boyfriend's dominant role:

> Vi går på brede grusstier på Fælleden, er omkransede af den. Omkring den de nye reservater. Alle de nye bygninger. Glasfacaderne, der spejler det hele kaster sol over det hele. (…) Bunkerne gør det hele uigennemskueligt. Man kan nemt fare vild her, hvis man går væk fra de brede grusstier. Det siger du til mig. Du går hele tiden en halv meter foran mig, har en mærkelig bestemthed i dine skridt. Jeg tror godt jeg ved hvorfor, men jeg påtaler det ikke. (Falk Jensby 2016, 42)

> We walk on broad gravel paths in the Common, surrounded by it. All around it is the new reservations. All the new buildings. The facades of glass mirroring everything cast sun over everything. (…) The bushes make it all opaque. It's easy to get lost here if you leave the broad gravel paths. That's what you tell me. All the time you are walking half a yard ahead of me, a strange determination to your steps. I think I know why, but I'm not addressing it.[21]

What the protagonist has guessed is that he is to be put at the disposal of other men in the cruising scrubs of the Common—we shall return to this—but what should also be noticed are the terms in which *Amager Fælled* is described. The commons are surrounded by "new reservations" ("nye reservater"), meaning the new neighborhood called Ørestad, which is also Nordenhof's point of departure.

Labeling Ørestaden a "reserve" may imply that Ørestaden can be viewed as a place that is "protected from damaging external influences, and wherein an activity may be carried through without any hindrances or disturbances" (cf. the general definition of the word "reserve"). But calling a neighborhood a "reserve" carries no positive connotation. Here a specific kind of people live (those with means or those without any means), and whereas a natural reserve is created for the protection of biodiversity, the neighborhood-as-reserve constitutes a homogeneous and uniform environment—so the texts proceed to describe it as a world of reflections (the glass facades mirroring everything, throwing sunlight onto everything): in the reserve one "looks into the mirror and thinks it is a window," as Sarah Schulman so poignantly puts it (Schulman 2013, 28).

But in *TECHNO* the couple is moving away from the glass facades, into the confusion, impossible to survey, of scrubs and thickets:

> Du tager min hånd, fører mig med ned ad stien. Buskadset har groet sig ind i plænerne i en sådan formation, at hele denne gruppering ligger skjult for de mennesker, der går ude på de brede grusstier. Det er derfor, brødre kan gå frit herinde, agre frit herinde. Det er derfor de ligger nøgne på tæpper på tomme pladser og venter på hinanden herinde. (Falk Jensby 2016, 42)
>
> You take my hand, leading me down the path. The shrubbery has grown its way into the lawns in such a formation that this entire grouping lies hidden from the people walking the broad gravel paths. This is why brothers can move freely here, act freely here. This is why they lie naked on blankets, in empty spots, waiting for each other here.

"Brothers" are what the protagonist's partner calls other homosexual males, and the scrub is primarily an excellent cruising place because it protects the men from the gaze of passers-by. Again, this possibility of freedom comes out of *Amager Fælled*'s specific environment—*it is simply a result of the place's vegetation*, which—in the wording of Lea Løppenthin's poem—is a pattern that wants to use us. The protagonist is placed in the scrubs with his behind bared, and several men pay him a visit at the partner's instigation. Indeed, the vegetation itself serves as the point of departure of a Jean Genet-like string of images,[22] beginning as the protagonist sets his eye on a certain branch, while at the same time a number of different actors penetrate him:

> Jeg kan ane et træ bag ved busken. En af dets største grene er knækket af, ligger et sted hvor jeg ikke kan se den. Men nu dette: Træets åbne sår, hvorfra det sveder en tyk harpiks. Den flyder brun ned ad stammen, køber ud langs andre grene. Drypper ned i busken foran mig. Jeg ser harpiksen sive langsomt ned langs buskenes stilke, ned ad grene, sive ned i jorden og mærker hænder på mine balder. Mærker, hvordan de skiller dem ad, skaber frit udsyn til min endetarmsåbning. Jeg bliver eksamineret. Spytklatten, der spyttes, tungen, der borer sig ind i min endetarmsåbning, forstår jeg som en godkendelse. (Falk Jensby 2016, 44)
>
> I glimpse a tree behind the bush. One of its largest branches has broken off, and lies in a place where I can't see it. But now this: The tree's open sore from which it is sweating a thick resin. It is floating brown down the trunk, running along other branches. Dripping into the bush in front of me. I am watching the resin slowly sieving along the stalks of the bushes, down branches, sieving into the ground, and sense hands on my buttocks. Feel how they are parted, creating a free view of my anal orifice. I am examined. The gob of spittle being spit out, the tongue drilling its way into my anal orifice, this I understand as approval.

The string of images unites the thick resin with the human spit that is introduced into the anus—resin and spit united by the brown color, as anal sex often leads to the secretion of feces-colored liquids, and since many men come inside the I we are getting quite a wet affair on our hands:

> Jeg kan ingenting lige nu. Bare mærke lage løbe overalt: Jeg kan ikke undgå følelsen af,
>   at jeg skal ligge her i den gennemsigtige harpiks [sæden] resten af mine dage. (Falk Jensby 2016, 48)
>
> Right now I can do nothing. Just feel brine running everywhere: I cannot avoid the feeling that I will lie here, in the see-through resin [the semen], for the rest of my days.

That, though, is not going to be the case. It is time to go home—and the resin-dripping branch has to be carried along:

> Det grønne blad, indhyllet i harpiks. Jeg siger til dig, at vi kan knække den gren af busken, tage den med hjem. At vi kan erstatte orkidéen med den. Du siger okay. Vi kan tage i centret på vej hjem og købe en vase til den. Du går hen til grenen. Dine stærke hænder, albueleddet. Du knækker grenen af, giver den til mig. Harpiksen smitter af på min hånd, får grenen til at klistre sig fast. Vi går ud af det lille buskads. (Falk Jensby 2016, 48)
>
> The green leaf, covered in resin. I am telling you that we can break that branch off the bush, bring it home. That we can use it to replace the orchid. You say okay. We can go to the mall on our way home, and buy a vase for it. You go over to the branch. Your strong hands, the elbow joint. You break off the branch, you hand it to me. The resin stains my hands, makes the branch stick. We leave the small thicket.

The almost over-symbolical branch is therefore placed in the living room, and the I consults his phone, finding an index of "all plants at Amager Fælled" ("samtlige planter på Amager Fælled") (Falk Jensby 2016, 49).

The branch is discovered to be of giant knotweed, whose Latin name is *Fallopia sachalinensis*. The name fallopia connotes—to the I and his partner—phallus,[23] which is clearly understandable given the circumstances. Looking into the plant index reveals that fallopia is the plant family whose Danish name is *Silver rain* (Fallopia), whose species have arrow- or spear-formed leaves. It is hardly necessary to mention what the common connotations of arrows and spears are, the gliding of the signifier being as easy to grasp as a gliding can be.

The point of this entire passage is of course, once more, that it is the specific space of *Amager Fælled* that makes the encounter of bodies possible—or perhaps even furthers it—unsanctioned by the reign of private property, or any other regulatory mechanisms for that matter. The string of images giant knotweed-resin-spear-sweat-semen simply underlines the impact of the environment upon the body that participates in it. This is made quite explicit: "the resin stains my hand, makes the branch stick to it" ("harpiksen smitter af på min hånd, får grenen til at klistre sig fast") (Falk Jensby 2016, 48).

In the novel the episode on *Amager Fælled* is an unequivocally positive experience in the mind of the I narrator. There is no coercion at all involved in what is happening—no one is taking anything they are not supposed to take. The gangbang in the cruising thicket of *Amager Fælled* is a 100% ethical act. The I is not even taking drugs, though he often does.

The ethical aspect of the episode on *Amager Fælled* is, very importantly, highlighted by the contrast it offers to another event in *TECHNO*. An event that proves completely destructive to the I, since it involves the worst kind of coercion, namely rape. The I is raped by a guy that he has brought home (his partner is in Berlin), and who almost tries to strangle him, triggering a powerful anxiety that will demand treatment and on top of it all ruin the relationship with his boyfriend.

But in the scrubs of the commons there is no coercion—there may even be some kind of community, an experience that the novel, although in a very different manner, shares with Asta Olivia Nordenhof's and Lea Løppenthin's texts on *Amager Fælled*. In Nordenhof, a feeling of belonging with the surroundings is established, a concord that simply *needs* to be shared, not only with those present, but also with those absent ("must write to morten! must write to bjørn!," "må skrive til morten! må skrive til bjørn!"). In Løppenthin the position of enunciation is collective, cf. "we" ("vi") and "the Tetris formation" ("Tetris-formationen"). And the group perspective is significant in Liv Sejrbo Lidegaard as well, whose debut in 2015 was a volume of poetry that quite simply carried the title *Fælleden*.

Liv Sejrbo Lidegaard: The Common as Common Ground

The first suite of poems of the volume is called "Close up/close by" ("Tæt på"), and in the suite's second part we once again find ourselves on or around *Amager Fælled*. The first passage goes thus:

> har ikke været alene i flere uger. ikke siden en morgen jeg vågnede
> op på en bænk og frøs, gik hen til et bål, der var en der gav mig en
> jakke og en cola. har samlet nogle blå kornblomster. vi gik og ledte
> efter brænde ved stranden. sover let, det er lyst hele tiden. (Lidegaard 2015, 15)

> haven't been alone for weeks. not since a morning when i woke/up on a
> bench freezing, went to a campfire, somebody gave me a/jacket and a coke.
> have gathered some blue cornflowers. we walked around looking/for firewood on the beach. sleeping lightly, it's bright all the time.[24]

The tone of voice is at one and the same time matter-of-factish and slightly un- or de-realizing. The I has been alone, but is now together with somebody who has fed her (coke) and warmed her (a jacket). It is midsummer in Scandinavia (bright all the time, cornflowers), something which may enhance the slightly euphoric state in which the I finds herself. In the first passage we might just be anywhere during the Nordic summer—but the next passage makes it clear that we are likely to be in Amager—on the commons from which the book borrows its name:

> flyene er lige over os, flyver tæt på som fuglene. teltet lugter af
> døde myrer og sidste års græs. vi har hængt vasketøj til tørre i
> krattet. da jeg vågnede lå mine venner omkring mig og sov.
> (Lidegaard 2015, 15)

> the planes are right above us, flying close by like birds. the tent smells of/dead ants and last year's grass we have hung laundry out to dry in/the thicket. as i woke up, my friends lay sleeping around me.

So the I has gone camping of sorts with her friends, and it is true that planes fly very low over the commons, since the airport is only a few kilometers away. But the question is what valorization is given to this air traffic. The planes are "close by as the birds" ("tæt på som fuglene"), but the equation of "the planes" ("*flyene*") with "birds" ("*fuglene*") does not really seem to pose a problem. In the next passage we find the following: "is it orange a sunset or reflecting the lights of the city. the water smells of bog. the planes drown our voices. we cannot start washing our hands now. the air sticks to my skin" ("er det orange en solnedgang eller byens genskær. vandet lugter af mose. flyene overdøver os. vi kan ikke begynde at vaske hænder nu. luften klæber til min hud"). There is a lot to notice here. First, the text works using paratactical, de-hierarchized syntax. All statements are juxtaposed, the text employs lower-case letters. Second, the sunset or the reflection of the city lights, like the planes and birds, is a phenomenon that is described in terms of continuity. One cannot tell what is "natural" and what is "unnatural"—nor is there any point in telling them apart, since "we cannot start washing our hands now"—nothing is pure ("the water smells of bog" and the air "sticks" to the skin). Nothing is pure and the idea that something is able to or would have to be pure is not one with which this kind of environmentally conscious poetry is working. To the pure all things are pure—but here we are rather, like in Nordenhof, getting *dirtier*. Not being able to wash one's hands is of course both a real experience (there is no clean water nearby) and a stock phrase about not wanting to accept one's guilt, like Pontius Pilate. In this case guilt has to do with global warming. Longing for the pre-industrial world is not an option in this text, a point that does not imply that it merely accepts the critical state of the planet. It also speaks of what it is that the group on the commons are "rehearsing" ("øver sig på"), namely "survival" ("overlevelse"). It is as if the camping group were *preppers* at heart, a position, it has to be said, of abandon.

However, a dynamics evolves within the group, something that barely resembles unmixed, isolationist (deep ecology) resignation. This becomes especially clear from the suite's final passage:

> driver langt ned ad stranden. svømmer og vader tilbage mod
> strømme. løber så hurtigt vi kan. ikke fordi vi har travlt. ikke
> fordi vi vil komme først. det er ikke en dans. det er et løb. det er
> ikke et håb, det er et forsøg. rundt om hinanden. salt, sand, maver,
> vand, tang, alger, småsten, skaller, øjenbryn, eller hjemve, eller
> vinden som havet for et øjeblik siden. (Lidegaard 2015, 20)
>
> drifting long down the beach. swimming and wading back
> against the stream. running as fast as we can. not because we are in a hurry. not
> because we want to be first, it's not a dance, it's a run. it's
> not a hope, it's an attempt, around each other. salt, sand, bellies,
> water, seaweed, pebbles shells, eyebrows, or homesickness, or
> the wind like the sea a moment ago.

These lines are quite an accurate description, not of the pattern of movement of an individual, but of that of a group—a pattern of movement which earlier on, speaking of Løppenthin's poem, I described as a Deleuzian Caucus-race: a perfect example of nomadic distribution. It is NOT a dance (a dance has rules), there are no winners and no losers ("not because we want to be first," "ikke fordi vi vil komme først"), nor is it a teleological movement (there is no "hope" ["håb"])—but it is an *attempt* in which the group of bodies even blends together with the rest of the place's physical environment, like small particles of sand that stick to a humid body.

In the already quoted interview from *Information*, Lidegaard has other interesting proposals about the significance of the Common. The interview was not in fact conducted because of the book of poetry, but because *Amager Fælled*, as I write this, is threatened by invasion: part of the area is simply to be laid out for housing purposes. Besides pointing to the Common's importance as a place to stay "because it has no economical value," this is what Lidegaard answers when asked by the journalist about the threatened biodiversity of the site. "There is quite a special fly called the *Xanthogramma festivum* out here, isn't there?" asks the journalist, and Lidegaard answers:

> Yes. And this is a difficult argument to make. A small fly, why would it be important that it doesn't disappear? In a way it doesn't matter, on the other hand it absolutely does matter. And this is partly what has driven me to writing this book. The need for some answers to this question. We are used to thinking about what has value, a kind of utilitarian thought that might be difficult to argue against, just as it is difficult to argue for a space that doesn't have any use. But I have experience of watching places being destroyed she says and refers among other things to the part of Ørestaden that has already been built. (Villesen 2016)

According to Lidegaard, *Amager Fælled* represents an area without *utility*. A place that does not matter, seen from the viewpoint of the capital, though this does not mean that the capital would not like to make it valid and useful by granting it capital value. It is, however, a place that really does matter seen from the perspective of contemporary Danish literature.

The conclusion must be admissible that the four authors I have mentioned here make a tremendous investment, both in a quite literal, palpable manner and symbolically, in a place known as *Amager Fælled*. And we may now perhaps answer the question why it is that this particular *place*, this *space of given reference*, provides the stuff of dreams for other communities and other ways of being in the world than the one offered to us by late capitalist society.

Amager Fælled as Political Utopia

As it has been stressed, *Amager Fælled* is almost in Copenhagen—it is a relatively easy matter for many of the city center inhabitants to go there. At the same time, the very name *the commons* has a distinct set of connotations both in a Danish and in an international context, nor is *Amager Fælled* the only "common" in Copenhagen. The most well known, and the one that is of greatest relevance to us here, is the area known as *Fælledparken* or the "Commons Gardens"—but which is in fact the old *Nørre Fælled* or "Northern Common." A green area which is probably best known for housing the International Workers' Day, as well as for being adjacent to the city stadium, formerly known as *Idrætsparken*, by know reduced to the commercial-colloquial *Parken*. *Nørre Fælled* was the scene of one of the most important events in Danish political history: "The Battle of the Common" (*Slaget på Fælleden*), which took place on May 5, 1872—only a year after the defeat of the Paris Commune. The Danish workers' leader Louis Pio had called for a grand rally with a view to igniting a revolution,[25] but was arrested the day before the meeting, and Copenhagen's director of police banned the rally. Notwithstanding, thousands of workers gathered on *Nørre Fælled*, where fighting erupted between workers, police, and hussars who charged the workers with drawn sabers. No one was killed, but many were wounded, and the Battle of the Common must be characterized as the single most violent event in the history of Danish workers. This story bears no relation to the literature of which I am writing here—and then again it does. It is impossible to speak of "the commons" in a Danish context without connoting in one way or another the Battle of 1872, or at least the workers' movement. And while *Nørre Fælled* was a battlefield in the past, *Amager Fælled* may become one in the future. On Sunday, September 16, 2016, more than 2000 people demonstrated against the plans to build high-rises of approximately 260,000 m² on the most biologically vulnerable part of *Amager Fælled*. The protest took the shape of people taking each other's hands and forming a protective human chain around the salt meadow. It was a quiet protest, and no revolutionary leaflets were circulated, but it is a form of protest that does seem to be able to gather rather a large number of people, to which it must be added that it is in some cases the last remaining resort. On that Sunday on Amager, a future injustice was symbolically "prevented from happening." But this form of protest has been used in other cases, in which the need for protection has been otherwise acute.[26] So a new battle of the commons may be under way. And contemporary Danish literature contributes to the articulation of what we might perhaps term the place's virtual resources—those returning qualities in places that are brought forth in the writing of texts, and which the geocritical-Deleuzian perspective helps uncover. They are first and foremost:

- An experience of community and solidarity—not just between humans but with the surroundings as such.
- The experience of an open (nomadic) space in which the movements of the body are not regulated in advance, and wherein the human relationship with the surroundings is marked by continuity.

- A space where biodiversity is able to thrive without being enclosed. The Commons is not a reservation.
- A site free from coercion, where there is room for exchange that cannot be capitalized.

This is quite a lot at one and the same time, but it is striking how interconnected the questions and the thematics of these texts are. Amager and *Amager Fælled* as late capitalist utopia-machines?

The last chapter in the history of Shitty Island most definitely remains to be written.

Notes

1. All translations are mine unless other translators are mentioned.
2. This text does not intend to provide a comprehensive literary history of Amager as a motif. Although this would in fact be a welcome thing, my emphasis will still be on contemporary literature. Two other depictions of Amager in Danish literature that are both extremely interesting and rather ambiguous should, however, not go unmentioned: Hans Christian Andersen's (2004) *Fodreise fra Holmens Canal til Østpynten af Amager i aarene 1828 og 1829*, and Klaus Rifbjerg's *Amagerdigte* (1965).
3. *Vidensindsamling Natur 2013 Amager Fælled, Biomedia, Rapport til Københavns Kommune*. Written by Anders N. Michaelsen and Johanne Bak, Biomedia and Lars Andersen. Handed in for publication.
4. *Blót* is the Old Norse name for sacrifice.
5. In Denmark, the corresponding reorganization of agriculture is known as *udskiftningen* and takes place around 1800; it has its own local history.
6. See, for instance, *Capital*, I, chapter 27. My account, however, primarily follows Silvia Federici's analysis of the enclosure's significance as presented in Federici's (2004) book *Caliban and the Witch: Women, the Body, and Primitive Accumulation*.
7. For examples of the World Bank driving people away from areas of common exploitation, see, for instance, Silvia Federici and George Caffentzis: "Commons Against and Beyond Capitalism" (2013).
8. As is well known, Timothy Morton (2007) has suggested that we stop speaking of "nature" and start speaking of "the environment" instead. In short, nature is automatically framed as an "outside," whereas we are inextricably entangled with our environment, the latter notion being of course a basic assumption of ecology.
9. It is the book that has attracted the greatest amount of comment. In the newspaper *Information*, May 5, 2014, the author of these lines described

it as eco-critical in the article "Litteratur der gør den økologiske bevidsthed sanselig"; Jens Kramshøj Flinker analyses it in terms of an ideological critique of neoliberal developments in society, whereas Tue Andersen Nexø (2016) has an almost opposite interpretation of it as a rebuttal of the welfare state. See Jens Kramshøj Flinker (2013): *Litteratur i 00'erne—en ny ideologikritik* and Tue Andersen Nexø: *Vidnesbyrd fra velfærdsstaten*.
10. Translated by Susanna Nied to whom I wish to express my warmest thanks.
11. "*Lovgivning vedrørende Ørestad*" ("Legislation concerning Ørestad") was voted in 1992. The "unused" areas of Amager were considered far too valuable for them just to be left to lie, and on March 11, 1993, *Ørestadsselskabet* (The Ørestad Company) was founded, its mission being to manage the growth of the newly founded district.
12. The construction of the metro has been marred by numerous "scandals": social dumping, corruption, messy accounts and lack of tax payments, illegal firings, and so on. This is, according to the Danish social scientist Bent Flyvbjerg, inevitably the case in large public construction projects, but as he says in an interview with *DJØF-bladet* (January 19, 2014) an untamable desire for recognition and profit prevents the initiators from drawing a lesson from the sins of the past: "Politicians adore mega-projects like monuments. They provide media attention, both when they are started, and when there is a ribbon to cut. At the same time, the huge financial scope of these projects means that there is a lot of money to be made by a lot of actors. Consulting firms, construction firms, lawyers, labor and management, and finally engineers, who love the projects because they are innovative and groundbreaking and may become drivers of the development of technological know-how that can be sold abroad."
13. Morton's ecology is above all dark because it includes the ugly or unbeautiful—not just butterflies and oaks but fried chicken and beer cans are also part of the environmental circuit.
14. Translation by Peter Borum and myself. My thanks to Lea Løppenthin for providing a very helpful draft.
15. In *Poetics of Relation* (2000, 59) Édouard Glissant (becoming thereby complementary to Deleuze and Guattari) distinguishes "arrowlike" territorialization—for instance that of colonization—from "wandering," "circling" territorialization—for instance that for which the wandering poet stands. This corresponds fairly well to what Westphal says about territorialization in *La Géocritique* (2007, 87–96), since he also has need of a non-conquering concept of territorialization.
16. Rosi Braidotti strongly stresses that "nomadic subjectivity" has nothing to do with being a refugee or having no fixed residence. See Rosi Braidotti: "By Way of Nomadism" in *Nomadic Subjects: Embodiment and Sexual Difference in Contemporary Feminist Theory*, 1994.

17. It is telling that the need for biopolitical control of reproduction, which in Federici's compelling analysis forms the basis of the witch trials, fosters ideas of nocturnal sex orgies in unenclosed spaces (Federici 2004, 192–8).
18. See http://www.religion.dk/andre-religioner-og-trosretninger/hvad-bygger-asatroende-deres-religions-paa-i-sag.
19. In *Homoseksuel Sex-Guide København* one finds the following description in a review of *Amager Fælled*: "Location: Large Natural Reserve in Amager." There are two good places: http://findvej.dk/55.65406,12.5698?zoom=16&maptype=3 and … http://findvej.dk/55.65013,12.5687?zoom=16&maptype=3. "Time: on principle all day from 9 AM until 10 PM. Activity: moderate to high … mostly in summer. Who goes there: mostly between 25 and 75 years old. … MY ASSESSMENT FROM 1–6 STARS: **** (super nice natural surroundings with lots of space—but too many exhibitionist nudists and sometimes too little action)." http://sol.dk/debat/homoseksuel-sex-guide-k%C3%B8benhavn.
20. When Ursula Andkjær Olsen and I edited the first issue of the journal *Kritik* in the spring of 2013, the theme was "gentrification." We had a hard time finding Danish contributors, and the notion itself was subjected to a devastating critique from the literary editor of Denmark's largest cultural newspaper *Politiken*, the very idea of problematizing "gentrification" being regarded as viewing matters from an elitist perspective. Much has changed since then, but it is obviously difficult for the Scandinavian welfare model to accept the questioning of prevalent models of urban planning.
21. All translations from *TECHNO* are by Peter Borum and myself. They have been approved by Niels Henning Falk Jensby.
22. See the famous vaseline passage from the *Journal du voleur* (1982)—brilliantly analyzed by Derrida in *Glas*, 1974.
23. In fact, it refers to the Italian sixteenth-century scientist Gabriele Falloppio, so from this perspective there is no reference to the erect penis. Then again, Falloppio is known, among other things, for being the first to describe a condom in scientific terms.
24. All translations by Liv Sejrbo Lidegaard.
25. In the pamphlet calling for the rally, entitled "Maalet er fuldt" (Pio 2016; "Our cup is full"), it says, among other things: "Should we allow ourselves to be led like lambs to the slaughter by Capital? Should we suffer that our enemies stop our advance, perhaps for years on end? No, the workers of Copenhagen cannot in all decency let this pass! Let us therefore gather together; governments are anytime prone to hold a review of those of their subjects whom they sacrifice on the altar of war-madness at the first given occasion in order to satisfy their ambition. So let us then muster all free workers, all who will help us in the struggle against capital; then we shall

know our own power and the weakness of our enemies; gathered in the thousands we will state our claims and promise each other to stand shoulder by shoulder until victory is ours! But you, worshippers of gold! You, blood-suckers of the poor! You shall be met once again with the clamor: 'For millenia you have been pouring us a bitter drink of life; beware, our cup is full! Let not a single drop fall into it or—it overflows!'" https://www.arbejdermuseet.dk/wp-content/uploads/2016/10/2402140_kilde-1-2.pdf.
26. http://politiken.dk/debat/ECE2475611/behoever-lykke-at-vaere-synonymt-med-selvtilstraekkelighed-for-danskerne/. This article by Danish writer Carsten Jensen (2014) describes an attempt to save two Afghan children from being deported by forming a protective circle of human bodies around them at Copenhagen Airport.

REFERENCES

Andersen, Hans Christian. 2004. *Fodreise fra Holmens Canal til Østpynten af Amager i aarene 1828 og 1829*. København: Det Danske Sprog- og Litteraturselskab.
Braidotti, Rosi. 1994. By Way of Nomadism. In *Nomadic Subjects: Embodiment and Sexual Difference in Contemporary Feminist Theory*, 1–41. New York: Columbia University Press.
Culler, Jonathan. 1981. Apostrophe. In *The Pursuit of Signs: Semiotics, Literature, Deconstruction*, 135–155. Ithaca: Cornell University Press.
Deleuze, Gilles. 2004 [1969]. *The Logic of Sense*. Translated by Mark Lester with Charles Stivale, edited by Constantin V. Boundas. London: Continuum Impacts.
Deleuze, Gilles, and Félix Guattari. 1980. *Capitalisme et schizophrénie 2: Mille plateaux*. Paris: Les Éditions de Minuit.
Derrida, Jacques. 1974. *Glas*. Paris: Editions Galilée.
Falk Jensby, Niels Henning. 2016. *TECHNO*. København: Gyldendal.
Federici, Silvia. 2004. *Caliban and the Witch: Women, the Body, and Primitive Accumulation*. New York: Autonomedia.
Federici, Silvia, and George Caffentzis. 2013. Commons Against and Beyond Capitalism. *Upping the Anti: A Journal of Theory and Action* 15 (September): 83–97.
Flinker, Jens Kramshøj. 2013. *Litteratur i 00'erne—en ny ideologikritik*. Hellerup: Spring.
Genet, Jean. 1982 [1949]. *Journal du voleur*. Paris: Gallimard.
Glissant, Édouard. 2000 [1990]. *Poetics of Relation*. Translated by Betsy Wing. Ann Arbor: University of Michigan Press.
Heiberg, Johanne Louise. 1944 [1891]. *Et liv gjenoplevet i Erindringen 1842–49*, vol. II. København: Arkiv for dansk litteratur.

Jensen, Carsten. 2014. Behøver lykke at være synonymt med selvtilstrækkelighed for danskerne? *Politiken*, December 7.
Lidegaard, Liv Sejrbo. 2015. *Fælleden*. København: Gyldendal.
Lindegaard, Hanne. 2001. *Ud af røret? Planer, processer og paradokser omkring det Københavnske kloaksystem 1840–2001*. PhD thesis, DTU.
Løppenthin, Lea Marie. 2014. *nervernes adresse*. København: Gladiator.
Marx, Karl. 1867. *Das Kapital, I*. Otto Meissner: Hamburg.
Michaelsen, A.N. et al. 2014. *Vidensindsamling Natur 2013 Amager Fælled*. Biomedia foril Københavns Kommune. January. http://www.avlu.dk/wp-content/2014/09/Vidensindsamling-Natur-Amager-Fælled-2013.pdf.
Morton, Timothy. 2007. *Ecology without Nature: Rethinking Environmental Aesthetics*. Cambridge, MA and London: Harvard University Press.
Nexø, Tue Andersen. 2016. *Vidnesbyrd fra velfærdsstaten*. København: Arena.
Nordenhof, Asta Olivia. 2013. *det nemme og det ensomme*. København: Forlaget Basilisk.
Olsen, Ursula Andkjær, and Elisabeth Friis. 2013. *Kritik*, "Gentrificering," no. 207. København: Gyldendal.
Pape, Morten. 2015. *Planen*. København: Gyldendal.
Pio, Louis. 2016 [1872]. *Maalet er fuldt*. https://www.arbejdermuseet.dk/wp-content/uploads/2016/10/2402140_kilde-1-2.pdf.
Rifbjerg, Klaus. 1965. *Amagerdigte*. København: Gyldendal.
Schulman, Sarah. 2013. *The Gentrification of the Mind: Witness to a Lost Imagination*. Berkeley, Los Angeles, London: University of California Press.
Westphal, Bertrand. 2007. *La Géocritique: Réel, Fiction, Espace*. Paris: Les Éditions de Minuit.

OTHER RESOURCES

"Lovgivning vedrørende Ørestad" ("Legislation concerning Ørestad"). 1992. https://www.retsinformation.dk/eli/ft/199112K00024.
DJØF-bladet. 2014, January 19. http://www.djoefbladet.dk/blad.aspx?y=2014.
Villesen, Kristian. 2016. Slaget om Fælleden. *Information*, October 8. https://www.information.dk/mofo/farvel-sidste-sted-omkring-formaaet-lade-vaere-fred.

Open Access This chapter is licensed under the terms of the Creative Commons Attribution 4.0 International License (http://creativecommons.org/licenses/by/4.0/), which permits use, sharing, adaptation, distribution and reproduction in any medium or format, as long as you give appropriate credit to the original author(s) and the source, provide a link to the Creative Commons licence and indicate if changes were made.

The images or other third party material in this chapter are included in the chapter's Creative Commons licence, unless indicated otherwise in a credit line to the material. If material is not included in the chapter's Creative Commons licence and your intended use is not permitted by statutory regulation or exceeds the permitted use, you will need to obtain permission directly from the copyright holder.

CHAPTER 3

Mapping a Postmodern Dystopia: Hassan Loo Sattarvandi's Construction of a Swedish Suburb

Cristine Sarrimo

The Million Housing Programme is the name of a well-known housing development in Sweden. It was initiated by the Social Democratic government in 1965. The aim was to build one million apartments to rectify the shortage of housing and to improve the standard of living. Between 1965 and 1975, approximately one million apartments were built in small towns and outside the city centers of the largest cities (Gråbacke and Jörnmark 2010, 236–7).

Today, in the mindset of people and in public discourses, the Million Housing Programme areas are often apprehended as places of social unrest, unemployment, problems related to migration and poor schooling—places where the idealized Social Democratic welfare state is demolished or has failed (Ristilammi 1997, 75).[1] Certain areas have become stigmatized, and even perceived as spaces outside "real" Sweden. In *Expressen*, one of the largest Swedish tabloids, an article series about suburbs is introduced as follows:

C. Sarrimo (✉)
Lund University, Lund, Sweden

© The Author(s) 2020
K. Malmio, K. Kurikka (eds.), *Contemporary Nordic Literature and Spatiality*, Geocriticism and Spatial Literary Studies, https://doi.org/10.1007/978-3-030-23353-2_3

Nearly half a million live in a Sweden that is forgotten, abandoned but at the same time at the center of the debate. It is about parallel societies, scared police officers, conflicts with religious signatures and networks of criminals that have the power. It is about economic poverty, social vulnerability and a galloping gap with the rest of society. But also about the inhabitants' struggle for a better future. (Moreno 2016, 8; Trans. CS)

The above excerpt summarizes a widespread picture of certain suburbs in contemporary media: especially those located in the urban areas of the largest cities in Sweden. The word "suburb" has even become a metonymy in media discourses telling the "entire" story of deprived childhoods and marginalization. In France, a comparable representation of *la banlieue* is detectable in mainstream media: there is a "reductive view promoted in the mass media of '*la banlieue*' (without the plural 's') as a 'singular' (i.e., undifferentiated) space of alterity" (Prieto 2013, 107). In a manner similar to that of Sweden, discussion of the "*crise des banlieues*" in France "almost invariably turns to talk of immigration and minorities" (Prieto 2013, 108).

Many artists, musicians and authors have first-hand experience of living in a Million Housing Programme area. One out of four people in Sweden now lives or has earlier lived in one of these areas. One of them is the author Hassan Loo Sattarvandi, who in his novel *Still* (Sattarvandi 2008) portrays a Million Housing Programme area called Hagalund, which is located north of the city center of the capital Stockholm. The purpose of this chapter is to analyze Sattarvandi's construction of Hagalund with the aim of mapping the novel's dystopian space.

Sattarvandi was born in 1975 in Tehran and came to Sweden when he was three years old. He grew up in Hagalund. The area is mostly known for its eight light blue skyscrapers located on a hill. The blue buildings are interconnected with footbridges overarching spacious yards. In Stockholm, Hagalund is often called Bluehill [Blåkulla n.d.], the place where witches are said to fly on their brooms on Easter Eve. It is also called Blowinghill [Blåskulla] due to the spacious yards where the wind is said to constantly blow. When building these skyscrapers at the beginning of the 1970s, a former working-class suburb consisting of small wooden houses dating from the 1890s and onward was demolished. Hagalund is thus a multilayered cultural historical site, but in *Still* its history is absent. In the novel the skyscrapers, footbridges and yards are the main sites and they play a pivotal part in how the protagonists perceive the place in which they move around. The novel is mostly narrated in the present tense, which is one of its main features, showing that the space constructed is characterized by the loss of memory, and the absence of both a past and a future.

To grasp how the novel's dystopian space is constructed and what the term "dystopia" entails, the theoretical framework is informed by the geocriticism of Bertrand Westphal (Westphal 2011), Eric Prieto's study on the postmodern poetics of place (Prieto 2013), and Fredric Jameson's concept *cognitive mapping* (Jameson 1988, 1992). According to Westphal, geocriticism is geocentric, multifocal, stratigraphic and polysensorial. This means that the primary focus is a geographical site that is possible to locate on a map. The place analyzed is viewed as an accumulation of different historical strata, which necessitates a multifocal approach, that is, other texts and representations than literary ones must be taken into account to broaden the perspectives on the site chosen. Finally, the sensorial perceptions of place consist of the auditive, olfactoric and tactile, and not just the visual. Literature and other art forms can thus contribute to diversify the understanding of individuals' sensorial perceptions of place (Westphal 2011, 111–47).

Eric Prieto prefers to use the term "place," making the following distinctions: "Place, then, will be understood (…) at the most general level, to designate any geographical site (of any size, scale, or type) that is meaningful to someone, for whatever reason. (…) A site does not become a place until a person comes along and enters into a meaning-generating relationship with it" (Prieto 2013, 13). Following Prieto, "place" in this chapter will be used to designate a site distinguishable on a map or in the landscape: Both Hagalund and Stockholm exist in reality and can be visited and perceived. Having said that, Sattarvandi's Hagalund is a literary representation. To underscore its representational and discursive functions, the terms "space" and "spatiality" will be used. The dystopian space Sattarvandi constructs in his novel will in this chapter be understood as a postmodern one inspired by Prieto's study on postmodern literary places and Fredric Jameson's view on how globalization and a late capitalist society can affect the individual's conceptions of and relation to place (Prieto 2013; Jameson 1992).

Geography as Destiny: A Cage of Exile—Socially Deprived and Culturally Appropriated

Still, the novel's title, has similar significations in both Swedish and English: calm, quiet, smooth and something that stands still (including the stillness of death). The main character and first person narrator is a young man called Nemo. There is no traditionally structured plot culminating in a cathartic solution. The novel is mostly narrated in the present tense in a constant flow without any dots, and depicts Nemo and his few male friends, their movements, dialogues, their drug abuse and sometimes violent behavior.

Due to the present tense, *Still* seems to take place in a constant "here and now" without any past or future, which creates a feeling of claustrophobia. The young men never leave Hagalund. Unemployed, with no studies, no leisure time and no family ties, they have no reason to go to the Stockholm city center or elsewhere. If their movements were traced on a map, they would mainly be limited to passing back and forth over the footbridges connecting the yards between the light blue buildings. Occasionally, the friends use the elevator to go up to an apartment, and at times they go down to the building's cellar or garbage room, where they use drugs. The geographical and physical environment is a very limited part of the suburb Hagalund:

> (…) några timmar senare—efter jag gjort en hel del menlösa och helt intetsägande saker—gick jag från första gården till den andra gården, från andra gården till den tredje gården, från den tredje gården till den fjärde gården, allt var så identiskt—så lika, ibland visste jag inte ens var jag var, var jag stod, vad jag såg, vem jag såg och allt omkring mig var byggt på samma sätt, med samma färger och vi som gick omkring i detta gick i samma takt, med samma blick, och samma—samma—samma och inne, innanför bröstet vaknade tristessen mer och mer och paniken spred sig ut i kroppen och känslolösheten var där och inget kunde döva den nu, tänkte jag och när vi alla hade gått runt så i några varv satte jag mig på den första gården och bara väntade på att någon skulle se mig och fråga—hur allt var, vad händer (…) *det var en exakt lika tråkig och menlös dag i exil som alla andra dagar*, men just den här dagen var något menlösare, något tråkigare och helt olidlig att andas igenom (…) (Sattarvandi 2008, 121–2; Italics CS)

> (…) a few hours later—after I did some bland and completely meaningless things—I walked from the first yard to the second yard, from the second yard to the third yard, from the third yard to the fourth yard, everything was so identical—so similar, sometimes I didn't even know where I was, where I stood, what I saw, who I saw and everything around me was built in the same way, in the same colors and we who walked around in this, we walked at the same pace, with the same gaze, and the same—same—same and inside, inside the breast, aridity awoke more and more and panic spread in the body and apathy was there, and nothing could deaden it now I thought, and when we all had gone around like that a few turns I sat down in the first yard and just waited for someone to see me and to ask me—how everything

was going, what's happening (…) *it was just as boring and empty a day in exile as all the other days*, but this day was a bit more pointless a bit more arid and completely excruciating to breathe through (…)[2]

Depending on the lack of a traditional plot, there are few markers of time passing and no movement forward by the characters. They have no ambitions except finding and taking drugs; there is no individual or psychological development. Only daylight and twilight indicate that time passes. "Exile" is the word highlighted in the quotation above, and it sums up the life Nemo and his friends are living. They move in a limited space as in a prison. Everything stands still in a literal sense.

The focus of the novel is geocentric, that is, it solely depicts a limited part of the suburb of Hagalund. The rest of Hagalund and the area outside the suburb are described as a distant noise. Sweden and the world outside Sweden are never an integrated part of the diegesis. The "world" is exclusively present through other inhabitants in Bluehill, who are racified or attributed another nationality than Swedish: they are called Greeks, Poles and Gooks, but never portrayed. Romani people are pictured as enemies to the main character Nemo, who bullies a disabled Romani boy.

"Sweden" as a nation is only present in *Still* by billboards with election slogans; there is obviously an election to come but Nemo and his friends take no part in it. The nation is also present through well-known discourses about migration and the suburbs. They are voiced in the novel by an omniscient narrator, by Nemo and one of his friends, Saladin. Critical views on cultural appropriation are put forward in the novel, expressed by an implied critical authorial voice. These views, however, never affect the life world of the suburb or the inhabitants of the "prison." A production company is making a music video with a hip hop group whose members live in Bluehill, and the cameraman in charge of the film is ridiculed:

> *Grabbar*, sa han och pekade mot det fjärde huset, *det skulle vara bra om vi kunde få med båda husen på den sidan—det ger ett jävligt coolt förortsintryck—lite getto och om man håller kameran så här, då ser husen helt enorma ut—det skulle se jävligt maxat ut* (…) *Kom igen nu—killar*, sa den tunnhåriga snubben bakom kameran, *attityd, attityd, attityd, förort, förort, förort, attityd—kom igen nu—visa att ni är tuffa, farliga och att ni kommer från gettot, det ska bara skriiiiiiiika förort—den här videon ska filma rakt på pucken—rakt in i verkligheten, farliga blickar som ska skrämma tittaren* (…) (Sattarvandi 2008, 30–1; Italics original)

Guys, he said and pointed toward the fourth house, *it would be nice if we could film both houses on this side—it will make a hell of a cool impression of the suburb—a bit ghetto and if you hold the camera like this, the houses look completely enormous—that would look fucking great.* (...) *Come on now—guys*, said the thin-haired dude behind the camera, *attitude, attitude, attitude, suburb, suburb, suburb, attitude—come on now—show that you are tough, dangerous and that you come from the ghetto, it must blaaaaaaaaaast out suburb—this video must film right on—right on reality, dangerous gazes that must scare the viewer* (...)

The cameraman uses one of the most worn-out metaphors of the contemporary Swedish suburb—the melting pot—and thus shallowly connects it to migration and celebrates its presumed exoticism: "*Det är förbannat synd att man inte är från förorten, det är här det händer*—(...) *förorten är grejen, förorten är maxad, kulturerna möts, exotisk mat och—och—alla exotiska kulturer som bara möts i en gryta*" (Sattarvandi 2008, 32; Italics original). ("*It is too bad that you don't come from the suburb, it's here that everything happens*—(...) *the suburb is the thing, the suburb is the coolest, the cultures meet, exotic food and—and—all exotic cultures that only meet in a pot*").

At the beginning of the twenty-first century, novels and poetry called "immigrant literature" written by so-called immigrant authors were discussed in the literary public sphere in Sweden. The appearance of these concepts was, according to the Swedish literary scholar Magnus Nilsson, a consequence of critics reading literature through an "ethnic filter." Certain authors were identified as representatives of an imagined contemporary multicultural society, which led to a discriminating, homogenizing and racifying attitude toward them, as well as to a reductive understanding of their works (Nilsson 2010, 15–53). These attributes—immigrant literature and immigrant author—were therefore criticized and ironically depicted, not least in novels by authors who had been ethnically identified and hence read as telling authentic stories of contemporary immigrant experiences. Instead, Nilsson offers a class oriented and social reading of these works, arguing that the authors are defying the "ethnic filter" and contesting the contemporary Swedish view of the multicultural society, which basically is an imagined ideologically constructed space (Nilsson 2010, 80–135).

In *Still* there are recognizable traces from this debate about immigrant ethnic culture when Nemo's friend Saladin gives voice to what can be defined as a cultural appropriation of the experiences and reality of Bluehill inhabitants:

3 MAPPING A POSTMODERN DYSTOPIA: HASSAN LOO SATTARVANDI'S... 61

(...) *de vill ha förortshumor, de vill ha Gringo, de vill ha skitsnack och piss—du vet, förut trodde jag att jag levde i verkligheten, sen kom den rakt upp i mitt ansikte varje dag—jag läste om den, jag hörde den och det var alltid de som sa att den äntligen var här—verkligheten är här—nu kan man höra den, nu kan man se den och nu kan man läsa den på riktigt och på deras språk, med deras ord—verkligheten har äntligen visat sig för oss, sa de och där satt jag mest och undrade om jag var verklig, fanns jag här och nu—eller var jag lika falsk som det de kallade verkligt?* (Sattarvandi 2008, 99–100; Italics original)

(...) *they want comedy from the suburb, they want Gringo, they want bullshit and piss—you know, before I thought that I lived in reality, then it came right in my face every day—I read about it, I heard it and it was always them who said that it was here at last—the reality is here—now you can hear it, now you can see it and now you can read it for real and written in their language, in their words—reality has at last shown itself to us, they said and I sat there and wondered if I was real, did I exist here and now—or was I as false as that what they called real?*

The words chosen by Sattarvandi echo the discourse on culture from the suburb which has accompanied not only certain literature but also music and comedians: The deprived voice from the margin is supposed to tell the true story from the suburb which has never been heard before. The point made by Sattarvandi has also to do with power relations, where the classes in power appropriate the voices from the suburb:

(...) *och helt plötsligt blev min verklighet en jävla disneyvärld där mina erfarenheter, dina erfarenheter och varenda jävla människas erfarenheter i förorterna blev en produkt som såldes ut till medelklassen av medelklassen—vafan har hänt nu—ingct är verkligt längre, det som vi ser finns inte, det vi känner existerar inte längre—vi är inte längre oss själva, vi finns inte längre, vi har suddats ut av dem—ju längre tiden går, desto mer suddas vi ut, desto mindre finns vi och ändå påstår man det motsatta hela tiden—ibland undrar jag, eftersom de alltid skriver om hur verkligt det helt plötsligt blev, om jag någonsin har varit verklig* (...) (Sattarvandi 2008, 100–1; Italics original)

(...) *all of a sudden my reality became a fucking Disney World where my experiences, your experiences and every fucking human's experiences in the suburbs became a commodity that was sold to the middle class by the middle class—what the fuck has happened now—nothing is real any longer, the things we see don't exist, the things we feel don't exist anymore—we are no longer ourselves, we don't exist anymore, we have been wiped out by them—the longer time passes, the more we are wiped out, the lesser we exist and yet they claim the opposite all the time—sometimes I wonder, because they always write about how real it suddenly became, if I ever been real at all (...)*

As formulated by Saladin, Nemo's friend, reality is at stake: Who has the power to publicly voice experiences from the margin, in this case, the suburb? When the inhabitants are not heard, their reality is silenced twice over: first due to no interest, second due to appropriation by agents in power. Consistently, the characters are portrayed as ruled by external forces beyond their control; "everything" is said to have destroyed Nemo without his consent. He has no power over his own decisions and his circumstances. He moves in nothingness, staring into a void:

> (...) och sen gick vi (...) tillbaka in i intet, där vi gick halvdöda fram och tillbaka över broarna och några timmar senare (...) gick [vi] (...) förbi de gråtande blåa husen och in i ett tomrum där vi stod och stirrade vilset omkring oss—de blåa husen, den tomma gatan och den tysta hopplösheten som skrek mitt i alla dessa valplakat som omringade oss med ... (Sattarvandi 2008, 199)

> (...) and then we went (...) back into nothingness, where we walked half dead back and forth over the footbridges and a few hours later (...) [we] went (...) past the crying blue houses and into a void where we stood staring disoriented around us—the blue houses, the empty street and the silent hopelessness screaming in the midst of all these election slogans surrounding us with ...

Nemo is Latin for Nobody, but is also the main character in Jules Verne's *Twenty Thousand Leagues Under the Sea*. In Verne's novel Nemo is a prince from India who after a major catastrophe lives on his submarine Nautilus where he rules as sovereign. He is described as a genius who chooses to live outside society and who rejects the rules of other humans. Sattarvandi's Nemo is Nobody, living in limbo or in exile. But in contrast to Verne's Nemo, Sattarvandi's Nemo has no status as a genius, nor does he live in the suburban limbo by his own choice. He is trapped. Verne's novel seems to be used as a contrasting feature by Sattarvandi; his Nemo lives in a dystopian space without any anchoring points, and has no "submarine" allowing him to move and travel around.

Nemo experiences a fundamental alienation in relation to the place where he is living, indicating a loss of situatedness. His lived experience does not fit into any encompassing understanding of the place he is occupying, whereas the camera man is an agent with the means to decide how to depict the suburb and its inhabitants. Places and spaces on a larger scale such as the city and the nation are absent in the novel and hence give no meaning to Nemo and his friends. There is no position from where they can have a detached critical view of themselves or society. Sattarvandi shows the consequences of living in a place exempt of kinship, meaningful activities and future projects. The space described is detached from the inhabitants; it only exists, and does not give Nemo and his friends any meaningful or fulfilling experiences, leaving them disoriented and underscoring their marginalization.

There is a fundamental lack of interrelatedness between the inhabitants and the environment, one of the main points that Jameson makes when identifying the spaces of the postmodern. He uses the term "cognitive mapping," arguing that individuals in a postmodern society have difficulties in locating themselves and in cognitively mapping their position: "this alarming disjunction point between the body and its built environment (…) can itself stand as a symbol and analogon of that even sharper dilemma which is the incapacity of our minds, at least at present, to map the great global multinational and decentered communicational network in which we find ourselves caught as individual subjects" (Jameson 1992, 44). Hence, it is impossible to encompass and to grasp the power structures governing one's lived experiences, a significant theme in the novel, the protagonists being governed by faceless forces called "they" and "them" (Sattarvandi 2008, 222). It is nevertheless important to stress that the act of mapping cognitively is also "applicable in other historical moments in which an individual's ability to grasp his/her relationship to the external world is in crisis" (Goddard 2014, 32). It is not unique for a late modern or postmodern situation. On a general level, the act of perceiving and being able to map one's environment is a basic and necessary human capacity without which it is difficult to exist.

In his analysis of Mehdi Charef's novel *Le thé au harem d'Archi Ahmed* (1988), Prieto discusses what he calls geography as destiny, asking why Charef has written a novel confirming many of the "negative stereotypes that have emerged around immigrants and the suburban poor." This is because the novel is mainly "about place, and more specifically, about the '*effet de lieu*' (…) pushed to its deterministic extreme" (Prieto 2013, 121). Charef's novel is accordingly "a story about stasis—even entrapment" as well as about "environmental determinism" (Prieto 2013, 124). This also holds true for Sattarvandi's novel: it is not about immigrants or ethnicity, but a novel showing how a certain place determines some of its inhabitants.

Prieto argues that certain French novels depicting the suburbs tend to describe the protagonists' positions in terms of "interstitiality, inbetweenness, and lack" (Prieto 2013, 113). In these French novels the characters have no anchoring points and are obliged to invent their own "roots" (Prieto 2013, 113). The concept of the *entre-deux* has "taken on a particular importance in the current, transitional (postmodern, postcolonial, globalizing) moment of world history." As these interstitial places "all too often" are "thought of in terms of what they lack or what is wrong with them," Prieto's effort is to emphasize "the overlooked productive potential of in-between places" (Prieto 2013, 1). In the novel *Still*, Nemo and his friends are living in a similar space in between the city and the nation; they are free floating in a limbo, but the search for roots or anchoring points is never an issue. The novel *Still* solely depicts a space of lack and interstitiality.

To interpret Sattarvandi's dystopian space more productively amounts to situating the novel in the wider social and ideological context of contemporary Swedish immigration and housing policies. As stated above, suburbs such as Hagalund have been identified as places of unrest, related to migration and poverty. Magnus Nilsson argues that Sattarvandi in *Still* criticizes a contemporary *imagined* multicultural society that understands social inequality in ethnic terms that make social and class-based issues invisible (Nilsson 2010, 157). The issue of interpreting certain suburbs as socially deprived will be further elaborated in the concluding discussion.

The Sensorial Flight into Another Dimension: Drugs and Music

Nemo's and his friends' solution to their predicament is to try to leave limbo, the place that stands still, although their eventual destination is unknown. One night there is a power outage in Hagalund:

> *Kolla, allt försvinner.* Vi ställde oss upp i en ring med ryggarna mot varandra och det blev mörkare och mörkare och Foggy undrade: *Är det strömavbrott?* Kanske, tänkte jag och vi vände oss mot varandra, stirrade upp mot himlen och stjärnorna blev klarare och Leo log och sa att den där stjärnan som lyser lite mer än alla andra, det är ingen stjärna, det är en planet, och omkring oss skalades verkligheten av sig själv och det var nästan som om vi stod på en

plats som inte fanns längre, som med tiden skulle dö och vi svävade bort från denna förruttnade plats och upp mot himlen, slingrade om varandra, likt ormar, svävade vi upp mot himlen och det enda vi lämnade kvar efter oss var våra fotspår och våra andetag och vi svävade bort dit där inget stod still (Sattarvandi 2008, 228; Italics original)

Look, everything is vanishing. We stood up in a circle with our backs against each other and it became darker and darker and Foggy wondered: *Is it a blackout?* Maybe, I thought and we turned toward one another, staring at the sky and the stars became clearer and Leo smiled and said, that star which shines a bit more than the others, that is no star, it's a planet, and around us reality was stripped away by itself and it was almost as if we were standing on a place which didn't exist anymore, as if time would die and we floated away from this decayed place and up into the sky, intertwined, like snakes, we floated into the sky and the only thing we left behind were our footsteps and our breath and we floated away to where nothing stood still

The novel ends with the above quote without a final dot which shows that this story is never-ending. Nemo and his friends dream about floating away into the sky intertwined "like snakes": no individual autonomy or unique identity is called for; instead a utopian collective animal-like experience of leaving the earth for a dimension characterized by movement is described. A pivotal thematic in *Still* is this flight from a place that stands still into another dimension. The senses are often used to depict the flight and flying. Thus, there is a sensorial characterization of spatiality that can be understood as a polysensorial construction of space in Westphalian terms.

Traditionally, sight, hearing, touch, smell and taste are viewed as external senses, all of which are activated in the novel. As mentioned, the first person narrator Nemo and his friends are addicted to drugs. The drugs constitute, besides music, the foremost unifying force within this group of friends: their main concern is how to afford drugs, who might have drugs, where to consume them and what will happen when taking them. To describe the sensations when consuming pot, alcohol or Rohypnol, Sattarvandi juxtaposes Nemo's perceptions with beating music:

(…) när jag öppnade ögonen igen stod jag i en soffa, mittemot mig dansade Ivan, Foggy till vänster om mig och Saladin satt skrattande på golvet och musiken pumpade ut och mina armar hängde livlöst ned för sidorna, knäna vek sig och huvudet hängde ned mot bröstet och musiken pumpade ut— *Then I heard the turbine go, yeah, out of my window was the sunset*—och i musiken försvann jag bort bakom ögonlocken, det kalla på insidan av bröstet spred sig och mellan pekfingret och långfingret brände jointen till och skrattet ekade ut över rummet och beaten pumpade på och jag log, grät, skrattade och grät, *bambambambambambam bambambambambambam klapp klapp so I started to dance, without wearing no seatbelts, we all started to dance, without wearing no life vest, bambambambambambam bambambambambambam klapp klapp—my plane noise went down,* och vi skrattade och Ivan höjde musiken och dansade och hoppade och jag lutade mig tillbaka mot väggen och kände pulsen långsamt gå ned i samma takt som beaten och Foggy spydde ut magsyra på glasbordet och jag fortsatte att dansa med huvudet hängande mellan axlarna, ögonen rullade under halvt slutna ögonlock och när jag lutade mig mot väggen puttade Caspian till mig, skrattade tillgjort och slog mig på axeln (…) (Sattarvandi 2008, 85–6; Italics original)

(…) when I opened my eyes again I stood on a sofa, opposite to me Ivan was dancing, Foggy on my left and Saladin sat laughing on the floor and the music pumped and my arms were hanging lifeless down my sides, my knees buckled and my head hung against the breast and the music pumped—*Then I heard the turbine go, yeah, out of my window was the sunset*—and I disappeared into the music behind my eyelids, the coldness inside my breast spread and between my forefinger and my middle finger the joint burnt and the laughter echoed in the room and the beat pumped and I smiled, cried, laughed and cried, *bambambambambambam bambambambambambam klapp klapp so I started to dance, without wearing no seatbelts, we all started to dance, without wearing no life vest, bambambambambambam bambambambambambam klapp klapp—my plane noise went down,* and we laughed and Ivan raised the music and danced and jumped and I leaned against the wall and felt the pulse slowly go down in the same pace as the beat and Foggy threw up gastric acid on the glass table and I continued to dance with my head hanging between my shoulders, my eyes rolling under half-closed lids and when I leaned toward the wall Caspian pushed me, laughed artificially and hit me on the shoulder (…)

The lyrics of the music are from the single "Manila," with electronic music created by the Swiss composer Beat Solèr. The song is about a plane crash where all the passengers, instead of panicking, start to dance. The singer is Michael Smith, a 12-year-old boy from Compton in the south Los Angeles area. Compton is well known for the hip hop group N.W.A and the group's second album was called *Straight Outta Compton* (1989). On YouTube Smith performs to the lyrics of "Manila" at the same time as an animation shows rabbits dancing in a plane and ends with them jumping off the wings (YouTube n.d.).[3]

The quote above is an illustrative example of how Sattarvandi narrates sensorial perceptions. Nemo sees his friends dancing and being intoxicated and one of them throws up; the smell can easily be imagined. It is cold in his breast and he gets his finger burnt by the joint. He disappears into the music behind closed eyes and feels his pulse slowing down to the electronic beat. His heart beats at the same pace.

The taking of drugs in the novel is often accompanied by beating music: this is to underscore the flight from the place and the sensations of nothingness drugs and music trigger. Intoxicated, Nemo vanishes into another dimension and momentarily leaves the world. Sight, hearing, touch, smell and taste are senses directed toward the environment, that is, they allow us to navigate and communicate and to register where we are located with our bodies. Nemo's aim is not to advance his corporeal situatedness, or to enhance his consciousness about his location; on the contrary, his desire is to disconnect himself from the place he is currently occupying. The aim of his cognitive mapping is thus paradoxical: he does not search for anchoring points, he strives to loosen them completely. The cold sensation of nothingness when affected by drugs paralyzes him; at the same time, his immediate environment occupies his consciousness, contrary to his wishes:

> (…) och där inom mig skrek de tomma intetsägande höghusen i sin blåa falska fasad och jag öppnade ögonen, jag låg på golvet och hon gränsle över mina höfter och Saladin skrek (…) *hahahahaaaaaaaaaaaaaaaaaaaaaaaa aaaaaaaaaa, de där horungarna* (…) *Om man bara kunde flyga, flyga iväg—försvinna, bara bli någon annan och—då skulle det vara lite enklare och de här linjerna skulle inte spela någon roll, de här gränserna skulle suddas ut—inget skulle finnas kvar, men de skulle försöka få tag på oss, riva oss, klösa oss och kasta ned oss hit igen* (…) *men det skulle inte gå längre— vi skulle bara försvinna bort—flyga vår väg och de skulle bara stå kvar där och stirra förvirrat—som—de—korkade—jävla—idioter—de—alltid— kommer—att—vara*———— *de skulle alltid*———— *vara- aaaaaaaaaaaaaaaaaaaaaaaaaaaaaaaa* (Sattarvandi 2008, 42, 44–5; Italics original)
>
> (…) and there inside me the hollow skyscrapers screamed in their blue false frontage and I opened my eyes, I lay on the floor and she straddled over my hips and Saladin screamed (…) *hahahahaaaaaaaaaaaaaaaaaaaaaaaaaaaaaa aaaaa, those children of whores* (…) *If you only could fly, fly away—disappear, become someone else and—then it would be a bit easier and these lines would not matter, these borders would be effaced—nothing would remain, but they would try to catch us, scratch us, claw us and throw us down here again* (…) but it

would not succeed any longer—we would just vanish—fly away and they would just stand there and stare confused—as—the—stupid—fucking—morons— they—always—will—be———— they would always———— beeeeeeeeeeee eeeeeeeeeeeeeeeee

The image of the skyscrapers in Hagalund invades his consciousness when it is not sufficiently intoxicated. When it is, the omniscient narrator shows how this consciousness gradually changes the pace to one resembling the music beat: *bambambambambambam bambambambambambam klapp klapp*.

Thus the thematics of flight and flying, escape and entrapment are pivotal in the novel, as is the vertical structure. Looking out from one of the apartments in the skyscraper does not give a satisfactory overview of the world; it just enhances the feeling of distress and nothingness. No panoramic encompassing perception of the suburb, city or nation is available to Nemo and his friends (Wistisen 2013, 8). There is no topos from which the main character Nemo can perceive something new or revelatory that would change his depressing situatedness. Being in Hagalund amounts to being powerless, subjected to a power that never shows itself; it is a faceless anonymous power without any clearcut agency. It is called "they" and "them" (Sattarvandi 2008, 222) and is never used to mobilize any effort to escape the cage.

STILL: A "CARTOGRAPHIC" NOVEL? MUSIC AS A LOCAL-GLOBAL SUBURBAN DYNAMICS

Music has another function in the novel besides being an integral part of the characters' perceptions when taking drugs, which lead to sensations of flight and escape. The critical view on cultural appropriation and unequal power relations commented upon above can be understood as a critique of how cultural expressions today are part of a culture industry which markets and labels artists according to preconceived notions. The cameraman ridiculed when screening the hip hop group in Hagalund is in this respect a symbolic representative of the contemporary global music industry. In *Still* there are several references to contemporary popular music.[4] Thus, the lyrics and beats constitute a main source of intertextuality in the novel, which merits being thoroughly investigated. In this context, another aspect of this intertextuality will be addressed, namely its "cartographic" or spatial function.

Fredric Jameson has argued that in late capitalist or postmodern society "the phenomenological experience of the individual subject—traditionally the supreme raw materials of the work of art—becomes limited to a tiny corner of the social world." The individual's "lived experience" no longer "coincides with the place in which it takes place." According to Jameson, this leads to a "growing contradiction between lived experience and structure, or between a phenomenological description of the life of an individual and a more properly structural model of the conditions of existence of that experience" (Jameson 1988, 349). Hence, there seems to be a "gap" between the individual's perceptions of place and his or her understanding and interpretation of this place.

In *Still*, it is clear that the cognitive mapping of Nemo and his friends is alienating. The space of exile, which is Sattarvandi's version of the suburb of Hagalund, is disconnected from the city of Stockholm as well as from the nation. Hagalund is an enclosed local space which in this chapter is interpreted as a postmodern dystopia, though another interpretation of the novel's alienating local situatedness is possible. Sattarvandi's Hagalund is mapped according to a local-global scale due to the several references made to globally transmitted popular music.[5] The ridiculous cameraman and the hip hop group he is filming underscore this dynamics. Hagalund is a well-known site for Swedish hip hop artists, as is Compton in the south Los Angeles area, the place referred to in the Swiss electronic music discussed above. Thus, an interrelationship between Hagalund and Los Angeles as well as Switzerland is constituted through music. Music is also used to underscore the thematics of violence in the novel. When Dire Strait's rock ballad "Tunnel of Love" is playing on Nemo's radio in his apartment, he is having a violent fight with his friend over a former girlfriend (Sattarvandi 2008, 169). Instances such as these show how cultural expressions such as music can be an "important component in the cognitive mapping process" (Goddard 2014, 33). This holds true for literary texts as well, "as instances of fantasies or storytelling" (Goddard 2014, 33). In *Still* the protagonists' cognitive mappings of music beats are mainly paralleled with the sensations of drug addiction and bodily pain. The common denominator of Nemo and his friends is this global space triggered by the music they are experiencing together. In this respect, a sort of community is created in situations when their interactions are accompanied by music. The crucial point is that this postmodern space is not at all grounded in the national, nor solely in the local, but precisely in the local-global, which is detectable through the references to music.

Following Prieto's chronology of postcolonial place models, one could argue that the space of exile in *Still* corresponds to a contemporary postcolonial experience: the nation is no longer "the primary scale of place narrative," nor "the emphasis on the neighborhood as a way to contest essentializing visions of the nation as an undifferentiated whole," but rather "the niche, which emphasizes the place of (…) society within the global cultural ecology" (Prieto 2013, 183). "The niche" is not defined by national borders, but is scaled locally globally. A similar place model is detectable in *Still*.

In this respect, *Still* is a cartographic novel, that is, defined by its local-global scale and not by being grounded in the nation nor in the neighborhood in an essentializing manner. It should be clear, too, that *Still* is no *Bildungsroman*. There is no psychological growth or coming of age, no phenomenologically fulfilling identity formation; on the contrary, the spatiality in the novel is an integral part of the characters' loss of the past, the future and of humanity. Consistently, the characters are portrayed as ruled by external forces beyond their control, "everything" is said to have destroyed Nemo without his consent (Sattarvandi 2008, 169). Referring to French *banlieues* novels, Prieto promotes Jameson's view on cognitive mapping. These French novels—like *Still*—can be understood as "dramatizations of the attempt to break out of a naïvely phenomenological perspective and enter into the more worldly 'cartographic' perspective that Jameson promotes: after the *Bildungsroman*, the *Kartografroman*" (Prieto 2013, 190).

To Situate a Postmodern Dystopia Stratigraphically: A Concluding Discussion

Two aspects of Westphal's geocritical conceptualizations, which were briefly mentioned in the introduction to this chapter, are stratigraphy and multifocality. The former term is borrowed from geology and archeology, meaning that the place studied should be viewed as an accumulation of earlier moments and different historical strata. To be able to do this, a multifocal view is necessary. The place Hagalund will therefore be put in relief to other texts than the novel *Still*, hopefully leading to a more complex understanding of the place under scrutiny.

In Sattarvandi's case it is a narrow, not to say claustrophobic, picture of Hagalund he gives us: a cage in which some of its inhabitants are entrapped and where the rest of the world is absent. An anonymous power practices its discipline on them by undermining their own possibilities to escape. Nemo and his friends seem to be their own worst enemies—checking to see that none take any steps to change their situation. Power is internalized and functions in a self-regulatory way; they seem to have a "wall in the head" (Hanley 2012, xiii).[6]

The question is, what would the difference be between Sattarvandi's postmodern dystopia and a historically situated Hagalund? To discuss this, a brief historical account of Hagalund is necessary. The area belonged to an estate before parts of its land was sold as plots. During the end of the nineteenth century, houses were built on these plots and a municipal community was established in 1899. The association The Friends of Old Hagalund (n.d.), whose aim is to cherish old Hagalund's legacy, summarizes its character on its website:

> At most 6,000 inhabitants lived in this area. Hagalund probably represented the country's foremost example of a mixed suburban municipality, where larger apartment buildings stood side by side with small privately owned houses, and a primitive rampant development. (…) During the years 1966–1975 the municipality underwent a total makeover. Almost all houses were demolished and a skyscrapertown, a part of the Million Housing Programme, came in their place. The area is now more known as Bluehill. (Trans. CS)

Many of the citizens who bought the plots and constructed houses were artists and craftsmen. They helped each other to build and adorn their houses in a variety of styles. Often three houses were built on each plot due to the housing shortage. Most of the houses had shops facing the streets. The artist Olle Olsson Hagalund (1904–1972), a naivist painter, protested against the demolishment of Hagalund in the 1960s. It is to his merit that a few of the old houses still exist, one of them being his own house, now a museum. On the Stockholm County Museum (n.d.) website, one of the visual representations of the old and the new Hagalund is telling: in one photograph the turquoise color of the Olsson museum, a two-story wooden house, is pictured in front of Bluehill's skyscrapers.

A cultural historical account of Hagalund is given on the museum's website. Here the architects, Ragnar Westrin and Stefan Szejnman, and their vision of Bluehill, is presented: "The vision was that the buildings should be perceived as gigantic Atlantic passenger liners on their way to a new modern society where people could live with light, air and greenery."

Despite the fact that "people opposed the large scale" when they were built, "today we esteem the buildings as majestic landmarks of highly cultural historical value and national importance." When the houses were built, the architect Bo Ahlsén and the artist Lars Abrahamsson were assigned to adorn the frontages: "The skyscrapers' glazed sheet metal in blue enamel waver in heaven's nuances and is contrasted with the clinker bricks of the groundfloors." This artistic effort is said to "join the street space and create an overall milieu that makes Bluehill a Million Housing Programme area of national importance."

The museum's presentation differs radically from Sattarvandi's version of Bluehill, and the metaphorics are telling. The architectonic vision is typical of a functionalistic view of a new social democratic society: the citizens must leave the old world behind them and embark on a journey toward a bright new future. Implicit in the architects' vision is that the old world that should be left behind is not light, filled with air and green fresh colors. It seems to be implied that the old Hagalund is the opposite to the new one: dark and suffocating.

According to the Friends of Old Hagalund, traditional Swedish popular movements expanded in the area in the beginning of the twentieth century, including youth organizations, Social Democratic associations and temperance societies. In 1909, the year of the general strike in Sweden, Hagalund had a general strike committee, showing that there was political and organizational commitment in the municipality. This story is not told by Sattarvandi, whose characters are pictured as cut loose from history and from political engagement. The postmodern society in Sattarvandi's version is an unhistorical and futureless location, which indicates a break with history when the Million Housing Programme was carried out.

In public discourse there are contradicting views of the area. On Flashback (2017), one of Sweden's largest chat forums, one user asks what it is like to live in Bluehill. The answers are well-known opinions about Swedish Million Housing Programmes: not enough Swedes, too many immigrants, noisy, downtrodden, high crime rates, unsafe, but also beautiful views from the modern, large and well planned apartments, nice neighbors, excellent public transport, close to the Stockholm city center.

Still was published in 2008. At this time, there was—and still is—an ongoing gentrification of the suburban areas of Stockholm due to the shortage of housing. A major sign of gentrification is rental apartment buildings being transformed into housing societies. Hagalund was built in the 1970s. The first housing society, called Bluehill (Blåkulla), was established there in 1983. To become a member in such a society, one has to pay the former tenant of the apartment the price set by the housing market; it is not rare that with potential buyers bidding, the prices go up. Housing societies are becoming more common in Sweden and rental apartments increasingly scarce. In the first housing society in Hagalund there were 439 apartments of which 38 were rentals. The society's website tells that the society owns the land on which the buildings stand, and that the society sells each rental apartment when tenants move.

These discourses about Hagalund including Sattarvandi's literary dystopia—the cultural value of Bluehill, the area's historical past worth commemorating and the ongoing gentrification countered by futurelessness and deprivation—create a multifaceted, contradictory and common picture of a Western postmodern urban space in transformation. It contains ingredients typical of Sweden's conversion to a Social Democratic welfare state: when building a new equal society one should preferably look forward and not back to be able to leave poverty behind you. To move to a Million Housing Programme area was "a chance to become modern and a force in the Swedish modernization project" (Ristilammi 1997, 78; Trans. CS).

In Sattarvandi's narrative construction of Hagalund, this ideal future, symbolized by the eight clear blue skyscrapers, has not yet come. Sattarvandi's depiction is more attuned with the presumed darkness of the old Hagalund, which was demolished when the Million Housing Programme area was built. Sattarvandi's Bluehill is not gentrified or viewed as a cultural history worth preserving. *Still* is not constructed chronologically, following a line of progression, common in narratives about modernization, as in the story told by Stockholm County Museum: in its version Bluehill has become a part of a national cultural history. Time stands still in *Still*, as do the citizens depicted. When chronos is not an issue, topos is what is left: in Sattarvandi's version this topos is not a utopian space of modernity but a postmodern cage of exile only worth destroying. Nemo and his friends dream of flying away and Nemo has visions of completely demolishing the skyscrapers: "hela gatan låg i ruiner—husfasaderna var bortblåsta, fönsterrutorna ut- eller inslagna och betongplattorna var upprivna" ("the whole street was in ruins—the walls were blown away, the windows were smashed and the concrete slabs were torn up") (Sattarvandi 2008, 31).

The visions of flight and escape in *Still* stand out as ironic and sinister when compared to the modern architectural vision of the Million Housing Programme, where citizens would presumably embark on a journey to a brighter future when moving to the light blue skyscrapers. The postmodern dystopia of Sattarvandi and the modern utopia of the Million Housing Programme stand in stark contrast. Put in relief with Olle Olsson Hagalund's naivist paintings of the old working-class Hagalund, the sense of an early modern Swedish vision or utopia is underscored. In many of Olsson Hagalund's paintings a small scale municipality is depicted. Small wooden houses with gardens are shown, and streets where citizens happily walk, sometimes chatting with each other. The same café, shop and church appear in several paintings. These paintings capture an atmosphere of community, peace and security. Three different visions of the same geographical site are thus detectable in the material discussed: the early modern, modern and postmodern.

The stratigraphic and multifocal approach acknowledges that a specific geographical site is constructed by a complex network of political and architectural visions, literary narratives and artistic representations, as well as by discourses projected over a long period of time on certain urban areas such as the Million Housing Programmes. When built in the 1970s, these areas were associated with "social otherness"; it was here that the socially "underprivileged" lived hopefully heading toward a more privileged future. From the 1990s onward they became increasingly associated with "ethnic otherness" or areas for "non-Swedes" (Ristilammi 1997, 75).

Above Prieto's postcolonial models of place were discussed which led to identifying *Still* as a cartographic novel on account of it being scaled by local-global dynamics. The modern vision of Hagalund, the "chance to become modern" and "a force in the Swedish modernization project" (Ristilammi 1997, 78) is grounded in the nation, so is the museum's claim that Bluehill today is a site of national cultural importance. But how should one understand the discourses on ethnic otherness projected onto urban areas such as Bluehill?

In the introduction to this chapter a passage from a Swedish tabloid was quoted saying that certain suburbs are "parallel societies" with religious conflicts and criminals in power. The inhabitants are poor and socially vulnerable. A "galloping gap with the rest of the society" is detectable according to the journalist who wrote the series of articles introduced with the passage quoted (Moreno 2016, 8–14). Thus, in this tabloid, certain suburbs are constructed as sites "outside" society and the nation. These statements correspond with Sattarvandi's postmodern dystopia: in *Still* Hagalund is a space in between the city and the nation; it is a limbo without any anchoring points.

Thus, the nation is no longer the scale of Sattarvandi's "place narrative" (Prieto 2013, 183). Nor does he see the neighborhood as a way of situating the protagonists in a more favorable position. Olle Olsson Hagalund offered images of the neighborhood as an exemplary space of community, whereas Sattarvandi's dystopian limbo is situated within a "global cultural ecology" (Prieto 2013, 183) linked to globally transmitted popular music.

When discussing Mehdi Charef's *banlieue* novel, Prieto encounters an ethical dilemma, even though he does not use that notion himself. If the scholar draws the conclusion that a novel like Charef's or Sattarvandi's is about geographical determinism, how should he or she handle the question of emancipation, change and social mobility? Prieto chooses to call Charef's novel a tragedy, "implying a deterministic sense of inevitable submission to an implacable destiny" (Prieto 2013, 123). The thematics of immobility, flight and escape are central in *Still*; Sattarvandi tells a story about confinement and stasis with no way out for Nemo and his friends. In Charef's novel, Prieto detects the same thematics (Prieto 2013, 123–4). If no escape route or change is in sight, are these two novels complicit in reproducing stereotypical discourses on the suburb and its male immigrant inhabitants? Is *Still* but one among many other contemporary discourses constructing the suburb as an ethnic and social otherness?

Prieto solves this dilemma by arguing that Charef "pivots from the ethnic to the geographical theme," highlighting what Prieto calls "the place effect" (Prieto 2013, 125–6).[7] The thematics of mobility and immobility in the novel needs to be viewed as a spatial element. Social mobility is connected to geographical mobility, and to obtain change one needs to move from the place which entraps you (Prieto 2013, 126–7).[8] Charef shows rather than tells how geography is destiny in a certain suburb in France. Sattarvandi, for his part, does not tell the reader what political or ideological conclusions to draw, but shows in a similar manner as Charef how a specific place exerts power over a few of its male inhabitants. In this respect, *Still* too is a postmodern tragedy telling the story of how social inequality is place-bound.

Notes

1. Per-Markku Ristilammi argues that the suburb has been viewed first as a modern otherness, later as a social one, and now as a place for ethnic otherness.
2. All translations of *Still* are mine.
3. Seelenluft—Manila (official video). The composer Solèr uses the stage name Seelenluft.

4. In Sattarvandi's *Still* references are made to among others: Ini Kamoze's "Hotstepper" (149), Pretty Ricky's "Call Me" (157), Pink Floyd's "Another Brick in the Wall" (164–169), House of Pain's "Jump Around" (165–166), Dire Straits "Tunnel of Love" (169), Bruce Springsteen's "The River" (170), Chet Baker's "The Thrill is Gone" (182), Aaliyah's "We Need a Resolution" (201), Daddy Yankee's "Gasolina" (212) and Bob Sinclar's "World, Hold On" (215).
5. See Endnote 4 above for music references made in the novel.
6. Lynsey Hanley (2012) writes how growing up in one of Britain's largest council estates affected her self-esteem and how she had to struggle with what she defines as the wall in her head.
7. Prieto refers to the French sociologist Catherine Bidou-Zachariasen (1997) who has shown what effects *le territoire* has on inhabitants in urban areas in "La Prise en compte de l'effet de territoire' dans l'analyse des quartiers urbains."
8. Prieto refers to the French sociologist and novelist Azouz Begag (2002), who links social mobility to the need for geographical mobility in *Les Dérouilleurs: Ces Français de banlieue qui ont réussi*.

REFERENCES

Begag, Azouz. 2002. *Les Dérouilleurs: Ces Français de banlieue qui ont réussi*. Paris: Mille et une Nuits.

Bidou-Zachariasen, Catherine. 1997. La Prise en compte de 'l'effet de territoire' dans l'analyse des quartiers urbains. *Revue Française de Sociologie* 38 (1): 97–117.

"Blåkulla". n.d. Website of the Housing Society Blåkulla [Bluehill]. Accessed June 22, 2017. http://www.blakulla.net.

Flashback. 2017. https://www.flashback.org/t2474810.

Goddard, Jeanette E. 2014. Plotting One's Position in Don Quijote: Literature and the Process of Cognitive Mapping. In *Literary Cartographies: Spatiality, Representation, and Narrative*, ed. Robert T. Tally Jr., 31–46. New York: Palgrave Macmillan.

Gråbacke, Carina, and Jan Jörnmark. 2010. The Political Construction of the 'Million Housing Programme': The State and the Swedish Building Industry. In *Science for Welfare and Warfare: Technology and State Initiative in Cold War Sweden*, ed. Per Lundin, Niklas Stenlås, and Johan Gribbe, 233–249. Sagamore Beach, MA: Science History Publications.

Hanley, Lynsey. 2012 [2007]. *Estates: An Intimate History*. London: Granta Books.

Jameson, Fredric. 1988. Cognitive Mapping. In *Marxism and the Interpretation of Culture*, ed. Cary Nelson and Lawrence Grossberg, 347–360. Urbana: University of Illinois Press.

---. 1992. The Cultural Logic of Late Capitalism. In *Postmodernism or the Cultural Logic of Late Capitalism*, 1–54. Durham: Duke University Press.
Moreno, Federico. 2016. Knarket, klanerna och kyrkan tog över i centrum. *Expressen*, June 30, pp. 8–14.
Nilsson, Magnus. 2010. *Den föreställda mångkulturen: Klass och etnicitet i svensk samtidsprosa*. Hedemora: Gidlund.
Prieto, Eric. 2013. *Literature, Geography, and the Postmodern Poetics of Place*. New York: Palgrave Macmillan.
Ristilammi, Per-Markku. 1997. Betongförorten som tecken. In *I stadens utkant. Perspektiv på förorter*, ed. Karl-Olov Arnstberg and Ingrid Ramberg, 75–85. Tumba: Mångkulturellt centrum.
Sattarvandi, Hassan Loo. 2008. *Still*. Stockholm: Albert Bonniers förlag.
"Stockholm County Museum." n.d. Accessed June 22, 2017. http://stockholms-lansmuseum.se/sok-bilder/fotosamlingar/?idno=ldng2014-0559.
"The Friends of Old Hagalund." n.d. Accessed June 22, 2017. http://hagalunds-vanner.com/om-foreningen/om-gamla-hagalund/.
Westphal, Bertrand. 2011. *Geocriticism: Real and Fictional Spaces*. Translated by Robert T. Tally, Jr. Basingstoke: Palgrave Macmillan.
Wistisen, Lydia. 2013. En sång om Trojas murar. En analys av maskulin identitet och utanförskap i tre samtida svenska förortsskildringar. *Tidskrift för litteraturvetenskap* 43 (3–4): 5–16.
YouTube. n.d. Seelenluft—Manila (Official Video). Accessed June 22, 2017. https://www.youtube.com/watch?v=mh2SiGuDT1A.

Open Access This chapter is licensed under the terms of the Creative Commons Attribution 4.0 International License (http://creativecommons.org/licenses/by/4.0/), which permits use, sharing, adaptation, distribution and reproduction in any medium or format, as long as you give appropriate credit to the original author(s) and the source, provide a link to the Creative Commons licence and indicate if changes were made.

The images or other third party material in this chapter are included in the chapter's Creative Commons licence, unless indicated otherwise in a credit line to the material. If material is not included in the chapter's Creative Commons licence and your intended use is not permitted by statutory regulation or exceeds the permitted use, you will need to obtain permission directly from the copyright holder.

CHAPTER 4

Living Side by Side in an Individualized Society: Home, Place, and Social Relations in Late Modern Swedish-Language Picturebooks

Kristina Hermansson

One of the most common narrative patterns in children's literature begins with the protagonist leaving home on an adventure and ends with his or her return home (Nikolajeva 2004; Nodelman 2008). Home is associated with safety and feelings of security, compared to the more dramatic but also potentially dangerous ("away"). Home is situated in a familiar, private space in contrast to the public or semi-public spaces in which various adventures take place. In this chapter, I explore the written and visual constructions of characters and social relations in relation to place, focusing on the above-mentioned narrative pattern in a selection of contemporary Swedish-language picturebooks published in Sweden and Finland between 2006 and 2014. What characterizes the interplay between place and social relations in these works? How does the presentation of place

K. Hermansson (✉)
University of Gothenburg, Gothenburg, Sweden

© The Author(s) 2020
K. Malmio, K. Kurikka (eds.), *Contemporary Nordic Literature and Spatiality*, Geocriticism and Spatial Literary Studies,
https://doi.org/10.1007/978-3-030-23353-2_4

shape the presentation of characters and social relations, and vice versa? How is the basic home-away-home pattern negotiated and renegotiated?

Picturebooks from the 2000s tend to increasingly blur conventional boundaries between children and adults. Sandra Beckett claims that contemporary picturebooks "play an essential role in the crossover phenomenon" often dealing with "adult," dark, and painful themes, especially in Scandinavian countries (Beckett 2002, 2). Furthermore, these works also tend to mock conventional forms of children's narrative by using literary features such as polyfocalization, irony, and a complex interplay between visual and verbal aspects (Beckett 2002, 17). As I intend to demonstrate in the following, the selection of picturebooks analyzed in this chapter exploits and reshapes the basic home-adventure-home pattern.

My material consists of three Swedish-language picturebooks from the 2000s which examine aspects of living together side by side, though not in the same home or family. All three titles address the home and social relations, though from slightly different perspectives and in different ways. The specific titles examined are *Milja och grannarna* (Sandelin 2006; "Milja and the neighbors"), *Sonja, Boris och tjuven* (Lindström 2007; "Sonja, Boris, and the thief"), and *Tilly som trodde att …* (Staaf 2014: "Tilly who thought that …").

These works address questions that are dealt with by late modern cultural theory, such as individualism, social isolation, and the emphasis on security (Beck 1992; Bauman 2000; Brown 1995). The three titles investigate the possibilities of cohabitation in different places: a row of terraced houses, a campsite, and an apartment building and its surroundings. The characters and their social relations depicted are intertwined with written and visual spatial elements, though the spatial aspects of social relations are thematized even on the narrative level. The similarities in both themes and narrative structures in the current examples make this a productive literary corpus to examine from the point of view stated above. During the 2000s and especially the last five years, there have been several picturebooks on the topic of neighbors, often focusing on various kinds of environments, living conditions and family constellations.[1] This tendency should be set against the backdrop of an increasing strive for a more inclusive and socially engaged children's literature, dealing with social relations and diversity from different aspects and perspectives (Hermansson and Nordenstam 2017).

Milja och grannarna starts by depicting the protagonist's inner vision of what it ought to be like to live in a terraced house, in contrast to her own experience. The plot in "Sonja, Boris, and the thief" is set in a semi-public place, in a temporary community, while "Tilly who thought that …" depicts people living in the same apartment building or in one case outside on the street. All together these books thematize the art of living together in the same place, side by side though not under the same roof or in the same family. By examining the presentation from a spatial point of view, I intend to shed light on how the presentations of place also shape the presentations of characters and social relations, and vice versa.

In the analysis, I will primarily draw on Doreen Massey's theories of space and place, especially her concept of *throwntogetherness*. According to Massey, space should be imagined as open, multiple as well as performative or challenging (Massey 2005). This concept is not unlike the established spatial theories of Henri Lefebvre (1991). While Lefebvre intends to expose the production of space in late capitalism on a universal basis, Massey instead focuses on particular processes, adding parameters other than class, such as gender and ethnicity (Massey 2005). With her concept of throwntogetherness, she aims to illuminate places as events, "the unavoidable challenge of negotiating a here-and-now (…) a negotiation which must take place within and between both human and nonhuman" (Massey 2005, 140). A place or, as in this case, a written and visual presentation of a place in a picturebook, is hence regarded as an event, a performance that takes place in a certain context. This means that although the plot and characters are set in certain places, the spatial presentation cannot be comprehended separately but only in relation to other parameters. Following Massey, I put no particular effort into differentiating "space" from "place," using both terms more or less synonymously. However, place is often used in a broader sense, while space or spatial instead functions in more abstract, analytical ways (Massey 2005, 185). Following both Lefebvre and Massey, space is not regarded as an empty vessel but as something people do based on specific discursive premises. A place has no inherent reality but, according to Lefebvre, is being *produced* and, adding Massey's reasoning on the subject, also *reckoned* in its *specific* manifestations in time and space (Lefebvre 1991). What makes Massey particularly relevant to my present aims is her emphasis on the connections between place and social relations: "Places pose in particular form the question of our living together" (Massey 2005, 151). Further, she focuses on various power relations and was among the first to apply intersectional perspectives (Rönnlund and Tollefsen 2016, 49). This is also in line with the aims and means of this chapter.

When analyzing picturebooks, my current theoretical starting point entails regarding place as an iconotextual performance. The notion of *iconotext* was coined by Kristin Hallberg in 1982 and refers to the interplay between verbal and visual aspects (Hallberg 1982, 165). The main aim of my study is to examine how places and social relations are presented in writing as well as visually in the selected picturebooks. The starting point in spatial theory is intertwined with a desire to explore the presentation of social relations in order to enlighten both obstacles and opportunities in the imagination and in the organization of social relations in general. As Massey puts it: "The political corollary is that a genuine, thorough, spatialisation of social theory and political thinking can force into the imagination a fuller recognition of the simultaneous coexistence with others with their own trajectories and their own stories to tell" (Massey 2005, 11).

BROKEN NEIGHBORS: A SHACKLED COMMUNITY

Milja och grannarna explores the theme of living side by side in a row of terraced houses in a Finnish or Nordic setting. The story is told from the viewpoint of Milja, a six-year-old girl who lives with her parents:

> När Milja ska somna om kvällarna funderar hon ibland på hur det ser ut hemma hos grannarna. Hon skulle så gärna gå in till dem och titta, men hon får nöja sig med att se in genom fönstren i smyg. (Sandelin 2006, spread 3)

> When Milja is about to fall asleep in the evenings, she sometimes ponders how things might look in the neighbor's houses. She would love to peep into their houses to see for herself, but she has to content herself with looking through the windows in disguise. (Trans. KH)

The spread visually presents Milja's gender-biased imaginations of her neighbors: Mr. Marudd is lifting weights, Miss Alopeus is watering her plants, and Jonas the librarian is reading a book about ghosts, dressed in black and portrayed as looking almost like a vampire. Behind the picture of Jonas situated in a gray thought balloon, there is a spider web further enhancing the supposed mysterious profile of the librarian.

The adult characters are generally presented as caricatures rather than individualized persons, everyone being annoyed at their neighbors' behavior. According to the narrator, the only one who Milja has visited from the outset is Miss Alopeus. However, by means of an omniscient narrator, the reader gains an insight into the homes and lives of all the characters. Miss Alopeus works in a perfume store. She uses her vacuum cleaner to block what she regards as disturbing noise from her neighbor, Jonas, a librarian who plays the saxophone. Mr. Marudd lives with his dog and is annoyed at both Alopeus and Jonas on account of the noise they produce. Jonas, on the other hand, is irritated by Marudd's early morning habits. The reader is informed of this by the narrator, focalizing different characters on different spreads, though first and foremost on Milja. The fact that Mr. Marudd is wearing a jumper with the text "Suomi" (Finland) and a print of the Finnish flag, contributes to presenting this spry, winter-loving character as well as accentuating the national setting.

When the neighbors meet outside their houses, they do not say hello to one another, even though they have been living side by side for several years. This fact, as it is presented by the narrator, is contrasted to Milja's ideal vision of what it would be like to live in a terraced house, with a shared flowerbed and all the neighbors taking turns shoveling snow and sometimes inviting one another for a cup of coffee or tea. On the spread visually depicting Milja's imaginary row of houses, the façade is white and red and the setting is full of green trees, flowers, and happy people. Even the cats seem content, looking at each other with a symbolic heart hovering above one of them. In contrast, the next spread visualizes how things really are, according to the narrator focalizing Milja. In this picture, the façade is gray, the trees have no leaves, and the people look unhappy and walk in different directions. They all seem isolated and the atmosphere conveyed is depressing.

After several spreads telling of the neighbors' trouble coping with one another's behavior, there is one spread depicting Miss Alopeus on a chilly winter's day as she walks to the shopping center. In the snowy background, Milja is sledding down a hill. On the right page it is shown how she slips on a patch of ice and falls, presented in simultaneous succession (Nikolajeva and Scott 2001, 139–40). The linear plot is depicted by four examples of Miss Alopeus in various positions, to be read as a sequence. The following spread contains ten separated visual scenes depicting the approach of Jonas, who also falls when trying to help his neighbor. Image number ten shows both of them lying on top of each other, with his feet on her head. While the visual presentation presents the fall in detail, the surrounding verbal text adds a background from Jonas's perspective, but also contains a bit of dialogue. For the first time, out in the street in a public space, the two neighbors say hello. But as Jonas tries to help Miss Alopeus to her feet, he slips on the same icy patch. The next spread presents Mr. Marudd on his way to the grocery store. He falls in exactly the same spot, though this is pictured in close-up, showing the three neighbors piled up on top of each other.

Marudd's dog informs Milja about what has happened, while she helps the injured neighbors get to hospital. Eventually they end up in the same room, unable to move. Trapped in one space, shackled to their beds, they are unable to avoid one another's characteristics and habits. This situation makes them even more irritated with one another. As Massey writes, "the chance of space may set us down next to the unexpected neighbor" (Massey 2005, 151). In this part of the book this chance is taken to the extreme, since neighbors, in denotative terms, are now situated not only in the same row of terraced houses under the same roof, but literally side by side. The only character joining this group of people voluntarily is Milja, the young protagonist who from the outset is presented as a curious person with a huge interest in her neighbors. However, when she offers neighbors pastries, the social tensions dissipate: "You are even closer neighbors now," she says ("Ni är ännu närmare grannar nu, säger hon") (Sandelin 2006, spread 21).

Happiness emerges in the room as the neighbors start eating, smiling at one another, and talking with each other. As Jonas, almost completely wrapped in ABC bandage, plays the saxophone, colorful flowers come out of the instrument in the picture.

On the last spread, the neighbors are portrayed in an almost utopian community, playing and barbecuing together in perfect harmony. Though, the terrace house in the background still looks like a prison, beige and grey with dark windows. Once again, sharing a meal is presented as an almost emblematic expression of a positively contested throwntogetherness, bridging individual differences and former conflicts as well as singular habitations. The neighbors are no longer shackled in the same room, with legs and arms in casts or socially or physically separated. They are presented outdoors in their intimate neighborhood, voluntarily sharing time and space with people they had not originally chosen to cohabit with but had tried to avoid. They have returned home, yet they are pictured at another much more colorful place than the gloomy one initially presented. Even the environmental setting is transformed. The final spread contains not only happy people having a barbecue, but also flowers, stars, and music. Milja has attained new knowledge of her neighbors, but the transformation presented is much more ample: it involves the social relations and thus, the entire community (Fig. 4.1).

Fig. 4.1 Linda Bondestam's illustration in *Milja och grannarna* (2006), by Annika Sandelin and Linda Bondestam

At the Campsite: Cohabitation and a Criminal Manhunt

Recurring themes in the picturebooks of the prominent Swedish author and illustrator Eva Lindström are control and loss—be it a loss of friends, gloves, or even a forest. In Lindström's *I skogen* (2008; "In the forest"), these themes, specifically, an attempt to control the environment leading to its loss, are taken to extremes since the forest simply goes on vacation.

The themes of loss and the vain pursuit of control are intertwined with a significant aspect of Lindström's mode of visual expression: messiness. There is no central perspective in the visual presentations: people, animals, and things seem scattered in both sparse and cluttered environments, whether a forest or a hotdog stand. Using watercolor, gouache, and graphite, Lindström creates flat settings in which things happen simultaneously, like scenery or a visual palimpsest, adding layer on layer without a clear hierarchy. Humans and animals are mixed. According to Elina Druker, Lindström's picturebooks parody the detective genre by intertwining absurd subtexts (Druker 2011). Furthermore, according to Ulla Rhedin, they cast light on children's concrete way of thinking (Rhedin 2013).

Sonja, Boris och tjuven (Sonja, Boris, and the thief) is a twisted detective story in the form of a picturebook. The front cover shows a bold man wearing orange sweatpants and a yellow sweater and a woman with gray hair and a ballet-inspired outfit. Behind the human couple there is a tent, a small table, and a camping stove. There are also several trees in gray, blue, and purple. The landscape looks Nordic, despite the intense, artificial colors. The place, as the reader is soon informed, is a campsite inhabited by the human couple Sonja and Boris as well as various humanized animals wearing clothes. Björnen ("The Bear") is the owner of the campsite, a bare-chested guy wearing blue sweat pants and flip flops. Though he plays an important part in the story, he is not referred to in the title, which, besides the two human beings, refers to the anonymous, not clearly defined, antagonist, "tjuven," the thief.

The sociologist and philosopher Zygmunt Bauman uses the tourist as a metaphor to illustrate the condition of postmodern life. The tourist, according to Bauman, moves through spaces that other people inhabit. Bauman describes the current state of modern society as a campsite open for everyone who has a tent or caravan and enough money to pay the rent: "Guests come and go, none taking much interest in how the site is run, providing that they have been allocated a plot big enough" (Bauman 2001, 104). Nobody demands anything from the site manager except to be "left alone and not interfered with" (Bauman 2001, 105). Perhaps Nordic campsites differ in this respect, but at least campers seem to spend a lot of time together and even make friends in this modern kind of *heterotopia*, borrowing Foucault's concept of a momentarily realized utopia (Foucault 1984). Furthermore, the campsite could be regarded as a spatial manifestation of the modern distinction between work time and leisure time (Bjurström 2011). It is a piece of cultivated, commercialized nature where people spend a certain time away from their ordinary lives—that is, if they are tourists like Boris and Sonja and not permanent campers.

The plot is simple: Things are disappearing at the campsite and Sonja, Boris, and Björnen are searching for them. It is possible even for a toddler to figure out from the pictures who most likely is the thief, though it is not commented on in the text and one cannot be completely sure. Soon Sonja suspects that the things have been stolen. After she declares this, the characters start looking for a thief rather than for the lost items. A canine character called Schäfer (i.e., German shepherd) puts up a poster reading "AKTA ER FÖR TJUVEN" ("BEWARE OF THE THIEF") (Lindström 2007, spread 5). However, the poster contains a picture of himself. Despite his name, this dog, judging from the visual information, is clearly not a German shepherd but most likely a bulldog. This is only one example of how the written and visual texts clash, creating an iconotext that employs counterpoint—to apply Nikolajeva's categories of text/picture relations. Counterpoint means that the words and images question each other in a creative way (Nikolajeva 2000). In this case, the presentation of the dog mocks the idea of an alignment between name and identity. Besides, German shepherds are common police dogs, and this character acts like a private investigator rather than a police officer (or a police dog).

The written presentation completes the visual one by reflecting the part of the text that cannot be discerned in the picture: "Vänd Er med förtroende till Mej om Ni ser något som är borta" ("Turn confidently to Me if you see something that is gone") (Lindström 2007, spread 5).

This is doubly ironic. Intertextually, the poster resembles a typical wanted poster, which usually contains a picture of the suspected criminal. However, as the reader is later informed, the self-appointed detective and the criminal turn out to be one and the same. Furthermore, philosophically, one may ask oneself whether something that is "gone" can actually be seen. This is not meant as linguistic nitpicking, but points toward a general existentialist theme in Lindström's writing: things and people disappear, despite the characters' vain struggles to maintain control.

The traces of suspected crimes disrupt the campsite as a place of temporary harmonious coexistence. Fear is growing, and everyone starts suspecting each another. Soon the police are called in. A male human character arrives, with gray hair, jacket, glasses, and a magnifying glass, recalling a stereotypical detective. He starts, though seemingly not very wholeheartedly, searching for the thief. The character is portrayed with typical detective attributes. The story contains a fair amount of irony targeting the detective genre. The adult reader might also find somewhat ironic the comments indirectly referring to what sociologists call a "risk society," that is, "a society preoccupied with the future (and also with safety), which generates the notion of risk" (Giddens and Pierson 1998, 209), or put another way, a "community of anxiety" (Beck 1992, 50). Ironic references to this theme can be found on the spread depicting how Björnen locks a strongbox locker in a bigger strongbox (Fig. 4.2).

Fig. 4.2 Eva Lindström's illustration in *Sonja, Boris och tjuven* (2007)

Björnen reckons that Schäfer will guard the place, but things still keep on disappearing. Soon even Schäfer vanishes.

The fact that three sandwiches disappear when Björnen has his back turned in the camping café is noted as peculiar by the narrator. From the picture of the café interior, however, one can tell that the mouth of the dog standing in front of the table where the sandwich was seems crammed full. By means of such an expanded *text-picture relationship*, to use Nikolajeva's terminology, the reader gains more information than the mere text reader. Significant clues as to the detective mystery are to be found in the pictures (Nikolajeva 2000, 22).

Sara Ahmed claims that fear *does* something: "it re-establishes distance between bodies whose difference is read off the surface" (Ahmed 2004, 63). Ahmed discusses fear from a spatial political point of view, recalling that those who in fact have the least reason to fear crime often tend to fear it the most. According to Ahmed, this has to do with the fear of openness itself, a fear of "spaces where bodies and worlds meet and leak into each another" (Ahmed 2004, 69). This reasoning, I would argue, could be connected to Massey's concept of throwntogetherness, a notion of space as performative and effecting or interplaying with social relations. At the campsite in Lindström's book, characters meet with others and the thefts mean that everyone gets more involved with one another, participating in the same project of finding the thief. Simultaneously, however, suspicion grows, disrupting the happy communion presented on the first pages.

In *Sonja, Boris och tjuven* differences between species are emphasized, as the human police detective takes charge, outmaneuvering Björnen, who owns the campsite, and thus wields economic power. The threat gradually escalates, and the next day it is discovered that there has been a burglar in the café: the strongboxes have been stolen from the office and the whole area is a mess, with broken items and footprints everywhere. The thief's presence has been made visible by these traces. Boris becomes a suspect. His footprints cause the detective to perform a speech act, hailing Boris as a suspect subject: "Du där! (...) Jag får be dig följa med. I lagens namn" ("Hey you! ... Follow me! In the name of the law") (Lindström 2007, spread 8). Despite Sonja's protests, the police take Boris to the police station. This passage could be used as an illustration of *interpellation* in the sense the French philosopher Louis Althusser uses the term. Althusser even uses a similar, often quoted, example of a police hailing a suspect to explain the ideological process of interpellation (Althusser 2014).

A striking feature of the visual presentation of the campsite is that almost all the doors are ajar, as are the windows and tents, blurring the boundary between inside and outside, mine and yours. This conveys an open, welcoming attitude, connoting community rather than individualism, comfort rather than security. This positive presentation of place is soon juxtaposed, however, to a spread depicting the hearing of Boris and Sonja. Behind the well-lit table where the hearing takes place, there is a door with a huge lock. The right-hand part of the spread shows the building from the outside, with closed doors. The right page depicts the outdoor environment and contains no humans. The page is completely gray, except for two trees in different shades of yellow. There are sharp angles everywhere, no messiness but emptiness. The bicycle parking lots contains no bikes, the doors are locked. The only living being present on this part of the spread is a profile looking like Boris that can be seen through a window.

Then we are back at the campsite. The detective has cordoned off the scene of the crime. The theatrical dimension characterizing the book becomes even more profound in this picture of two people watching the detective while he performs his investigation.

In the small community depicted, the thefts cause living beings of different species to come together in their quest for the thief. Sonja does not help her partner Boris when he needs her testimony not to be arrested; instead, she says that she was asleep when the burglary took place, so she cannot provide an alibi. Later, though, she finds an indication that Schäfer and not Boris is guilty, and calls the police. But, as mentioned above, Schäfer has disappeared.

Eventually, a common space is established on the ground between the separate tents at the campsite. Boris has been set free and has returned to the campsite. The incidents seem to have brought the characters closer together. Sonja, Boris, and the detective are sitting down on the ground, remarkably relaxed and content judging from the picture. Björnen stands at the back, holding a tray of buns. None of them any longer seems interested in solving the case; instead the dialogue is about Boris's experiences in the cell. However, the final words paradoxically claim that detective action is still going on, though less intensely: "Utredningen går långsamt framåt. Ännu har ingen tjuv åkt fast" ("The investigation is slowly proceeding. Yet no thief has been caught") (Lindström 2007, 12).

This is only one example in which, to use Nikolajeva's terminology, elements of counterpoint escalate into an ambivalent text-picture relationship. The clash between written and visual information produces a certain amount of uncertainty, and there is no corrective to lean on (Nikolajeva 2000, 22). This collision is related to the mild kind of irony characterizing the picturebook or even Lindström's production in general.

The ending contains almost classical ingredients, recalling that of Tove Jansson's 1952 picturebook *Hur gick det sen?* ("What happened after?"), published in English as *The Book about Moomin, Mymble and Little My*. In Jansson's book, on the last spread everyone is sitting on the ground, drinking lemonade. "The adventure is over," Druker commented on this ending in her dissertation on pictures in this and other modern picturebooks, including Jansson's (Druker 2008, 95). What is the case, however, in Lindström's book? If Boris is to be regarded as the protagonist, he has clearly completed an adventure, first being forced from his temporary home, put in a cell, and eventually returned to the campsite. However, against the backdrop of Massey's concept of throwntogetherness and her reasoning on place as an event, it is possible to submit that the camping site including its inhabitants is the most profound protagonist. Not only Boris, but the place has been transformed, from the first presentation of a casual community characterized by openness and diversity to a micro version of the risk society in which suspicion grows and social relations crack. Finally, it has once again become a place of relaxed social intercourse. As discussed above, the story mocks the idea of a proper (detective) plot as well as heroic individualism.

Even though the detective riddle remains unsolved at the end, the most prominent characters except for Schäfer are finally gathered, having coffee and cake. Actually, the thefts do not seem to bother them anymore. The story ends by showing a content little community, now also including the nonresidential police detective. Sharing a meal outdoors is part of the happy ending.

Burglaries take place, but the important thing seems to be what one makes of that. The voluntary, positive situation of throwntogetherness at the campsite eventually triumphs over the fear of crime. According to Massey, this term refers to an "event of place in part in the simple sense of the coming together of the previously unrelated, a constellation of processes rather than a thing" (Massey 2005, 141). The final spread depicts a new appropriation of place, giving it new meaning. The place once again functions as an arena of communion where both old and new inhabitants are eating cake together.

However, even in this almost utopian local community, power relations can be discerned, though they are not commented on. Regarding gender, it is notable that the suspect, the actual (or most likely) thief, and the police detective are all male. Furthermore, the written text tells us that Sonja has made the cake, while the male animal character Björnen simply defrosted some buns in the microwave oven. Yet they both in different ways help reclaim the campsite as a place for enjoyment and community, including newcomers.

Different Flats, Same House: Where You Live and Who You Are

Emma Adbåge is a well-established writer and a frequent illustrator of picturebooks. In *Tilly som trodde att ...* ("Tilly who thought that ..."), the pictures were drawn by Adbåge and the text was written by Eva Staaf, here debuting as an author. If *Sonja, Boris och tjuven* mocks the traditional detective plot, this genre lacks a plot. It is based on various settings and various social relations, or more precisely different kinds of *homes* connected by a narrator focalizing on the young protagonists Tilly and Tage. The significance of class regarding social environments as well as social relations is suggested by the visual presentation of each flat and its inhabitants, but it is not verbally commented on.

The front cover presents a picture of an apartment building from the outside. On the back cover of the book, the apartment building is depicted from another angle, showing balconies and a front door through which a person is about to pass. A dog is peeing on the messy ground. Through the windows, people of different ages can be seen. The first spread seems to show the view from the apartment where Tilly and Tage live, an urban landscape of colorful apartment buildings, a playground, a school, and a swimming center. The right-hand page shows Tilly's room, where she and her friend Tage are sitting on the bed:

> De bor i ett hus de är vana att bo för de har bott där sen de föddes.
> De vet inte exakt hur det är att bo någon annanstans (...)
> Tilly och Tage vet inte exakt hur det skulle kunna vara att vara någon annan.
> Har man tur, kan man kanske få veta det. (Staaf 2014, spread 1)

> They live in a house where they are used to living because they have lived there since they were born.
> They don't know exactly how it is to live somewhere else (...)
> Tilly and Tage don't know exactly what it would be like to be someone else.
> If you're lucky, you might find out. (Trans. KH)

The written text makes spatial aspects central to the presentation of characters and social relations. The narration also has a spatial structure, following Tilly's movements through different apartments, outside, and to the swimming center. Each home is presented from Tilly's and Tage's points of view, particularly in their dialogues. They eventually find out that not everyone has a room of their own and that families come in very different forms. Several single parents do occur, though there are no same-sex couples. The characters are strikingly white, considering the diversity regarding other aspects. On the other hand, all characters except from the homeless man live in the same house.

The home of Tilly's friend Loppan is depicted as a place where many things are allowed, where one can remove the cushions from the couch or play with real biscuits and apples. The picture shows Loppan's mother, wearing sweatpants revealing her stomach with the waistband of her underpants visible. She stands at a desk, drinking tea while the kids play in the very messy apartment. The floor is full of stuff and through the door one can see a bedroom with an unmade bed.

The next spread depicts Tage's home. In contrast, this picture show a perfectly organized kitchen with the blinds pulled down. On a chair sits a neatly dressed woman with glasses, while Tilly and Tage sit on the sofa looking at each other in a worried way: "Tages mamma säger att allt inte är roligt här i livet. Att det är något man lär sig när man blir större" ("Tage's mum says that not everything in life is fun. That is something that one learns as one gets older") (Staaf 2014, spread 3). The anxiety is manifested in several ways in the darkened room, and the written text tells of the ticking clocks. The text as well as the visual depiction of the setting emphasizes the mother's negative stance toward life. Or, to put it another way, the material order reflects and emphasizes the depressive disorder.

The next spread depicts Tilly's meeting with a homeless man sitting in the street and begging for money. She asks her mum to give him money, though she only brought her credit card. When the mother explains to Tilly that it is a card loaded with money, Tilly thinks it would be even better to give it to the beggar. The mother, though, just continues walking.

The scene with the beggar is re-enacted later on, as Tilly, on her way home, returns to the spot where she first saw the homeless man. This time, Tilly's mother is more proactive in avoiding him. From Tilly's perspective, the written text informs the reader that the mother seems to be having a problem with her shoelaces. The visual presentation shows the mother apparently tying her shoelaces somewhat away from Tilly and the beggar. In the following dialogue with Tage, the two friends talk about why people do not help one another, though even small children know that one ought to. The question goes unanswered, and Tage describes it as a good but hard one.

At the swimming center, another manifestation of inequality is brought to the fore. One of the children, Boris, has not brought a swimsuit or towel, and the written text says that he never has. This surprises Tilly, who thought that all parents would read the messages from the teacher. On the left side of the spread depicting the swimming pool, Boris sits to the left of Tilly by the pool, not part of the happy fellowship of bathing kids. Tilly is wearing a towel, and has just left the others for a while. The right side of the spread depicts the dressing room, in which Boris sits crouched on a bench, looking at the others. In this picture, he is spatially marginalized because he does not have a bathing suit. However, the written text might indicate, at least for the adult reader, that this is only one expression of a more thorough marginalization related to his family situation. However, the swimming teacher overlooks the pattern that is obvious to Tilly and simply tells Boris to remember his bathing suit next time.

Later, Tilly and Tage show up at Sonja's place, a friend who, according to the narrator as well as to Sonja herself, has everything. Tilly finds out that no parents are at home. Sonja claims that she has no mother and that her father is usually away traveling, so her grandmother takes care of her. Tilly, the written texts informs, had so far supposed that every child has a mum and a dad. Obviously, she is unaware that there are several kinds of family constellations.

In some homes, living together does not work properly, though this does not bother the competent, young protagonists who adapt themselves to any circumstances. The spread about Peppe's place shows a very dirty bathroom. Peppe's father never cleans and the household has run out of toilet paper, so Tilly wipes herself with a dirty sock from the laundry. In the picture, Tage and Tilly are happily playing in the dirty bathtub. In the next spread, they have entered Freddie's home where lots of different people mix: Freddie's family is like "ett knippe gräs" ("a bundle of grass") in comparison with Tilly's explicit idea of a family as a constellation with "en början och ett slut" ("a beginning and an end") (Staaf 2014, spread 11).

The differences between homes surprise the young protagonists, but except for the situation of the beggar, they are not understood as manifestations of inequality. Like Milja in *Milja och grannarna*, Tilly notices the differences between people while not really valuing or categorizing them, though Tilly and Tage do reflect on these differences.

From Tilly's and Tage's point of view, the reader 'enters' many different homes and meets their different inhabitants. One by one, Tilly's prejudices are challenged, especially regarding adults who do not behave "properly" or exactly the way she expected. Lack of care of one's home is highlighted as a sign not only of otherness, but—at least for the adult reader—as a sign of low socioeconomic status and/or dysfunction.

Mimmi lives in an extremely messy apartment. In the picture, we find that her tattooed mother is smoking below the kitchen fan, wearing a thong partly visible above her jeans. On the table, there is an emptied piggy bank and an ashtray. The socioeconomic status of this family is stressed by the written description of a lack of food: no fruit, no sweets, no cookies, no milk (Fig. 4.3).

Fig. 4.3 Emma Adbåge's illustration in *Tilly som trodde att...* (2014), by Eva Staaf and Emma Adbåge

In the utopian final spread, Tilly and Tage go on an excursion with their preschool, visiting the beggar's spot on the street alongside a building. In the visual presentation, all the children and their preschool teachers have gathered round the homeless man and share their food with him. The written text informs us that the children give him all they have and that the event becomes like a party. In the picture, most people are smiling. The beggar and Tilly are sitting side by side, looking at each other.

In this spread, people, as illustrated in the visual and written narrative, enact a temporary communion on the street. Following Lefebvre's reasoning, this collective appropriation of a public place, in this case by the preschool group, could be regarded as the transformation of dominating space into lived space. The place might in the end be comprehended as a carnivalesque re-domination of a certain spot, earlier appropriated by the homeless person and now turned into a happy community. However, even when the socially most marginalized and exposed character is the center of others' attention, he does not utter a word and remains completely anonymous. As the preschoolers enter his non-home and turn it into a picnic spot, he is simultaneously given the function of being a peculiar point of interest, an excursion destination. Tillys final reflection is neither about him nor about inequality. The verbal text focus her assumption about adult food preferences, that now is challenged. This leads to the conclusion that, fortunately, one cannot know everything.

Eventually, Tage and Tilly as well as the reader have gained some insight into their neighbors' various living conditions. However, they are not presented like the traditional protagonist moving away from home, experiencing an adventure and then returning home again. This is rather an episodic picturebook in which the title character and her friend function like commentators reflecting on the episodes and settings presented. The eventual 'home coming' takes place out in the street, where the social relations and the place is altered. The formerly most marginalized person has now become the center of the event.

Reproducing Places: Final Reflections and Conclusions

The literary examples analyzed above end, as mentioned, with characters coming together, sharing a meal on the ground. In Lindström's *Sonja, Boris och tjuven*, the burglaries have an obvious effect on the environment and on social relations that are transforming in a direction toward what sociologists would call a risk society. However, in the end the story takes another turn, replacing the former increasing anxiety with a calm reunion.

In the last spread, Sonja and Boris are sitting down together along with the detective while Björnen offers them buns. No one seems to be at all worried even though the case has not been solved. The only one missing is the suspected burglar, Schäfer, who has mysteriously disappeared, similar to the way things mysteriously started to disappear at the outset. However, ultimately no one seems to be bothered either about him or the things lost. It is not stated whether things are still disappearing, or whether it is the anxiety that has vanished. Instead, a relaxed community is highlighted. The characters are depicted as enjoying one another's company.

This ending recalls the final spread in *Tilly som trodde att…*: the two protagonists are gathered outdoors with the preschool group, not at a campsite but out on the street next to the man who used to ask for money. They are having a picnic, sharing their food with the beggar.

In all three examples that have been analyzed, the stories end by presenting more or less temporary gatherings in which the characters are having a meal together outside. This is where the adventures end, not back in the protagonist's individual homes but in outdoor communions at collectively appropriated places, in public or in semi-public areas: on a campsite, in the street, or in the yard.

In all these examples, eventually humans—and in two cases nonhumans as well—both children and adults from different backgrounds come together outside on the ground, if only momentarily. No one has returned to his or her private habitation. Yet a common home is established within the communities presented.

By applying Massey's theories of place and the concept of throwntogetherness, it becomes clear that the presentation of place in these picturebooks cannot be fully comprehended independent of the presentation of social relations, or the other way round. The analyzed works end on an almost utopian note, depicting places from earlier in the books in a new or renewed light, and consistently positively contested. However, these places have in various respects been changed just as the social relations have been. *Sonja, Boris och tjuven* eventually re-establishes the laidback community of the camping site in a somewhat new constellation. In *Milja och grannarna*, it is Milja's imaginary neighbor kinship that is realized. Finally, in *Tilly som trodde att …*, a communion including a preschool group and a homeless man takes place out in the street, or at least the center-periphery relations are shifted. In this sense, the presentation of place in Massey's terms, including characters and their social relations, form a collective protagonist. In all three cases, the characters eventually share a meal outdoors. Hence, the presentations of places and social relations are intertwined, mutually conditioned, and transformed. Eventually, individualistic isolation and (adult) suspicion toward one's neighbor is overcome on public or semi-public ground.

NOTE

1. There are other contemporary examples that could have been added in this study. The motif of neighbors, especially in apartment blocks, has become increasingly common during the last decade, for example: *Hela huset* by Anna Bengtsson (2007; "All of the house"); *Stig tittar ut* by Ann-Christine Magnusson (2011; "Stig peeps out"); *Ett hus med många dörrar* by Sanna Juhlin (2013; "A house with several doors"); *Huset som vaknade* by Martin Widmark (2017; "The house that woke up"); *Kompisen i hissen* by Minette Lidberg (2017; "The friend in the elevator"); *Nyckelknipan* [The title is difficult to translate since it is a wordplay, fusing the words for "bunch of keys" with "trouble"] by Sanna Mander (2017); and *I huset där jag bor* by Lena Sjöberg (2018; "In the house where I live"). They relate in different ways to the home-adventure-home structure, since they present different kinds of denouements. The covers of the books by Bengtsson, Juhlin, Lidberg, Mander, Sjöberg as well as the one by Staaf analyzed in the chapter show blocks of apartments, thereby visually emphasizing the main motif of the books that in various ways thematize social relations in a late modern society. My selection for the article aims to present a broad spectrum of narration as well as various forms of living together, while still relating to the home-away-home pattern in somewhat similar ways in order to make a comparative analysis more fruitful.

REFERENCES

Ahmed, Sara. 2004. *The Cultural Politics of Emotion*. New York: Routledge.
Althusser, Louis. 2014 [1969–1970]. *On the Reproduction of Capitalism: Ideology and Ideological State Apparatuses*. London: Verso.
Bauman, Zygmunt. 2000. *Liquid Modernity*. Cambridge: Polity.
———. 2001. *The Individualized Society*. Cambridge: Polity Press.
Beck, Ulrich. 1992. *Risk Society: Towards a New Modernity*. London: Sage.
Beckett, Sandra. 2002. *Crossover Picturebooks: A Genre for All Ages*. New York: Routledge.
Bengtsson, Anna. 2007. *Hela huset*. Stockholm: Alfabeta.
Bjurström, Erling. 2011. *Fritidens rum: Topografiska perspektiv på ungdomars fritidssocialisation och ungdomspolitiken*. Stockholm: Ungdomsstyrelsen.

Brown, Wendy. 1995. *States of Injury: Power and Freedom in Late Modernity*. Princeton: Princeton University Press.
Druker, Elina. 2008. *Modernismens bilder: den moderna bilderboken i Norden*. Diss. Stockholm: Stockholms universitet.
———. 2011. På jakt efter de ting som flytt. Den främmandegjorda vardagen i Eva Lindströms böcker. In *Barnlitteraturanalyser*, ed. Maria Andersson and Elina Druker, 41–54. Lund: Studentlitteratur.
Foucault, Michael. 1984 [1967]. *Of Other Spaces: On Utopias and Heterotopias*. Translated by Jay Miskowiec. http://web.mit.edu/allanmc/www/foucault1.pdf.
Giddens, Anthony, and Christopher Pierson. 1998. *Conversations with Anthony Giddens: Making Sense of Modernity*. Cambridge: Polity Press.
Hallberg, Kristina. 1982. På jakt efter de ting som flytt. Den främmandegjorda vardagen i Eva Lindströms böcker. Litteraturvetenskapen och bilderboksforskningen. *Tidskrift för litteraturvetenskap* 3–4: 163–168.
Hermansson, Kristina, and Anna Nordenstam. 2017. A New Niche in Children's Literature. Norm-Crit Picture Books in Sweden. *LIR. Journal: Performing the Child. Power and Politics in Children's Literature and Culture* 9: 97–120.
Jansson, Tove. 1952. *Hur gick det sen?(Boken om Mymlan, Mumintrollet och lilla My)*. Stockholm: Geber.
Juhlin, Sanna. 2013. *Ett hus med många dörrar*. Färjestaden: Vombat.
Lefebvre, Henri. 1991. *The Production of Space*. Oxford: Basil Blackwell.
Lidberg, Minette. 2017. *Kompisen i hissen*. Bromma: Opal.
Lindström, Eva. 2007. *Sonja, Boris och tjuven*. Stockholm: Alfabeta.
———. 2008. *I skogen*. Stockholm: Alfabeta.
Magnusson, Ann-Christine. 2011. *Stig tittar ut*. Bromma: Opal.
Mander, Sanna. 2017. *Nyckelknipan*. Helsingfors: Schildts & Söderströms.
Massey, Doreen. 2005. *For Space*. London: Sage.
Nikolajeva, Maria. 2000. *Bilderbokens pusselbitar*. Lund: Studentlitteratur.
———. 2004. *Barnbokens byggklossar*. Lund: Studentlitteratur.
Nikolajeva, Maria, and Carole Scott. 2001. *How Picturebooks Work*. New York: Garland.
Nodelman, Perry. 2008. *The Hidden Adult: Defining Children's Literature*. Baltimore: Johns Hopkins University Press.
Rhedin, Ulla. 2013. Kaos och ordning. Att berätta ur barnets perspektiv och våga möta barndomens mörker. In *En fanfar för bilderboken!* ed. Ulla Rhedin et al., 37–63. Stockholm: Alfabeta.
Rönnlund, Maria, and Aina Tollefsen. 2016. *Rum: samhällsvetenskapliga perspektiv*. Stockholm: Liber.
Sandelin, Annika. 2006. *Milja och grannarna*. Helsingfors: Söderström.
Sjöberg, Lena. 2018. *I huset där jag bor*. Stockholm: Rabén & Sjögren.
Staaf, Eva. 2014. *Tilly som trodde att …*. Stockholm: Rabén & Sjögren.
Widmark, Martin. 2017. *Huset som vaknade*. Stockholm: Bonnier Carlsen.

Open Access This chapter is licensed under the terms of the Creative Commons Attribution 4.0 International License (http://creativecommons.org/licenses/by/4.0/), which permits use, sharing, adaptation, distribution and reproduction in any medium or format, as long as you give appropriate credit to the original author(s) and the source, provide a link to the Creative Commons licence and indicate if changes were made.

The images or other third party material in this chapter are included in the chapter's Creative Commons licence, unless indicated otherwise in a credit line to the material. If material is not included in the chapter's Creative Commons licence and your intended use is not permitted by statutory regulation or exceeds the permitted use, you will need to obtain permission directly from the copyright holder.

PART II

Where Do You Feel? Spaces, Emotions, and Technology

CHAPTER 5

Love, Longing, and the Smartphone: Lena Andersson, Vigdis Hjorth, and Hanne Ørstavik

Christian Refsum

The smartphone is arguably the most important of various technological devices restructuring the experience of space and time in late modernity. It regulates rhythms for attention and relaxation, communication, participation, and isolation. It is both an extremely important device for communication across distances and a thing we become emotionally attached to. For more and more people it is the last thing we look at before going to sleep and it wakes us up in the morning. If we need to switch the sound off, we can keep it close to our bodies and be alerted by its vibrations. It has a visual, auditive, and haptic component. It contains our calendar, phone book, and address book, and serves as a platform for all kinds of information, business, and entertainment. It is an extension of our eyes and ears, as well as a means of structuring and organizing our reality. In modern cities more and more people can now be observed looking down into a screen as they stroll down the street, perhaps they are navigating with Google Maps, or they might be watching a YouTube clip posted on Facebook by a so-called friend.

C. Refsum (✉)
University of Oslo, Oslo, Norway

© The Author(s) 2020
K. Malmio, K. Kurikka (eds.), *Contemporary Nordic Literature and Spatiality*, Geocriticism and Spatial Literary Studies,
https://doi.org/10.1007/978-3-030-23353-2_5

The smartphone is an example of what Giorgio Agamben calls a *dispositif*, usually translated into the slightly misleading word *apparatus* in English. The term, taken from Michel Foucault, resonates with Hegel's concept of "positivity" as well as with Martin Heidegger's *Gestell*. What is common, according to Agamben, to these concepts is that:

> (...) they refer back to [the Greek word] *oikonomia*, that is, to a set of practices, bodies of knowledge, measures, and institutions that aim to manage, govern, control, and orient—in a way that purports to be useful—the behaviors, gestures, and thoughts of human beings. (Agamben 2009, 12)

And later in the same essay:

> I shall call an apparatus literally anything that has in some way the capacity to capture, orient, determine, intercept, model, control, or secure the gestures, behaviors, opinions, or discourses of living beings. (Agamben 2009, 14)

This broad definition of "apparatus" thus becomes more operative than both the Heideggerian *Gestell*, which designates a certain enframing of reality,[1] and the Foucauldian *dispositive*, consisting of heterogeneous elements in complex relational systems exercising power, though not from a fixed or stable source.[2]

According to Agamben, processes of subjectification and desubjectification take place in the interaction between, or rather in a fight between, "living beings" and various apparatuses. Such fights go on all the time. For example, in religious practices, both the sacrifice and the confession serve as apparatuses. In sacrificing or confessing, the sinner regains a renewed or strengthened subjectivity at the same time as he adapts to society. Agamben argues that through modern technology, such as the mobile phone,[3] subjectification becomes more and more abstract. Modernity is characterized by a constant adding up of apparatuses, which leads to a proliferation or dissemination in the processes of subjectification (Agamben 2009, 15). The problem is that processes of subjectification and desubjectification seem to become mutually indifferent, and so desubjectification does not give rise to the recomposition of a new subject, except in larval or, as it were, spectral form (Agamben 2009, 21). This could very well be the case with the cell phone (*Telefonino*, in Italian, which Agamben confesses to hate), as well as the more advanced smartphone, which is a platform for performing all the functions of a computer. Such apparatuses would appear to be tools for agency and subjectification, but for Agamben the opposite is the case. The mobile phone turns living beings into objects of control. In *24/7: Late Capitalism and the Ends of Sleep* (2014), Jonathan Crary argues similarly that our consumption of more and more information takes place within what Foucault called "a network of permanent observation" (Crary 2014, 47). For him, the smartphone is just one of many devices which confirms and enhances a cultural situation defined by capitalism's constant aim to maximize profit. Through interactive media, capitalism works 24 hours a day:

> (…) capitalism is not simply a continuous or sequential capture of attention, but also a dense layering of time, in which multiple operations or attractions can be attended to in near-simultaneity, regardless of where one is or whatever else one might be doing. So-called "smart" devices are labeled as such less for the advantages they might provide for an individual than for their capacity to integrate their user more fully into 24/7 routines. (Crary 2014, 84)

While we are using the networks for our own needs and entertainment, our attention is captured, often in preprogrammed routes. This happens in a cultural climate where engagement, participation, and interaction are highly praised values. The economic principle of maximizing productivity and profit has crept into our private lives. Users of smart devices are deprived of time gaps, zones for relaxation, meditation, and sleep—all crucial for positive subjectification. According to Crary, all means are used to minimize sleep, recuperation, and inactivity. As a result, people are getting tired and depressed. We are unable to sleep properly during the nighttime, and are too tired to work well during the day. Crary can be criticized for nostalgia and for overstating his argument, but whatever the scope of the problem is, I think his arguments deserve to be discussed.

My contribution to this discussion is to highlight some literary descriptions of how the cell and smartphone are media for expressing, mirroring, producing, and structuring emotions like love and longing. I will leave the question of control and the explicit critique of neoliberalism aside, and stress instead on how mobile phones are apparatuses for capturing and holding attention. They are apparatuses for *availability*, a word that gives slightly different connotations from that of control, but which is also related to it, since availability is an important precondition for modern control systems.

First, mobile phones open up the possibility of simultaneous communication at any time, (without any guarantee that such communication actually will be established). Second, mobile phones are apparatuses for producing subjects who understand themselves as constantly *available*. A third aspect by which the mobile phone influences the temporality of love and longing is that it weakens our sense of being tied to a certain place, a certain time, and a certain situation.

The reason we accept entering into a state of availability typical for the world of smart devices is that we expect to get something in return. Agamben is clear that even if it were possible to fight the mobile phone, it would be pointless, since "[A]t the root of each apparatus lies an all-too-human desire for happiness" (Agamben 2009, 17). For contemporary love studies it is of wide interest to investigate how the desire for happiness manifests itself, and how it is met in the interaction with the apparatus. Much has already been done in examining ideologies of happiness. Sara Ahmed has criticized the "imperative" to be happy in *The Promise of Happiness* (2010) and Lauren Berlant has analyzed how *Cruel Optimism* (2011) might prevent us from making important decisions that can change our lives for the better. Within critical theory there is widespread skepticism about the role of new media in relation to promises of happiness. Zygmunt Bauman has argued in *Liquid Love: On the Frailty of Human Bonds* (2003) that mobile phones and other network technology take part in a wider and problematic process in Western societies where communication is separated from relationships. Scholars with a special interest in how new media actually works often have a more positive approach. Sunil Manghani (2009) has, for example, argued for reading text messages of love like a form of minimalist love poetry. He also criticizes Bauman for not seeing how texting can draw people together, creating new forms of intimacy. And even the harshest critics of new technological apparatuses must admit a certain positive potential.

When Agamben (2009, 21) claims that desubjectification does not give rise to the recomposition of a new subject, except "in larval or, as it were, spectral form," the formulation is deeply ambiguous. The specter/ghost is usually seen as an effect of the past, but it might also signal a power which is yet to be realized, some sort of change, as in Marx's famous opening of the communist manifesto: "A specter is haunting Europe—the specter of communism." The connotations of the word "larval" are more positive than those of the specter, since no butterfly evidently will emerge without first being a larva. Despite Agamben's overtly pessimistic view on modern technology, his pessimism is not unconditional. In my interrogation of literary cell and smartphone experiences, I aim to contribute to a deeper understanding of the issues raised by Agamben, Bauman, and Crary. But first it is necessary to say a few words about how the language of love and longing has been developed in epistolary literature.

THE LANGUAGE OF LOVE AND LONGING

The sentimental novel from the eighteenth century is to a large extent an epistolary genre. Richardson's *Pamela; or, Virtue Rewarded* (1740), Rousseau's *Julie, ou la nouvelle Héloïse* (1761), Goethe's *Die Leiden des jungen Werthers* (1774), and Laclos's *Les Liaisons dangereuses* (1782) are only the most famous in a genre mapping emotions of attachment, love, and longing through fictive letters. The letter seems to be a privileged sentimental form for the simple reason that the discourse on love presupposes *separation and longing*. Love letters are written while the lovers are apart. And in the process of longing the lovers use letters (in the double meaning of this word) to give shape and meaning to their affects, to become loving subjects. The discourse on unsuccessful love is far more extensive than that of consummated love. This also seems true of other genres. Fairytales often end by stating that the two lovers, after trials and suffering, "lived happily ever after." We are not told what actually happens or what the lovers feel during this "ever after." Comedy celebrates couples coming together in the end, but the dramatic stuff is all about obstacles. The highly influential Swiss cultural theorist Denis de Rougemont also underlines the crucial status of longing within the language of love in his classic *Love in the Western World* (1940), which centers on the legend of Tristan and Isolde. Roland Barthes makes a similar point in his *Fragments d'un discours amoureux* (1977), using Goethe's *Werther* as a primary example of obsessive, impossible love.

In the digital age, the epistolary genre has become an anachronism. Letters and epistolary texts still convey and arouse emotions, but the conditions for the success of the sentimental novel have more or less been removed. As conventions for communication have now been redefined by smart devices, as well as by new applications like email, Skype, the internet, and FaceTime, the kind of separation that motivated the traditional letter no longer exists. What happens with the discourse on love and longing in this situation? Some answers seem obvious. Communication is speeded up and is often fragmented, and in the era of the smartphone, pictures, voice, and sound become equally important as writing. The discourse on love developed in epistolary literature will hence change. To investigate such changes one would have to investigate the technology and use of smart devices in a systematic way, which is beyond the scope of this chapter. Instead, I shall discuss three novels by three highly praised contemporary Nordic female writers. In my examples, the role of the cell and smartphone is described with a literary sensibility related to the old media regime of literature. In none of these examples do mobile phones play a particularly important role. The heroines in the books are not, for example, on Tinder. But references to mobile phones can still contribute to a better understanding of the issues raised above.

Restless Longing in a Standby Mode

Lena Andersson's novel *Egenmäktigt förfarande—en roman om kärlek* (2013/2015; *Wilful Disregard: A Novel About Love*) has been much debated in Sweden and Norway because of its descriptions of a stereotype called *Kulturmannen* ("The Culture Man"), a man with cultural capital, a huge network, influence, often to be seen at cultural gatherings, and attracting younger women who admire him. They listen to him, but he does not listen to them. He engages with them, but is not willing to commit himself.[4] The Culture Man in Lena Andersson's novel, the artist Hugo Rask, is a rather flat character, contrary to the female protagonist, the poet and essayist Ester Nilsson. What touched me with the novel was the description of Ester's plunge into love as passion in the sense of suffering. Ester falls in love, but is confused since Hugo, the man she loves, is unwilling to commit himself to her—nor, however, does he clearly reject her. She is left, therefore, with an exhausting and destructive sense of hope. She waits for Hugo to call, for him to respond to her long philosophical SMS messages and her emails. She writes: "Ju mer du tiger desto mer talar jag, det är hegelskt" (Andersson 2013, 103) ("The more you stay silent the more I speak, it's Hegelian") (Andersson 2015, 95). The situation becomes unbearable and she leaves Sweden for Paris. Paris, however, turns out to be a city that one should *not* visit to cure heartache (as if that would come as a surprise to anyone). It is as if she actually wants to suffer. She wanders around in the city of love, waiting for Hugo to reply to her text messages:

> Varför fattade hon inte att avgrundsångesten över ett obesvarat SMS var densamma varje gång och enda sättet att undvika den var att inte skicka några? (Andersson 2013, 118)[5]

Why could she not grasp that the abysmal anguish of an unanswered text was the same every time and the only way to avoid it was not to send any? (Andersson 2015, 110)

In one way there is nothing special with Ester, Paris, or the mobile phone, for the novel describes a well-known feeling of longing very convincingly. However, the mobile phone holds the longing person in a *permanent standby mode*, and this is Esther's problem throughout the entire book: there is no way for her to find peace. At any moment, the phone might ring; she is always on her guard. Then, suddenly, walking around in Paris, it actually rings. Hugo Rask's name appears on the display. She prepares herself, pushes the button, and hears his voice, as well as some other voices in the background, but he cannot hear her even if she screams back at him. He has called her without knowing. But she cannot believe that the call was accidental. She interprets the call as a sign that he actually needs her as much as she needs him, perhaps without knowing it, as a sign of deeper and stronger feelings.

In Friedrich Kittler's (1999) psychoanalytically inspired media theory, transmissions of images can be understood as experiences of the imaginary, whilst transmissions of sound connects us to the Lacanian real—to a sort of proximity characterized by an overwhelming materiality which cannot be subsumed under the symbolic order established by language. The mobile phone thus combines absolute distance and extreme closeness much more effectively than for example a letter. Hugo's voice—processed by the apparatus—establishes a strong spectral presence across the continent. It is partly a presence beyond understanding, which rules out any communication. In this scene, Andersson brilliantly captures the vulnerability of the modern neoliberal subject: potentially always connected, always affected, potentially very close to other persons, but at the same time, very, isolated, very alone.

Longing for a Voice

In *Snakk til meg* (2010; "Speak to Me") by the Norwegian writer Vigdis Hjorth, the protagonist Ingeborg is middle aged. Her husband passed away many years ago, and her son has left her to study in Stockholm. Ingeborg travels to Cuba. She meets a man whom she marries, and after many difficulties with the immigration authorities manages to get to Norway. The novel partly describes how their relationship develops before he leaves her, and partly how she tries to establish contact with her son in Stockholm, before the son shouts into his cell phone that he never wants to see her again (Hjorth 2011, 260). The book is seemingly written as diary notes or as a long letter to her son, perhaps after he has broken contact. Ingeborg, like Ester in *Egenmäktigt förfarande*, is connected to the literary world. Ester is a critic and Ingeborg works in a public library. They are both working with the written word on a daily basis, and for both of them writing is an important means of dealing with emotions as when they experience longing. They both try to communicate through the written word, and suffer from a lack of response. The words give order to their lives, but an order which is not sufficient to interpret their deepest longings and fears, and which eventually fails in the attempt made to communicate with the beloved.

Ingeborg waits for letters, telephones, and text messages from Havana and Stockholm, and like Ester she is trapped in a sort of cruel optimism. She realizes how her cell phone occupies her attention and tries to defend herself by leaving it at home when she goes to work so as not to look at it constantly (Hjorth 2011, 220). But eventually it is too tempting to take it along with her. The "promise of happiness" that Agamben saw as crucial in the appeal of the apparatus, is too strong to resist, even if she tries.

The particular social effect of this promise can be compared to a description of longing in a previous novel by Hjorth from another technological age, when the promise of happiness worked differently. In the novel *Om bare* ("If Only") from 2001, the female protagonist is in love and awaits a telephone call from her unreliable lover. Since she does not have a mobile phone, she stays at home, afraid that he might call when she is out. Here the promise of happiness leads the protagonist into isolation. In *Snakk til meg*, written ten years later, Ingeborg, like Ester in *Egenmäktigt förfarande*, is free to go wherever she wants, but remains in a psychological prison of waiting. This is partly an individual choice, but it is also a result of historical and culturally variable conventions and expectations. When Hjorth wrote *Snakk til meg* in 2010 it was not taken for granted in Norway that everyone would be reachable by mobile phone during working hours, even if it was common. Leaving one's mobile phone at home would not therefore be considered strange. In Norway in 2018, however, many would consider it impolite not to carry a mobile phone and be unreachable. It is striking how technology in its initial phase appears to be an opportunity, but becomes redefined as a duty once it is used by the majority of people. Its social significance is thus radically altered. The mobile phone becomes a much more powerful apparatus for interpellation and social control once it implies the command of availability.

The relationship between Ester and Hugo in *Egenmäktigt förfarande* exemplifies perfectly how the question of availability is also a question of power. Ester is constantly available for Hugo, whereas he is in a position where he can choose to be available when it pleases him. Ingeborg in *Snakk til meg* is also trapped in a waiting mode. Both Ingeborg and Ester make themselves available and both of them try in vain to make contact with a loved one who does not respond. (In Ingeborg's case this is most noticeable in her relationship with her son.)

Ingeborg's uncertainty about how to approach her son and her lover is also reflected in her understanding of the conventions of the apparatus. She worries constantly about when and how she should send messages, both to her husband, Enrique, and to her son, Torgrim. The turning point comes on the last pages of the novel when Torgrim, after having rejected her calls and messages for a long time, suddenly calls back and screams that he never wants to speak to her again. After that she writes:

> Det er deg jeg savner. Det er fraværet ditt som gjør vondt. Smerten man føler ved et tap er målestokken for håpet man har hatt. Å vite hvordan du har det. Høre stemmen din en gang til, skal det aldri skje?
> Hvordan var det for deg? Jeg vil så gjerne høre, skal tåle alt, vær så snill, snakk til meg! (Hjorth 2011, 262)
>
> It is you that I miss. It is your absence that hurts. The pain you feel from a loss is a measure of the hope you have had. To know how you are. To hear your voice once more, will it never happen?
> How was it for you? I would so much like to hear, I can take anything, speak to me!

Even if the telephone conversation comes as a shock, and strikes her with pain, it is contrasted with the even worse impersonal effects of text messages. Here is a quote about longing for contact, from a few pages earlier:

> Opplevde månedene etterpå nærmest som en kjærlighetssorg. At du ikke svarte, ikke lot høre fra deg vondt *som om du hadde sendt en SMS om at alt var over*, som om du gjorde det slutt, uten forklaring, sånn opplevde jeg det: uten årsak. (Hjorth 2011, 254; My italics)
>
> Experienced the following months more or less like a heartache. That you didn't reply, didn't give a sign hurt *as if you had sent an SMS saying every-*

thing was over, like if you broke up, without explanation, that's how it felt: without reason. (My italics)

The SMS is here used as a simile for rejection (*as if you had sent an SMS saying everything was over*)—and due to the short format—a sort of empty, cold rejection impossible to fully comprehend. A text message thus serves as a paradoxical simile for not getting any message at all. However, the passage also indicates that, not only is the break up via SMS painful, it is similar to no message at all. In the context it is clear that waiting for a call is *like* an endless series of breakup messages. The silence of a mobile phone is in one sense similar to no communication, but in another sense the silence is worse than it would have been without the mobile. For with the mobile phone we have the possibility of communication in all environments and at any time, and therefore we also have the complete and utter rejection at all times and everywhere. The mobile phone is thus an apparatus for keeping its user in a state of cruel optimism, hoping and waiting, preventing the subject from taking control over her own life. Most of Ingeborg's life is lived in a waiting mode. She tries to console herself, thinking that he will make contact:

> (…) Sånn beroliget jeg meg selv og ventet på den angrende telefonen, den unnskyldende mailen, postkortet, det kom ikke. (Hjorth 2011, 255)
>
> (…) This is how I calmed myself and waited for the regretful phone call, the apologetic email, the postcard, it didn't arrive.

As is clear in this passage, the phone is in no way the only apparatus that nurtures the hope of reconciliation and happiness. It is just one item of technology among many that serve a similar purpose. The mobile phone continues to serve functions that were earlier met by other apparatuses, but it also introduces new ones. It partly coexists with and partly displaces other apparatuses.

The (Im)Possibility of a Meeting

Ruth, the protagonist in Hanne Ørstavik's novel *Det finnes en stor åpen plass i Bordeaux* (2013; "There is a Big Open Square in Bordeaux"), is an artist from Oslo who goes to Bordeaux to set up an art exhibition. She has a boyfriend, Johannes, in Norway, who is an art historian from the west coast. He says that he loves her (Ørstavik 2013, 17), but refuses to have sex with her, drinks too much, is unfriendly and often neglects her calls and messages. The plan is that he will come to Bordeaux with her, but he starts to drink, and things do not go according to plan. One night, while having dinner with her friend, Abel, Ruth suddenly receives a picture message from Johannes showing a half-naked woman standing on a table in a strip club. Underneath the picture, he writes.

> Her er jeg nå. (Ørstavik 2013, 153)
>
> Here I am now.

The picture upsets her, and she and her friend move on to another bar to have another drink. Here she reflects on her situation:

> Hun [her friend, Abel] ser på meg som om hun forstår, eller at det er helt greit, helt åpent, virker det uansett som. Det merkelig store ansiktet hennes. Men hun er så langt borte, jeg registrerer det bare, jeg er bak en hinne, inne hos meg selv, når ikke gjennom til de andre, det er bare han som når meg her. Som sender meg bilder her. Som sender meg ingenting her, her inne, hvor han er det eneste jeg venter på, som ikke kommer. Jeg lar meg gli ned krakken, tar veska, går mot døra (…). (Ørstavik 2013, 178)
>
> She [her friend] watches me as if she understands, or finds it okay, completely open, it nevertheless seems. Her remarkably large face. But she is so far away, I just notice it, I am behind a film, inside, at my place, cannot come through to the others, it is only he who can reach me here. Who sends me pictures here. Who sends me nothing here, inside here, where he's the only one I'm waiting for, who doesn't come. I let myself slip off the stool, take my bag, walk towards the door (…).

The repetition of the Norwegian word *her* (here) is of course an ironic reminder that there is no "here" in a traditional sense, neither for Johannes, nor for Ruth. What "here" refers to is an imaginary space defined not only by the actual setting but also by the picture she has seen as well as her memories and fantasies.

In the remaining 40 pages of the book Ruth wanders about in Bordeaux, speaks with Abel, thinks of Johannes, and of a love relation between Abel's daughter Lily and her relationship to a boy, Ralph. She sends and receives text messages to and from Johannes, and she speaks into his telephone answering machine. Ørstavik's prose combines all the various planes of *her* (here) in a presentation of a simultaneous imagined reality (historical time, past, present, future).

After receiving the picture from the strip club, she decides to go to a strip club herself. She wants to take a photograph of a stripper and send it to Johannes as if to establish a common experience of "here"—of being in a similar place. His message, "Here I am now," is both a rejection and an invitation: it communicates first *I am not with you*, but it also communicates that he actually *is with her* in another sense, since he thinks of her and sends her this message when looking at the naked body of a stripper in Norway. He wants her to know all about himself—including his less sympathetic sides, what he has earlier called his pornographic desire—something that fits well with what Ruth has thought of as a robust openness between them. The picture he sends thus represents a highly ambivalent declaration of love. It also breaks down traditional borders between absence/presence as well as private/public.

She is not allowed to take photographs in the club she visits so she leaves. It is not possible to establish a common "here" with him. He misses his plane and when she calls him the next morning he says that he will come, something he subsequently fails to do.

The book is about actual and imagined meetings. It lingers on the imaginary. The title of the book, *Det finnes en stor åpen plass i Bordeaux*, refers to a square where Ruth fantasizes about meeting Johannes. The square serves as a symbol for openness and vulnerability. In earlier times executions were carried out there. Ruth's fantasies represent a longing for a radical, dangerous openness that she has felt in the presence of Johannes— in meetings that have been strong and good, but that have also implied a risk of decapitation, a fatal self-destruction. Ruth, both the person and the artist, seeks a deep existential confrontation with Johannes. She wants and needs him, regardless of the pain caused by their contact, despite his unsympathetic behavior and rejection of her, it seems. She is kept in a waiting mode for messages and phone calls as she wanders about in Bordeaux at night. But her waiting does not seem as futile or destructive as in *Egenmäktigt förfarande* or in *Snakk til meg*. What is so skillfully described in the novel is how Ruth opens up mental spaces, where reality, dreams, and visual projections transgress geographical, psychic, and gender boundaries. This is clear from the beginning of the novel when we meet Ruth the artist as she reflects on a picture she has gotten in her head:

> I bildet går jeg ut av en vogn, bøyer meg, og går ned de to trinnene. Jeg vet ikke om jeg er mann eller kvinne. Jeg har svarte klær, bukser, ser det ut til, jeg ser bare det, nedover beina, og skoene, svart lær. Det er en hestedrosje. Det er ved en stor åpen plass, med trær langs tre av sidene. (Ørstavik 2013, 12)
>
> In the picture I leave the wagon, bend, walk down the two stairs. I don't know whether I'm a man or a woman. I have black clothes, trousers, as it seems, that's all I see, covering my legs, and my shoes, black leather. There's a horsecab. It's by a big open square, with trees along three sides.

This passage demonstrates how Ruth analyzes her situation not only in letters and words, but also in mediated and imagined pictures. What is striking about the image is that it presents a mode of existence beyond traditional distinctions ("I don't know whether I'm a man or a woman"). It thus opens up a process of desubjectification and a wide range of possible subjectifications. A page later, she thinks about a mental image from New York, two girls in underwear, one of them resembling her daughter. These are just two examples of how various forms of referentiality are combined in the book, leaving the reader with the experience of a highly reflexive imaginary work of art. It is as if all the impulses obtained and processed by the artist, who is also the protagonist and narrator, play out roles in a complex drama of desubjectification and subjectification. In the last part of the book communication via the smartphone starts to dominate Ruth's actions and thoughts. But the complex imaginary of the book leaves the reader with the impression that Ruth's waiting and longing has a strong creative potential.

Conclusion

These three novels all contain passages that indicate how the cell or smartphone might function like a new sense organ and how it frames personal, intimate experiences. For the three longing protagonists the cell or smartphone can be considered an extension of the self, an object of proxemics in Roland Barthes's (2012, 111–13) sense of the term.[6] The mobile phone is kept close to the body in every situation in order to transmit signals across distances at any time. All the novels deal with the relationship between geographical and mental distance in modern relationships and in all of them the mobile phone plays an important role in negotiating distance. The themes of availability, uncertainty, waiting, and longing are combined to form the dominant chord in all the examples. And in all of them the main protagonists at times seem to lose connection with the place they are in. Ingeborg in *Snakk til meg* is neither completely in Cuba, neither in Stockholm, nor in Norway. Ester in *Egenmäktigt förfarande* is neither completely in Paris, nor in Hugo Rask's atelier in Stockholm. Ørstavik's repetitions of the word "here" clearly indicate that the question of place is both crucial and impossible. These people are out of place.

All the female protagonists enter a waiting and longing mode. Through the mobile phone they make themselves constantly available, and they all try to establish contact with a man who doesn't respond in a manner that gives them the confirmation they want and expect. As de Rougemont (1983) has shown, male lovers have often found themselves in a waiting and longing position in Western literature, especially in the courtly tradition, where a knight desires a lady who is married. Such histories have been especially important for the development of romantic ideals in Western culture. The reflexivity of Petrarch and Dante take its cue from the absence of the beloved. And the topos of a man in love with his own capacity for suffering due to experiences of impossible love became an early cliché. Cervantes, for example, made fun of his hero playing the stereotypical role of a man who suffers from an impossible love in *Don Quixote*. And both male and female fictional heroes have repeatedly been destroyed by unreciprocated love. Seen in this context, it is striking how the unrequited love stories of contemporary female Nordic heroes fall into a well-known literary pattern. In a culture with a high degree of equality between the sexes, several female writers describe a situation of longing and waiting with deep roots in the male Western discourse of love. The female contemporary writers presented here also create self-reflexive art works which linger on the experience of separation, longing, and the impossibility of meeting. In addition, the works open up a discussion on how the temporality of love and longing changes as the conditions for communication and the negotiations of space change.

The smartphone is a platform for a wide range of messages and sense experiences. It captures all the mental layers which have been described in Friedrich Kittler's (1999) media theory: symbolic text messages, imaginary pictures of realities and dreams, and "the real" of the materiality of the apparatus and the mediated voice. In Ørstavik's novel, there is a strong emphasis on the imaginary dimension. In Lena Andersson's novel, as well as in Vigdis Hjorth's, there are passages that reflect on the directness and frightening reality of the voice, as well as on the neutral arbitrariness of symbolic text signs.

Waiting and longing are psychic dispositions that might lead to stagnation and renewal, to desubjectification and new subjectification. In this respect, mobile devices serve various functions. The apparatus marks an affective, intimate space and carries a hope of happiness. It might function as an apparatus for communication, liberation, and subjectification. Examples can no doubt be found in contemporary literature, film, or TV series. My examples point, however, in a more pessimistic direction. Here the apparatuses are shown as devices for keeping the female protagonists in a constantly waiting position, in a virtual prison that is carried around everywhere, depriving them of time gaps where they are not available, gaps for rest, recreation, reorientation, and sustainable subjectification. *Egenmäktigt förfarande* describes this cultural situation and its heartbreaking consequences. The novel describes a state of mind where there seems to be no way out of the waiting and longing mode. Ester has found the perfect apparatus to keep her in this longing position. However, it is important to see that a waiting and longing mode is not necessarily a passive mode. Ester is a highly reflective writer. Like the frustrated Provençal troubadours from the twelfth century, she suffers from unconsummated love, but does gain self-reflexivity instead.

All the novels contain passages where desubjectification seems to pave the way for a renewal of the self. This perspective seems particularly relevant for the two Norwegian novels written in the first person, *Snakk til meg* and *Det finnes en stor åpen plass i Bordeaux*. In both books there is a genuine concern to open up a shockingly dangerous but also potentially liberating mental space. When Ingeborg's son Torgrim shouts: "I never want to see you again" in *Snakk til meg*, Ingeborg's whole frame of reference breaks down, establishing a new open space where she has to reorient herself. She has lost Enrique, and now she has lost Torgrim, and for the first time she is confronted with fierce anger. It is a personal catastrophe, but also potentially liberating, since it requires a radical reorientation. For the first time she is forced to respond in a manner that will not conform to established roles of attachment. Her frames of reference for playing the role of the loving, waiting, longing subject become impossible and she has to build a new frame. From this point on, a possibility of a new subjectification arises.

Even though waiting and longing is also a major theme in *Det finnes en stor åpen plass i Bordeaux*, it does not dominate in the same way as in the two other books. One possible reason is that the book has an artist as a protagonist, who is constantly in a process of renewal and reformulation of her own sensibility and understanding. Her thoughts, as they are presented in the novel, are not solely centered on her contact with Johannes, except in some of the last parts of the book. It rather seems as if her interest in Johannes is part of a larger experimental and open attitude to the world and to various life forms. The book also relates to all sorts of mediated messages, photos, pictures, exhibitions, and sounds, leaving the impression that Ruth lives in a world of opportunity and potential freedom.

As already mentioned, the protagonists in my novels have all grown up in an old media situation, one not defined by mobile media. Young people, who have grown up with smart devices and have integrated the new media as extensions of their subjective sensibility, who don't read novels, would perhaps describe their experiences of love and longing differently than in my examples. A media theorist might object to my perspective by claiming that my examples convey an outdated understanding of love and communication. But the experience of not being at the height of the dominant media regime is a reality that most of us live with. I would argue that the experience of not being up to date actually *is* the dominant experience of engaging with communication technology in late modernism. This reality is a valuable subject matter for investigation in itself, and contemporary novels tell stories of this reality.

Notes

1. In "The Question Concerning Technology" Heidegger defines *Gestell* as "the essence of modern technology (…) which is itself nothing technological" (Heidegger 1977, 20). *Gestell*, in English, means "enframing (…) the gathering together of that setting-upon which sets upon man, i.e., challenges him forth, to reveal the real, in the mode of ordering, as standing-reserve" (Heidegger 1977, 20).
2. "What I'm trying to pick out with this term is, firstly, a thoroughly heterogeneous ensemble consisting of discourses, institutions, architectural forms, regulatory decisions, laws, administrative measures, scientific statements, philosophical, moral and philanthropic propositions—in short, the said as much as the unsaid. Such are the elements of the apparatus. The apparatus itself is the system of relations that can be established between these elements" (Foucault 1980, 194). Even if Foucault's *dispositif* can be associated with the political economy of the household, Foucault tends to see the *dispositif* as a strategic means which serves a particular purpose in a conflict.
3. Since I refer to texts from different stages in late modernity, I sometimes refer to cell phones and at other times to smartphones, depending on the

text I am referring to. I use "mobile phone" as a term covering both cell and smartphones. The enormous differences in the technology and potential use of mobile phones will only be taken into consideration where they are relevant to my argument.
4. The Swedish writer Åsa Beckman introduced the stereotype *Kulturmannen* in an essay in the Swedish newspaper *Dagens nyheter*, April 27, 2014. She sees *Egenmäktigt förfarande* as an exemplary study of the Culture Man. The term was later picked up by several other writers and critics, the most influential perhaps being Ebba Witt-Brattström in her collection of essays *Kulturmannen och andra texter* from 2016.
5. Translations from the Scandinavian texts are my own except for Lena Andersson's novel, which was translated into English by Sarah Death in 2015.
6. In an essay on Roland Barthes, "Proxémie," Reinhold Görling (2018, 267) suggests that the lamp, the bed, and the smartphone can be considered extensions of what we understand as ourselves, as interfaces for the transference of affects.

References

Agamben, Giorgio. 2009. *What Is an Apparatus? And Other Essays*. Edited by Werner Hamacher. Translated by David Kishik and Stefan Pedatella. Stanford, CA: Stanford University Press.

Ahmed, Sara. 2010. *The Promise of Happiness*. Durham and London: Duke University Press.

Andersson, Lena. 2013. *Egenmäktigt förfarande: en roman om kärlek*. Stockholm: Natur & Kultur.

———. 2015. *Wilful Disregard: A Novel About Love*. Translated by Sarah Death. London: Picador.

Barthes, Roland. 2012. *How to Live Together: Novelistic Simulations of Some Everyday Spaces*. Translated by Kate Briggs. New York: Columbia University Press.

Bauman, Zygmunt. 2003. *Liquid Love: On the Frailty of Human Bonds*. Cambridge: Polity Press.

Berlant, Lauren. 2011. *Cruel Optimism*. Durham and London: Duke University Press.

Crary, Jonathan. 2014. *24/7: Late Capitalism and the Ends of Sleep*. London: Verso.

Foucault, Michael. 1980. "The Confession of the Flesh" (1977) Interview. In *Power/Knowledge Selected Interviews and Other Writings, 1972–1977*, ed. Colin Gordon, 194–228. New York: Pantheon Books.

Görling, Reinhold. 2018. Proxémie/Proksemikk. In *Living Together: Roland Barthes, the Individual and the Community*, ed. Knut Stene-Johansen, Christian Refsum, and Johan Schimanski, 267–277. Bielefeld: Transcript Verlag.

Heidegger, Martin. 1977. The Question Concerning Technology. In *The Question Concerning Technology and Other Essays*, 3–35. Translated by William Lovitt. New York and London: Garland Publishing, Inc.

Hjorth, Vigdis. 2001. *Om Bare*. Oslo: Cappelen Damm.

———. 2011 [2010]. *Snakk til meg*. Oslo: Cappelen Damm.

Kittler, Friedrich. 1999. *Gramophone, Film, Typewriter*. Translated, with an Introduction, by Geoffrey Winthrop-Young, and Michael Wutz. Stanford, CA: Stanford University Press.

Manghani, Sunil. 2009. Love Messaging: Mobile Phone Texting Seen Through the Lens of Tanka Poetry. *Theory, Culture & Society* 26 (2–3): 209–232.

Ørstavik, Hanne. 2013. *Det finnes en stor åpen plass i Bordeaux*. Oslo: Forlaget Oktober.

Rougemont, Denis de. 1983 [1940]. *Love in the Western World*. Translated by Montgomery Belgion. Princeton, NJ: Princeton University Press.

Open Access This chapter is licensed under the terms of the Creative Commons Attribution 4.0 International License (http://creativecommons.org/licenses/by/4.0/), which permits use, sharing, adaptation, distribution and reproduction in any medium or format, as long as you give appropriate credit to the original author(s) and the source, provide a link to the Creative Commons licence and indicate if changes were made.

The images or other third party material in this chapter are included in the chapter's Creative Commons licence, unless indicated otherwise in a credit line to the material. If material is not included in the chapter's Creative Commons licence and your intended use is not permitted by statutory regulation or exceeds the permitted use, you will need to obtain permission directly from the copyright holder.

CHAPTER 6

"Never Give Up Hopelessness!?": Emotions and Spatiality in Contemporary Finnish Experimental Poetry

Anna Helle

In the past decades, the Finnish poetry scene has been vital, dynamic, and full of life. Poets of different ages have worked concurrently. Young poets have come along one after another, and they have brought out new ideas and aesthetic outlooks. Moreover, senior poets have had a vital role in formulating and reformulating the poetics of the twenty-first century. Influences have been taken from various directions. In experimental poetry, one source of inspiration has been Finnish avant-garde poetry from the 1960s, and the influences of (post)-structuralist theories as well as new American poetry have also been evident.

    This chapter focuses on a small array of recent Finnish poetry and especially on experimental poetry. The poems are written by Karri Kokko (b. 1955), Tytti Heikkinen (b. 1969), and Eino Santanen (b. 1975). I have chosen the poems on the grounds of how they deal with different aspects of contemporary Finnish society. I interpret the poems in the context of late modern Finland, the geographical place and cultural area in which the

A. Helle (✉)
University of Turku, Turku, Finland

poems have been written, published, and received. The poems discuss twenty-first-century Finnish issues: some deal with finance capitalism, while others tackle social problems and unsatisfactory subject positions. The poems, moreover, express, describe, and arouse different kinds of emotions, which are typical of contemporary Finnish poetry (Blomberg et al. 2010). In these poems, the emotions are closely related to how it feels to live in today's Finland. However, there is often an ironic twist, too, as in the title's quote "Never give up Hopelessness," taken from Heikkinen's poem.[1]

By approaching the poems in the context of late modernity and from the viewpoint of emotions and spatiality, I wish to analyze how contemporary Finnish poetry deals with the surrounding society. I aim to answer the following questions: What do the poems talk about? What kinds of emotions are there in these poems? What is the role of spatiality in them? How are the poems connected to the surrounding world? Spatiality in this chapter does refer not only to late modern Finland as a place and a cultural area but also to Finnish literature (poetry, to be more precise) as a public space in which emotional and potentially political topics are experienced and dealt with.

Experimental Poetry and Postmodernism

Experimental poetry is understood here as the kind of poetry that seeks to extend the boundaries of poetry and raises fundamental questions about the nature of poetry itself (Bray et al. 2012, 1–2). Poetics refers to the "creative principles informing any literary, social or cultural construction."[2]

The poetry that I deal with can be characterized more precisely as postmodern, although the term "postmodern" is rarely used in Finnish discussions concerning recent poetry. The reasons for neglecting the term are not self-evident. Nevertheless, from the 1980s onward, the notion of postmodernism has been frequently used in relation to the postmodern novel and I suppose that the term has become somewhat overused. This may well be the case beyond the boundaries of Finland as well. Brian McHale, for instance, has noted in *The Obligation toward the Difficult Whole* (2004, 1–2) that the word "postmodernism" is not very often used when talking about the latest American poetry.[3]

Be that as it may, postmodernism in poetry can imply many things. It can mean recycling already existing texts, or making pastiches. Different styles can be mixed and combined with texts that deal with contemporary ways of living and writing. Postmodern poetry, moreover, often uses unpoetic material (Haapala 2013, 182). Joseph Conte (1991, 9) has stated that in comparison with modernist poetry, postmodernists see the language as a more plastic medium that can be reshaped and employed for multifarious purposes. Although this opinion can be challenged by referring, for example, to the highly modernist *Waste Land* (1922) by T. S. Eliot, which mixes different languages, registers, voices, and cultural images, I argue that in a broader perspective this kind of poetics is rarer in modernist poetry and more prevalent and dominant in postmodernist poetry.

Moreover, while modernists often longed for the lost promise of cultural renaissance, postmodern poets more commonly see the world as irreversibly chaotic and out of control (Conte 1991, 9). Some theorists emphasize the anguished nature of postmodern poetry, while others highlight its playful and liberating aspects (Conte 1991, 9; Hoover 2013, xxix). In the poems that I scrutinize here, there is always a humorous or ironic tone even if the contents are otherwise serious.

One postmodern feature that is common to all the poems discussed in this chapter is that the speakers of the poems are evidently artificial constructions (see Conte 1991, 43–4). The selected poems also utilize citation techniques or recycle found material, and all of them are based on an experimental approach to composition. Moreover, due to the artificially constructed speakers, the contents of the poems cannot be seen as direct expressions of the inner life of the poets. All this is typical of postmodern poetry (Hoover 2013, xxix–xxx).

The relationship between the experimental poems that I inspect here and questions of spatiality is complex. To begin with, the poems use different kinds of found material. Kokko's *Varjofinlandia* (2005; "Shadow Finlandia") is made up of texts that have been taken from Finnish blogs dealing with depression, while Heikkinen's poems recycle material found from Finnish blogs in which teenage girls write about their lives. Santanen's bank-note poems, on the other hand, have been written on 20 euro bills, that is, found objects that belong to the public domain.

The poems chosen play with the notions of intimate and public spaces and question the borders between them. In the original contexts, the source materials of Kokko's and Heikkinen's poems deal with intimate matters of private persons. They were, however, already public when the poets found them on the internet and modified them into poems that are public in a very different sphere. This conceptual move, the shift from one realm to another, changes the nature of the texts and the way in which readers respond to them. Santanen's poems, for their part, use bank notes as a public space in order to criticize the problems of present-day capitalism. Writing poetry on bank notes makes the two very different public spaces of poetry and money collide.

POETICS AND POLITICS OF EMOTION

The language of the poems that I scrutinize here is emotionally charged, which is why I suggest that they employ a kind of "poetics of emotion." Today, the theoretical toolbox available for analyzing literature, emotions, and affects is more than well stocked. There are several central concepts such as affect, emotion, feeling, and sentiment, among others, and a multiplicity of ways for defining them (e.g., Helle and Hollsten 2016; Seighworth and Gregg 2010; Nussbaum 2001, 22–3; Keen 2011; Deleuze 2012, 63; Massumi 2002; Ahmed 2004; Ngai 2005). In this chapter, I use the concept of emotion to refer to different kinds of human sentiments, or to feeling something in relation to other people, thoughts, or situations.[4] Emotions can be purely mental or they may have bodily dimensions. They are often conscious, but it is also possible that subjects do not always know how they feel (Ahmed 2004, 5–11).

Interestingly enough, the American literary scholar Fredric Jameson (1991, xix–xi) has stated that postmodern culture (by which he refers both to postmodernist literature and art, and to late modern society marked by capitalism) is witnessing a waning of affect. Jameson (1991, 10–5) argues that he does not claim that all affect, feeling, or emotion has vanished in the postmodern era. However, in postmodernism the subject is "dead" or decentered in the way that art can no longer express its feelings.[5] He also states that along with the end of the centered bourgeois subject we might be liberated from the kind of subject's anxieties but also from "every other kind of feeling."

Reading the postmodern poems that I have selected—and the most recent Finnish poetry in general—makes the notion of the waning of affect problematic. As I see it, the twenty-first-century Finnish postmodern poetry is replete with emotions, and this is one of the main reasons why the poems are thought provoking and political. Jameson published his famous book on postmodernism already in the early 1990s and he dealt with cultural phenomena of the 1960s. Hence, the difference between my understanding and that of Jameson's may be the result of the temporal gap between the 1990s and the present day but also of focusing on dissimilar texts. While Jameson refers to artists and writers such as Andy Warhol (1922–1987), Jean-Luc Godard (b. 1930), John Cage (1912–1992), and Thomas Pynchon (b. 1937), my material consists of Finnish poetry written in the twenty-first century. Over the past few decades, both theoretical conceptions and postmodernist literature have altered.

It is nevertheless true that postmodern poems rarely express directly the feelings of the poets. I see this, however, as a question of poetics, not as a sign of the death of the subject. The fact that the speakers of the poems that I scrutinize here are artificial constructions and the poems themselves are often made by copy-pasting found material does not eradicate the affective force of the poems. I suggest, on the contrary, that emotions have an important role in connecting the poems to the surrounding world.

The politics of emotion refers to the ways in which things are made political through emotions (Ahmed 2004). Emotions are everywhere, and literature has a crucial role in reflecting and discussing the emotions that circulate in our rapidly changing culture and society. For instance, fictional characters live through affective experiences, and they react emotionally to the circumstances in which they live. Literature offers means to verbalize and comprehend obscure and problematic emotions. It also serves as a public space where affective issues can be brought into discussion.

Approaching contemporary literature from the viewpoint of emotions is important. It has been assumed that the affective climate of contemporary culture is transforming along with the societal transition from the industrial to the post-industrial phase (e.g., Clough 2007, 2–3). Raymond Williams's (1988, 146) notion of the changing structures of feeling is worth remembering here. His basic idea is that groups of people may experience life in different ways, and that experiences are structured. The structures are mobile, and they change in time and in relation to the surrounding society. Literature as an instance of cultural meaning-making participates in expressing, molding, and interpreting the changing affective climate. Although all of the poems discussed in this chapter are Finnish, I suppose that they express the kinds of structures of feeling that are recognizable in many other late modern societies too.

Varjofinlandia and the Voices of Finnish Depression

The latest Finnish poetry often builds a space to deal with negative emotions. Karri Kokko's *Varjofinlandia* is a perfect example of this since it is a collage made of material found from Finnish blogs dealing with depression.

Kokko is a Finnish experimental poet who has published 16 literary works. All of his works (except for the debut collection *Uno boy*, 1982) have been published by alternative Finnish publishers instead of established publishing houses. Despite his somewhat marginalized status in relation to established literary institutions, Kokko has a relatively visible role in the Finnish twenty-first-century poetry scene. He is also known as a literary critic and journalist, and has had several blogs. He participates actively in poetry events and keeps inventing new approaches to poetry.

The genre of *Varjofinlandia* is not self-evident. It consists of 61 pages filled with successive sentences cut off from blog texts and rearranged into an artwork. It could therefore be seen as prose literature. Another possibility is to see it as prose poetry or procedural poetry, as I do; I read *Varjofinlandia* here as a long postmodern poem that uses the New Sentence Technique.[6]

The name "Varjofinlandia" refers of course to Finland. The name of the country is "Suomi" in Finnish but it is called "Finlandia" for example in New Latin. The name connects Kokko's work to a specific geographical place, Finland. Finland is also a certain cultural area marked by its location in the North between Scandinavia and Russia, and is one of the Nordic welfare states. The word "Finlandia" has, however, particularly solemn connotations, because it is used, for example, in Jean Sibelius's *Finlandia Hymn* (1900), which is almost a national anthem in Finland—Sibelius (1865–1957) himself was a world famous Finnish national composer. Moreover, the most distinguished Finnish literary prize for novels is the Finlandia Prize.

With the prefix "Varjo-" ("Shadow"), *Varjofinlandia* aims to question the elevated connotations of "Finlandia." The name can therefore be interpreted in several ways. It may refer to the dark sides of the official Finland, or it can be read as a statement according to which the neglected voices that express malaise should be heard by the wealthy part of the nation. In relation to the Finlandia Prize,[7] it may also refer to marginal or marginalized literature (such as experimental poetry) that flourishes in the shadows of the best-selling novels that fill the shelves of bookshops.

Varjofinlandia is a postmodern dramatic monologue in which a decentered subject reflects on his or her emotions. A dramatic monologue is, of course, a poem that consists exclusively of the speaker's speech and in which the speaker is obviously someone else than the author of the poem. In fact, the speaker of *Varjofinlandia* can be characterized as a "pseudo-center" of the poem, to borrow the notion of literary scholar Juri Joensuu

(2012, 183) who has used it in relation to search engine poetry. The next passage speaks about a particular emotion, misery or sadness, and possibly about disappointment, too:

> Suhteellisen surkea olo. Jossain on jotain vikana, kun annan pompotella itseäni noin, kohdella näin. Olen epäonnistunut jossain, koska en kerta kaikkiaan osaa tehdä itseäni onnelliseksi. (Kokko 2005, 18)
>
> Feeling quite miserable. There is something wrong when I let other people bounce me and treat me like this. I have failed in something because I just can't make myself happy. (Trans. AH)

Varjofinlandia's speaker continuously describes his or her depression and complains about his or her miserable life—the gender of the speaker remains unclear, or it keeps changing.[8] Besides, the speaking I is evidently a construction because the whole work is made of text fragments found from blogs. One could also claim that there is a multitude of speakers in *Varjofinlandia*. Due to the form of the work—there are no divisions into paragraphs or into stanzas—I tend to think, however, of one multiple speaker. "Multiple" refers here to one entity that includes many, as in Deleuze and Guattari's concept of multiplicity (see Massumi 1992, 6). Consequently, the impression of the speaker is not very coherent.

Every now and then, the reader can observe small breaks or ruptures in points where fragments from different sources have been placed together:

> Päivät mä olen liian väsynyt ajattelemaan tai tekemään mitään ja yöt mä pyörin sängyssä hiestä märkänä ja ajattelen ja ajattelen ja ajattelen. Sillon kun mä en pysty nukkumaan, asiat on aika huonosti. Mä en oo nukkunut viikkoon. Mä en pysty nukkumaan. Auta. Paljon on clämässä murheita. Heräsin hikisenä ahdistaviin uniin. Jouduin eilen miettimään liikaa, liikaa, liikaa ja tulin levottomaksi. Että voi olla vaikeaa. Lievää alakuloa. Väsyttää ihan tuskaisesti. Onpa voipunut olo. (Kokko 2005, 21–2)
>
> In the daytime, I am too tired to think or do anything, and during the night, I toss and turn in my bed all sweaty and I think and think and think. When I can't sleep, things go wrong. I haven't slept for a week. I can't sleep. Help. There are many worries in the life. I woke up all sweaty because of distressing dreams. Yesterday I had to think too much, too much, too much and I got nervous. How difficult can it be? Feeling slightly melancholic. I am horribly tired. Feeling exhausted. (Trans. AH)

The speaker goes through various emotions, such as exhaustion, worry, anxiety, and melancholy. The speaker uses colloquial language, which creates a sense of intimacy, and he or she repeats certain words as if to emphasize the fraught situation. Moreover, the somewhat floundering progression is part of the aesthetics of *Varjofinlandia* and it underlines the artificial nature of the speaking I. For example, the sudden appeal "Help," addressed to an unknown receiver, catches the reader's attention. This kind of style also highlights each sentence and makes one think of the huge number of Finnish people (or indeed people throughout the world) who suffer from depression.

Due to the way in which *Varjofinlandia* has been created—by copying, pasting, and reorganizing found sentences—it has a documentary feel. The material comprises thoughts of real people who have discussed their mental health issues in blogs. The book can therefore be read as an expression of a certain kind of subjectivity in present-day Finland. It is the kind of subjectivity that for some reason or another fails to keep up with the actions of the surrounding society.[9] The method behind *Varjofinlandia* is also interesting from the viewpoint of public space. Kokko has taken thoughts and emotions that other people have expressed publicly on the internet. He has anonymized them and transformed them into conceptual poetry in which the original, allegedly authentic voices have been turned into an obviously constructed speaker. This play between the two public spaces—blogs and printed poetry—highlights the tension between private and public on the internet.

What has all this to do with the politics of emotion? To begin with, *Varjofinlandia* is full of negative emotions expressed by the speaker. Of course, depression is not merely an emotion—it is a mental problem that can be diagnosed—but living through depression partly means living through negative emotions that make life difficult and unsatisfactory. The speaker is exhausted and anxious, but the reader never really gets to know why, making the reading experience primarily oppressive.

The negative emotions are closely tied to *Varjofinlandia*'s critical stance toward the Finnish welfare state. The topic of depression is rather serious considering that depression is one of the biggest problems of Finnish public health. Every fifth Finn suffers from depression during his or her lifetime, and depression is the most common reason for sick leaves in Finland. In fact, the number of burnouts in working life—often diagnosed as depression in Finland—is on the increase due to changes in work causing precarious positions and growing demands for efficiency.[10]

The dull and grinding emotions related to depression are utilized in *Varjofinlandia* in an effective way to arouse contradictory emotions in readers. To begin with, the book is somewhat boring, but then again, so is living through depression. In this sense, the poetics of *Varjofinlandia* amplifies the affective tone of its content. On the other hand, the "poetics of boredom" connects Kokko's work to American postmodern poetry. Experimental poet Kenneth Goldsmith (2008, 146), for instance, has stated that his own works—which are often conceptual in nature and resemble Kokko's works in many ways—are so boring that even he himself is reluctant to read through them.

Nevertheless, the repetitive and excessive way in which the work deals with depression also creates ambiguous emotions and humorous tones. One could say that *Varjofinlandia*'s "tongue is seriously in its cheek," as Paul Hoover (2013, xxx) has described postmodern American poetry. The amusement does not derive from the contents of *Varjofinlandia*, at least not directly. The topic of depression is not funny, and the speaker mainly speaks about it in serious ways.[11] The comic effect is rather due to the procedure by which the book has been made. Putting numerous complaints of single speakers together creates an impression of an inconsistent speaker who endlessly harps on about problems that in the end start to seem somewhat banal. Private suffering turns into a generic discourse, and this has two consequences. Firstly, as the complaining voices are detached from the original context of the blogs, the tone of the text becomes more ambivalent or ironic. Secondly, the effect created is both serious and amusing at the same time.

As Linda Hutcheon (2003, 9–11) has noted, irony can mean different things: either saying something else than what you mean, or leaving something unsaid so that the receiver has to interpret the hidden meaning. I suggest that the latter meaning is better suited to describing *Varjofinlandia*, because it does not provide the reader with any interpretive frame that would help to contextualize the content. With irony there are two participants, the one who ironizes and the one who interprets, and ultimately it is always up to the interpreter to decide whether something is ironic or not. Hence, irony is risky because not everyone understands it. It is also difficult to direct the receiver to interpret the ironic message in the desired way (Hutcheon 2003, 10–11).

Most importantly, Hutcheon (2003, 14–15) writes about the emotional ethics of irony, which is intriguing from the viewpoint of *Varjofinlandia*. Hutcheon states that even though irony is often seen as a vehicle that "engages intellect rather than emotions," irony may also arouse various emotions in the receiver, such as uncertainty, humiliation, or embarrassment, to mention but a few. Irony is often used to affect the receiver emotionally, but it can also lead in the opposite direction and distance the reader from the text.

How should the irony of *Varjofinlandia* be interpreted? What would be its ironic edge? As I see it, Kokko's work gives a voice to an anonymous mass of depressed Finns and criticizes the Finnish welfare state for its inability to solve the problem. On the other hand, it plays with the stereotypical assumptions of the Finns as a miserable nation by condensing and exaggerating the experiences of depression into one book. Far from disdaining the problems that depressed people have to live through in real life, *Varjofinlandia* offers its readers a possibility to see the topic from an ironic, distanced viewpoint and, at certain points, also through humor. This offers a fresh and challenging perspective on one of the most serious problems of Finnish society.

Fatty XL and Finnish "Social" Flarf

My second example of experimental poetry dealing with present-day Finnish problems is Tytti Heikkinen's flarf poem "On Par with Whales." Heikkinen is a Finnish experimental poet who uses material found from the internet in her poetry. She has published three poetry collections, and her debut volume, *Täytetyn eläimen lämpö* (*The Warmth of the Taxidermied Animal*), was nominated for the Helsingin Sanomat Prize for the best literary debutant of the year in 2008. *Helsingin Sanomat* is the most widely read Finnish newspaper. A selection of her poems from her first two collections has been translated into English under the title *The Warmth of the Taxidermied Animal* (2013). In this chapter, I use the English translation.

Flarf refers to the kind of experimental poetry that draws material from the internet by using odd search terms and then selecting and modifying it into poetry; the procedure has been called "Google sculpting" (Epstein 2012, 311, 318). Gary Sullivan, who coined the term, defines flarf as "a kind of corrosive, cute, or cloying, awfulness. Wrong. Un-P.C. Out of control. 'Not okay'" (Magee et al. 2003). According to him, the word can also be used as a verb "to flarf," and in this sense the meaning of the word is "to bring out the inherent awfulness, etc., of some pre-existing text" (Magee et al. 2003). Furthermore, the already mentioned Goldsmith

(2011, 4) emphasizes the brutality of flarf by stating that it is based on using the "*worst*" results of Google searches: "[t]he more offensive, the more ridiculous, the more outrageous the better." In flarf, the already public material is transferred into a different kind of public space. Bringing graceless and vulgar content from the internet to the realm of poetry is unexpected, causing unease in the reading.

Flarf in its original American form is primarily humorous. However, Finnish flarf has been called "social flarf" because it discusses social problems such as drug abuse, obesity, and violence (Rantama 2010). Finnish flarf is therefore more political than its American counterpart. While it is typical for all flarf to express and arouse forceful emotions, Finnish flarf is more empathetic than American flarf, and American flarf has even been accused of using uneducated, racist, or populist language to mock and ridicule those who use this kind of language (Sullivan 2008, 194).[12] Finnish flarf also uses so-called bad language, albeit in a more sensitive way.

Heikkinen's "On Par with Whales" is the opening poem of the "Fatty XL" poems,[13] which have been put together from material found in internet chat forums and blogs where teenage girls write about their lives (Pollari 2013, 4). The poems are in many ways similar to Kokko's *Varjofinlandia*, not least because the poems have been constructed with the help of internet search engines. Fatty XL poems, too, are dramatic monologues in a similar way to *Varjofinlandia*. The style of Heikkinen's poems, however, is rougher and more provocative. This is how the poem begins:

> Fuck i'm a fatty when others are skinny.
> Also Im short, am I a fatty or short? Wellyeah
> I'm such a grosss fatty that it makes no sens ….
> My Woundedness has let the situation get
> this way tht the fat squeezes out etc. Now I'm
> putting distance btwn me and everything, because I've been so
> disappointed in my self, cause from the "greedy"
> I think of a greedy fatty and then I get mad. Panic
> rises in my chest, a tremor. Everything is so terrible
> , outside its wet and icy, It's cold when I.
> lay here and im an undisciplined fatty.
> .This morning smeone I know was fucking aroundAbout how I'm such a fatty
> and I hadto punch them BTWN THE eyes … they spit back at me
> and I got a horrible pigsnot on the bag of my neck. After that
> I gothome super hungry. (Heikkinen 2013, 79)

Although the poem mixes together multiple sources, "On Par with Whales" is coherent in the sense that it could be spoken—or rather written—by one person.[14] Heikkinen's artistic output shows here; she has searched for a certain kind of material and she has selected, reorganized, and (possibly) rewritten it in order to convert it into poetry. This poem's play with the notion of intimate and public is layered in a similar way to *Varjofinlandia*. Individual teenage girls have written about their life and sentiments on the internet sites, thus sharing them in public communities. The poet has used this publicly available material by merging the numerous voices into one poetic I called "Fatty XL." The result is quite puzzling; "On Par with Whales" reproduces collective speech under the guise of a speaker who clearly resembles the traditional speaking subject.

The more or less coherent form of dramatic monologue has certainly influenced the affectivity of the poem. It creates a sense of intimacy, an illusion of somebody expressing directly her thoughts and feelings, and in dramatic monologue, this someone can tell her story entirely from her own viewpoint. All this encourages the reader to identify or empathize with the speaker, an identification strengthened by the many narrative elements in the Fatty XL poems.

The flarf elements are highly visible in "On Par with Whales." The use of a four-letter word at the very beginning ("Fuck I'm a fatty") introduces the reader to the somewhat unusual register of the poem. The poem also uses language typical of internet chat forums. There are abbreviations such as "BTWN" for "between" or "abt" for "about." There are also many misspellings, such as "I" written in lower case at the beginning of the poem, or separate words typed together like in "wellyeah," all typical features of internet language. The style of the speaking I, moreover, is unpolished, to say the least; she does not aim at impressing what she might call highbrow readers, quite the contrary.[15]

Fatty XL expresses her emotions in an overflowing manner, and this may touch at least some readers (Helle 2015). The poem is also interesting from the viewpoint of social class and intersectionality. The girl called Fatty XL seems to incarnate many of the negative stereotypes related to working-class girls and women—Joensuu (2012, 181) has even used the term "white trash" when writing about the Fatty XL poems. To begin with, her language is vulgar and she speaks very openly about everything; about her fatness, about her humiliating sex experiences, about her mother's alcohol abuse and sex life, and so on. Niina Pollari (2013) who has translated Heikkinen's poetry into English calls Fatty XL therefore an "over-sharer," a person who discloses too much about herself. Fatty XL's spelling mistakes also point to stereotypical ideas about the working classes, hinting at a low education.[16]

The Fatty XL poems are emotionally charged, dealing with present-day social problems in a provocative way. She can be seen as a victim of the weight loss industry, as Laura Joyce (2014) has noticed in her essay. Fatty XL sees herself as too fat and she would like to lose weight, feeling anger, frustration, self-loathing, and shame about her body. The Fatty XL poems connect to a wider context of fatness discourses in late modern Western culture (see Harjunen 2009; Helle 2015). We have constructed certain medical and cultural standards for normal weight, and fatness is usually seen as a problem or as something to be ashamed of. Fatness discourses permeate society as a whole, urging everyone to judge and control their own bodies, sometimes in unhealthy ways. Young girls are especially vulnerable in this regard, and different kinds of eating disorders are increasingly current. As Joyce points out, Fatty XL "has adapted entirely to the weight loss industry's dangerous cycle" (Joyce 2014).

The fact that the Fatty XL poems have been created by recycling material from internet forums generates a kind of "reality effect." The styles and topics of the poem both imitate and borrow from those found on the internet. This gives the poem a documentary character akin Kokko's *Varjofinlandia*. In many ways, Fatty XL is the incarnation of a certain kind of subject in late modernity. She is lonely and isolated, and seems to live her life primarily through the internet. The poem does not, however, merely recycle the discourses found from the internet. As flarf poetry, it also comments on them by bringing out their "inherent awfulness" (Magee et al. 2003), namely unhealthy ways of speaking about weight and one's own body. But despite the sad themes of the poems, they are nonetheless hilarious. The outspokenness and excessive emotions of the speaker together with the rough language (and other humorous elements such as misspelling) are likely to make at least some readers laugh.

Eino Santanen's Bank Note Poetry and Finance Capitalism

The third example, Eino Santanen's bank note poetry, deals with present-day capitalism by manipulating the ideological features of both bank notes and capitalism. The poems, published in an anthology called *Tekniikan maailmat* (2014; "Worlds of Technique"), have been written with a typewriter on 20 euro bank notes. Santanen has published five collections of poetry beginning from 2002, *Tekniikan maailmat* being the fourth. It won the prestigious Tanssiva karhu poetry prize awarded by the Finnish national broadcasting company YLE.[17]

There are altogether eight bank-note poems in the anthology, and they speak about money, economy, and love. The material bases of euro notes connect the poems to the euro zone, that is, countries that belong to the monetary system of the European Union. The Finnish language in which the majority of these poems have been written (some are in English) ties them more specifically to the Finnish cultural area.[18] Bank notes belong both to the public and to the private sphere. They are essentially public because they represent the common monetary system. At the same time, bank notes can be someone's private property.

Santanen's poems make use of bank notes, Euros, as public space, as a publishing platform on which to display and distribute poetry. They also play with the idea of the special relationship people have with owning money (Fig. 6.1).

> 1./Sinä tunnet tämän/setelin nyt. Tämä/seteli on kädel-/läsi nyt. Tämä/seteli on sinun,/rakas ja tärkeä,/nyt.
> Vaihtaisit sen korkeintaan/seteliin, jolla on arvoa./Vaihtaisit sen korkeintaan/nautintoon, jolla on arvoa/Tai korkeintaan/suuressa hädässä./Tämä seteli on pian 6:n/askeleen päässä/sinusta,/kuten muukin maailma./Sano sille: Hei hei/seteli./Se ei vastaa. (Santanen 2014, 30)
>
> 1./You can feel this/note now. This/note is in your hand/now. This/note is yours,/beloved and important,/now.
> You would only change it/for a valuable note./You would only change it/for valuable pleasure/Or only/in a very difficult situation./This note will soon be 6/steps away/from you,/like the whole world./Say to it: Bye bye/note./It does not answer. (Trans. AH)

This poem called "Tunneseteli" ("Emotional Bank Note") is the first poem in the bank note poetry section. It is a good example of these poems as it contains many of the central themes of the bank-note poems. It speaks about emotions, it refers to money's exchange value, and it presents money as providing the potential for pleasure. The speaker of the poem remains undefined, and the "you" of the poem refers to the user of the money, the bearer of the bank note. The speaker of this poem is estranged in a different way than in Kokko and Heikkinen; the source of the voice remains unknown. The emotion of love in the poem is one-sided:

Fig. 6.1 Eino Santanen's artwork "TUNNESETELI / X20602643123", part 1/2 in *Tekniikan maailmat* (Santanen 2014, 30)

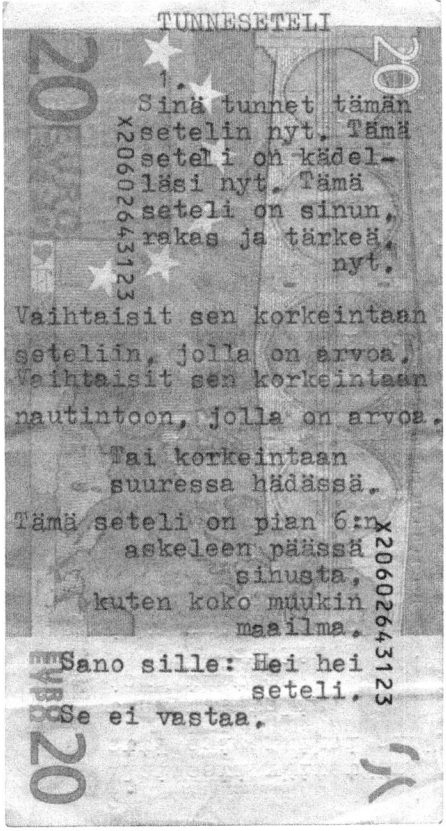

according to the speaker, the note is "beloved and important" for the bearer, but the note is mute and makes no response (Fig. 6.2).

The theme of love is even more evident in another poem called "L24680445062 Tunnistaa Osa 1/2" ("L24680445062 Recognizes Part 1/2"):

> Minä rakastan sinua/kuin seitsemäätoista kirjainta/minä rakastan sinua/ kuin kolmea Sanaa/Numeroiden pyörteenä/minä/sinun numerosi kohtaan//Minä sanon sinun nimesi/Se on kolme sanaa. (Santanen 2014, 32)

> I love you/like I love eight letters/I love you/like I love three words/As a whirl of numbers/I/encounter your numbers//I say your name/It is three words. (Trans. AH)

Fig. 6.2 Eino Santanen's artwork "L24680445062 TUNNISTAA", part 1/2 in *Tekniikan maailmat* (Santanen 2014, 32)

In this poem, love and money intertwine. The speaker of the poem pretends to be the bank note itself. Hence, an official object, the bank note, is humanized or personalized. It addresses the speech to the bearer of the note. Once again, the experimental poem confuses the boundaries between private and public.

The talk about love evokes the discourse of love poetry, and Finnish readers may be reminded of Pentti Saarikoski's famous love poem "Minä rakastan sinua" ("I love you") published in *Mitä tapahtuu todella?* (1962, "What is actually going on?"). Saarikoski (1937–1983), one of the Finland's best known and most established poets, began his career as a modernist but soon started to transform poetic language by introducing material from everyday life and from political discourse. Saarikoski was an ardent communist and a celebrity known for his four marriages and problems with alcohol. In addition to referring to Saarikoski, Santanen's poem also expresses our fascination with money in the capitalist cultures in which we live.

However, the content of the bank note's love talk remains empty and without point. "Minä rakastan sinua" ("I love you") are merely "seventeen letters" or "three words" ("eight letters" in the English translation). The poem, in fact, only pretends to speak to the bearer, and the bearer could be anyone, and of course the note is endlessly passed from one person to another (Fig. 6.3).

Fig. 6.3 Eino Santanen's artwork "L24680445062 TUNNISTAA", part 2/2 in *Tekniikan maailmat* (Santanen 2014, 32)

The lines "As a whirl of numbers/I/encounter your numbers" refer to the second part of the same poem ("L24680445062 Recognizes Part 2/2"):

Minna Maria Johanna Kari 160372-098F
Pekka Tapio Korhonen 240153-011A
Olavi Erik Johannes Laine 100588-298H
Tuula Kaarina Saastamoinen 291248-329C

FI86 8000 2381 4045 78 021169-118S
FI13 3939 0032 8392 43 270376-102R
FI89 4055 3120 0680 69 310741-0328
FI19 1011 5000 7121 86 080666-132H
(Santanen 2014, 33)

The "whirl of numbers" refers to number 20, the value of the note, and to the serial number of the note L24680445062. These numbers are juxtaposed with the social security numbers and bank account numbers of—presumably—fictional people.

From the viewpoint of finance, the individual user of money can be anyone, and the humanity of the user can be reduced to series of numbers. However, people tend to project feelings onto money and to the possibilities it offers. Although the poems speak about love they do not arouse affectionate or tender emotions in the reader. Rather, the tone of the poems is ironic because all the talk about love is hollow. The emotions that the poems are more likely to arouse are suspicion and amusement.

Santanen himself has stated in the anthology's afterword that the banknote poems participate in the discussion on finance capitalism and its recurrent crises, as well as nature and status of money in contemporary finance capitalism.[19] The poems' comment on finance capitalism, however, is not self-explanatory but needs to be construed.

Finance capitalism refers to the form of present-day capitalism in which most accumulation of financial resources takes place within the financial market. It has been the dominant force in the global economy since the end of the twentieth century. Nowadays, business is mainly based on the trade of financial products such as bonds, stocks, futures, and other derivatives and on creating new financial instruments. The value of money is detached from concrete, material bases; the value of stocks, for instance, is mostly based on speculation. Whereas trade used to be based on selling manufactured or acquired goods, today it is based on selling money, credit, debt, and bonds. In the old days, profit was pursued in the long run, while nowadays it is more likely that short-term gains are sought.[20]

Santanen's bank note poetry comments on the vague value of money. In the same way in which the value of money can change rapidly in the financial market due to speculation and the reactions of speculators (Marazzi 2011), the value of a bank note can change if you write poetry on it. However, it is not precisely clear how the value of a note changes when you write a poem on it. The note may become invalid if it is thought to be damaged. Or its value may rise if it is seen as a prized artwork. In this case, the value of the note is based on other things than the material base of the 20 euro note. Moreover, the future value of the bank-note poem is itself speculative: its value as an artwork will be determined by how recognized Santanen will be as an artist and how established the bank-note poem will become.

There is a conceptual element in Santanen's bank note poetry. It is not criminal to tamper with bank notes in the euro zone, at least not in Finland, but the Bank of Finland considers it unethical. There is also resistance and rebellion in Santanen's poems. They comment on the capitalist society in which money is not only a medium of exchange but has almost mythical dimensions, a potential that could be realized in the form of pleasure, happiness, or success. Santanen's poems criticize this way of thinking by suggesting that even if we project our emotions, dreams, and hopes onto money, money itself has no emotions and will never reply.

Poetics and Politics of Twenty-First-Century Finnish Experimental Poetry

Twenty-first-century Finnish experimental poetry absorbs influences and inspiration from international trends but also formulates its own poetic principles. Contemporary poetry deals with timely questions concerning Finnish society and the Finnish way of life, although not to the exclusion of other themes. As I see it, innovative ways of using (found) language and found material (bank notes) open up a playful space where language is used for both poetic and political purposes.

The poems have also proven themselves interesting from the viewpoint of spatiality. The examined poems merge private and public spaces in a multitude of ways. Intimate confessions made by individuals on the internet have been used as poetic raw material in Kokko and Heikkinen, being turned into art that is both conceptual and documentary. In Santanen, public and private spaces intermingle when bank notes are used as a platform for poetry that speaks about the emotions humans have about money. The play with the borders of private and public in poetry makes visible the layered structures of reality.

There is also a multitude of emotions in the poems discussed in this chapter. Kokko's and Heikkinen's poems deal with negative emotions expressed by discontented speakers, while Santanen's poems adopt the conventions of love talk in an ironic way. These emotions are closely connected to the topics the poems address. The poems aim at shaking or disturbing readers, provoking them to think about certain aspects of our way of life. There are, however, humorous aspects to the poems as well. The excessive and repetitive form of *Varjofinlandia* is grating but also amusing, and the excessive emotional outpourings in Heikkinen's poem are hilarious and stupefying at the same time. Santanen's humor is based on the conceptual idea of writing poems on bank notes and on the play with the notions of you and I in a poem.

What, then, would be the political message? In the context of late modernity, the poems seem to take a stand on several issues typical of present-day Finnish society and culture. First, there are the different forms of malaise dealt with in the poems, such as depression and eating disorders that are alarmingly common in Finnish society. Secondly, the poems also criticize the Finnish welfare society and capitalism.

Kokko's and Heikkinen's poems can be read as a playful, modified, and amplified testimony of the downsides of living in twenty-first-century

Finnish society. The speakers of the poems are more or less alienated, and the fact that they talk about their issues on the internet makes one think of loneliness. The viewpoint of Santanen's poems is slightly different because they are closely connected to the economic or financial system that we live in. Under the somewhat cheerful or playful surface of the poems, there is an important and profound message to be found. Santanen's poems question the central role we have given to money in our late modern culture. The poems point out that as such, money is empty and can offer no meaning for life.[21]

NOTES

1. The quote is from the poem "Always the same thing" (Heikkinen 2013, 81), from the "Fatty XL" series. The first poem of the series will be discussed in this chapter along with other poems. The misspelling is deliberate.
2. *Oxford English Dictionary*, "poetics."
3. McHale uses the term himself, as does Paul Hoover in *Postmodern American Poetry* (2013).
4. In psychology, the concept of emotion refers to certain conscious sentiments, although the exact number of them varies in different theories. According to Suzanne Keen (2011, 6), a literary scholar who focuses on emotions in her work, there are seven primary emotions (anger, sadness, fear, surprise, disgust, contempt, and happiness) and eight secondary emotions (empathy, compassion, shame, embarrassment, envy, guilt, hatred, and comfort in belonging).

    In addition, the concept of emotion often implies the idea of narrativity; the individual who experiences an emotion knows the reason that has caused it (see Altieri 2003, 2–4). The psychology-based definition with its limited number of strictly defined emotions narrows the scope of the concept too much, which is why I prefer not to use it here. The definition provided by Sara Ahmed (2004), for instance, is broader and more flexible.
5. According to Jameson, the feelings of a subject in modernism were often related to alienation and anxiety, as in Edvard Munch's *The Scream* (1893).
6. See McHale 2004; Silliman 1987; Lehto 2005. The New Sentence technique is a poetic technique invented by Ron Silliman (1987). In this technique a poem is created by combining phrases that have been found from different sources, thus generating a new unity.
7. In addition to the Finlandia Prize, there is also the *Varjofinlandia* ("Shadow Finlandia") award. The Helsinki-based (academic) bookstore Akateeminen

kirjakauppa gives the prize every year to the book that has sold the most in the store. In relation to these awards, the name *Varjofinlandia* can be read as ironic; Kokko's work could never have become a bestseller.
8. In one passage the speaker says "Peniksessäni on mustelma" ("There is a bruise on my penis"), but in another "Tällaisina hetkinä minä kiitän vallitsevaa sukupuolijärjestelmää, jossa saan olla heikko ja herkkä ja avuton" ("In moments like this I am thankful for the prevailing gender system in which I am allowed to be weak and sensitive and helpless"), which seems to refer to a female speaker.
9. Other Finnish poets, too, have dealt with mental issues in their poems. Harry Salmenniemi's *Texas, sakset* (2010, "Texas, scissors"), for instance, discusses mental problems and medicalization, among other things.
10. See Mustosmäki et al. 2016, 13; Rikala 2013, 17–18; Jakonen 2015, 110–13.
11. There are, however, some comical details in *Varjofinlandia*, for example when the speaker says that he/she is so distressed that his/her teeth are numb (Kokko 2005, 25).
12. Sullivan brings this out in his ironic essay "My Problems with Flarf," which is composed of other people's critical stances toward flarf.
13. The poems were originally published in Finnish in a collection titled *Täytetyn eläimen lämpö* (2009), and some of them have been published as English translations in *The Warmth of the Taxidermied Animal* (2013).
14. Although the poem quite obviously replicates written internet language, I still use the conventional terms "speaker" and "speaking I."
15. The language of these poems deviates not only from the standard language but also from more traditional poetic language. It foregrounds certain linguistic elements, for example, features of internet language that are unlikely in a poem. One could even say that the language of "On Par with Whales" parodies the presumptions of foregrounding poetic language by transforming the informal internet language into poetry.
16. For stereotypical views on working-class women, see Skeggs (2004, 100–5).
17. There are also bank-note poems in Santanen's latest collection *Yleisö* ("Public"), published in 2017. They deal with capitalism, but also with questions of nationality, civil rights, and religion. The collection was published after this chapter had been written, and hence its poems are not discussed here.
18. In the anthology, the poems have been published as scanned black-and-white images. In addition to them, Santanen has issued bank-note poems by means of YouTube (see https://www.youtube.com/watch?v=IfpRZe29VFY). Together with Tatu Pohjavirta, Santanen has also

made another video of the bank-note poems for the Kipinä art exhibition (held in Fiskars, Finland, in 2013): https://vimeo.com/67806791.
19. The poems also deal with other unwanted consequences of present-day capitalism, such as unemployment.
20. Marazzi 2011, 2015; Ahokas and Holappa 2014, 127–31; Kocka 2016, 110–18. Ahokas and Holappa call the current phase of capitalism (beginning from the 1960s) "money manager capitalism," linking it to finance capitalism.
21. The chapter was written as a part of "The Literary in Life" project (285144), funded by the Academy of Finland.

REFERENCES

Ahmed, Sara. 2004. *The Cultural Politics of Emotion*. New York: Routledge.
Ahokas, Jussi, and Lauri Holappa. 2014. *Rahatalous haltuun. Irti kurjistavasta talouspolitiikasta*. Helsinki: Like.
Altieri, Charles. 2003. *The Particulars of Rapture: An Aesthetics of the Affects*. Ithaca and London: Cornell University Press.
Blomberg, Kristian, Henriikka Tavi, and Teemu Manninen. 2010. 2000-luvun runous. *Tuli & savu* 4/2009. http://www.tulijasavu.net/2010/03/2000-luvun-runous/.
Bray, Joe, Alison Gibbons, and Brian McHale. 2012. Introduction. In *The Routledge Companion to Experimental Literature*, ed. Joe Bray, Alison Gibbons, and Brian McHale, 1–18. London and New York: Routledge.
Clough, Patricia Ticineto. 2007. Introduction. In *The Affective Turn: Theorizing the Social*, ed. Patricia Ticineto Clough and Jean Halley, 1–33. Durham and London: Duke University Press.
Conte, Joseph M. 1991. *Unending Design. The Forms of Postmodern Poetry*. Ithaca and London: Cornell University Press.
Deleuze, Gilles. 2012. *Spinoza. Käytännöllinen filosofia*. Translated by Eetu Viren. Helsinki: Tutkijaliitto.
Epstein, Andrew. 2012. Found Poetry, 'Uncreative Writing,' and the Art of Appropriation. In *The Routledge Companion to Experimental Literature*, ed. Joe Bray, Alison Gibbons, and Brian McHale, 310–322. London and New York: Routledge.
Goldsmith, Kenneth. 2008. A Week of Blogs for the Poetry Foundation. In *The Consequence of Innovation: 21st Century Poetics*, ed. Craig Dworkin, 137–139. New York: Roof Books.
———. 2011. *Uncreative Writing: Managing Language in the Digital Age*. New York: Columbia University Press.
Haapala, Vesa. 2013. Lyriikka. In *Johdatus kirjallisuusanalyysiin*, ed. Aino Mäkikalli and Liisa Steinby, 157–251. Suomalaisen Kirjallisuuden Seura: Helsinki.

Harjunen, Hannele. 2009. *Women and Fat: Approaches to the Social Study of Fatness.* Jyväskylä Studies in Education, Psychology and Social Research 379. Jyväskylä: The University of Jyväskylä.

Heikkinen, Tytti. 2013. *The Warmth of the Taxidermied Animal.* Translated by Niina Pollari. Notre Dame, IN: Action Books.

Helle, Anna. 2015. Pitikö runouskin vetää ihan läskiksi?' Tytti Heikkisen 'Ryhävalaan tasoa' -runon affektiivinen vastaanotto. *Avain* 4: 67–83.

Helle, Anna, and Anna Hollsten. 2016. Tunnetko kirjallisuutta? Johdatus suomalaisen kirjallisuuden tutkimukseen tunteiden ja tuntemusten näkökulmasta. In *Tunteita ja tuntemuksia suomalaisessa kirjallisuudessa*, ed. Anna Helle and Anna Hollsten, 7–33. Helsinki: Suomalaisen Kirjallisuuden Seura.

Hoover, Paul. 2013. Introduction. What Is Postmodern Poetry? In *Postmodern American Poetry. A Norton Anthology*, ed. Paul Hoover, xxix–lvii. New York and London: W.W. Norton & Company.

Hutcheon, Linda. 2003 [1994]. *Irony's Edge: The Theory and Politics of Irony.* London: Routledge.

Jakonen, Mikko. 2015. Talous ja työ prekaarissa yhteiskunnassa. In *Talouden uudet muodot*, ed. Mikko Jakonen and Tiina Silvasti, 92–121. Into: Helsinki.

Jameson, Fredric. 1991. *Postmodernism, or the Cultural Logic of Late Capitalism.* Durham: Duke University Press.

Joensuu, Juri. 2012. *Menetelmät, kokeet, koneet. Proseduraalisuus poetiikassa, kirjallisuushistoriassa ja suomalaisessa kokeellisessa kirjallisuudessa.* Poesia: Helsinki.

Joyce, Laura. 2014. The Register of Candied Decay. *3:AM magazine.* http://www.3ammagazine.com/3am/the-register-of-candied-decay/.

Keen, Suzanne. 2011. Introduction: Narrative and the Emotions. *Poetics Today* 32 (1): 1–53.

Kocka, Jürgen. 2016 [2014]. *Kapitalismin lyhyt historia.* Translated by Timo Soukola. Helsinki: Gaudeamus.

Kokko, Karri. 2005. *Varjofinlandia.* Helsinki: Poesia.

Lehto, Leevi. 2005. Jälkisanat. In *Varjofinlandia*, ed. Karri Kokko. Helsinki: Poesia.

Magee, Michael, Mohammad K. Silem, and Gary Sullivan. 2003. The Flarf Files. *Electronic Poetry Center*, 2003. http://epc.buffalo.edu/authors/bernstein/syllabi/readings/flarf.html.

Marazzi, Christian. 2011. *Capital and Affects: The Politics of Language Economy.* Los Angeles, CA: MIT Press.

———. 2015. *Finanssikapitalismin väkivalta.* Translated by Eetu Viren. Helsinki: Tutkijaliitto.

Massumi, Brian. 1992. *A User's Guide to Capitalism and Schizophrenia. Deviations from Deleuze and Guattari.* Cambridge, MA: Swerve Editions.

———. 2002. *Parables for the Virtual: Movement, Affect, Sensation.* Durham and London: Duke University Press.

McHale, Brian. 2004. *The Obligation Toward the Difficult Whole: Postmodernist Long Poems*. Tuscaloosa and London: The University of Alabama Press.
Mustosmäki, Armi, Tomi Oinas, and Timo Anttila. 2016. Abating Inequalities? Job Quality at the Intersection of Class and Gender in Finland 1977–2013. *Acta Sociologica*. http://journals.sagepub.com/doi/abs/10.1177/0001699316657580.
Ngai, Sianne. 2005. *Ugly Feelings*. Cambridge, MA and London, UK: Harvard University Press.
Nussbaum, Martha. 2001. *Upheavals of Thought: The Intelligence of Emotions*. Cambridge: Cambridge University Press.
Oxford English Dictionary. http://www.oed.com/.
Pollari, Niina. 2013. Translator's Introduction. In *The Warmth of the Taxidermied Animal*, ed. Tytti Heikkinen, 4–5. Translated by Niina Pollari. Notre Dame, Indiana: Action Books.
Rantama, Vesa. 2010. Sallad, dallas. Review of *Texas, sakset* by Harry Salmenniemi. *Kiiltomato* 8.3.2010. http://www.kiiltomato.net/harry-salmenniemi-texas-sakset/.
Rikala, Sanna. 2013. *Työssä uupuvat naiset ja masennus*. Doctoral Dissertation. Tampere: Tampere University Press.
Salmenniemi, Harry. 2010. *Texas, sakset*. Otava: Helsinki.
Santanen, Eino. 2014. *Tekniikan maailmat*. Helsinki: Teos.
Seighworth, Gregory J., and Melissa Gregg. 2010. An Inventory of Shimmers. In *The Affect Theory Reader*, ed. Melissa Gregg and Gregory J. Seighworth, 1–25. Durham and London: Duke University Press.
Silliman, Ron. 1987. *The New Sentence*. New York: Roof.
Skeggs, Beverley. 2004. *Class, Self, Culture*. London: Routledge.
Sullivan, Gary. 2008. My Problems with Flarf. In *The Consequence of Innovation: 21st Century Poetics*, ed. Craig Dworkin, 193–197. New York: Roof Books.
Williams, Raymond. 1988. *Marxismi, kulttuuri ja kirjallisuus*. Translated by Mikko Lehtonen. Tampere: Vastapaino.

Open Access This chapter is licensed under the terms of the Creative Commons Attribution 4.0 International License (http://creativecommons.org/licenses/by/4.0/), which permits use, sharing, adaptation, distribution and reproduction in any medium or format, as long as you give appropriate credit to the original author(s) and the source, provide a link to the Creative Commons licence and indicate if changes were made.

The images or other third party material in this chapter are included in the chapter's Creative Commons licence, unless indicated otherwise in a credit line to the material. If material is not included in the chapter's Creative Commons licence and your intended use is not permitted by statutory regulation or exceeds the permitted use, you will need to obtain permission directly from the copyright holder.

PART III

Which Language Do You Use? Spaces of Language and Text

CHAPTER 7

Stavanger, Pre- and Postmodern: Øyvind Rimbereid's Poetry and the Tradition of Topographic Verse

Hadle Oftedal Andersen

In this chapter, I will suggest a reading of two quite unique contemporary Scandinavian long poems, using topographic verse, a tradition predating Romanticism, to shed light on the specific way in which the concept of place is unveiled in them. Because the tradition of topographic literature approaches the questions of place and space in ways we are not familiar with today, the presentation of this tradition's main features may in itself be seen as an interesting, perhaps even necessary, supplement to current theoretical developments on these topics. The main point of my reading, however, is to show that the deliberations on the genre of topographic verse, with the implications that follow from this perspective, will make it possible to identify how the poems in question position themselves as transposings of premodern thinking onto postmodern society.

Øyvind Rimbereid (b. 1966) is arguably the most celebrated poet in Norway today. He debuted in 1993, with the first of three books of prose fiction published in that decade. These were all relatively short works of

H. O. Andersen (✉)
University of Helsinki, Helsinki, Finland

© The Author(s) 2020
K. Malmio, K. Kurikka (eds.), *Contemporary Nordic Literature and Spatiality*, Geocriticism and Spatial Literary Studies,
https://doi.org/10.1007/978-3-030-23353-2_7

high-quality literature; they were well received by critics and in glimpses were very good, but all in all they were not particularly out of the ordinary. Then he changed from prose to poetry, with *Seine topografiar* (2000; "Late Topographies"), followed by *Trådreiser* (2003; "Thread-travels"). These books placed Rimbereid in the vanguard of Norwegian literature and paved the way for his masterpiece, *Solaris korrigert* (2004; "Solaris Corrected"), which as early as 2007 was regarded as one of the 24 most important Norwegian works of literature in history. Since then he has published a further four books of poetry, of which *Jimmen* (2011) has received by far the largest amount of acclaim.

Late Topographies, *Solaris Corrected* and *Jimmen* all depict Rimbereid's hometown Stavanger on Norway's southwestern coast, and they are all written in some form of Stavanger dialect. In this, Rimbereid has opened up something of a small wave of dialect poetry in Norway.[1] It may also be argued that he has had an influence on the growing number of Norwegian poems written in the long poem tradition, as the title poem of *Solaris Corrected* spans 37 pages and *Jimmen* has one 54-page-long text.

But why long poems about Stavanger?

Rimbereid finished his university studies in 1994, with a master's thesis focusing solely on the Swedish poet Göran Sonnevi's long poem "Sjostakovitj, 1976" (1979). As a student, he was an active member of a small society, the Rhetorical forum (Retorisk forum), in which Georg Johannesen (1931–2005) was the central figure. Johannesen was himself a brilliant poet, a former literature researcher and the most prominent expert on rhetorics in Norway. After deconstruction and French feminism lost their momentum, rhetorics became the *it* thing to do in humanistic faculties across Scandinavia at this time.

If there is one thing that sets the interest in rhetorics in Norway apart from the rest of Scandinavia, it is a smaller degree of interest in the theory of public speech as found in the classics like Cicero and Quintilian, and a much greater interest in various genres of text, speech and language-centered philosophy that occurs after this, all the way up to rhetorics falling out of favor when Romanticism sets in. Among these other genres are several forms of literature from before Romanticism which have fallen under the horizon of common understanding of what literature is: genres like homiletics (the theory of religious preaching), epistolography (the theory of writing letters) and so on. Of the more literary genres, topographic literature is probably the most noticeable, along with religious psalms. As I have written in my doctoral thesis *Kroppsmodernisme* (2005;

"Body Modernism"), the focus on the body in the Scandinavian literature of the 1980s gave way to an increased interest in the spatial area toward the end of the decade that followed. As in the 1980s, the 1990s poems tend to be short. They identify a smaller place, say a garden, and use it as a starting point for a phenomenological exploration of the way we conceptualize the world through interaction with it.

Against this backdrop of the currents of the time and of personal interests, it is easy to see the logic of Rimbereid's choice in turning to long poems dealing with the Stavanger area. Especially if one considers the often-repeated mantra in the 1990s that postmodern literature had changed from quoting earlier modernist form to quoting pre-Romantic form: "Late topographies" may be read as "late *modern* topographies," thus implying the term late modernism as it is often used instead of postmodernism.

Topographic Verse

In an essay from 2006, Rimbereid himself makes public the connection most relevant to us. The essay's title is "Om det topografiske diktet. Eller i stedet for en poetikk" ("On the topographic poem. Or instead of a literary program"). This text is first published in Rimbereid's up until now only collection of essays, *Hvorfor ensomt leve* (2006; "Why live in solitude").

The topic of his essay is not the topographic poem as this term is understood in the English tradition, where it covers poems of the seventeenth and eighteenth century describing parks and the like. What Rimbereid is referring to in his title is what one would call topographic *verse*, although he actually writes at least as much about prose in his essay.

This literary program opens with a longer paragraph called "Stedet i mennesket" ("Place in man"). We are presented with the following description of the relationship between the literature he is about to describe, and the program behind his own writing:

> Poetikk? Ikke presist. Heller: Om det som finnes under skriften min, som motiv og tradisjon, idet diktet slynger seg nedover pc-skjermen. Denne opplyst poetiske mellomverdenen, som selv forsøker å slynge et lys over en verden der ute, en verden som i mitt tilfelle ofte har handlet om steder, byer, landskap og geografier—konkret og faktuelt, med så fortid, nåtid og framtid. (Rimbereid 2006, 79)

Literary program? Not quite. Rather: On that which lies underneath my writing, as motif and tradition, as the poem meanders itself downwards on the PC screen. This illuminated, poetic middle world, which itself tries to shed a light on a world out there, a world which in my case has often been about places, cities, landscapes and geographies—specific and factual, with its past, present and future. (Trans. HOA)

As a present-day writer, Rimbereid approaches his writing with a modern understanding of creativity, society and humanity. The topographic literature predating Romanticism, he describes, is a tradition which inspires him, which he writes himself into, partly in the sense that his own texts may be seen as a continuation or an update of it, and partly in the sense that it provides ways of writing which, when used again today, provides both interesting form and interesting perspectives. Rimbereid's poems are results of a fruitful dialogue between the author and his horizon on the one hand, and the topographic tradition on the other.

Rimbereid's essay, quoted above, then continues with a presentation of a number of *exempla* from the Norwegian wing of this tradition. He starts with prose, and I paraphrase:

1. Olaus Magnus: *Historia de gentibus septentrionalibus* (1555). The text is written in Rome, where Olaus was exiled after the reformation. This description of the North focuses on culture and commercial life, plus military-strategic advice and insights, as it is possibly meant as preparation for a counter-reformation. But it is also filled with melancholia. In this text, we are presented with a new way of composition, with points toward later poetic works: thematic rather than chronological organization. Topics are placed paratactically, side by side, and each topic draws in a lot of anecdotal detail.
2. Absalon Pederssøn Beyer: *Om Norigs rige* (1567; "On the Country of Norway"). This is probably written as part of the ongoing conflict with the Hanseatic League. Classic rhetorics are in use, including the view of the world as a human life, with its current state described as old and sleepy. Digressions and anecdotes occur *en masse*.
3. NN: *Hamarkrøniken* (probably around 1570; "The Hamar Chronicle"). Hamar, where the Catholic bishop had his seat until the Reformation in 1536, is described as being in its terminal stage. The text takes the shape of an elegy and/or an ode, although it does not conclude in heaven, but on earth. The structuring element is a

wanderer who explains what he sees, the focus being on the actual topography. This is an unstable world, where magic and superstitions are included.

After these prose texts, Rimbereid turns to poetry. I continue paraphrasing:
Poetry was first written in Latin, as it was not yet understood how to make metric verse in Germanic languages. "Diktverkene ble tenkt og komponert ut fra et likhetsprinsipp som kan virke fremmed sett med et moderne blikk, som helst oppsplitter verden. Genrene fungerte den gang som arenaer mer for tematiske kombinasjoner og krysninger enn for konsentrater" ("The poems were conceived and composed based on principles of similarity that may seem strange from a modern perspective, which tends to divide the world. The genres at that time worked as arenas for combinations and crossings rather than areas of concentration"). (Rimbereid 2006, 109; Trans. HOA)

Rimbereid finishes with Petter Dass's *Nordlands trompet* (1739; "The Trumpet of Nordland"). This long poem has been seen as an authentic expression of the joy of mentioning, of bringing forth through language. There is a fuzzy border between inspiration from the Latin tradition and inspiration from folklore, local song traditions and more. I may add that to Norwegian readers, it is well known that this text opens by addressing everyone living in the recently populated county of Nordland, and goes on for a little short of 100 pages to describe various aspects of geography, commercial life, nature and so on.

As the essay presents the tradition in the mode of classic rhetorics, through *exempla* rather than synthesis, it will be more or less coincidental if more specific aspects of the tradition found in Rimbereid's poetry are actually mentioned in the essay. But before we continue our investigation by looking closer at *Solaris Corrected* and *Jimmen*, there are two more general points to be made: First, topography in this tradition is to be understood in a wide sense, where all aspects of nature and culture are relevant. Second, there is a sense of urgency in these texts, related to the changing tides of history. Most if not all of the texts above are descriptions of topographies at times of dramatic societal change.

But first of all: How does this older tradition relate to the interest in place and space in recent years?

Place and Space in Topographic Verse

If we are to understand how place and space are perceived in this older literature, we must bear in mind that it is written before phenomenology and before the Romantic or Kantian understanding of the sublime. Because topographic verse is older than Romanticism, it has no concept of a hypersensitive poetic subjectivity, and hence no interest in describing the reception of sensory data of chosen surroundings and the emotional response to these either.

The word "landscape" has its origin in the Golden Age of Dutch painting in the seventeenth century (Oxford English Dictionary). With a precursor in the more idyllic Italian painting of rural topography, this may be seen as the first time real or real-like topography is structured specifically in accordance with the human eye. Topography becomes landscape, the object changes from what is to what is perceived. This, one might say, is where the history leading to our understanding of place and space begins.

But if one looks closer at Golden Age paintings, they are, although staggeringly realistic compared to most if not all earlier art, still filled with elements that open up for potential interpretations. As a parallel to the vanitas motifs of the same era—these are after all Baroque paintings—the landscapes depicted often feature elements which might easily be seen as representations of human death. In his essay "Gjenferdets ruin" (1994; "The Ruin of the Ghost"), Norwegian writer Tor Ulven reflects on a ruin in a landscape by Jacob van Ruisdael (c. 1629–1682), one of the foremost Dutch painters of the seventeenth century:

> Den er det arketypiske bildet på livets forgjengelighet og usselhet, den er omgitt av brukne trær, sprukne gravmæler, vann som strømmer og blir borte like ubønnhørlig som tiden går, og vi med den, henimot døden. (Ulven 1997, 162)
>
> It is the archetypical image of life's perishability and frailty, it is surrounded by broken trees and cracked grave inscriptions, water streaming and disappearing as unstoppable as time passes, and we with it, towards death. (Trans. HOA)

This coexistence of realism and allegory is very understandable if one contemplates how educated people of this time would be familiar with the *quadriga*, the system of reading the Bible on four different levels: moral, literal, allegorical (as an enhanced metaphor describing something in the real world) and anagogical (as an allegory describing the afterlife). And this is where the Dutch Golden Age landscape painting and the tradition of topographic verse converge: They both describe the local reality, and this is done in part for the sheer joy of it, and in part to open up reflections on the larger questions of life and the afterlife as they unfold in the specific place represented.

The reality of what is described in topographic verse plays an important role, as it situates the description in this world, and thus transforms the question of Biblical interpretation into a question of interpreting the place of the depicted topography within the same biblical tradition. And as such, it is easy to understand why descriptions of topography and descriptions of human praxis go hand in hand in this literary tradition, for these two things have not been separated yet. In the same way as the Dutch paintings are filled with people and buildings, so too are topographic verses. The people go about their business, in their unreflecting everyday way, and it is the role of the poet to open up the dimensions of this reality toward other levels of existence. For this, the inclusion of other dimensions of existence is the understanding of place and space as inherited from medieval times, and possibly even earlier.

As we will see in a later section, *Jimmen* is a prime example of the coexistence of levels: The depiction of Jimmen and his owner's work is realistic, but the owner's transformation into a horse at the end must be read allegorically. In the same vein, the title poem "Solaris Corrected" ends with the subject of the poem leaving his body, in true anagogical fashion.

Solaris Corrected

The title poem in *Solaris Corrected* is set almost 500 years into the future. The text is written in a Stavanger dialect which has been heavily modified to imply the intermediate language history. My ad hoc translation into English will hide all of this, so even if you need to read the following translation to understand the content, I hope you will also take a look at the original text as it is quoted first. Here is the opening of the poem, addressing the reader in a fashion resembling poetry predating Romanticism:

> Wat vul aig bli
> om du ku kreip fra
> din vorld til uss?
> SKEIMFULL, aig trur, ven
> du kommen vid diner imago
> ovfr oren tiim, tecn, airlife,

all diner apocalyptsen
                    skreik-
mare. OR din beauty draum! NE
wi er. NE diner ideo! DER
aig lefr, i 14.6, wi arbeiden
onli vid oren nanofingren,
dei er oren total novledg, wi arbeiden
so litl, 30 minutes a dag. AIG seer an
miner fingren, part of organic 14.6,
men veike, dei er som seagrass ...
SO ku aig begg din vorld
begynning, start uss
up igjen? KU det!
         SKEIMFULL aig er. SO
                    wat
vul du bli
om wi ku kreip fra
uss til deg? (Rimbereid 2004, 9–10)

WHAT would I be
if you could crawl from
your world to us?
Shameful, I think, when
you come with your images
of our time, signs, aeronautics,
all of your apocalyptic
                    night-
mare. OR your beautiful dream! NE
we are. NE your ideas! WHERE
I live, in 14.6, we work
only with our nano-fingers,
they are our total knowledge, we work
so little, 30 minutes a day. I look at
my fingers, part of organic 14.6,
but weak, they are like seagrass ...
SO could I beg your world
to begin starting us up again? I COULD!
         SHAMEFUL I am. So
                    what
would you be
if we could crawl from
us to you? (Trans. HOA)

Rimbereid is following the guidelines for public speech according to classic rhetorics here. This is the *exordium*, the opening of the speech, where the speaker addresses the audience to show his *ethos* and win their attention and trust (*captatio benevolentiae*).

What we read is a version of Stavanger dialect filled with influences from other languages around the North Sea basin. These influences are not limited to loanwords, or even code switching to another language for words that already have a counterpart in Norwegian, but include changed grammar, like aspects of English syntax and the use of the French "NE" to mark negation, along with phonetic changes like English diphthongs in words like "aig" and "skeimfull" ("eg" and "skamfull" in Stavanger dialect).

As the offshore oil industry plays such a dominant part in present-day Stavanger, these language changes function as an implication that this activity—which crosses territorial lines between Britain, Germany and Norway—has become the one overpowering cultural feature in Stavanger. There is also a clear connection between this identification of offshore activity as the main cultural influence, and the fact that the persona in "Solaris Corrected" carries out his work on the bed of the ocean: This is the most obvious way in which Rimbereid's poem represents an extrapolation of the Stavanger we know today. But in addition to this, Rimbereid's language of the future shares characteristics with the language of the literature predating Romanticism. Written language in these earlier days was filled with foreign words and phrases, and with inconsistent spelling.[2] It is with the National Romantic project that the written language first reaches its stability, with consequent spelling based on etymological studies and domestic spelling of loanwords. This point is further underscored paratextually, as the book is equipped with Jacob Ziegler's primitive, premodern map of Scandinavia from 1532 on the dust jacket and on the last two pages.

But these acknowledgments of relation to the old tradition of topographic verse give important information to the reader, because "Solaris Corrected" is not a pastiche: We are presented with the Stavanger region of the future through the temperament, reflections and everyday life of a person who is staged in a dramatic monologue or persona poem. As we see in the opening of the poem quoted above, this person is equipped with the kind of imagination and sensitivity we might identify as the modern subjectivity only found in literature written from the Romantic era onward. This is remarked upon later in the poem, when a medical examination concludes that the persona has "noko for staerk production/af eigne picts" ("a slightly too high production/of his own images") (Rimbereid 2004, 41; Trans. HOA). This leads to the following exclamation on his part, regarding his wife who is a photographer:

WAT vul da Shiris breyn vera?
WAT nevrons exist flammande i henna?
WAT konclution vul innsirkla henna? (Rimbereid 2004, 41)

WHAT would then Shiri's brain be?
WHAT neurons exist flaming in her?
WHAT conclusion would encircle her? (Trans. HOA)

If his imagination is diagnosed as a slight illness, then her "konclution," her diagnosis, would obviously be that of a severe mental illness. This means that the society described is one where the Romantic or (post) modernist poetic imagination has completely fallen out of favor. What we see is thus that this future society represents a return to the understanding of art predating Romanticism—art as *techne*, as handicraft without the modern concept of creativity.

At this point it should be noted that there are references in the poem to tourists coming to Norway to experience the beauty of nature. This means therefore people who are still living inside the Romantic and modern paradigm of landscape. As a photographer, Shiri is also somehow related to an aesthetic experience of the world. But the persona speaking in "Solaris Corrected" is not. His declaration of being "SKEIMFUL," ashamed, of his time is something he "thinks" he would be. And the rest of the poem focuses on his thoughts and deliberations on his life and his world. This is not an expression of feeling, it is—in the same way as the topographic literary tradition—the use of landscape as a starting point and a continued source of input for an extensive reflection on the state of the surrounding world.

Instead of one world, with one view of the world, we are presented with a specific view, associated closely with the society in question, namely "Organic 14.6." The specificity of this—that his girlfriend is not like everyone else, that he is a little bit different from the norm, and that there are other societies where the view of the world is qualitatively different, sits well with the rhetoric tradition: as behavior and society is shaped through *praxis*, these are not universally uniform. This is the big difference between the rhetoric tradition and the idealistic, philosophical tradition from Plato onward. And so the persona in "Solaris Corrected" is not the voice of everyone at his time in the future, but the voice of a specific person in a specific place. He is a rhetoric *exemplum* of his time, not a statistical everyone as we find them in modern statistics.

But he is an *exemplum* of a collective we, of people from Stavanger, probably of people from Norway, possibly even for people in the Western world (as the tourists are predominantly Russian and Chinese) in the future. He, the persona, is speaking on behalf of a culture when he suggests that his girlfriend would be diagnosed as mentally ill, in a poem dominated by the reflecting form since before Romanticism.

The thought this leaves us with is compelling: If creativity is presented as something of an illness in the future, does this mean that the age of creative imagination is merely an interregnum in our history? If the language of the future is described as destabilized in the same way as it once was, does this mean that we live with a blindness toward a fundamental instability within our systems of information and knowledge? In other words: Is the stability of the world we believe we are surrounded by a mere illusion, something that will inevitably fall back into what we regard as a chaotic and primitive life where we have no control? The scope of this article does not allow for further discussion of these questions, even if they are well worth a thought. But the obvious and short answer is that Rimbereid's poem indeed points toward an inherent destabilization within communication and culture itself.

Life as Work

Interesting, from our point of view, is what Audun Lindholm, editor of the highly influential periodical *Vagant*, suggests with reference to the title *Solaris Corrected*: that Rimbereid's correction of Stanislaw Lem's novel *Solaris* (1961), and Andrei Tarkovsky's 1972 movie loosely based on this, lies in Rimbereid's dismissal of the concept of travel in his vision of the future: "Rimbereid's book might (bearing the title in mind) be read as a comment on both Lem and Tarkovsky, and the correction seems to lie especially in the insistence on man being earthbound." ("Rimbereids bok kan (med tittelen in mente) leses som en kommentar til både Lem og Tarkovskij, og korreksjonen synes særlig å ligge i insisteringen på menneskets jordbundethet") (Lindholm 2008; Trans. HOA).[3]

Let us have another look at the sequence describing work in Stavanger in the future: "WHERE/I live, in 14.6, we work/only with our nano-fingers,/they are our total knowledge, we work/so little, 30 minutes a day. I look at/my fingers, part of organic 14.6." Nano-fingers are robotic arms, used to perform work on the atomic and molecular level. Later, we learn that he works with robots that perform work at the bottom of the ocean. Hence, the nano-fingers are placed on the robots. He looks at his fingers, which are "part of organic 14.6" in the same way as the robotic fingers are part of him. (A Norwegian reader will associate "14.6" with the way the ocean on the Norwegian continental shelf is divided into "blocks" for commercial activity, that is the oil industry.[4])

The above quotation is thought-provoking because there is a double relation in this passage, between robot and man on the one side and man and a place where several people live called "organic" on the other. And because this strikes a chord with what Aristotle writes about slavery. For Aristotle, as he writes in *Politics*, a slave is not defined as someone you own, but as someone who, like tools, is part of the master. As Giorgio Agamben explains in *The Use of Bodies: Homo Sacer IV, 2* (2016, 13), after having referred to this passage in Aristotle: "The slave is a part (of the body) of the master, in the 'organic' and not simply instrumental sense of the term, to such an extent that Aristotle can speak of a 'community of life' between slave and master."

Why does an educated writer like Rimbereid place "live" and "work" next to each other? What does he mean by stating that the nano-fingers are "our total knowledge"? Why is the worker "part of" society? And why is this society called "organic," the word Aristotle uses to explain how the slave is a part of the master's body?

This clustering of concepts goes to the core of understanding human beings as identical to their relationship with their surroundings through work. The persona presents himself as identified with a place where all they know is how to operate nano-fingers (as present-day Stavanger only knows how to pump up oil). He is made who he is by being a part of this society. As part of an "organic" master-slave relation, he is not his own, but as much an inseparable, unautonomous part of his place of work as the robots.

Note that "robot" is a word derived from Czech "robota," "serf-labor." The persona in "Solaris Corrected" only operates the fingers on these serfs, these robots, for half an hour a day, but this is still what he himself regards as the all-important aspect of his existence. At the end of the poem, his physical presence is relinquished, as he is—probably—transported through an elevator down to an empty oil reservoir at the bottom of the North Sea and transferred into an "abstract-faktical" duplication of himself (Rimbereid 2004, 39–40). Maybe because his work is not needed anymore, but explicitly because he has been told that this is humanity's last hope for survival after the planet has been made uninhabitable by human activity.

As the concept of humans changing shape because robots take over their jobs is also present at the conclusion of the other object of our investigations, *Jimmen*, there is good reason to believe that this is Rimbereid's suggestion or question: If humans are defined by their work, and by their partaking in "organic" work societies, then perhaps there is no defining aspect, nothing to make them human, after work is gone. At least humans would have to be defined in a different way, as yet unknown to us.

The persona in "Solaris Corrected" reflects on this:

DET seis i Bibl at
"love stand ovfr all ting."
MEN stand du onli i love,
haf ne andre gifts, hendels, arbeid
du da risk
    standa og standa og standa. (Rimbereid 2004, 34–5)

IT says in the Bible that
"love stands above everything."
BUT if you only stand in love,
have no other gifts, happenings, work
you then risk
    standing and standing and standing. (Trans. HOA)

As we have seen earlier, the reference in the opening of the poem goes to what Aristotle writes on slaves. According to Agamben, the concept of "labor" as something one can buy and sell is introduced in Roman times. The Greeks only trade in the result, in the product. But their slavery, their "organic" view of the master-slave relationship stands at the beginning, as the starting point for this definition of man through work. So the reference in "Solaris Corrected" connects the end of work with the beginning of work, in a way similar to the way language was reflected upon: What we see as part of the stability of our world is again presented in a way that both describes its future ending and points toward its beginning, which again means that our world—indeed, our own personality, our humanity—does not have the kind of eternal permanence both we and our philosophical tradition take for granted.

The biblical allusion goes to 1 Corinthians 13. This famous passage lists skills and knowledges, and disregards them all in relation to *agape* (in modern translations, *agape* is changed to "love," so Paul's insistence on the supremacy of the reciprocal love between man and God is obscured). We note that the persona in "Solaris Corrected" turns Paul's disregard for praxis around 180 degrees: he asks what love/*agape* is if you have no earthly skills. The anagogical level of "Solaris Corrected" is thus presented in the negative, as something pointed at but placed as a poignant absence within the world as it is unfolded in the text.

And by this, we are back at present-day Stavanger, a town defined by the oil industry, with people defined by the oil industry, speaking a language defined by the oil industry. Historical occurrences shape the world, and the world shapes us, to a point where the lack of presence of an afterlife in the secularized society must be addressed if the text is to live up to its ambition of being topographic verse, with an anagogical level in place.

But tradition shapes us, too. And here is another possible reason for the title: Stanislaw Lem published the novel *Solaris* in 1961. Jean-Michel Jasiensko published the French translation of *Solaris* in 1964. Boris Niremburg directed the movie *Solaris* in 1968. Joanna Kilmartin and Steve Cox published the English translation of *Solaris* in 1970. Andrei Tarkovsky directed the movie *Solaris* in 1972. Steven Soderbergh directed the movie *Solaris* in 2002. Lem has expressed disappointment, to say the least, with the movies as well as with the English translation. This only highlights the fact that all these versions make for destabilization. Like all the versions of the same story you might find in literature before the modern concept of creativity is established—with Shakespeare at the center of the Western canon, although only a handful of his plays have an entirely original plot (Mabillard 2000)—*Solaris* drifts around in our culture as something that has taken shape after numerous times and places.

In Tarkovsky's version, human scientists look down in the ocean and see their own metaphysical aspirations mirrored. In Rimbereid's "corrected" version, the people of Stavanger look down in the ocean and see their aspirations mirrored as oil work. Even transcendence is to be obtained down there, in empty oil and gas reservoirs. But this eternal existence after leaving the body behind, in the computer-generated reality under the sea bed, is just another aspect of the anagogical level the "Solaris Corrected" persona sees no point in. He reflects on this, and comes to the conclusion that the only thing one could do would be to talk to other people. And that is, to him, like when love is just to be "standing and standing and standing." An afterlife without *praxis*, without the physical weight of work, is of no interest to him.

Jimmen

Turning now to the book depicting Stavanger's past, we will be able to follow a path ending up in a position neatly mirroring that of the future in "Solaris Corrected": *Jimmen* takes its name from a horse. Together with his owner, he walks the streets of mid-1970s Stavanger, collecting food waste used for pig fodder. Once a week, they empty latrine buckets in those backyards where there are still outhouses. Throughout the poem, the owner and the horse take turns as speaking persona. But even if the owner occasionally expresses himself as if he spoke directly to the horse, there is no indication that they can understand each other. So this is not a dialogue, but rather two dramatic, internal monologues intertwined.

The owner's language is traditional Stavanger dialect, while the horse's language might best be described as Old Norse, with simplified syntactic structure and some rather obvious limitations to his vocabulary. As modern Stavanger dialect—like all language in Norway, in Iceland and the Faroe Islands—descends directly from Old Norse, the impression is that the horse's language is an archaic form of human speech:

> Høyrer eg no
> gode herren
> koma nedåt sti
> og burtåt stallen mine heimars.
> Han mun opna veggar tvo
> og ljoset skal då rida stort
> med taumar gull
> og munnbet silver. (Rimbereid 2011, 7)

> Hear I know
> the good master
> come down the path
> and to stable mine home's.
> He may open walls two
> and the light will then ride large
> with reins gold
> and mouthpiece silver. (Trans. HOA)

The age of horses lasted longer in Norway than most places in Northern Europe. Due to trade restrictions, one needed an import license to buy a car until 1960, and private cars did not become commonplace until a decade later. In 1970, only 70,000 of the 300,000 farms in Norway had a tractor. As the 1970s progressed, motorized vehicles rapidly became all-dominant. One could still see the occasional horse and carriage even in relatively big towns like Stavanger, but by 1975 this would be very rare, and almost have the same function of civilizatoric embarrassment as the aforementioned outhouses.

As man and horse in the time of cars, Jimmen and his owner are living anachronisms. This is underlined when they view the first condeep platform being towed out of Stavanger on its way to the Norwegian oil fields in the North Sea (this happened in 1975). The horse of old times is contrasted with the production of fuel for cars in present age.

Rimbereid makes use of the parallel between the towing boats and the horse in front of the carriage. This is further expanded when Jimmen tries to tow a car with engine trouble, but fails because he is old. The age of the horse is coming to an end, both literally and allegorically.

There are also references to the owner's sister. In a "muttering" way, as if all readers were intimate with the Stavanger region, it is mentioned that she lives at Dale, but not that Dale is a huge mental hospital. She is religious, knitting for the church bazaar, which means that she is a member of a Free Church congregation. This makes her a form of living anachronism as well. From the 1930s onward, Stavanger was a town with a lot of activity of this kind. But by the 1970s, the active members were senior citizens, typically old ladies, and today most if not all of these religious societies are gone.

As in "Solaris Corrected," we are introduced to the society through personas who are not describing the topography in the catalogue fashion of the old topographic verse, but rather through monologues which make us see the world from their perspective, not expressively as is the norm from Romanticism onward, but through their observations and their accompanying reflections on them.

The choice of time frame, the dawn of the oil industry in the Stavanger region, is of course no coincidence. By choosing the horse and his owner as the basis for a description of the rapid introduction of a new era in the up to this point rather backward Stavanger region, the poem succeeds in following up on one of the main traits of the old topographic literature: to describe a society as it is changing, and to make both old and new and the contrast between them clear to see.

The world's first industrial robot was introduced by the Norwegian company Trallfa in 1961. Commercial production followed in 1969, and was moved into a new facility outside Stavanger in 1975—the same year Jimmen and his master observe the first condeep platform. At the end of the poem, Jimmen's owner seeks out this new factory. When he comes out again, Jimmen is nowhere to be seen, and the owner's language goes through gradual changes until he speaks like Jimmen has done earlier.

Jimmen has been overtaken by cars. Now his owner is being overtaken by robots. And the untimeliness of his existence is demonstrated through a fall out of the language of the contemporary and into the archaic language of the horse, and of a society long gone. At the same time, there is immense urgency here. Jimmen and the owner are not only confronted with a change, but with a civilizatoric jump from religion and horses to oil and cybernetics.

The mirroring effect of the endings of "Solaris Corrected" and *Jimmen* are striking. We were presented with a man disappearing at the end of the oil age. Now we are introduced to a man who disappears at the start of the same era. In sum, these two poems constitute a beginning and an end to what is today the identity of Stavanger and of Stavanger people, namely the oil industry and the work related to it.

The connection between the two is further underlined in a sequence in *Jimmen* where the horse contemplates the reins with which the owner controls him, and wonders if his master is controlled by invisible reins from the people in the houses where they collect garbage. As we understand, this touches upon the same question of work and identity, of "organic" relations as I discussed in relation to "Solaris Corrected."

In sum, the old horse in the last days of the horse in Stavanger, together with his master in the last days of this kind of work, points not only to a personal disappearance, but to a disappearance on a larger scale: The horse and the man collecting biowaste is not only an *image* which has disappeared from Stavanger. It is something which has stopped taking place in Stavanger. In the same vein, the man of the future disappearing into a computer-generated reality is representative of a culture which stops taking space. This disappearance into the future resembles *virtual reality*, but in a radicalized form, where there is no outside, no "world of bricks and mortars" anymore.

Stavanger, Pre- and Postmodern

Were we ever modern? When reading really old texts, we are often struck by the way science is mixed up with other sectors of human intellectual activity. But we have greater difficulties in identifying this blurring of the border of objective knowledge when dealing with our own time. Most obviously, we will find the understanding of the human psyche frighteningly primitive, even as recently as with Freudian psychoanalysis and the practice of lobotomy. And if lobotomy has been replaced by electroshock treatment, we still do not know exactly how to do this or why it works.

Even in the hardest of sciences, like physics, the element of insecurity is staggering. We expect dark matter, but we cannot be surer of the existence of this *terra incognita* than we once were of a large inhabitable continent south of Australia.

To a person who has lived through the 1980s, with its postmodern skepticism toward the ideology of progress, the pit to fall into as a consequence of this understanding is that of new age nonsense and alternative medicine. The cynical, thoughtful way of looking at it is to reflect on the relativity of knowledge and systems of information as an integral part of our existence.

By pouring present-day Stavanger into the old tradition of topographic verse, in ways which make the presence of the latter clear to see, Øyvind Rimbereid makes us see how a specific position in time and space affects us, and how we in turn affect not only the view of this space, but indeed the way this space unfolds, the way this space comes to function as an objective environment for other people and, indeed, for entire cultures.

Stavanger in the past of *Jimmen*, in the present of *Late Topographies*, and in the future of "Solaris Corrected" is a continuum of human *praxis* which is specific to this place, but has its roots in traditions leading all the way back to the origin of our civilization. The depiction of our civilization may in certain aspects lean rather heavily on metaphysical beliefs, but even these are rooted in space, in time and in tradition, for Rimbereid has not invented the questions posed by the personas in his poems. He has merely relocated them, to his own specific place. And pointed toward a future where it will come to an end, where we leave "organic" work relationships and, thus, leave the physical space we have been filling through our *praxis*.

Notes

1. Of the new wave of poetry written in Norwegian dialect, Erlend O. Nødtvedt's *Bergens beskrivelse* (2011; "Depiction of Bergen") is of special relevance, as it is structured as the same kind of dialogue with a tradition predating Romanticism that Rimbereid, as we will see in this chapter, makes use of a decade earlier.
2. Norway was part of the twin kingdom Denmark-Norway from 1536 to 1814. A purist wish to abolish the huge number of borrowed words, or at least give them domestic spelling, was introduced in Denmark-Norway in the middle of the eighteenth century (Spurkland 1987, 60). Danish was introduced as a separate subject in schools in 1775. Ole Malling published *Store og gode Handlinger af Danske, Norske og Holstenere* (1877; "Great deeds by Danes, Norwegians and Holstenians"). And, as a language history reads: "Myndighetene gjorde stavemåten i den til gjeldende norm, og med et hadde dansk fått en offisiell rettskriving" ("The authorities made the spelling in that book normative, and on account of that, Danish had an official spelling") (Spurkland 1987, 61).
3. "Solaris Corrected" has been commented upon in passing in many articles on contemporary Norwegian and Scandinavian poetry. In addition to this, Lindholm's and four other articles focus solely on "Solaris Corrected." None of these five articles has been published in scientific, peer-reviewed publications.
4. In the most comprehensive systematization of ancient sources, Matthew Dillon and Lydia Garland's *Ancient Greece: Social and Historical Documents from Archaic Times to the Death of Socrates* (2nd ed. 2000), we find a paragraph corresponding to section 14.6, namely "14.6 Aristotle on the Writing of History." I quote: "It is also clear from what we have said that the work of a poet is not to tell what has happened, but what might or could happen either probably or inevitably. (…) For this reason poetry is more scientific and serious than history, for poetry speaks general truths, and history particular facts. By general truths I mean the sorts of things that a certain type of person will say or do either probably or inevitably (…)" (Dillon and Garland 2000 [1997], 509). If this is not a mere coincidence, it means that Rimbereid is situating his character not only geographically but also within canonic, classical thinking on literature and history.

References

Agamben, Giorgio. 2016. *The Use of Bodies: Homo Sacer IV, 2*. Translated by Adam Kotsko. Stanford: Stanford University Press.
Andersen, Hadle Oftedal. 2005. *Kroppsmodernisme*. Helsinki: University of Helsinki.

Dillon, Matthew, and Lydia Garland. 2000 [1997]. *Ancient Greece. Social and Historical Documents from Archaic Times to the Death of Socrates.* 2nd ed. London: Routledge.
Lindholm, Audun. 2008. For aig veit existen af vorld. In *Norsk litterær kanon*, ed. Janike Kampevold Larsen and Stig Sæterbakken. Oslo: Cappelen Damm. http://www.vagant.no/for-aig-veit-existen-af-vorld-om-solaris-korrigert/.
Mabillard, Amanda. 2000. What Inspired Shakespeare? *Shakespeare Online*, August 20, 2000. http://www.shakespeare-online.com/faq/shakespeareinspired.html.
NET Bible (New English Translation). https://www.biblegateway.com.
Oxford English Dictionary (OED). http://www.oed.com.
Rimbereid, Øyvind. 2004. *Solaris korrigert.* Oslo: Gyldendal.
———. 2006. *Hvorfor ensomt leve.* Oslo: Gyldendal.
———. 2011. *Jimmen.* Oslo: Gyldendal.
Spurkland, Terje. 1987. Språkutviklingen før 1814. In *Vårt eget språk. I går og i dag.* Vol. I, ed. Egil Børre Johnsen, 20–65. Oslo: Aschehoug.
Ulven, Tor. 1997. Gjenferdets ruin. Skepsis 5/1994. *Essays*, 162–4. Oslo: Gyldendal.

Open Access This chapter is licensed under the terms of the Creative Commons Attribution 4.0 International License (http://creativecommons.org/licenses/by/4.0/), which permits use, sharing, adaptation, distribution and reproduction in any medium or format, as long as you give appropriate credit to the original author(s) and the source, provide a link to the Creative Commons licence and indicate if changes were made.

The images or other third party material in this chapter are included in the chapter's Creative Commons licence, unless indicated otherwise in a credit line to the material. If material is not included in the chapter's Creative Commons licence and your intended use is not permitted by statutory regulation or exceeds the permitted use, you will need to obtain permission directly from the copyright holder.

CHAPTER 8

The Poetics of Blank Spaces and Intervals in Selected Works of Elisabeth Rynell

Antje Wischmann

The poetry collection *I mina hus* (2006, "In My Houses") appeared after the successful novel *Hohaj* (1997, *Schneelandschaft* 2002),[1] which made the Swedish author Elisabeth Rynell known to a wide readership. It is not hard to discern motifs common to both her poetry and prose, such as descriptions of landscapes that speak to a number of sensory perceptions, seasonal cycles and intensive snapshot images. In the poems of *I mina hus* a suggestive technique of gaps for the reader's imagination is applied in the blank spaces: there are white spaces in the midst of the "poetic body" that create enjambments and ensure a striking overall layout. The blank space is a characteristic example of "textual form as sign" (Sabel and Glauser 2004, 6) and a counterpart to the inscription: "Hundar/ser exakt/det vi själva inte ser [ ][2] Min hund/hade en blick/rätt ur den gamla världen [ ]" ("Dogs/see precisely/what we can't see [ ] My dog/had a gaze/reaching out of the old world [ ]") (Rynell 2006, 8).[3] This lacuna is referring to what is not be seen by humans; it establishes an analogy between the non-visual and the non-representational. But the

A. Wischmann (✉)
Department of Scandinavian Literature and Culture, Universität Wien, Wien, Austria

blank space can also be an interval or a pause and has sometimes an iconic function: "Jag kan känna/hugget in [ ]/i livet [ ]," ("I can feel/the cut/ [ ] into life [ ]") (Rynell 2006, 27). The experience of a "cut" seems to be performed within the linear writing and reading process. At the same time the blank spaces relate to each other, build up their own framework, as a kind of silent para-code, beside the textual.

In Rynell' s prose, a fusion of prose and poetry, the author inserts blank spaces as well, in two different ways: as lacunae like [ ] and as a kind of imaginary space between the story lines, when the focalization shifts from person to person or from the first-person narrator to a character. The readers have to relate the story lines to each other in order to grasp their personal interpretation of the novel (*Hohaj* and *Hitta hem*, 2009; "Finding home"). Especially in *Hitta hem*, the story lines first appear to be independent of each other because the main character Hild is living in the 1960s and her historic counterpart Mala in the seventeenth century. But after the readers have learned about passage or portal figures entering different (text) worlds, they will probably guess that Mala is a character in a literary text, written by the young author Hild. The melodramatic novel *Hohaj* even combines three focalizations: the first-person narrator (living in the twentieth century) has lost her husband, and this tragedy is mirrored in a love story of two outsiders, the female servant captured by her violent father (Inna) and the roaming poor seasonal worker (Aron), probably a Romani traveler or a Jew. Has the first-person narrator herself composed the traumatic story of Inna and Aron as part of a metanarrative and metafictional project? Readers will no doubt take different views on this. Literary scholar Thomas Seiler, for example, works on the assumption that Inna and Aron are characters invented by the writing first-person narrator (Seiler 2004), helping her to overcome her life crisis. The novel's levels are intertwined, with connections and passages to each other, and the readers may move in and out of the three character's parallel worlds: "Det finns portar i verkligheten./Går man in genom en av de portarna/kommer man ut i en annan berättelse./Hur många portar det finns, vet ingen" (Rynell 2009, epigraph, corresponding to page 5) ("There are portals in reality./ If you go through one of these portals,/you emerge into a different narrative./How many of these portals there are, no one knows").

In a striking way these portals or passages are used both as narrative and as metaphorical concepts in Rynell's texts. Blank spaces and lacunae are "unprinted" space entities, but they can appear as signs with different meanings or may even be omissions, for example, remnants of deleted words or letters: without doubt, they are never "quiet," but always say something to the readers. During reception, blank spaces and lacunae enfold as "space[s] of reader response" (Heitmann 2012, 217), analogous to the "Leerstellen" by the reader response literary theorist Wolfgang Iser in 1972. He analyzed how "Leerstellen" in the reader's reception generate additional meanings, sometimes as an intended supplement or emphatic enrichment.

In Rynell's text a lacuna is the smallest possible format of a blank space within the sentences of a poem. On an intratextual level the blank space between the poems and the book chapters offers imaginative space in order to complete the text by means of the reader's reception. Having the protagonists of Rynell's *Hohaj* and *Hitta hem* in mind, the recipients have to decide how they will relate the threads to each other: Which narrator is the creator of Inna's or Mara's level? Answering this question depends on the interpretation of the novel as a whole. This narrative-structural example illustrates that my particular focus will be (a) on the positioning of material text/blank space/space of response as spatial entities and their relations to each other and (b) on the meaning which is generated by these relational processes.

What interests me, in other words, is the process of placing, that is, of "positioning with respect *to space* (Anordnungen *zu Räumen*)," in this case with respect to spatiotextual entities, even more than the "positioning of entities *in space* (Anordnung der Gebilde *im Raum*)" (Löw 2004, 46; italics original). Michel Foucault's term "relations among sites" (1984, 2, in French "relations d'emplacement") also deals with placing processes and the relations between placings. Relational space (in contrast to the common spatial concept of the container; Löw 2001, 2004) is always constituted by the interaction of space and time. First, I will examine the spatiotextual composition of the "opening" and the two "closing" poems of *I mina hus*, entering and then leaving the "textual houses" of Rynell's poems. In the second part I want to discuss the relationship between the correlations of blank spaces and intervals to Rynell's narrative profile as a modernist writer.

THE TEXT-AS-BUILDING METAPHOR IN *I MINA HUS*

There is, of course, a long tradition of comprehending the text-as-building, as one can live in a world of words and a universe of texts. The materials of language can be compared with building elements, for example, words can be compared with stone bricks; lines with the rafters of the roof; the page's paper with real estate grounds; the title of a chapter with the room of a building, or a floor or section. In the depicted world the cellar of a house may represent the hidden unconsciousness or repressed feelings, the loft can signify utopian thought or bohemian lifestyle, and so on. It is easy and productive to compare an architectural object with "textus" (tissue, weave) as both are artifacts.

Gaston Bachelard's phenomenological notion of *La poétique de l'espace* (originally in 1957) could be truly inspiring, if it did not rely on the rather limited concept of spatial containers.

Often the beginning of a text may be conceptualized as an entrance, as an opening to the fictional world. In Rynell's text, by shifting focalization the ending of one narrative thread can open up for another and to the imagined space of the reader's response. A lacuna in a poem opens up this space of reception, but this is even more so with the concrete blank space of the layout and the temporal intervals of a poetic text because the language of poetry is much more "foregrounded" than that of prose.

The 30 poems in *I mina hus* spread across five chapters, constructing their own textual spatiality as houses of poems. Further, houses function as frameworks just as the houses of Rynell's poems operate as a medium for reader's perceptions, they form the material condition of their conception of the social world and their surroundings.

On the one hand, the poems are two-dimensional texts on two-dimensional pages, while on the other they establish a (metaphorical and literal) text-as-building: a unique form of textual housing. The textual-spatial shape of the poems is, therefore, as important as their description and representation of space. The textual form as such becomes a theme and an object of reflection. This kind of textual spatiality, involving type and script, is called *Schriftraum* in German (Doetsch 2015, 73–87), which always encompasses both layout and the bodily act of writing and/or physical printing.[4]

When it comes to the arrangement of Rynell's lyric texts—elements of textual spatiality such as templates and typography—what we need to investigate are context and the relations between stanzas, lines, phrases and words. With their mutual relations in mind, we need to analyze the concrete placings of text on the page. The focus, then, must be on the positioning of select compositional elements vis-à-vis textual spatiality, elements that construct intra- or intertextual connections before the readers' eyes. The house of a text can only establish a temporary ensemble, the result of placings and positionings within language and literary texts.

In Rynell's works, the house mostly operates as a form or framework that facilitates positioning and placing. Further, the house becomes a model for material language and for language as a medium. Rather than through division into chapters, *I mina hus* is structured by simple graphic sketches of tiny houses. These outline images are used as an alternative numbering system, much like Roman numerals: from 1 single house to 5 adjacent houses (Rynell 2006, 69), 15 sketches in all. But rather than standardized logotypes, these sketches show traces of "manual treatment," combining drawing and inscription: two short lines for windows, another for the centrally positioned door. The ambiguity of the title is striking: "In my houses" now inevitably also means "in my poems" or "in my writings," which are rendered as one-of-a-kind and temporary artifacts. The title and the layout entrench the analogy between house and text or building and literary work. Just as the rooms in a building are connected by corridors or passageways, so the blank spaces are interconnecting openings between the texts, having concrete and metaphorical significance: leaving a given house means entering another locational or spatial domain. The outside of one construction could be part of the inside of another spatial unit; these shared elements may at times be the actual page of a book, or may refer to other pages and books. Compared with material books or pages, texts have neither clear endings nor distinct borders.

Leaving a building might also mean entering a larger structure or understanding that the interior space is always subsumed by a surrounding space or opens into an exterior space. Leaving a textual building means entering something else, something different—perhaps another building or a (temporary) world outside the text. It is according to this opening and contextualizing principle that Rynell's writings build on earlier textual buildings, integrating them or amalgamating them into an expanding arrangement of texts.

A poem's context can lead us into the neighboring poetic text. The lines of a poem can open up both into the diegetic site (the depicted place), the layout of the page and the "Schriftraum" or to places experienced by readers. From a character's internal point of view we may not immediately be able to judge the dimensions of the space encompassing a house. Is the spatial unit of a house essentially defined by its territorial extension or "container" or is it perceived through relational space? What could actually be the outside of the inside, just a further sphere of another inside, nested in one another?

The first poem in *I mina hus* provides the volume with an epigraph, which introduces the themes of nostalgia, vanishing places and temporary constellations. The volume thus begins by indicating strategies of textual interlinkage and possible paths of interpretation.

TRASTARNA HAR INTAGIT TRÄDTOPPARNA

Ur den blöta [   ] nyväckta jorden
ännu kall av snösmältning
föds rabarberna långsamt
i ett baklänges upprullande
med fotspjärn nere i det svarta

Världens ansikte
är inte läsbart [   ] vi måsta berätta oss
fram [   ] Vittnandet
en andra
födelse

[   ] Blodet
hinnorna
[   ] [   ] den tunga närande efterbörden
faller
och ett träd längst inne
i det blå
som vi äter oss grymtande fram
genom. (Rynell 2006, 4)

THE THRUSHES HAVE OCCUPIED THE TREETOPS/out of the moist [   ] newly awoken earth/still cold from the melting snow/the rhubarb plants are slowly born/by unfurling themselves backwards/pushing themselves up from a foothold down in the blackness//the face of the world/is not readable [   ] we have to narrate ourselves/forwards as we go along [   ] Witnessing/another/birth//[   ] The blood/the shells [   ] the rich nourishing afterbirth/falls down/and a tree deep within/in the blue/that we gruntingly eat our way/through

The dynamism of the new rhubarb shoots resembles an arabesque alive with energy. The linear moving forward of the text is both illustrated and realized in a performative forward movement. In the first stanza the lacuna is introduced as a temporal interval, slowly shifting from the neutral "moist" to the pathos of "newly awoken earth." The connotations of this pause are hesitation and thoughtfulness. Like the third omission after "go along" the first marks the positioning of a temporal unit, almost as if the lyrical I was searching for an adequate expression. The next blank space is iconic because of the analogy between the unreadable and the invisible. The last stanza is obviously beginning with two intervals, within an enjambment from the last word of the second stanza ("birth"), illustrating the process of creation step by step; here preparing for the primitivist identification with an organism of nature.

In the last poem, at the volume's "exit," we are returned to the summery beginning—and are perhaps meant to pass through a portal leading to a landscape of memory, which reveals an epiphany, though it immediately erases it, even overriding, silencing and fading out the text through a self-reflexive deixis ("här," "here"). The allegoric reading ends with the whiteness of the page.

JUNI

Och tvärs genom denna tunga grönska
ser jag ett ansikte
[ ] vittra
som om vinden
när den för ett ögonblick gick genom lövverket
suddat ut det

ögonen [ ] munnen [ ] de exakta läpparna [ ] allt omändrat
kringrört [ ] utplånat

Jag vet inte efteråt
om detta ansikte någonsin funnits [ ] Kanhända
var det bara en bild i lövverket
framstampat ur en inre bild [ ] ur
hjärnans lövverk [ ] hjärnans
bländverk
en önskan [ ] en längtan efter
ett ansikte

jag säger sedan till natten: träd
mig nära

och natten färdas i löven
ankrad vid en enda [ ] ytterligt tunn
fågelröst

som ur intet sprider sina toner
genom det bleka
grönskimrande mörkret [   ] Att allting
är så tillfälligt [   ] så skört
så lätt att utsudda här. (Rynell 2006, 83–4)

JUNE/And through the midst of the dense greenery/I see a face/[   ] weather/as if the wind/when it moves for a moment through the foliage/obliterates it//the eyes [   ] the mouth [   ] the precise lips [   ] everything altered//mixed up [   ] wiped out//Afterwards I don't know,/whether there was ever such a face [   ] Perhaps/it was just an image in the foliage/generated from an inner image [   ] from/the cerebral foliage [   ] the brain's/illusion/a desire [   ] a longing for/a face//then I tell the night: come/close to me//and the night moves forward through the leaves/anchored in a single [   ] particularly faint/birdcall/which broadcasts its notes out of the void/through the pale/green-shimmering darkness [   ] that everything/is so temporary [   ] so fragile/so easily erasable here

The momentary appearance of a face evokes the theme of an "imagination," one that can traverse the boundary between an internal idea and a phenomenological perception in both directions; it may be located both within and outside the perceiving subject. In this way images are projected onto the perceived environment, while one's own perception seems called into question as the possible result of wishful thinking. Characteristically, this poem hints metaphorically at two lines and thus—in accordance with a musical metaphor—two voices: the spatiotemporal forward movement of the night occurs in alignment with a bird's call. However (in contrast to the novels), this linear orientation cannot be related to a narrative and is thus only partially comparable to the novels' alternating narrative perspectives.

Not only do the distinct blank spaces in "June," as visualized omissions, accentuate the recipient's need for interpretation, they also draw attention to the technique itself, that is, its poetic and "foregrounding" function. The blank spaces resist fluent reading, so it is impossible to appropriate the poems according to the "line-as-breath" principle (Hansson 2011, 47).[5] They slow down the reading process, not least because the multiple references engendered by the enjambments must be examined in succession. This results in a reading experience characterized by running forward and running backward, which unsettles the chronology of the perceptual process: initially a face might look out from behind the greenery, then the text jumps to a face that is "absent yet again," because the components of the face, flanked by four blank spaces, cannot be reconstructed in retrospect.

The locational adverb "här" (here) guides one's attention not just to the scenography and the place of the subject, but also to the space on the page that remains blank beneath the summer-focused vanitas. The highlight of the summer marks a turning point; the certainty of the seasonal rhythm already reminds one of the summer's loss; the intensity of the epiphanic moment therefore corresponds with the notion of death, emptiness and silence.[6] By opening the poetic textual building to its typographical environment, the blank space is also compared with the loss of textual signs or the outer world as a universe encompassing totally different codes.[7] The blank spaces after "inner image" and "desire" again correspond with the figure of non-resemblance, referring to phenomena which can hardly be put into words.

At the epilogue "conclusion" of the collection, the poem "Över" ("Over") presents a text-specific variant of obliteration: the elliptical lines indicate that the movement that plays such a prominent role here is coming to a stop. Stasis is setting in. As if along a nerve pathway, the textual buildings leads the reader's gaze across the poem's spatiotextual boundary into the extratextual world. In other words, the layout visualizes the text's capacity (through a linguistic code and an iconic symbol for linearity) to point beyond itself as a poem.

> ÖVER
> när det är över
> och vattnet lägger sig blankt
> som om
> aldrig en vind [   ] en
> rysning
>
> och ingenting stör
> ögats resa
> ut
> [   ] synranden tunn [   ] en nervtråd utspänd. (Rynell 2006; Unpaginated, corresponding to page 85)
>
> OVER/when it is over/and the water grows calm/as if/never a wind [   ] a/quiver//and nothing disturbs/the eye's journey/beyond/[   ] the gaze's narrow edge [   ] an outstretched nerve fiber

The last words—as an illusionary thread—make an attempt to leave the textual space, as if the "outstretched nerve fiber" was extending into the extraliterary world. This self-reflective and metapoetic method suggests a belief in "formal mimesis," by translating a physical phenomenon into a typographical counterpart: the line as a nerve. If one tried to visualize this transgressive movement, out of the embodied text, it would be a line, crossing the paper margin of the page ("edge"). This approach reminds one of the open endings in novels, because the characters of the embedded narrations establish the horizons for the characters of the frame narration (about the nameless female writer in *Hohaj* and Hild in *Hitta hem*). The concrete outside of a text may nevertheless correspond with the inner diegesis, and perhaps the extraliterary world is sometimes the most fictional world.

SCRUTINIZING MODERNIST FOUNDATIONS IN THE FUSION OF POETRY AND PROSE

The metaphor of a thread is part of the basic modernist repertoire in that it highlights constructedness as such (e.g., textus as tissue or weave). As the thread of life or fate and as a narrative guideline, it is also deployed in the third stanza of the well-known poem "Coda" (1938) by the famous modernist Swedish poet Gunnar Ekelöf (1907–1968), though in addition here emphasis is placed on a linear, irreversible orientation as a feature common to text and life: "Vad vore händelsernas vävnad utan/den röda tråden, ariadnetråden,/försvunnen då och då men alltid invävt!" ("What would the weave of events be without/the red thread, the thread of Ariadne,/vanished now and then, but always woven in!" Translated by Larsson and Nathan 1982). This maxim emphasizing the importance of a strong narrative is the epigraph to Rynell's essay collection *Skrivandets sinne* (2013; "The Sense and the Senses of Writing"). In this work the author coins the term "human narrative" ("människo-berättelse"), which, in a metaphorical sense, relentlessly highlights the directed, dynamic and compressed character typical of the components of the "textus": "ett myller av trådar som löper framåt och bakåt, uppåt och nedåt som i en väv" (Rynell 2002, 100) ("a tangle of threads running forwards and backwards, upwards and downwards as in a weave"). Here we can discern a central line, a narrative thread, namely the "human narrative thread" (Rynell 2013, 39). Yet in neither the poetic nor the novel texts should we think in terms of a "'naive thread" (solely in the sense of a focus that one ought to maintain): the blank spaces, intervals and threads always signalize that the texts (and the author) are aware of their self-referentiality from their "beginning." Readers are automatically confronted with this poetic method, intuitively taking part in the performance of material language and, in both her poetry and prose, confirming the perception of language as a medium.

Nonetheless, in an essay on her argument about coherent or shattered narratives with Sara Lidman (1923–2004), who advocated the shattering of narratives (in the 1980s and 1990s, Wischmann 2014, 52–9), Rynell presents herself as a less experimental author, upholding a view of literature as a vigorous organism. Lidman is one of the most renowned classical modernists, known for her critical left-wing documentary prose (e.g., *Gruva*, "The Mine," 1968). In Lidman's late novels (e.g., *Oskuldens minut*, "Minute of Innocence," 1999) the characteristics of her work have gradually become grotesque and distorted, whereas Rynell still takes the principle of the organism more seriously. This prompts her to describe her narrative as a "viljekropp med obändig muskulatur," which possesses "en egen levande och tvingande kraft" (Rynell 2013, 37) ("a will-based body with an untameable musculature"; "an autonomous, living and compelling power"). Rynell favors clearly identifiable narratives, suggesting that she is a fairly traditional writer, at least in some ways. Her recurring critique of civilization entails a number of anachronistic features or throwbacks to early modernism: because she ascribes language to a primeval sphere and to a state of pre-consciousness, many of her texts tie the use of language directly to concepts of femininity, corporeality and ethnicity.[8] By referring explicitly to the Finland-Swedish and Swedish early modernist poets Edith Södergran (1892–1923) and Harry Martinson (1904–1978) in *Skrivandet sinne*, she encourages criticism of postmodern (or post-postmodern) life and artistic conditions, expressing a quite skeptical attitude to technology, consumerism and rationality. Here the similarities to Lidman's or Harry Martinson's literary and political engagement are plainly evident.

Rynell is undoubtedly a representative of eco- and feminist criticism, and her "modernist project" has to be understood in terms of a "renovation" or a late modern "retake" (Hassan and Hassan 1983; Eco 1985). Her work is deeply rooted in the literary debates on the nexus of the body and language of the 1980s and 1990s (Eglinger 2007). Transferring vitalism to a new era and integrating it with an awareness of inscriptions enables her poetry to "vitalize" textual spatiality and highlight the theme of embodied texts. The fact that the text, having entered the world, behaves in a creaturely way, looking at writers or readers and picking up a scent like an animal (Rynell 2013, 65), can only be explained if we assume that the anthropomorphization (on the premise of the texts' self-referentiality, see above) extends even to the self-reflexive unfolding of poems. In Rynell's poetry the graphic of the houses (as visual titles of the sections) claims that the poems could be conceived as if they were textual houses. In the novel *Hitta hem* a variety of story lines derives from the forest, as a tangle of springs and paths: "(...) det sprang upp berättelser ur den [skogen] som det springer upp källor ur marken. Berättelser som längs alla spår och stigar föddes och färdades, nästan som ett folk av berättelser som också de var en del av skogen" (Rynell 2009, 106) ("Narratives welled up from the forest like springs gushing from the ground. Narratives that were born of the trails and paths and traveled along them, almost like a people of narratives forming part of the forest"). The narrative and the poetic topology are more important than the depicted geographic places or topography.

In accordance with this nature-exoticizing concept of language, living bodies, natural elements and creatures even communicate on their own initiative, with no particular addressees: "Granar är retoriska figurer" or "en kväll så fullskriven av tecken" (Rynell 2006, 11, 9) ("Pines are rhetorical figures"; "an evening written full of symbols"). Characteristically, natural phenomena are always already symbolic entities, and they constitute a typographical landscape.

Rynell's compositional principle, as I have elaborated it here, is a variant in its own right when compared, for example, with Danish poet Inger Christensen's (1935–2009) novel *Azorno* (1967). In this ostentatiously fragmented novel, the depicted places and conflicts between characters are fused in several sequential permutations, creating a system of spatiotemporal units and establishing a unique set of rules, which recalls the Scandinavian (mostly Danish) poetry governed by script system principles ("systemdigtning") of the 1960s and 1970s (Hejlskov Larsen 1971). In Christensen's novel, several narrating and writing figures alternately compete for the status of creator of that which has been narrated (Wischmann 1998). In a less complicated way this applies to *Hohaj* and *Hitta hem* as well. Which "thread" foregrounds the other? Which diegetic world is meant to be fictional/fictitious? These questions may be hard to answer. Even the textual building metaphor is applied by Christensen, for example, in a very famous poem ("Vandtrapper," "A Staircase of Water"), while material chapters are explicitly compared to the steps of a stone staircase (Christensen 1969, 45–6).

Yet in the framework of these works as a whole, as soon as we notice the genre-spanning attributes of Rynell's poetry and prose, we begin to pay due attention to their compositional intricacies. Rynell's late modernist novels emphatically revolve around a subject that writes, while concurrently being re-written by its texts. Both the textual buildings and the intertextual housings have an impact on both the production and the reception of Rynell's texts. The blank spaces and intervals have a spatio-temporal spell on the reader's reception: They are invited to spend some time to adapt poems and prose and to transform them into a highly personal reception experience.

Notes

1. There is no translation in English.
2. The [ ] symbol indicates a distinct blank space in the layout.
3. All translations in this chapter are by Antje Wischmann, in intense dialogue and negotiation with the translator Alex Skinner.
4. Doetsch calls the bodily gesture "Scription" (Doetsch 2015, 73–87).
5. Hansson understands the likes of William Carlos Williams and Allen Ginsberg as "line-as-breath" poets.
6. "Denn das Schöne ist nichts als das Schrecklichen Anfang, den wir gerade noch ertragen" (Rilke 1923, 11) ("For beauty is nothing but the beginning of terror that we are barely able to endure").
7. At the same time, the presentist "here" represents a verbal hinge to the title of the epilogue poem: "Över" ("Over"); as concluding vignette, this text is located outside the pagination. The poetics of empty spaces or signifiers referring to empty spaces is applied in a similar way by Ann Jäderlund in the early 1990s (see Brandt 2011, 2014).
8. Techniques of self-exoticization also appear in the poem "Poeten som smet" (Rynell 1988, 30).

References

Bachelard, Gaston. 2014 [1957]. *Poetik des Raumes*. Translated by Kurt Leonhard. Frankfurt a.M.: Fischer.

Brandt, Tatjana. 2011. 'Kroppen med de dubbla pulsarna.' Karneval och tomrum i Ann Jäderlunds diktsamling *Snart går jag i sommaren ut*. *Tidskrift för litteraturvetenskap* (1): 25–40.

———. 2014. *Livet mellan raderna. Revolt, tomrum och språkbrist i Ann Jäderlunds och Agneta Enckells tidiga poesi*. Helsingfors: Helsingfors universitet. https://helda.helsinki.fi/bitstream/handle/10138/144089/livetmel.pdf?sequence=1.

Christensen, Inger. 1969. Vandtrapper. In *Tekster fra slutningen af 60'erne*, ed. Vagn Lundbye, 45–46. Copenhagen: Borgen.

Doetsch, Hermann. 2015. Schrifträume. In *Handbuch Literatur und Raum*, ed. Jörg Dünne and Andreas Mahler, vol. 3, 73–87. Berlin: De Gruyter.

Eco, Umberto. 1985. Innovation and Repetition: Between Modern and Postmodern Aesthetics. *Daedalus, Journal of the American Academy of Arts and Science* 114 (4, fall): 161–184.

Eglinger, Hanna. 2007. *Der Körper als Palimpsest. Die poetologische Dimension des Körpers.* Freiburg: Rombach.

Foucault, Michel. 1984. Of Other Spaces: Utopias and Heterotopias. Translated by Jay Miskowiec, *Architecture Mouvement Continuité* (October): 1–9. http://web.mit.edu/allanmc/www/foucault1.pdf (print source Michel Foucault, and Jay Miskowiec, *Diacritics*, vol. *16, no. 1: 22–7*).

Hansson, Gunnar D. 2011. Var slutar texten? Behöver man tala? In *Var slutar texten?* ed. Gunnar D. Hansson, 42–84. Gothenburg: Gothenburg University Press.

Hassan, Ihab, and Sally Hassan. 1983. Introduction. In *Innovation/Renovation*, ed. Ihab Hassan, 3–12. Madison, Wisconsin: The University of Wisconsin Press.

Heitmann, Annegret. 2012. Die Medialität des Aphorismus. In *Am Rand. Zur Poetik des skandinavischen Aphorismus*, ed. Katarina Yngborn et al., 213–244. Freiburg: Rombach.

Hejlskov Larsen, Steffen. 1971. *Systemdigtningen. Modernismens tredje fase.* Copenhagen: Munksgård.

Larsson, James, and Leonard Nathan (eds). 1982. Coda. Translated by James Larsson, and Leonard Nathan. In *Songs of Something Else. Selected Poems of Gunnar Ekelöf*, eds. James Larsson, and Leonard Nathan, 33. Princeton: Princeton University Press.

Löw, Martina. 2001. *Raumsoziologie.* Frankfurt a.M.: Suhrkamp.

———. 2004. Raum – Die topologischen Dimensionen der Kultur. In *Handbuch der Kulturwissenschaften*, ed. Friedrich Jaeger and Burkhard Liebsch, vol. 1, 46–59. Weimar: Metzler.

Rilke, Rainer Maria. 1974 [1923]. *Duineser Elegien.* Frankfurt a.M.: Suhrkamp.

Rynell, Elisabeth. 1997. *Hohaj.* Stockholm: Bonniers.

———. 1988. *Sjuk fågel. Dikter.* Stockholm: Bonnier.

———. 2002. *Schneelandschaft.* Translated by Verena Reichel. Munich: Piper.

———. 2006. *I mina hus.* Stockholm: Bonniers.

———. 2009. *Hitta hem.* Stockholm: Bonniers.

———. 2013. *Skrivandets sinne. Essays.* Stockholm: Bonniers.

Sabel, Barbara, and Jürg Glauser. 2004. Einleitung. In *Text und Zeit. Wiederholung, Variante, Serie. Konstituenten literarischer Transmission*, ed. Barbara Sabel and Jürg Glauser, 5–12. Würzburg: Königshausen und Neumann.

Seiler, Thomas. 2004. Figuren des Fremden in der skandinavischen Gegenwartsprosa: Herbjørnsrud, Hermanson, Rynell. *Folia Scandinavica* 8: 17–25.

Wischmann, Antje. 1998. Inger Christensens Roman Azorno. In *Ästhetik der skandinavischen Moderne*, ed. Annegret Heitmann and Karin Hoff, 265–278. Frankfurt a.M.: Lang.

———. 2014. Performing Space – A Modernist *Hembygd*. An Exploration of Sara Lidman's Works. *Journal of Northern Studies*, edited by Umeå University and the Royal Skyttean Society et al. 8 (1): 37–66.

Open Access This chapter is licensed under the terms of the Creative Commons Attribution 4.0 International License (http://creativecommons.org/licenses/by/4.0/), which permits use, sharing, adaptation, distribution and reproduction in any medium or format, as long as you give appropriate credit to the original author(s) and the source, provide a link to the Creative Commons licence and indicate if changes were made.

The images or other third party material in this chapter are included in the chapter's Creative Commons licence, unless indicated otherwise in a credit line to the material. If material is not included in the chapter's Creative Commons licence and your intended use is not permitted by statutory regulation or exceeds the permitted use, you will need to obtain permission directly from the copyright holder.

CHAPTER 9

What Have They Done to My Song? Recycled Language in Monika Fagerholm's *The American Girl*

Julia Tidigs

"This is where the music begins" (Fagerholm 2009a, 1). So reads the very first sentence of Finland-Swedish[1] author Monika Fagerholm's novel *Den amerikanska flickan* (2004; Translated as *The American Girl* 2009). On the first pages of the novel, we find ourselves on the brink of the 1970s, and the American girl herself, Eddie de Wire, finds herself at the amusement park on Coney Island in New York. She enters a self-recording booth and sings, *a capella*:

> Titta mamma, de har förstort min sång.
> Det låter inget vidare. Det gör det inte. Men det betyder ingenting.
> Titta, mamma, vad de har gjort åt min sång. (Fagerholm 2005, 8)

> Look, Mom, they've destroyed my song.
> It does not sound very good. It really does not. But it does not mean anything.
> Look, Mom, what they've done to my song. (Fagerholm 2009a, 2)

J. Tidigs (✉)
University of Helsinki, Helsinki, Finland

This phrase, which appears here in two slightly different versions, returns throughout the novel. It is the novel's phrase above all other, and it is symptomatic in several ways: because it involves music; because it involves translation; because it travels between characters; because reiteration with variation is the way this novel works; and because the phrase comes from somewhere else—it is borrowed from Melanie Safka's song "What Have They Done to My Song, Ma"—and, through this intermedial connection, stands in relation to faraway places. It is the *leitmotif* of *The American Girl*.

I am not the first to pay attention to the song of the American Girl. Several scholars have discussed the role of music and/or reiterations in the novel. In the recent anthology of Fagerholm scholarship *Novel Districts* (2016), edited by Kristina Malmio and Mia Österlund, Lena Kåreland has treated the musical references of the novel as a form of "intermedial transformations"[2] and the role of music for the novel's tone as well as structure: Fagerholm "writes like a composer,"[3] Kåreland (2016, 27) declares. In her research on Fagerholm, Maria Margareta Österholm has mentioned the "sabotaged songs" (2012, 109) in *The American Girl*, and discusses the music in terms of gurlesque (Österholm 2016, 103–4, 111). Kaisa Kurikka (2016) has explored intertextual references and musical figures in connection to Fagerholm's use of repetition with variation in the novel *Diva* (1998) from the perspective of style and minor literature. Jenny Holmqvist (2016) has treated the use of repetition in *The American Girl*, and Bo G. Jansson (2013, 88–91) discusses Fagerholm's musical references and the use of repetition as postmodern traits which—among other things—link the novel's language to oral cultural expressions. Moreover, Anna Helle examines *The American Girl* as postmodern melodrama, as well as the links between death and affect in the novel and for its readers (Helle 2013, 2016). Helle draws attention to the use of reiteration with variation on the level of both phrase and story, and has also touched upon the importance of music and its connection to melodrama in the novel.[4]

Regardless of the ample previous attention that has been given to these features of Fagerholm's works, I do believe that there is more to explore, especially concerning the circumstance that many of the references and quotes in *The American Girl* are translated from other languages than the language of the novel, Swedish. Some of these quotes and references—though not all—are repeated. Some of them—though not all—are musical references. From the perspective of literary multilingualism, the translated quotes—often musical, often reiterated—appear to be on the edge, or rather, on the border zone of multilingualism, as I will show in the final part of this chapter. This is a zone where music, intermediality, translation, and multilingualism are in contact.[5] An added emphasis on translation, I argue, can further illuminate the linguistic practices of Fagerholm's novel, not least the spatiality of its language.

At a glance, it can seem that questions of language and translation are painfully absent in spatially oriented literary studies. In literary multilingualism studies, however, the use of multilingualism in the literary construction of different geographical places (and their inhabitants) have been put under investigation (see e.g., Tidigs 2009, 2014; Malmio 2011; Wirth-Nesher 2006; Pultz Moslund 2011). More importantly for the purposes of this chapter, literary multilingualism studies have paid ample critical attention to what, to a high degree, is a distinct spatial anchoring of languages in Western society during the last couple of centuries, namely nationalist language ideology. Just as conceptions of space are historically situated, as Robert T. Tally Jr. (2013, 17–42) has delineated, the manner in which language has been conceptualized in spatial terms as well as in relation to geographical places, has altered historically.

The birth of the modern nationally oriented conception of language involved a spatialized conception and anchoring of language in at least two distinct, yet related ways. The first involves the individual, the so-called native speaker, whose body becomes a *container* for the *mother tongue*. As Jacques Derrida (1998) and Yasemin Yildiz (2012, 6–14)—following Derrida—have emphasized, the nationalist conception of the mother tongue relies upon the idea of ownership of the native language, an ownership passed down from birth (through the mother). The "native" language of the individual is imagined to be spatially contained inside a body, and thus anchored physically in that body from birth. In this chapter, however, I will, through my reading of Fagerholm's novel, contrast this rather stationary conception of linguistic and emotional bindings with a conception of language that places movement at the center.

The other way nationalist language ideology has anchored language spatially is in terms of (geographical) space. Nationalism's motto of one language, one people, and one territory inscribes a mutual, fixed, relationship between language and geographical space through the (presumed) speakers of the "mother tongue" who reside there. Again, the idea of ownership is important, namely the collective ownership of the geographical nation(-state) on behalf of the people. Languages are imagined to *reside* in and intrinsically *belong* to a territory (in contrast to simply being spoken, to a various degree, by individuals who can stay in or move to or from a geographical area and also use languages in areas other than those where a language is most commonly spoken). It is significant that Gilles Deleuze and Félix Guattari (1986), in their attempt to make visible the processual, dynamic, power-fused, and unstable character of this spatial anchoring of language and place, use terms that contain the notion of *territory*: deterritorialization and reterritorialization. Although this chapter does not employ Deleuze and Guattari's terminology throughout, my investigation of literary language likewise puts a focus on movement and the temporal instability of spatio-linguistic constellations.

In *Cities in Translation*, Canadian scholar Sherry Simon explores the multilingualism of cities such as Montreal and Barcelona. Simon urges us to *listen* to the city: "Much of the abundant literature in recent decades has emphasized the visual aspects of urban life. And yet the audible surface of languages, each city's signature blend of dialects and accents, is an equally crucial element of urban reality" (Simon 2012, 1). This is in line with Bertrand Westphal's reminder of taking a "polysensuous approach" to geocritical studies: "Geocriticism promotes the empire of the senses, a polysensuous approach to places—places meaning concrete or realized spaces. Most of the time, places are perceived with our eyes, but it seems most appropriate to diversify sensing to include the sounds, smells, tastes, and textures of a place" (Westphal 2011, xiv). Although Simon's object of investigation is a non-literary city and mine is a literary text, I am inspired by both the implicit polysensuous approach of her study and her focus on the "*puntos suspendidos*, the areas of negotiation, the spaces where connections are created through translation" (Simon 2012, 2). Thus, I aim to explore Fagerholm's translated and borrowed phrases as precisely such polysensuous connective points where the Swedish of the novel is in dynamic contact with different languages outside of it.

In this chapter, I will first read Fagerholm's novel through its use of borrowed and translated phrases. What role do they play in the novel that they traverse? Thereafter, I will continue with a discussion of how this use of language affects the novel's readers by facilitating a reading/sounding experience and, by way of extension, challenges dominant conceptions of linguistic spatiality in Finland-Swedish literature.

Before these questions of multilingualism, translation, and spatiality are explored, however, the very practical conundrum that the question of translation poses for this chapter needs to be addressed. Most of the quotes that comprise the topic of this chapter come from English and appear in Swedish translation in Fagerholm's *Den amerikanska flickan*. Discussing them in English, and with references to the English translation, *The American Girl*, makes this multilingual factor almost invisible and difficult to grasp. I try to tackle this problem by offering the references to the novel in both Swedish and English; however, nothing can alter the fact that some readers see a text in Swedish with translated quotes in it, and some readers see an English text with English quotes in it. I will return to this question of translation and re-translation at the end of the chapter.

A Rumble of Borrowed Words and Sounds

Monika Fagerholm (b. 1961) is probably the most prominent writer in contemporary Finland-Swedish literature; she is also highly successful in Sweden, where she has received several of the most prestigious literary awards.[6] Fagerholm can also be considered a feminist cult writer with her coming of age novel *Diva* (1998). The novel *The American Girl* (2004) is, among many things, a story of love, friendship, and play between two girls, Sandra Wärn and Doris Flinkenberg, who become obsessed with the mysterious death of the American Girl, Eddie. Eddie is said to have drowned in a lake close to where Sandra and Doris live, but at the beginning of the novel, her body has not yet been found. In the end, it is the boisterous yet fragile Doris who takes her own life, while Sandra grows up to be a singer.

Multilingualism and linguistic heterogeneity has formed an important feature of Fagerholm's literary works since her debut with the story collection *Sham* in 1987. In *The American Girl* alone, there is much to explore: from the estrangement of Swedish by syntactic means that is Fagerholm's *tour de force* (see Dahl 2015), through the more "traditional," lexical multilingualism with occasional lines in English, German and French, and her sporadic use of dialectally marked language, to parodic episodes marked by "Swenglish" (see Fagerholm 2005, 343–7; this kind of language disappears in English translation, see Fagerholm 2009a, 355–9). For the purposes of this chapter, however, I will confine myself to the translated phrases.

As Kaisa Kurikka and Anna Helle have shown, the repetition of borrowed phrases, worn and torn when they travel between characters, is a central feature of Fagerholm's writing (Kurikka 2016, passim.; Helle 2013, 13ff.; Helle 2016, 84, 91). The many quotes from books, films, and songs are most prominently featured in *Diva* and in the diptych "The End of the Glitter Scene," comprising *The American Girl* from 2004 and *Glitterscenen* from 2009 (translated as *The Glitter Scene*, 2010). *Diva* is replete with quotes and intertextual references—one that has achieved cult status is the line from an Inger Lundmark poem, "*Det enda som hjälper mot tankar är hud*" ("The only help against thoughts is skin"). In *Diva*, an afterword with the heading "Loans, quotations" informs readers of the origin of some of the borrowed phrases, although the attribution is sometimes vague.[7] Not all loans are declared; for instance, the important recurring phrase "*Kom upp och se mig, få mig att le*" is not revealed to be a translation of "Make Me Smile (Come Up and See Me)" by Steve Harley & Cockney Rebel.

In *The Glitter Scene* repetition is driven to extremes in terms of both phrase reiteration and storytelling. In the Swedish original, *Glitterscenen* bears the subtitle "*och flickan hon går i dansen med röda gullband*"[8] ("And the girl joins the dance with red golden ribbons"; the subtitle is lacking from the English translation) and is *meta* in relation to its stylistic and narrative devices; it comments repeatedly on its own method—through music: "The folksong. A repetition in time and space. Such a different way of understanding time" (Fagerholm 2010, 80; "Folkvisan. En upprepning i tid och rum. Ett sådant annorlunda sätt att uppfatta tiden" Fagerholm 2009b, 69) (see also Kåreland 2016, 27).

If *The Glitter Scene* is a folksong, then an accurate description of *The American Girl* would perhaps be "sabotaged folk rock." In *The American Girl*, reiteration is crucial: the story of the mysterious death of the American girl Eddie de Wire is told time and again, in different versions. Musical references play an even greater role than in *Diva*, and in contrast to the folksong obsession of *The Glitter Scene*, the multilingual aspect is more prominent in *The American Girl*. To name but a few examples: the Tennessee Williams quote "Ingen kände min ros i världen utom jag" (Fagerholm 2005, 14–15; "Nobody knew my rose of the world but me," Fagerholm 2009a, 8–9); "*Jag är INTE kär. Det är bara ett tokigt skede jag genomlever nu*" (Fagerholm 2005, 389, see also 373) from 10cc's old hit "I'm not in love … it's just a silly phase I'm going through," (Fagerholm 2009a, 402, see also 386); "Hjärtat är en hjärtlös jägare" (Fagerholm 2005, 14, 2009a, 8), a variation of Carson McCullers's *The Heart is a Lonely Hunter*; "*Bergen lever upp till tonerna av musik*" (Fagerholm 2005, 247; "The hills are alive with the sound of music," Fagerholm 2009a, 254), the lead song of the musical *The Sound of Music*. Also noteworthy in connection to this is the circumstance that Eddie's distant relation, whom she boards with, is called Fröken ("Miss") Andrews.[9] There is Doris's nickname Doris Dag, which in English turns her into "Doris Day." And when

I read the phrase "*Bär Doris over mörka vatten*" (Fagerholm 2005, 15, 239), it always brings to mind the Swedish version of Simon and Garfunkel's "Bridge over Troubled Water," "Som en bro över mörka vatten ska jag bära dig" ("I will carry you/Like a bridge over troubled waters").[10]

There are many more of these kinds of phrases, including many Swedish quotes and song lyrics, which are recycled in the novel: the folksong "*Jag gick mig ut en afton uti en lund så grön*" (Fagerholm 2005, 309, see also 309–17; "*I walked out one evening, out into a grove so green*," Fagerholm 2009a, 319); Swedish early twentieth century poet Dan Andersson's "Omkring tiggarn från Luossa" that was made into a hit in the 1970s by popular Swedish folk group the Hootenanny singers (Fagerholm 2005, 243, 2009a, 250); "ÄR DET VERKLIGEN FREEED VI VILL HA … TILL VARJE TÄNKBART PRIS?" (Fagerholm 2005, 217; "IS IT REALLY PEACE WE WANT, AT ANY CONCEIVABLE COST?," Fagerholm 2009a, 241), the chorus of the hit "Fred" ("Peace") by leftist Swedish "progg" group Hoola Bandoola Band.[11] Doris's boyfriend Micke Friberg repeats "*Ingen kan älska som vi*," the title of an iconic Swedish youth film, admittedly from the 1980s, featuring the overplayed pop song "Inga kan älska som vi," "*No one can love like us*" (Fagerholm 2005, e.g., 318; Fagerholm 2009a, e.g., 328).

In the author's acknowledgments at the end of the novel, Fagerholm states that she has "at times taken the liberty of translating the lines from well-known musical pieces and from pop songs on my own, so as to be appropriate for the novel's plot" (Fagerholm 2009a, [509]). Here, Fagerholm explicitly acknowledges that song lyrics have been borrowed, incorporated, and translated, and that translation involves activity, choice, and metamorphosis.

A Song Fragment Travels Through a Novel

The entire 500-page novel starts "This is where the music begins" (Fagerholm 2009a, 1). This is, I argue, nothing less than a reading instruction: This is music. Read this book as you would listen to a song. Listen to it. If we do, what happens then to the song of the American girl?

In the introductory scene we are placed on Coney Island. Thus, even when reading the novel in Swedish readers know that the language surrounding the American girl, Eddie, is English: the italicized English line "*Do you need a place to crash?*" in the Swedish original also shows this

(Fagerholm 2005, 7, 2009a, 1). Readers are told that Eddie sings, and the song lines are also rendered in italics: "*Look, Mom, they've destroyed my song. (...) Look, Mom, what they've done to my song*" (Fagerholm 2009a, 2).[12] At this moment, however, the experiences of readers diverge. For when reading this, some readers will *hear* in their minds the following song lyrics, accompanied by Melanie Safka's voice:

> Look what they've done to my song, ma
> Look what they've done to my song
> Well it's the only thing that I could do half right
> And it's turning out all wrong, ma
> Look what they've done to my song (Safka 2015)

Melanie Safka's hit "What Have They Done To My Song, Ma," from 1970, has lent its first line to Fagerholm. For some readers—and I here speak of "real" readers, physical beings that experience the world through their senses, beings who have ties to different languages and different fields of association—for some of the novel's readers, the phrase is also a translated phrase, a phrase to recognize. Simultaneously as they/we read in Swedish, they/we hear this song, and not only the words but also melody, voice, accompaniment.

Here it is worthwhile to point out that Safka's lyrics themselves involve variation and translation, since the song is bilingual. The sixth verse is a translation of the first verse into French:

> Ils ont changé ma chanson, ma
> Ils ont changé ma chanson
> C'est la seule chose que je peux faire
> Et çe n'est pas bon, Ma
> Ils ont changé ma chanson. (Safka 2015)

At this point in the discussion it is important to note that the Melanie Safka connection in *The American Girl* is not a riddle waiting to be solved.[13] The phrase is not effective only in the light of its intermedial connection. Even if read without Melanie Safka, without a perspective of multilingualism, translation, or intermediality, and only as a Swedish phrase within the context of the novel, the phrase still constitutes reiterated, varied, and recycled language—language one can do something with.

What, then, is the presence of this song of the American girl in the novel? Eddie, in Coney Island, records it. The recording is brought to "the District" in Finland. There, the song is present as one of many fragments of names, words, and music that make up the history of the District.[14] The boy Bengt remembers the phrase from his talks with Eddie (Fagerholm 2005, 30, 2009a, 25). Doris and Sandra listen to Eddie's recording. When Sandra "hummed and spoke like Eddie had spoken," the song line is once again present: "*Look, Mom, they've destroyed my song*" (Fagerholm 2009a, 178). Doris "ALMOST started humming the Eddie-song, the American girl's song. She almost thought about telling—everything" (Fagerholm 2009a, 325). She tries to explain to her boyfriend that which Sandra would have understood directly, that the song is "A song that someone wants to sabotage" (Fagerholm 2009a, 325). Sandra, in turn, imagines her mother Lorelei Lindberg "singing the Eddie-song" (Fagerholm 2005, 462, 2009a, 478). The song wanders between characters who sing and speak its words differently, and for whom it functions differently. "Sandra sang and when she sang she felt it so clearly and strongly, she was not pretending to be the American girl, she was her" (Fagerholm 2009a, 174). The song is borrowed, and it has metamorphic qualities—to repeat, with variation, gives the characters possibilities to transform. But at the end of the novel, the song dies. This time, Sandra is in the self-recording booth on Coney Island and when she is about to sing she is lost for words, sees herself from the outside, and the whole situation becomes absurd.[15]

Recurring, commented upon, and often written in italics, the song about the destroyed song is present throughout the novel, and has the ability to express and forebode. Among other things, the central word of "mamma," "ma,"[16] draws attention to the ominous figure of the mother in the novel. Österholm has mentioned that the song expresses that which Doris and Sandra cannot speak of in direct words: how they both were abandoned by their mothers (Doris's mother who mistreated her badly, Sandra's mother who left when she and Sandra's father divorced).[17] The song of the American girl/Melanie Safka, however, also addresses itself directly to a mother, and is both foreboding and haunting.[18] The premature deaths of Eddie and Doris are connected to the song as well as with mothers, foster mothers, or mother figures. One could call "the mother" a black hole at the center of "The End of the Glitter Scene": she is a key figure associated with the role of victim as well as perpetrator,—a figure whose actions incite devastating chain reactions but also a figure that is always seen from a great distance. The perspective with Fagerholm is always that of the daughter, but the recurring song lyrics mean that the novel is haunted by the figure of the mother.

Reading the Novel as Song

The phrase from Melanie Safka's song is important for the novel when read solely within the frame of the book, namely for its characters and its theme, but it also alludes to an entire song. What happens with the reading of the book if we listen to that song?

For readers who hear the song when reading *The American Girl*, it sets the tone for the entire novel. In the song, there is a discrepancy between the light melody and the sinister lyrics, with metaphors that are taken literally and become grotesque.[19] This macabre effect is especially evident in the second verse:

> Look what they've done to my brain, ma
> Look what they've done to my brain
> Well they picked it like a chicken bone
> And I think I'm half insane, ma
> Look what they've done to my song (Safka 2015)

The girl in the song has had her brain picked until she is half insane—the simile "picked it like a chicken bone" is impossible not to imagine visually. *The American Girl* is a novel about stories: necessary stories, subversive stories but also dangerous stories, that can pick on your—or Doris's— brain 'til you're half insane.

Further on in the song, the third-to-last verse goes:

> Look what they've done to my song, ma
> Look what they've done to my song, ma
> Well they tied it up in a plastic bag and turned it upside down, ma
> Look what they've done to my song (Safka 2015)

As early as in the first verse, the song is an object that can be destroyed— that is also present in Fagerholm's Swedish translation. In the second-to-last verse, things are taken even further: here, the song is tied up in a plastic bag and turned upside down, sparking associations to asphyxiation. In the novel, the sabotage of a song, albeit a different one than Safka's, becomes literal when Doris shoots the doorbell of Sandra's house to pieces. This is the doorbell that plays "*Nach Erwald und die Sonne. Die Sonne. Die Sonne. Die Sonne*"[20] (Fagerholm 2009a, 68), a phrase that is closely connected to the stories Sandra tells about how her mother was swept away to the alps in her lover Heintz-Gurt's helicopter, stories with big holes in them but that keep picking on Doris's brain (Fagerholm 2009a, 83–9).

An additional important aspect of turning song into object is that the musical references in the book necessarily involve the transformation of transient auditory phenomena—words being sung—that are turned visual and objectified as printed letters on the page when written down. As such, the fragments of songs point toward an oral linguistic realm outside of the text, a realm with which the text is in contact.[21]

Here I return to the third verse:

> I wish I could find a good book to live in
> Wish I could find a good book
> Well if I could find a real good book
> I'd never have to come out and look at
> Look what they've done to my song (Safka 2015)

"I wish I could find a good book, to live in"—in several ways, this is just what happens. "There was this mushy side to Doris Flinkenberg. And in Doris Flinkenberg's head it was accompanied above all by different melodies that she snapped up a bit here and a bit there" (Fagerholm 2009a, 219–20).[22] Doris Flinkenberg, who lived in a realm of easy-listening pop and the stories of crime magazines, gets to live on in Sandra's songs of their games, friendship, and love when Sandra becomes a singer (see Österholm 2016, 111). For Doris the world turned out to be unlivable, a circumstance closely connected to the novel's theme of stories as necessary for survival and simultaneously potent and potentially lethal. But there is yet another dimension to living in the book: Fagerholm has given Safka's song a good book to live in, and not only that, she has placed the song center stage.

In media theorist Lars Elleström's terminology, the translated phrase from Melanie Safka's "What Have They Done to My Song, Ma" can be labeled a "simple representation of a media product" (Elleström 2014, 29).[23] Only the first line of Safka's song is present in Fagerholm's text, its origin is not mentioned and the song not described. However, this apparent "simplicity" does not equal lack of effect: as Elleström notes, "[o]ccasionally, for some perceivers, media representations such as these are not at all simple because they trigger far-reaching associations and interpretations" (Elleström 2014, 29). Indeed, above I have explored the significance of such associations and interpretations for the reading of the novel. Moreover, the form of the reference does not decide its relationship to the novel as whole: while the phrase itself is simple, its deployment in the novel, characterized by repetition with variation, is highly complex. The novel's use of the song is, I argue, only in small part to be viewed as a representation of a specific media product and more as a stylistic and narrative vehicle, a motor for its storytelling and transformation of language.

Language from Elsewhere

In the last part of the chapter I want to discuss what the translated and often repeated phrases do for the experience of reading the novel, as well as for the spatial anchoring—or, rather, dislodgement, of its language.

Borrowed scraps of language crisscross *The American Girl*, moving from character to character, from place to place, being recycled for new purposes. The translated phrases emphasize language as sprung from use, language as something collective, already used, already borrowed, always in transformation (see Deleuze and Guattari 2011, 8, 111 ff.). There is no reiteration without variation and transformation.[24] Already on the first page, "Look, mom, they've destroyed my song" is borrowed from somewhere else, Melanie Safka's song. And Eddie sings *a capella*—itself a variation. Of course, this inevitable mutability is not exclusive for intermedial references: it concerns all language. The translated quotes—that pop out, feel strange, feel familiar—only display this ever more clearly; they turn up the volume, so to speak.

In *Born Translated: The Contemporary Novel in an Age of World Literature* (2015), Rebecca L. Walkowitz turns traditional conceptions of original preceding translation, of what a literary work is, who its readers are, and what reader competence is all about, upside down. According to Walkowitz (2015, 4), literature can be "born translated" in different ways: it can be a question of works that are, for example, "*written for translation*, in the hope of being translated, but they are also often *written as translations* (…). (…) They are also frequently *written from translation*." A feature of so-called born-translated literature is that it "approaches translation as medium and origin rather than as afterthought. Translation is not secondary or incidental to these works. It is a condition of their production" (Walkowitz 2015, 3–4). This perspective, I argue, can illuminate a central aspect of *The American Girl* and its language.

In the beginning of *The American Girl*, there was translation: to take something that transforms in the process, and to extract something new from it. With translation and variation, Fagerholm can transport a tone, evoke a specific historical moment, awaken associations and moods among her readers, but also make the Swedish of her novel strange and new. This is a subtle affair. Walkowitz (2015, 32–3) emphasizes that the born-translated literature of late modernity is not defined by particularist language meant to be decoded by select, "competent" readers.[25] Instead, "contemporary novels have developed strategies of multilingualism designed for the foreign, nonfluent, and semifluent readers who will encounter them" (Walkowitz 2015, 44), for example the "narration" of languages, where the presence of foreign languages is signaled without the languages being represented directly in the text. *The American Girl* does something similar in its involvement with other languages: the translated phrases can be "decoded" in the sense that readers can recognize them from elsewhere, but the understanding or enjoyment of the novel is not dependent on readers doing so, nor do they make the novel less "approachable." The intertextual and intermedial connections are, however, a sign of the novel being born *in translation*. *The American Girl* begins in several languages, in several places, in several media.

Yet another effect of this overflow of references, clichés, reiterations, is that we start reading phrases that are *not* borrowed from another book, or film, or song, *as if* they were loans, as if they were translations, as if they were handed down, collective, recycled language—which in the end they are.

Walkowitz notes the way multilingualism and translation challenge the spatio-linguistic constructs of nationalism, where language and territory are locked together in ordered pairings: "Once literary works begin in several languages and several places, they no longer conform to the logic of national representation" (Walkowitz 2015, 30). In the early twentieth century, a Finland-Swedish language norm was established in linguist Hugo Bergroth's very influential *Finlandssvenska. Handbok till undvikande av provinsialismer i tal och skrift* (1917, "Finland-Swedish: A Handbook for the Evasion of Provincialisms in Speech and Writing"). Bergroth's ideal was a Finland-Swedish as similar to the Swedish spoken and written in Sweden as possible, and he explicitly urged writers of poetry and prose to learn to conform to this norm in their works. For a great part of the following century, the central question regarding the linguistic heterogeneity of Finland-Swedish literature was: How is Finland to be depicted entirely in the Swedish language, when life in Finland is rarely lived entirely (or even mostly) in Swedish? (See Ekman 2011, 34–47). When literary language did diverge from the Finland-Swedish language norm, either by inclusion of regionalisms or Finnish words or phrases, this linguistic heterogeneity was most often interpreted as a sacrifice of universal comprehensibility for the sake of authenticity, that is, showing readers how Finland-Swedes "really speak" (see Tidigs 2016).

Fagerholm's language, however, transgresses the paradigm of authenticity versus comprehensibility. Previously, Kristina Malmio (2012) has shown how Fagerholm opened up Finland-Swedish prose to the world with the help of pop culture in *Diva*.[26] In *The American Girl*, the transatlantic connection is visible from the start, both in the story and in the novel's language. This language, with its multitude of references, strange syntax and occasional Swenglish, is always language from elsewhere. For *The American Girl*—transatlantic, heterogeneous but in a non-organic manner—there is no given, no seemingly "organic" connection between word and place. The language of the novel is not about realistic depiction of life along the Finnish south coast; rather, it concerns tone, atmosphere, and time.

As mentioned at the beginning, the recycled language of the novel can be viewed as belonging to a border zone of literary multilingualism. Strictly speaking, in the case of the translated phrases, no foreign language is present on the page. It is, however, possible to read this kind of literary language as Yasemin Yildiz reads literal translations. In *Beyond the Mother Tongue: The Postmonolingual Condition*, Yildiz (2012, 144, 168) discusses the literary use of literal translations in Emine Sevgi Özdamar's works as a form of multilingualism that is simultaneously visible and invisible, and as a form that transforms *both* of the involved languages. In *The American Girl*, the translation from English transforms Swedish, and the Swedish translation is able to extract something new from the English.

Furthermore, the seeming lack of multilingualism, that is, the explicit presence of a foreign language, is valid only if we look solely at the book page and not consider the actual reading experience. In an article on intermedial connections between music and literature, Axel Englund has stressed how "the arts (…) exist simultaneously in the mind of the percipient" (Englund 2010, 79). If we consider the literary work not only as the text on the page but as the text in contact with a reader, that is, that the literary work comes into being in the meeting of text and reader, then we do find ourselves in a multilingual border zone. Then, *The American Girl* comes into existence in the meeting between text and all the texts and songs—among them Melanie Safka's—that are opened up inside readers. Elleström (2010, 23) has acknowledged the "inner sound experiences produced by the mind" of the reader of poetry. When coming into contact with intermedial references, the fact that the text consists only of printed words in Swedish, and that Eddie is said to sing *a capella*, does not stop some of the readers from hearing the music. In instances such as these, these sound experiences in the minds of readers concern not only words but also music, and not only the tenor of a voice but also accompaniment, rhythm, and so on. Readers/listeners do not disjoin sound from semantics in an abstract way, when they read and hear a song in their heads. Just as Sandra hears the echo of the voice of the deceased Doris in her head, just as the "mushy side" of Doris was accompanied by melodies, readers *hear* echoes of schlagers, pop songs, and folksongs. Through the presence of the song references, the literary work becomes a multilingual soundscape, created by and for every reader-listener in an endless series of slightly different versions.

Continuous Transformation

In this chapter I have explored the presence of translated and transformed song lyrics in *The American Girl* through a lens of translation, multilingualism, and spatiality. The borrowed, traveling, and collectively repurposed fragments of songs and phrases from English emphasize language as variation and transience. As Daniel Heller-Roazen expresses this ever-fleeting movement of language, in dialogue with Montaigne and Dante:

> The beginning and the ending of a tongue are perhaps best grasped in the terms afforded by Montaigne. They can be seen as nothing other than two moments in the course of the "continual variation" by which every language "runs away" from its speakers and "deforms itself," (…).
> (…) Hence the vanity of all attempts to slow or stop the fleeting course of languages. Whether they are nationalist or international, philological or ecological, such projects are united in the belief that speech is an object in which linguists can, and must, intervene to recall and conserve the identity from which it seems to be departing. In their aim to hold on to the forms of

speech a tongue has already cast off, such efforts are futile at best. One way or another, a tongue will continue in our time to change "by half," running away and deforming itself as it does, for a language, as Dante wrote, "can never remain the same," and, whether we like it or not, it will continue "every day," in the words of the essayist [Montaigne], to slip out of our hands. (Heller-Roazen 2005, 74–5)

In its emphasis on repetition with variation, Fagerholm's novel challenges the postulates of nationalist thinking about language and literature, forsaking the idea of linguistic stability so crucial to it. On account of its continuous reliance on translation, it also challenges the literary ideal of originality also crucial to modern literature. The translated fragments demonstrate language not as individual expression of the writer's soul but instead as a common resource of already used sentences, ready to be put to use, put into circulation again.

In its insistence on mobility and translation, Fagerholm's novel is distinctly late modern. The transatlantic language of the novel is on the move between people and places, not locked in a relationship to any certain place or to the body of any certain speaker. In *The Sociolinguistics of Globalization*, Jan Blommaert (2010, 2) acknowledges how globalization has "dislodged" "the traditional concept of 'language.'" The artifactualized image of language of modernity must, according to Blommaert, be replaced with "a view of language as something intrinsically and perpetually mobile, through space as well as time, and *made for* mobility" (xiv)—just like the language of Fagerholm's novel. Late modernity, and *The American Girl*, lets language have free reign with its focus on use instead of expression of identities, national or individual (in the form of the "mother tongue").

As mentioned in the introduction, *The American Girl* does not only begin in translation, it is also a novel that has been translated—into English among other languages. In translation, things start to happen with the originally translated phrases. In the case of the American girl's song, it is not only Fagerholm's translation-in-original, but also Katarina E. Tucker's English translation that make use of variation:

> She pushes Record and then she sings.
> *Look, Mom, they've destroyed my song.*
> It does not sound very good. It really does not. But it does not mean anything.
> *Look, Mom, what they've done to my song.* (Fagerholm 2009a, 2)

This is not the wording of Safka's song; when seemingly "returning" to English, the phrase does not return to its "original" wording.[27] The translation clearly privileges Fagerholm's Swedish version and not the English "original" phrases that were borrowed into it. I do not know if Tucker was aware of the connection to the Melanie Safka song when she translated these lines and chose "Mom" instead of "ma"; in the translator's acknowledgments at the end of *The American Girl*, Fagerholm's cooperation is mentioned (Fagerholm 2009a, [511]). In the end, however, it is strangely effective. When Walkowitz advocates a new definition of world literature for the late modern era, this is not the world literature dependent on nineteenth-century conceptions of it as "a container for various national literatures" that in themselves are seen as countable and separate entities, and as a literature which privileges a so-called primary or native audience (Walkowitz 2015, 30). Instead, Walkowitz argues for world literature as a "series of emerging works, not a product but a process" and which "privileges target: the analysis of convergences and divergences across literary histories" (Walkowitz 2015, 30).[28] She stresses: "a work may be produced several times, through adaptation, rewriting, and translation" (Walkowitz 2015, 31).

Seen from this perspective, Tucker's translation continues the work that Fagerholm's original work was already employed with: repetition, with variation. Fagerholm's Swedish translations are both same and different; they have already liberated themselves from the English "source." In English once more—as in translation into other languages—the phrases continue this movement whilst simultaneously carrying their past with them, like a note, or an echo.

Notes

1. Finland-Swedish/Finland-Swede (Swedish: *finlandssvensk*) is the accepted term for Swedish speakers from Finland. The coining of *finlandssvensk* in the 1910s was part of the formulation of national consciousness on behalf of Finland's Swedish-speaking minority, to a large extent as a result of the Finnish national awakening during the latter half of the nineteenth century (see Mustelin 1983).
2. Kåreland highlights the importance of intermediality in Fagerholm's works: "Intermedial transformations, that is the relationship and interaction between structures and devices from different art fields such as visual art, film and music, are typical of Fagerholm's authorship" (Kåreland 2016, 27).

3. "She transforms literature into music and the importance of music is prominent in her writing as an underlying structure. She writes like a composer, using a broken prose, where the sentences sometimes are unfinished and intertwined. In her texts, as in music, one theme attaches to another and the chords are repeated. Circles and repetitions of phrases and words go in and out of each other as themes in a piece of music" (Kåreland 2016, 27).
4. Helle primarily connects repetition with variation in the novel to the effect of ambiguity (Helle 2013, 13, 2016, 84, 91). On music and melodrama, see, for example, Helle (2016, 86).
5. Because I aim to examine the connections between translation and intermediality, it is important to make a distinction between the concepts: in this chapter, translation refers solely to the relationship between languages, such as Swedish and English. It is not used to describe intermedial relationships, such as the presence of song lyrics in a literary text or other kinds of intermedial connections. Thus, intermediality refers to the presence of musical references in the novel while translation refers to such references having been translated from one language to another.
6. In 2005, Fagerholm received the August Prize (Augustpriset) and the Göteborgs-Postens Literature Prize as well as the Aniara Prize for *The American Girl*, and in 2016, Fagerholm was the recipient of the Swedish Academy Nordic Prize, also referred to as "the little Nobel." She has also been the recipient of several Finnish literature awards.
7. For example, "har Jouko Turkka sagt någngång nånstans" ("has Jouko Turkka said sometime somewhere," Fagerholm 1998, [447]). Jouko Turkka (1942–2016) was a prominent Finnish theater director and writer.
8. The phrase comes from a well-known Swedish singing game, danced and sung at Midsummer or Christmas celebrations.
9. The name Fröken Andrews bears associations to the actress Julie Andrews, who not only played the lead role in *Sound of Music* but also in the stage production of the musical *My Fair Lady* (in the motion picture, Eliza Doolittle is played by Audrey Hepburn, who also played Holly Golightly in the adaptation of Truman Capote's *Breakfast at Tiffany's*, to which there are also Eddie references in *The American Girl*). In *My Fair Lady*, an important feature are sentences used for language instruction; in Fagerholm's novel, Fröken Andrews makes sisters Rita and Solveig repeat such phrases in order to learn English (Fagerholm 2005, 435, 2009a, 450).
10. "*Carry Doris over troubled water*" (Fagerholm 2009a, e.g., 9); "*Carry Doris over dark waters*" (Fagerholm 2009a, 245).
11. On the album, the song is called "Fred (till [for] Melanie)"—band member Mikael actually wrote the song as a response to the song "Peace Will Come (According to Plan)" by none other than Melanie Safka (www.

mikaelwiehe.se/komment_fred.htm). "Progg" refers to a left-wing and anti-commercial musical movement in Sweden during the 1960s and 1970s and should not be confused with progressive rock in general.
12. "*Titta mamma, de har förstört min sång.*"; "*Titta, mamma, vad de har gjort åt min sång*" (Fagerholm 2005, 8).
13. The Melanie Safka connection has been mentioned by, for example, Helle (2016, 86–7) and Österholm (2016, 105); the song was also sung onstage in the dramatic adaptation of *The American Girl* at Åbo Svenska Theater (Turku Swedish Teater) in 2007.
14. "The District and its history are also in the Winter Garden. Like pictures on the walls, names and words, music. (…) *Look, Mom, they've destroyed my song*" (Fagerholm 2005, 15, 2009a, 9).
15. "She starts singing. An old song. The Eddie-song, which it was once called./Look, Mom, what they've done to my song./They've destroyed it./But it is so stupid. Suddenly she has forgotten the words. The words to THAT song, it is almost unbelievable!/She stops singing, stops completely. Suddenly she sees herself from outside./What in the world is she doing standing there in the booth howling, all alone?/It is absurd" (Fagerholm 2009a, [502]). The heading of this chapter is called "The Day the Music Died. And I Started Living."
16. Melanie Safka's song uses "Ma"; Katarina E. Tucker's English translation of the novel most often employs "Mom."
17. The song "is a trigger for Sandra's transformation to the Marsh Queen but the song also expresses many of the unspoken experiences Sandra and Doris have in common, such as unresolved relationships to the adult women in their lives; they have both been abandoned by their mothers" (Österholm 2016, 105).
18. Helle (2016, 91) mentions the foreshadowing capacity of repetition in the novel, but does not address the example of the American Girl's song in this context.
19. See Helle, whose opinion of the lyrics differs from my own. In Helle's view, Safka's song is not particularly sad, but in the context of *The American Girl* the words sound sinister (Helle 2016, 87).
20. "Nach Ehrwald und die Sonne" is a cabaret number by legendary Swedish performer Povel Ramel.
21. Bo G. Jansson also mentions the song lyrics as a connective link between the text and oral cultural expressions (Jansson 2013, 91).
22. On the over-sentimentality of Doris, see Helle (2016, 94).
23. The distinction between a "simple" and a "complex" representation of a media product is not clear-cut. While Elleström describes the former as for example, a text that "briefly refers to a particular song" (Elleström 2014, 29), the latter "may be focused on a variety of characteristics: from formal

and more abstract traits to features that one tends to relate to content" (Elleström 2014, 31).
24. See Kurikka (2016, 49) on repetition in *Diva*: "Each time the phrase 'the cradle of Western culture' is used, its meaning is changed, while still maintaining the previous uses; thus, it becomes the source of a series of *differences* and repetitions. The only element that remains the same is the act of repetition. These repetitions can be conceptualized as *ritornellos*, refrains that bring about the rhythm and melodies of writing and simultaneously assemble various territories."
25. According to Walkowitz (2015, 32–3), who refers to Doris Sommer, "The exemplary works of non-translation studies tend to feature idiosyncratic diction, portmanteau words, or phrases that gather several national languages into a single sentence. (…) They are born untranslatable in the sense that they do not travel well and in fact often resist it."
26. Malmio specifically mentions how "*Diva* breaks the limits of national literature" through "the use of the 'unnatural' possibilities offered by American popular culture, and of science fiction" (Malmio 2012, 90).
27. A similar process has affected the 10cc quote, where the adjective "silly" (in the song) has gone via "tokigt" in *Den amerikanska flickan* (Fagerholm 2005, 389) to "crazy" in *The American Girl* (Fagerholm 2009a, 402).
28. The traditional conception of world literature that Walkowitz suggests a departure from in contrast "privileges source: distinct geographies, countable languages, individual genius, designated readers, and the principle of possessive collectivism" (Walkowitz 2015, 30).

References

Blommaert, Jan. 2010. *The Sociolinguistics of Globalization*. Cambridge: Cambridge University Press.
Dahl, Alva. 2015. *I skriftens gränstrakter. Interpunktionens funktioner i tre samtida svenska romaner*. Uppsala: Uppsala Universitet.
Deleuze, Gilles, and Félix Guattari. 1986. *Kafka: Toward a Minor Literature*. Translated by Dana Polan. Minneapolis and London: University of Minnesota Press.
———. 2011 [2004]. *A Thousand Plateaus: Capitalism and Schizophrenia*. Translated by Brian Massumi. London and New York: Continuum.
Derrida, Jacques. 1998. *The Monolingualism of the Other or The Prosthesis of Origin*. Translated by Patrick Mensah. Stanford, CA: Stanford University Press.
Ekman, Michel. 2011. *Mä vi blicka tillbaka mot det förflutna. Svenskt och finskt hos åtta finlandssvenska författare 1899–1944*. Helsingfors: Svenska litteratursällskapet i Finland.
Ellestrom, Lars. 2010. The Modalities of Media: A Model for Understanding Intermedial Relations. In *Media Borders, Multimodality, and Intermediality*, ed. Lars Ellestrom, 11–48. New York: Palgrave Macmillan.

―――. 2014. *Media Transformation: The Transfer of Media Characteristics Among Media*. New York: Palgrave Macmillan.
Englund, Axel. 2010. Intermedial Topography and Metaphorical Interaction. In *Media Borders, Multimodality, and Intermediality*, ed. Lars Elleström, 69–80. New York: Palgrave Macmillan.
Fagerholm, Monika. 1998. *Diva: en uppväxts egna alfabet med docklaboratorium (en bonusberättelse ur framtiden)*. Helsingfors: Söderströms.
―――. 2005. *Den amerikanska flickan*. Stockholm: Albert Bonniers förlag.
―――. 2009a. *The American Girl*. Translated by Katarina E. Tucker. New York: Other Press.
―――. 2009b. *Glitterscenen. Och flickan hon går i dansen med röda gullband*. Helsingfors: Söderströms.
―――. 2010. *The Glitter Scene. A Novel*. Translated by Katarina E. Tucker. New York: Other Press.
Helle, Anna. 2013. Tulkinnallinen horjuvuus ja affektit. Kuolema Monika Fagerholmin *Amerikkalaisessa tytössä* ja *Säihkenäyttämössä*. *Avain* 1: 5–22.
―――. 2016. When Love and Death Embrace. Monika Fagerholm's *The American Girl* and *The Glitter Scene* as Postmodern Melodrama. In *Novel Districts: Critical Readings of Monika Fagerholm*, ed. Kristina Malmio and Mia Österlund, 83–98. Helsinki: Finnish Literature Society.
Heller-Roazen, Daniel. 2005. *Echolalias: On the Forgetting of Language*. New York: Zone Books.
Holmqvist, Jenny. 2016. 'Skott, jag tror jag hör skott.' Bruket av repetition i Monika Fagerholms roman *Den amerikanska flickan*. *Tidskrift för litteraturvetenskap* 3–4: 79–95.
Jansson, Bo G. 2013. *Ljuga vitt och brett utan att ljuga. Den svenska prosaberättelsen i den postmoderna skärmkulturens tidevarv: filosofisk grund, innehåll och form*. Falun: Högskolan Dalarna.
Kåreland, Lena. 2016. Re-Imagining Girlhood. The Revision of Girls' Books in Monika Fagerholm's *DIVA* and *The American Girl*. In *Novel Districts. Critical Readings of Monika Fagerholm*, ed. Kristina Malmio and Mia Österlund, 25–37. Helsinki: Finnish Literature Society.
Kurikka, Kaisa. 2016. Becoming-Girl of Writing. Monika Fagerholm's *DIVA* as Minor Literature. In *Novel Districts: Critical Readings of Monika Fagerholm*, ed. Kristina Malmio and Mia Österlund, 38–52. Helsinki: Finnish Literature Society.
Malmio, Kristina. 2011. Ut i vida världen. Flerspråkighet i några finlandssvenska romaner på 1990- och 2000-talen. In *Både och, sekä että. Om flerspråkighet. Monikielisyydestä*, ed. Heidi Grönstrand and Kristina Malmio, 293–317. Helsingfors: Schildts.
―――. 2012. Phoenix-Marvel Girl in the Age of *fin de siècle*. Popular Culture as a Vehicle to Postmodernism in *Diva* by Finland-Swedish author, Monika

Fagerholm. In *Nodes of Contemporary Finnish Literature*, Studia Fennica Litteraria 6, ed. Leena Kirstinä, 72–95. Helsinki: Finnish Literature Society.
Moslund, Sten Pultz. 2011. The Presencing of Place in Literature: Toward an Embodied Topopoetic Mode of Reading. In *Geocritical Explorations: Space, Place, and Mapping in Literary and Cultural Studies*, ed. Robert T. Tally Jr., 29–43. New York: Palgrave Macmillan.
Mustelin, Olof. 1983. 'Finlandssvensk' – kring ett begrepps historia. In *Svenskt i Finland 1. Studier i språk och nationalitet efter 1860*, ed. Max Engman and Henrik Stenius, 50–70. Helsingfors: Svenska litteratursällskapet i Finland.
Österholm, Maria Margareta. 2012. *Ett flicklaboratorium i valda bitar. Skeva flickor i svenskspråkig prosa från 1980–2005*. Stockholm: Rosenlarv förlag.
———. 2016. The Song of the Marsh Queen. Gurlesque and Queer Desire in Monika Fagerholm's Novels *The American Girl* and *The Glitter Scene*. In *Novel Districts: Critical Readings of Monika Fagerholm*, ed. Kristina Malmio and Mia Österlund, 99–116. Helsinki: Finnish Literature Society.
Safka, Melanie. 2015 [1970]. *Candles in the Rain*. Talking Elephant Records.
Simon, Sherry. 2012. *Cities in Translation: Intersections of Language and Memory*. London and New York: Routledge.
Tally, Robert T., Jr. 2013. *Spatiality*. London and New York: Routledge.
Tidigs, Julia. 2009. 'Here I Am at Home – Here I Am in a Foreign Land'. Multilingualism, Modernism and (De)Territorialization in the Works of the Finland-Swedish Writer Elmer Diktonius. In *Europa! Europa? The Avant-Garde, Modernism and the Fate of a Continent*, ed. Sascha Bru, Jan Baetens, Benedikt Hjartarson, Peter Nicholls, Tania Ørum, and Hubert van der Berg, 359–372. Berlin and New York: Walter de Gruyter.
———. 2014. *Att skriva sig över språkgränserna. Flerspråkighet i Jac. Ahrenbergs och Elmer Diktonius prosa*. Åbo: Åbo Akademis förlag.
———. 2016. Litteraturens språkvariation, kritiken och det finlandssvenska rummets gränser. Kim Weckströms *Sista sommaren*, Kjell Westös *Drakarna över Helsingfors* och debatten om Finlandiapriset 1996. In *Språkmöten i skönlitteratur. Perspektiv på litterär flerspråkighet*, ed. Siv Björklund and Harry Lönnroth, 55–72. Vasa: VAKKI Publications.
Walkowitz, Rebecca L. 2015. *Born Translated: The Contemporary Novel in an Age of World Literature*. New York: Columbia University Press.
Westphal, Bertrand. 2011. Foreword. In *Geocritical Explorations: Space, Place, and Mapping in Literary and Cultural Studies*, ed. Robert T. Tally Jr., ix–xv. New York: Palgrave Macmillan.
Wiehe, Mikael. *Fred (Till Melanie)*. www.mikaelwiehe.se/komment_fred.htm.
Wirth-Nesher, Hana. 2006. *Call It English: The Languages of Jewish American Literature*. Princeton: Princeton University Press.
Yildiz, Yasemin. 2012. *Beyond the Mother Tongue: The Post-Monolingual Condition*. New York: Fordham University Press.

Open Access This chapter is licensed under the terms of the Creative Commons Attribution 4.0 International License (http://creativecommons.org/licenses/by/4.0/), which permits use, sharing, adaptation, distribution and reproduction in any medium or format, as long as you give appropriate credit to the original author(s) and the source, provide a link to the Creative Commons licence and indicate if changes were made.

The images or other third party material in this chapter are included in the chapter's Creative Commons licence, unless indicated otherwise in a credit line to the material. If material is not included in the chapter's Creative Commons licence and your intended use is not permitted by statutory regulation or exceeds the permitted use, you will need to obtain permission directly from the copyright holder.

PART IV

Is This a Possible Space?
Potentialities of Space

CHAPTER 10

"A Geo-ontological Thump": Ontological Instability and the Folding City in Mikko Rimminen's Early Prose

Lieven Ameel

In the Finnish author Mikko Rimminen's novel *Pölkky* (2007; "Woodblock"),[1] set in present-day Helsinki, one of the most disturbing occurrences is the appearance of a gradually widening hole in the skating rink in Kaisaniemi Park. The skating rink is under the supervision of the protagonist of the novel, and the threat posed by the hole is not only directed at the skaters, or at the hypothetical sense of achievement of the protagonist. As is suggested throughout the novel, the expanding hole and the steam rising from it are potentially of much more far-reaching consequences, intimating the possibility that not only the skating rink, but perhaps fictional Helsinki itself is being subjected to a slow but world-threatening upheaval. This event, which threatens the storyworld's spatial environment in Rimminen's second novel, echoes similar events in a range of postmodern literary texts. One parallel is the giant tiger roaming New York's underground in Jonathan Lethem's *Chronic City* (2009), which causes the sudden appearance of gaping holes in the city—a refer-

L. Ameel (✉)
University of Turku, Turku, Finland

ence which is of particular interest for its disturbance in the referential relationship with an identifiable urban environment. Like the hole in *Pölkky*, it presents an unreal and ultimately inexplicable occurrence that contrasts the narrated space and the referential world, but that also threatens the stability of the storyworld itself. Such disturbing events in late modern literature will be examined in this chapter as instances of ontological instability, and approached in terms of *folds* in narrated space. I will focus on Mikko Rimminen's early prose texts. One of the aims of this chapter is to propose a new reading of the author's early prose from the perspective of the texts' apocalyptic undercurrents, which have remained largely unappreciated, and to take into account a little-studied extract from an unfinished novel by Rimminen.[2]

The focus in this chapter is on how the relationship between the fictional city and its referential counterpart is both foregrounded and undermined in a way that destabilizes the ontological status of the storyworlds in question. The texts under discussion here display intimations of apocalypse, inviting the reader to consider whether the ontological instability is located in the perception of the focalizer or narrator, in literary space, or both. The key concepts that will be explored in the analysis of the literary space and storyworld are Brian McHale's *flickering effect* (1987) and Bertrand Westphal's *heterotopic interference* (Westphal 2011, 101). Gilles Deleuze's *fold* (1993) will be proposed here as a heuristic concept to describe how ontological instability in postmodern storyworlds is shaped. I argue that one of the advantages of this concept is the way it defies binary opposites, moving instead toward an understanding of spatial environments in postmodern storyworlds as acting on a holistic, if often paradoxical, continuous plane of meaning.

Cities as Folds

I want to start with a reflection on the relationship between the literary city and its referential counterpart in the literature of late modernity, tracing the potential of the fold for an understanding of postmodern space with the help of Brian McHale's thoughts on postmodernist literature, and Bertrand Westphal's subsequent reading of McHale. McHale, in *Postmodernist Fiction* (1987), has famously argued that postmodern literature is defined by ontological instability—by a profound uncertainty of what can be considered the knowable real in the storyworld. In terms of how space functions within postmodern literature, ontological instability is a feature first of all of the imagined storyworld, but also a characteristic of the referential relationship between the storyworld and the actual world. Brian McHale's (2003, 34) approach toward literary storyworlds is thus essentially engaged in complicating and weakening fiction's "external boundary." In postmodern literary representations of space, it has become increasingly difficult or indeed impossible for the reader to decipher the ontological attributes of the described spatial environment, or the precise referential relationship between the imagined storyworld and the actual world.

Drawing on the work of Roman Ingarden, Brian McHale refers to the metaphors of "iridescence" and "opalescence," coining the term "flickering effect" to describe the irresolvably ambiguous nature of storyworlds in postmodern fiction:

> Ambiguous sentences may project ambiguous objects, objects which are not temporarily but permanently and irresolvably ambiguous. This is not a matter, in other words, of *choosing* between alternative states of affairs, but rather of an ontological oscillation, a flickering effect, or, to use Ingarden's own metaphor, an effect of "iridescence" or "opalescence." And "opalescence" is not restricted to single objects; entire *worlds* may flicker. (McHale 2003, 32)

The visual metaphorizations of "flickering," "iridescence" or "opalescence" suggest that one reality is substituted for another, similar to lights going on or off, or as the angle of view changes. While McHale wants to move away from having to choose, the idea that worlds "flicker" continues to suggest an association with (electric) light, and of worlds subsequently being there and not being there, rather than a continuous and simultaneous state of affairs. In the present reading of postmodern spatialities and their ambiguous ontology, I would like, instead of these heuristic metaphors based on the realm of the visual, to draw on the work of Gilles Deleuze on Leibniz to propose the concept of the fold (Deleuze 1988).

In *Geocriticism* (2011), in the chapter on referentiality, Bertrand Westphal is to my knowledge the first to note the potential of the concept of the fold for analyzing questions of space in postmodern literature. Examining multiple worlds in postmodern literature, Westphal notes that "the representation of the referential world (…) in fiction engages in a process of interactivity between instances of heterogeneous nature brought together in the same world through an interface (…) which is also the means of connection between the elements of this world" and he adds that "this approach is something like the concept of the *fold*, developed by Leibniz in his theory of monads, and taken up by Deleuze in his book on Leibniz" (Westphal 2011, 99). Westphal links the concept of the fold to similar concepts used by McHale and Ingarden, but does not further develop or apply the concept.

THE FOLD: A STUDY OF APPEARANCE AND SUBSTANCE

In his study *Le pli: Leibniz et le Baroque*, Gilles Deleuze (1993) approaches the philosophy of Leibniz and the cultural thinking of the Baroque from the perspective of the fold. The fold is found, according to Deleuze, in the music, architecture, and sculpture of the Baroque, but most explicitly in the philosophy of Leibniz, both in terms of understanding the simultaneous existence of multiple worlds and in terms of the relationship between body and soul. The theological background of Leibniz's thinking, which may at first seem somewhat incompatible with early twenty-first-century literary storyworlds, is also crucial for understanding Deleuze's reading of Leibniz, who posits not a separation, but a linkage and continuation between different possible worlds, between the body and the soul, between appearance and substance, connected by way of a continuous plane, in which the way the plane is folded conditions the relationship.

The fold is a way of describing a world, or worlds, which are connected. Rather than seeing the world in terms of separate, individual units that get smaller the harder one looks (as in an atomist model), in the concept of the fold, "[t]he division of the continuous ought not to be considered as that of sand into grains, but as that of a sheet of paper or of a tunic into folds, in such a way that there can be an infinite number of folds, one smaller than the next, without the body ever dissolving into points or minima" (Deleuze 1993, 231). Conceptualizing the universe in terms of the fold is to think of a fabric that, by the infinitely complex manner in which it is folded, connects everything material and immaterial. The concept of the fold means that it is not necessary to posit a door, window, mirror, or other such separate connection between two different things—what we have is in essence a continuation of the same sphere or structure, folded in different ways: "(…) what Leibniz will continually assert: a correspondence, even a communication between the two levels, between the two labyrinths, between the coils of matter and the folds in the soul" (Deleuze 1993, 229).

For Leibniz, and for Deleuze, the fold is fundamentally a concept that examines the relationship between the body and the soul, a relationship which is described in the metaphor of the spatial interior and exterior:

> The infinite fold separates, or passes between matter and the soul, the facade and the sealed room, the interior and the exterior. For the line of inflection is a virtuality ceaselessly differentiating itself: actualized in the soul it is realized in its own way in matter. It is the Baroque characteristic: an exterior always on the exterior, an interior always on the interior. (Deleuze 1993, 242)

As a concept aimed at transgressing the distinction between interior and exterior, or superior (soul) and inferior (body), the fold as a necessary connection between two different levels provides a useful addition to the conceptual framework used for describing narrative worlds, their interrelations, and their relations to the actual world. In such a worldview, it is thus not necessary to posit a forced choice, or even a "flickering" between one possible world or another—ontological ambiguity is part of a storyworld "unfolding" as a reader moves along the lines of the text, as the film reel unfolds in the projector, or as a narrator or protagonist progresses in time and space.

Inevitably—and this has perhaps been underemphasized in research on postmodern literary ontological instability—the unstable relationship between literary space and its referent may have repercussions for the way in which readers view, in turn, the actual world. As Westphal points out, Brian McHale, in speaking of the interpretation between reality and its heterocosmic representation, "asks a fundamental question that literature formulates regularly. Where is the referent of fiction? What is it? What is its status?" (Westphal 2011, 88) And on the basis of fictional storyworlds, what status can be ascribed to the actual world as it is perceived? This implicit feedback-loop pointing back to the actual world is incidentally also one crucial repercussion of using the heuristic metaphor of the *fold*.

Before analyzing Mikko Rimminen's text, a few words should be said on the different kinds of referentiality Westphal discerns in literature, since the distinction between these different types will be of importance when looking at the ways in which Rimminens' three earliest prose texts posit an imagined Helsinki. In his examination of referentiality, Westphal distinguishes between three kinds of referential relationships, "three types of coupling": "homotopic consensus (knowing that pure conformity is a trick), heterotopic interference, and utopian excursus" (Westphal 2011,

88). "Homotopic consensus" describes a storyworld that would seem to conform closely to the referential world, as in the case of Dickens' London. "Heterotopic interference" refers to a literary text in which a recognizably referential space is radically transformed, as in the case of Henrika Ringbom's Helsinki novel *Martina Dagers Längtan* (1998; "The Longing of Martina Dager"), which adds a river to the center of the referential Helsinki (see Lappalainen 2016). "Utopian excursus," finally, conceives of a referential relation in which the literary space has irreversibly severed the links to a referential, recognizable space. As I hope to show, and following the framework of the fold, Mikko Rimminen's early prose moves gradually from a referential relationship that could be described in terms of a homotopic consensus, through a growing sense of heterotopic interference, toward utopian excursus. But between these different referential relationships, these "types of coupling," there are no clear-cut gaps or incisions—no sense of "uncoupling"—but rather a continuous operation on the same plane, as in the drapery of the storyworld gradually unfolding.

City Folds in *Pölkky*

The city in Mikko Rimminen's second novel *Pölkky* would seem to conform in the closest details to the actual city of Helsinki around the turn of the twenty-first century. And similar to the spatial environment in Rimminen's debut novel *Pussikaljaromaani* (2004; "The Tipplers' Novel," see below), urban space in the novel has an important role as a contextualizer and catalyzer of the plot developments. Part of the dynamics in *Pölkky* is constituted by the opposites composed by the narrator, who is clearly intimately acquainted with his part of Helsinki, and the protagonist, who seems to be utterly unfamiliar with the city on his arrival.[3] The presence of the narrator himself, an almost god-like eye hovering over, but also confined to, the Kaisaniemi area, seems at first the only anomaly in the novel in referential terms.

In the course of the novel, however, the spatial environments are increasingly bent out of the ordinary. The appearance of the hole in the ice of the skating rink is the first indication that cracks in the ontological ordering of the novel are opening up. In the terms used by Westphal, the hole presents a small, but gradually expanding instance of "heterotopic interference" (Westphal 2011, 101). Significantly, the narrator describes the appearance in world-changing terms, referring explicitly to the ontological aspects of the event when describing the sound coming from the hole as "a geo-ontological thump" (Rimminen 2007, 203). A strange thing is unfolding which threatens the normal order, and for which competing causes are given, none of which are ultimately convincing or conclusive. In the pages following the appearance, separate efforts are made to describe the enigmatic hole, and to find a reason for its appearance. It is interpreted alternatively as an "event of magical power," a "natural event" (Rimminen 2007, 204), while one character suggests it is a manmade disaster, caused by "a broken pipe," and notes that "the drainage network of the city is in an intolerably terrible state" (Rimminen 2007, 217). The cause or nature of the widening hole, however, remains unclear throughout the novel.

One way in which meaning is given to the event is by the use of personification. The sound accompanying the appearance is described as "swallowing" ("nielaisu") (Rimminen 2007, 203), implying the sound made by an animal or-human like creature, with the insinuation of the city (or its underworld) as the body. This personification of the spatial environment should be seen in the context of Rimminen's abundant use in the novel of body metaphors, often with violent and aggressive undertones—a metaphorization that has a long tradition in literature of the city (Mäkelä 2015, 12; see also Ameel 2014, 20–3). In the opening pages of the novel, which describe the arrival of the protagonist at the central railway station of Helsinki, the environment is introduced in threateningly personifying terms:

> Sumussa ... bussit olivat möhköytyneet luisiksi ja uhkaavan kookkaiksi organismeiksi ja rakennukset torin ympärillä näyttivät kuin kumartuneen nähdäkseen kulkijan tarkemmin mainoksenpunaisina hehkuvilla silmillään. (Rimminen 2007, 15)
>
> In the fog, the buses ... were chunkified into bony, threateningly bulky organisms and the buildings around the square looked as if they were crouching as if to better see the wanderer with their publicity-red smouldering eyes.

One particularly interesting feature of the personifying description of the environment in this opening scene is that it links the human-like attributes of the spatial environment not with the sentiments of the protagonist, but—rather uncannily—with the activities of the narrator, who stoops to better see the object of his scrutiny. The sense of threat ("smoldering eyes") sits uneasily with the overly chatty tone of the narrator. The sense added by these bodily metaphors is one of a threatening presence in the city, possibly identifiable with the narrator himself, which gradually, in the course of the novel, materializes in the form of the growing sink hole.

The fact that the hole is uncontrollably and incomprehensibly growing forms one of its world-threatening elements—what if it grows indefinitely? There is a second element of uncertainty, constituted by the steam rising from the watery hole, steam that is linked to the possible cause of the hole (a broken drainage or hot-water pipe?), but also to the possible effects of the hole. Throughout the rest of the novel, white steam is described as rising from the hole and folding into the fog that covers the city. (Rimminen 2007, 214) At the end of the novel, the fog—which the reader is entitled at this point to think is perhaps not unrelated to the hole—is again referred to, this time with explicit reference to the fog described in the opening pages of the novel:

> ... vallitsi kaikkialla jälleen riekaleinen sumu, jollainen kaupunkia tukahdutti jo kertomuksemme alussa ja joka tietysti, ikävä kyllä, vain vahvistaa käsitys- tämme siitä että loppu on nyt lähellä. (Rimminen 2007, 373)
>
> ... again, that ragged fog reigned everywhere, which stifled the city already in the beginning of our narration and which of course, unfortunately, only confirms our perception that the end is now near.

The end is near, because as competent readers, we can be expected to notice that, following the conventions of good storytelling, we are back where we began, in foggy Helsinki. But there are is also another possible interpretation, in which the actual end of the storyworld is near. The narrator claims that it is the presence of the fog which confirms that the end is near, and the wording could also be read as a suggestion that there is in fact a causal relationship between the fog and the end of the world. The description of Helsinki that immediately follows seems at first to confirm that the actual end of the world is at hand, and shows a city uncannily devoid of human presence—and it is in this sense that it looks forward, as I will show in the next section, to Rimminen's subsequent post-apocalyptic manuscript:

> Missään ei näkynyt ensimmäistäkään autoa, ihmistä, muutakaan nisäkästä eikä edes lintua, ja ainoat liikkuvat elementit maisemassa taisivatkin olla rata- pihalla sumun läpi tummana puikkona jostakin jonnekin siirtyvä yksinäinen veturi sekä juuri hiljaa sinne tänne huojahteleva sumu, johon edelleen vaisusti paikallaan ammottavasta lammikosta kohoava höyry sekoittui ja hävisi. (Rimminen 2007, 373)

There was nowhere even a car, or a human being, or another mammal or even a bird to be seen, and the only moving elements in the landscape were probably a lonely locomotive that moved from somewhere to somewhere in the railway yard through the fog like a dark stick and then that very fog that was swaying quietly here and there, and into which the steam, still rising lamely from the motionless gaping pond, mingled and disappeared.

Here, at the end of the novel, the reader is presented with a foggy Helsinki, but the referential relationship with actual Helsinki, which began in terms of a clear "homotopic consensus," has become increasingly complicated. It is a world on the brink of a new ontological realization, in which the fog from the beginning may be interpreted as the first sign and emanation of the "geo-ontological thump" of the hole, a phenomenon which is announced only halfway in the novel. This process gains further meaning when considered in relation to the prose texts published by Rimminen immediately before and after *Pölkky*.

Rimminen's Unwritten Apocalyptic Helsinki Trilogy: "An Extract from a Manuscript"

In *Pölkky*, the way in which the spatial environment gradually unfolds from a recognizable Helsinki to a world in which fog does not only visually veil the surroundings but is a force "reigning" and "stifling" the city—an influence emanating from a threatening, gaping hole—gains importance when considering the novel within the context of Rimminen's early prose, and more particularly, the prose texts written immediately prior to and after *Pölkky*. Upon close inspection, Rimminen's debut novel *Pussikaljaromaani*, his second novel *Pölkky*, and a third unfinished novel, would have together constituted an apocalyptic Helsinki trilogy, in which intimations of threat gradually grow and eventually materialize. Rimminen's third, unfinished novel has received little scholarly attention. Part of the manuscript was read by the author at the prose club "Prosak" in Helsinki (17 March 2009) and the same text was subsequently published in the literary periodical *Nuori Voima*, under the title "Katkelma romaanikäsikirjoituksesta" ("An Extract from a Manuscript") and with the introduction that it is the fourth chapter of a novel with the working title "Dear Brother" ("Hyvä veli"). The story is set in a Helsinki with post-apocalyptic features; only a hovering narrative eye, one man called Jeremias, and a dog are left in an otherwise deserted city, and more specifically in Hakaniemi, Helsinki.

Helsinki in the "Extract" has been "suddenly, mysteriously, and underhandedly apparently emptied, apart from the gulls" ("yhtäkkiä ilmeisesti lokkeja lukuunottamatta salaperäisesti tai -kähmäisesti tyhjentynyt") (Rimminen 2009, 2, 42), with Jeremias the only human being left to represent Helsinki's inhabitants, Finns, and possibly all of humankind (Rimminen 2009, 43). In this description, the possible emptying of the city as envisioned at the end of *Pölkky* seems to have become fact, and the narrator considers the possibility that Jeremias "might for example be something like 'the last man in the world'" ("saattoi olla esimerkiksi jotakin sellaista kuin 'maailman viimeinen ihminen'") (Rimminen 2009, 43)—a possible reference to a prototypical post-apocalyptic text, Mary Shelley's *The Last Man* (1826).[4] The fragment is not long enough to be able to say much about what would have been the attributes of a fully narrated storyworld, and, from the point of view of possible ontological instability, it would seem that a post-apocalyptic world—as depicted in the "Extract"—is inherently less ambiguous than a more open narrative environment that suggests the possibility of end-times without fully actualizing them, as in *Pölkky*.[5] What interests me here is how Rimminen's early prose texts move toward this dramatic end-time, with suggestions and intimations that the spatial environments of a thoroughly familiar Helsinki keep in their folds the possibility of a more disconcerting and threatening environment—the Helsinki that, in the "Extract" has "clicked" into something "unhabitual" (Rimminen 2009, 45). Similar to what happens in *Pölkky* (and, as I argue below, in *Pussikaljaromaani*), the only possible indication of any cause of the upheaval is given by a reference to the city's infrastructure in a manner that arguably transfers human attributes to the spatial environment, in a reference to a "fiery puff emanating from the Hanasaari power plant or somewhere" ("jostakin Hanasaaren voimalaitokselta kantautuvan ärhäkkään puuskahduksen") (Rimminen 2009, 45). In the "Extract," the referential relationship, in terms of the triad proposed by Westphal, has come close to one of "utopian excursus," in which the "narrative *unfolds* at the margins of the referent or around a projected referent in a derealized future" (Westphal 2011, 122; emphasis added). To trace this journey from a seemingly uncomplicated "homotopic consensus" to a disturbed relationship ("heterotopic interference") to an essentially otherworldly reality, it will be necessary to examine in closer detail Mikko Rimminen's debut novel *Pussikaljaromaani*, in which an apocalyptic undercurrent is arguably visible, especially in its play on the literal and metaphorical meanings of language in describing urban space.

To the End of the World: *Pussikaljaromaani*

In *Pussikaljaromaani*, a sense that all is not right in the city of Helsinki is repeatedly discernible in the spatial descriptions. The environment is recurrently read in phantasmagorical terms, suggesting that everyday environments provide points of entry into dream-like, otherworldly, highly eventful phenomena or environments, transformed by the visionary capacities of the main focalizer. This focalizer can be associated for most of the novel with one of the three young men, Marsalkka ("Marshall"). In one revealing example, during a tram journey from Kallio to Hakaniemi, a large office block with official agencies seems to the narrator to hide behind its walls a labyrinthine space where one could "wear down one's joints on spiral staircases drilling downward in the black mud of fundamental matter as if in a horror funfair DNA accelerator" ("kuluttaa nivelensä tomuksi perimmäisyyksien mustaan multaan kairautuvissa kierreportaissa kuin jossain kauhuhuvipuistomaisessa DNA-höykyttimessä") (Rimminen 2004, 169). The Lilliputian position of everyday citizens vis-à-vis official institutions and agencies, and the imagined attempt to gain access to their decision-making processes is projected into a metaphor (the "drilling spiral staircases") and a simile (the "DNA accelerator") of hyperbolic proportions that is in tune with the narrator's sympathy for the common man's plight in late modern society. One way to interpret such metaphorizations is to see them as in tune with an age-old "correspondence method" in city literature pioneered by Baudelaire (see Ameel 2014, 117–31; Keunen 2001), or with the rhetorical technique of pathetic fallacy, which transfers the feelings of the lyrical observer to (natural) spatial environments (see Evernden 1996). Yet somewhat disconcertingly there is also, I would argue, a sense that some of these descriptions are not to be taken unequivocally as metaphorical—that it remains unclear to what extent there is the possibility, within this ontological world, that there are *real* uncanny, threatening forces hovering at the edge of the focalizer's sight—and that the stairs in the building do not lead to a mundane cellar floor, but in actuality into "the black mud of fundamental matter." Once the reader becomes attuned to such a possibility, references to such a reading begin to abound—a realization that around the folds and edges of a representational Helsinki, there are references to a world with entirely different ontological conditions.

A sense of ontological uncertainty is enforced, for example, by recurrent references to the course of the sun in the firmament, in which the sun does not refer back to a succession of time that frames the events of this one-day novel in a logically developing and everyday experience, but in which, on the contrary, the trajectory of the sun is described as out of joint. Suggestions are made that the sun is stuck on its trajectory, or that its proximity threatens to ignite the earth (Rimminen 2004, 162, 154–5).[6] And when, at the dawn of a new day at the end of the novel, the sun is seen—almost unexpectedly—to rise again "amongst men in order to keep its promise, as is its habit," as if it were a heathen God, it looks to the narrator more like Armageddon than a new beginning: "[A]nd exactly there that disc caught some kind of cupola or bulge which made it look like a cheese spindle of Armageddon floating above the roofs" ("ihmisten ilmoille pitämään lupaustaan, tapansa mukaan, ja juuri siihen sen kiekon kohdalle osui joku kupoli tai pullistuma niin että se näytti joltain kattojen yllä leijuvalta harmagedonin juustosuikerolta") (Rimminen 2004, 321). In *Pussikaljaromaani*, a concrete sense of urban infrastructure under pressure is linked to water management and the threat of a Biblical flood—one sense in which it arguably looks forward to *Pölkky*.[7] The fairly uneventful events are punctuated, halfway through the novel, by a storm of considerable proportions that is followed by an electricity blackout, both of which are described as all-threatening and as incomprehensible in their causes and their effects. Typical of the hyperbolic language used to describe events in the novel, the exact arrival of the storm is described as "everything turning white for a moment," immediately followed by "a completely unreasonable crack as if all the trees of the city had been cut to pieces on the same stroke of the clock" ("(…) kaikki meni vähäksi aikaa valkoiseksi (…) tyystin kohtuuton räsähdys niin kuin kaikki kaupungin puut olisi isketty samalla kellonlyömällä pirstaksi") (Rimminen 2004, 210).[8] The subsequent lightning is described in terms of "a lightning bolt of certainly the whole range of southern Finland" and as resembling an "incomprehensible cosmic cabaret" ("varmaan koko eteläisen Suomen mittainen salama"; "jotain käsittämätöntä kosmista kabareeta") (Rimminen 2004, 236).

The storm is described literally as a "Biblical" event, "Biblical" too in the way in which it is experienced. For reasons that would take too long to describe, the main focalizer and protagonist Marsalkka suddenly starts running through the torrential rain, and the effect of the running, in combination with the rain, takes on quasi-physical proportions: "[T]ime and matter somehow began to curve around that running and despite the indisputable wormholiness, that quasi-physical phenomenon transformed itself quickly into something that somehow felt quite safe" ("aika ja aine rupesivat ikään kuin kaartumaan juoksemisen ympärille ja siitä eittämättömästä madonreikämäisyydestään huolimatta se kvasifysikaalinen ilmiö siinä muodostui nopeasti jotenkin turvalliseksi") (Rimminen 2004, 224). In a quasi-physical phenomenon with the "indisputable" characteristics of a worm hole, time and matter curve, which also has an effect on the experience of the environments: in a moment of epiphany, the nature of the city (or that part of the city) is revealed, with a sense of larger-than-life meaning imbued to everyday environments, which also, somewhat paradoxically, feels "safe":

> (…) koko se osa kaupunkia, koti, mäet ja harjut joiden rinteille suuret laatikkomaiset yksinelämisellä täyteenahdetut talot oli survaistu kuin vääriin koloihin pakotetut palikkatestikapineet tai jotkin jättiläismäiset nopat, (…). (Rimminen 2004, 225)

> (…) that part of the city, home, hills and ridges with on their slopes, large, box-like houses packed full with lonely living jabbed in their place as gizmos from a geometrical shape test forced into the wrong holes, or like giant dice, (…).

This depiction frames the everyday urban landscape as the result of a giant child at play, or as a monument to the power of blind fate (in the form of dice), reinforcing the feeling that the lives of the protagonists and the urban environments are subject to higher, unpredictable forces. Drawing on the work of Christopher Prendergast, the image of the city here as a set of toys for giants at play can be seen as an example of one of the two "most powerful narratives of the contemporary metropolitan condition: stories of end-time and stories of playtime." According to Prendergast, in stories of playtime, "the emphasis on accelerated falling apart (…) is redirected from (…) nightmare to fun, apocalypse to *bricolage*, ruins to waste, to the view of the city as playground and its debris as the material for a kind of urban *fort/da* game (…)" (Prendergast 1992, 207). Crucially, the play is here also a play on language, with humor as the dominant overtone, although there are also darker undercurrents and intimations of world-threatening upheaval.

When not much later in the novel there is a large-scale electricity failure, it is described as the advent of utter darkness, juxtaposed with the earlier total lightness:

> Se oli sellaista pimeää ettei kukaan osannut siihen mitään sanoa, sellaista joka vastaväitteittä nielee kaikki sanat jos siihen ryhtyy huutelemaan. (…) joka paikkaan tunkevaa pimeää, hyvin heikosti ymmärrettävää ja siten myös verraten kuohuttavaa (…). (Rimminen 2004, 269)

> It was the kind of darkness that nobody was able to add any word to it, a darkness that without objections would swallow all your words if you started shouting into it (…) darkness intruding in all places, very weakly comprehensible, and thus also relatively disturbing (…).

The only explanation that is offered for this sudden darkness is made by a man running past, emerging from and then returning to the darkness, who "shouted that a bomb had exploded in the center of the city" ("siinä pimeydessä juoksi joku mies ohi ja huusi että keskustassa on räjähtänyt pommi") (Rimminen 2004, 271). Ultimately, no explanation of any sort is offered, even after the lights return, and the possibility of a bomb is not disproved. Instead, the sense of possible world-threatening disaster is further exacerbated by hyperbolic descriptions of the consequences of the storm. The flooded streets are described in words reminiscent of the Biblical Flood, and the narrator considers the possibility that the lightning has brought the mechanical attractions at the *Linnanmäki* amusement park back to life.[9] A track cleaning tram looks "suspiciously" like "an infernal machine" (Rimminen 2004, 243), and violent and sudden noise leads the narrator to think that "the end of the world is nigh" (Rimminen 2004, 294). The city itself, or rather, the underground network of waste water drainage, is described in personified terms as uttering "gurgling" sounds "whenever a congested sewer tried to get a bit of breath"—again a foreshadowing of events in *Pölkky*. The everyday environment is described as if it contained windows into large-scale catastrophes, as if containing fold-like mirages of other worlds contained in this one. A case in point is the flooded crossroads in the inner-city district of Kallio, which to the narrator suddenly present a submerged epiphany:

> (…) siellä se häämötti, padonrakentamisen kuolettama kiinalaiskylä, rypäs kylmän veden täyttämiä huoneita joissa askareisiinsa jäykistyneet perheet leijailivat huonekalujen seassa hitaasti seinältä toiselle, lattiasta kattoon, ehkä myös ajasta iäisyyteen. (Rimminen 2004, 298)

> (…) there it loomed, a Chinese village put to death by dam building; a bunch of rooms filled with cold water, where families stiffened in their chores were drifting between their furniture slowly from wall to wall, from the floor to the ceiling, perhaps also from time to eternity.

The description is akin to the conceptualization, classical in city literature, of the city as *imago mundi* (see Ameel 2014, 22; Lilley 2009), containing all the diversity and splendor of the world. In this description, however, one corner of Helsinki contains within itself, as in a mise-en-abyme, a faraway corner of the world in miniature; not as a metaphor, but in a disturbingly literal sense.

The key source for a disturbing ontological instability, in *Pussikaljaromaani*, lies in the possibility of reading descriptions of the environment literally rather than metaphorically. Within the limited view of the focalizer, the world as it is seen and experienced from this highly localized and subjective position is indeed the world in its totality, and the novel makes repeated reference (often to comic effect) to the way in which, in popular usage, the "whole world" may hyperbolically refer to the limited world of the locutor. For example, when the focalizer sees his two friends disappearing behind a hill, he notes they "had managed to disappear behind the horizon a bit as if they had barged to the end of the world" ("ehtivät hävitä horisontin taakse vähän niin kuin ne olisivat tulleet rynnineeksi mailman laidalle") (Rimminen 2004, 216). Such arguments draw attention to the possibility of a literal reading of the novel, in which the world is indeed fully and wholly present in the perception of the narrator and/or focalizer—and how the threats to this experienced world are of a fundamentally ontological nature. Such a literary understanding of the text is also commensurate with the humor of the novel, which relies on the capacity to read figurative language literally, with consequences that are as comical as they are revelatory of the storyworld's possible ambiguous nature.

The conceptualization of a world as entirely dependent—even in ontological terms—on the focalizer's capacities can be contextualized not only within narrative studies, but also more broadly within theories of knowledge. It is a position that in philosophy has been associated with idealism, and evoked among others by the philosopher George Berkeley (1685–1753), a contemporary of Leibniz, whose thesis *esse est percipi* argues that to exist is to be perceived (Muehlmann 1995). The consequences of this position in a narrative context is that the storyworld ceases to exist when its main focal point ceases to observe; or that its ontological attributes become radically deformed once the mode of perceiving is radically affected, such as in the case of an intoxicated Marshall, running frenziedly through a Biblical torrent of rain. In apocalyptic city literature, it is often unclear whether the end of a fictional world is taking place in actuality, or whether it could stem from the focalizing or narrating center; as I have argued elsewhere, urban apocalypse tends to reside "in the perspective of the madman, or that of characters that are mentally incapacitated by distress, disease, or hunger. Confusion, despair, or illusion become projected upon the cityscape, and in such texts, the reader is guided to interpret the dystopian or apocalyptic cityscapes as a result of the protagonist's cognitive restrictions" (Ameel 2016).

In *Pussikaljaromaani*, apocalypse remains an implicit possibility, contingent on the reader's belief in the literal meaning of the narrator's statement. In *Pussikaljaromaani*, then, there are hints at the cracks and fissures in the stable storyworld, while in *Pölkky*, the hole in the ice rink can be seen as a disconcerting new spatial reality folding out of the habitual world, and into the air and fog enveloping the city. A city emptied of human beings is hinted at at the end of the novel, and in a sense, a radical "end" is realized with the very ending of *Pölkky*, in which the storyworld ends quite abruptly when its main focal point (though not its focalizer) steps out of that storyworld's boundaries and under a bus (Rimminen 2007, 384). In the "Extract from a Manuscript," the catastrophe has already occurred, and a new kind of ontological world has clicked into place.

Conclusion

In a conversation with the author (27.1.2017), Rimminen agreed that there is some basis for interpreting his first three prose texts as an apocalyptic trilogy (or trilogy moving toward the apocalypse), centered on Helsinki: "If I had published a novel written on the basis of that PROSAK extract, there would have been this structure, in which in Pussikaljaromaani there are hints; in Pölkky, it is already feared, and in the next novel, it would have already happened."

This narrative structure also sheds some light on the thematic understanding of these prose texts. Rimminen pointed out that in the three prose texts there is an important social context: *Pussikaljaromaani* posits the importance of a community, while *Pölkky* deals in part with human loneliness; in the last (unfinished) novel, with only one man left, it would not even have been possible to be lonely in company. The development in Rimminen's early prose texts can be seen from the perspective of the author's interest in the precariousness of community in late capitalist society, or in terms of his preoccupation with labor in its many forms (see

Mäkelä 2015; Ojajärvi 2013). What I have tried to suggest here is that the development in Rimminen's first three prose texts can also be read in terms of gradually escalating ontological tensions, which are also integral to the author's experiments with language and the role of the narrator. The spatial environments, although upon first encounter firmly referential to actual Helsinki, are presented as subject to incomprehensible forces that are hinted at, first, as a possibility in the linguistic realm—by taking metaphor literally—but that gradually appear as actual interferences in the ontological storyworld. In the course of the three texts, the spatial environment and its referential mode move, in the terms proposed by Westphal, from homotopic consensus—a close relationship to actual Helsinki—to a threatening sense of heterotopic interference, in the form of the hole in the ice rink, and eventually, in the "Extract," to a full-blown utopian excursus: a world in which the threatening intimations from the two novels seem to have become realized in a process of gradual unfolding.

Making sense of the changes in the referential relationship of the storyworlds in these three texts does not hinge on binary relations, on a choice between either a recognizable or a disconcertingly strange environment. Rather, the spatial environment appears as a continuous plane from which folds of different possible worlds gradually appear. Like spatial elements in the art of the Baroque—waves, curly hair moving out into the world—space is seen in *Pussikaljaromaani* and *Pölkky* to curve, as happens during the wild charge in the rain in *Pussikaljaromaani*, or in the steam curling from the ice hole into the fog enfolding all of Helsinki. The environment in the "Extract," by contrast, presents a more stable world, which has seemingly unequivocally "clicked" into something entirely unfamiliar.

The treatment of the urban spatial environment in Mikko Rimminen's early prose texts raises a number of issues that are of relevance for our understanding of space in postmodern literature in more general terms. An examination of Rimminen's prose texts confirms the notion, proposed by Brian McHale, that postmodern literature displays a conspicuous ontological instability: what at first appears to be a recognizable storyworld in the texts, with a firm referential relationship to actual Helsinki, turns out to be increasingly undermined by intimations of ontological disturbances. The distinction made by Bertrand Westphal between three types of "coupling"—"homotopic consensus," "heterotopic interference," and "utopian excursus"—is a helpful typology with which to examine the various kinds of referential relationships displayed by these texts. These relationships defy an understanding as being either true or not true—both in the internal coherence of the storyworld and in their relationship to the actual world—but can be approached more productively through the concept of the fold, as proposed by Deleuze: a concept that challenges binary oppositions, and that emphasizes the simultaneous presence of possibly contradictory worlds evolving on the same plane of meaning. Crucially, such an understanding of literary space and its referential relationship to the actual world, which refuses to make a dramatic distinction between actualized (or the real) and potential (or the imaginary), also draws attention to how the ontological instability of postmodern literature may in turn feed into readers' perspectives of their actual world, and may urge us to consider it in questions of simultaneously real and unreal, possible and actual.

Notes

1. All translations by the author unless stated otherwise.
2. Mikko Rimminen (1975) is a Finnish novelist known, amongst other things, for the idiosyncratic and innovative language of his novels, which tend to focus on the everyday lives of marginalized characters, often with absurdist undertones. His debut novel *Pussikaljaromaani*, a one-day novel set in the Finnish capital, has been compared to Joyce's *Ulysses* and the Finnish modernist classic *Alastalon salissa* (1933) by Volter Kilpi. Rimminen's third novel *Nenäpäivä* (2010; literally "Red Nose Day") was awarded the Finlandia Prize, the most prestigious Finnish literature prize. Rimminen has published four novels, none of which have been translated into English.
3. It is important to note that the narrator, although not a character in the story, has limited abilities in terms of perception and is unable to read the thoughts or inner emotions of the characters.
4. The figure of the "last man" is of course a pervasive one in the writing of the previous centuries, from Nietzsche to Fukuyama and beyond.
5. Marie-Laure Ryan is one of the theorists who has argued that a diversification of non-actualized possible worlds contributes to a narrative's tellability; see Ryan 1992; Hägg 2008. A narrative that leaves open the ontological status of a world possibly on the verge of collapse, with a range of possible multiple ontologies in the storyworld, would thus be inherently more tellable than a story in a post-apocalyptic setting, where the possible avoidance of catastrophe has been eliminated.
6. The reference brings to mind the myth of Phaethon, the son of the sun god, who was unable to control his father's chariot, and scorched the earth.
7. In *Pölkky*, too, the watery hole is referred to in terms of a Biblical flood, as a "small-scale Flood" ("pienimuotoisen vedenpaisumuksen") (Rimminen 2007, 216), and there are also references to drowning.

8. The lack of clarity about who or what is responsible for the dramatic events in the novel is enforced by the suggestion that time itself, or, literally, the striking of the clock, could have been responsible for cutting the trees in the simile.
9. The passage again draws on literal and figurative meanings of the same word—"life," which can denote both "life" and "noise."

References

Ameel, Lieven. 2014. *Helsinki in Early Twentieth-Century Finnish Literature*. Helsinki: Finnish Literature Society.
———. 2016. Cities Utopian, Dystopian, and Apocalyptic. In *The Palgrave Handbook of Literature and the City*, ed. Jeremy Tambling, 785–800. London: Palgrave.
Deleuze, Gilles. 1988. *Le pli: Leibniz et le Baroque*. Paris: Éditions de Minuit.
———. 1993. *The Fold: Leibniz and the Baroque*. Translated by Tom Conley. London: Athlone Press.
Evernden, Neil. 1996. Beyond Ecology: Self, Place, and the Pathetic Fallacy. In *The Ecocriticism Reader: Landmarks in Literary Ecology*, ed. Cheryll Glotfelty and Harold Fromm, 92–104. Athens: University of Georgia Press.
Hägg, Samuli. 2008. Lisää käyttöä mahdollisille maailmoille. *Avain* 2008 (3): 5–21.
Keunen, Bart. 2001. The Plurality of Chronotopes in the Modernist City Novel: The Case of *Manhattan Transfer*. *English Studies* 82 (5): 420–436.
Lappalainen, Topi. 2016. A Forest on the Edge of Helsinki: Spatiality in Henrika Ringbom's Novel *Martina Dagers Längtan*. In *Literature and the Peripheral City*, ed. Lieven Ameel, Jason Finch, and Markku Salmela, 149–163. London: Palgrave.
Lilley, Keith D. 2009. *City and Cosmos: The Medieval World in Urban Form*. London: Reaktion.
Mäkelä, Maria. 2015. Kognitiivinen realismi, kömpelö ruumis ja kielen todellisuus Mikko Rimmisen Pölkyssä. *Avain* 2015 (1): 29–49.
McHale, Brian. 2003 [1987]. *Postmodernist Fiction*. London: Routledge.
Muehlmann, Robert G., ed. 1995. *Berkeley's Metaphysics: Structural, Interpretative, and Critical Essays*. University Park: Pennsylvania State University Press.
Ojajärvi, Jussi. 2013. Työn syrjässä. In *Suomen nykykirjallisuus 2. Kirjallinen elämä ja yhteiskunta*, ed. Mika Hallila, Yrjö Hosiaisluoma, Sanna Karkulehto, Leena Kirstinä, and Jussi Ojajärvi, 154–156. Helsinki: Finnish Literature Society.
Prendergast, Christopher. 1992. *Paris in the Nineteenth Century*. Cambridge: Blackwell.
Rimminen, Mikko. 2004. *Pussikaljaromaani*. Helsinki: Teos.
———. 2007. *Pölkky*. Helsinki: Teos.

———. 2009. Katkelma romaanikäsikirjoituksesta. *Nuori Voima* 2009 (2): 42–46.
Ryan, Marie-Laure. 1992. *Possible Worlds, Artificial Intelligence, and Narrative Theory*. Bloomington: Indiana University Press.
Westphal, Bertrand. 2011. *Geocriticism: Real and Fictional Spaces*. Translated by Robert Tally. Basingstoke: Palgrave.

Open Access This chapter is licensed under the terms of the Creative Commons Attribution 4.0 International License (http://creativecommons.org/licenses/by/4.0/), which permits use, sharing, adaptation, distribution and reproduction in any medium or format, as long as you give appropriate credit to the original author(s) and the source, provide a link to the Creative Commons licence and indicate if changes were made.

The images or other third party material in this chapter are included in the chapter's Creative Commons licence, unless indicated otherwise in a credit line to the material. If material is not included in the chapter's Creative Commons licence and your intended use is not permitted by statutory regulation or exceeds the permitted use, you will need to obtain permission directly from the copyright holder.

CHAPTER 11

Uncanny Spaces of Transformation: Fabulations of the Forest in Finland-Swedish Prose

Kaisa Kurikka

The forest is a special space for the people of Northern Europe. As Emily Brady (2003, 22) has argued, the forest has a significant meaning in definitions of cultural identity in all Nordic countries; the forest is a space for solitude that enables (urbanized) people to encounter not only nature but also themselves. In Finnish literature the forest has been a recurrent theme for centuries. Depictions have varied from romantic notions of the woods as a magical environment to describing it as an important natural resource and commercial commodity. The Finnish forest is not only a holy site but also an environment of hard labor and a marked element of modern capitalism.

Finland is a country full of forests. The state economy depends on the success of forest industry to export, for example, the knowhow of forestry, products manufactured in pulp mills and paper factories; the forest industry is still the main natural resource in Finland. Forests, however, have always been important to Finnish citizens in other ways as well. The woods engender mythologized meanings dating back to the folklore gathered in

---

K. Kurikka (✉)
University of Turku, Turku, Finland

© The Author(s) 2020
K. Malmio, K. Kurikka (eds.), *Contemporary Nordic Literature and Spatiality*, Geocriticism and Spatial Literary Studies,
https://doi.org/10.1007/978-3-030-23353-2_11

Kalevala (1849), the Finnish national epic, and the poems of the *Kanteletar* (1840). This forest mythology, varying from a place of solitude to a natural resource to be profited from or to be exploited, is still reproduced in literature today. Because of its huge national importance, the forest has been written about a lot, whether focusing on the aesthetics or philosophical aspects of the woods (see, e.g., Sepänmaa et al. 2003), forest conservation (see Roiko-Jokela (ed.) 1997; Lähde 2015), or the literary depictions of the forest in climate poetry (see Lummaa 2008)—to name but a few examples. In this chapter, however, I will be discussing the ways in which the forest is regarded as an important space not only for humans but also for non-humans.

The starting point of this chapter is to elaborate on the ways in which the chosen examples of recent Finland-Swedish fiction depict the forest. I discuss the actualizations of this thematic in three works of Finland-Swedish prose fiction: *Gräset är mörkare på andra sidan* (2012; "The Grass is Darker on the Other Side") by Kaj Korkea-aho, *Camera Obscura* (2009) by Johanna Holmström, and *Martina Dagers Längtan* (1998; "Martina Dager's Longing") by Henrika Ringbom. They all testify to the enduring significance of the forest as a spatial image in Finnish literature. My discussion will take up similarities in the depictions of the forest in these texts, but it will also show how forests are understood as having special and multiple functions.

According to Pertti Lassila (2011, 20), who has studied depictions of nature and especially forests[1] in Finnish literature from the eighteenth century till the 1950s, Finnish literature regards nature and the forest as an alternative, as a contrast or as a counterforce, to human beings and their culture. In folk poetry the forest is seen as a holy place that differs from the sinful world of human beings (Tarkka 2005, 259). During the nineteenth century the poetry of Zacharias Topelius depicted forests and nature in connection with loving the homeland and as a metaphor and promise of the afterlife; Johan Ludvig Runeberg described nature as a book where God's greatness is manifested (see Lassila 2011, 126). Both Topelius and Runeberg have been canonized as national Finnish authors and their representations of forests are filled with nationalistic overtones.

In these literary depictions, which date back to past centuries, Finnish forests undergo a bifurcation, pointing either to other-worldly dimensions (whether to Christian or pagan beliefs) or to the material world inhabited by humans. This chapter argues that today forests are presented as a site to negotiate between the two poles of human and non-human entities, but instead of treating them as oppositions, contemporary fiction problematizes them by attaching itself along the moving line between them.

The title of Pertti Lassila's study is "The Blissful Forest" (*Metsän autuus*). In the introduction Lassila says that his main interest lies in the historical changes that have taken place in Finnish literature and its worldviews regarding nature. Lassila argues that in the literature of the latter half of the twentieth century—the period this chapter deals with—nature and forest have lost their credibility as an existential, spiritual, or ideological alternative to the culture of human beings. Lassila maintains that instead of remaining as an important existential and ideological site, nature has become commercialized, and it is treated as a place of recreational activities, adventure, and consumption in post-war fiction (Lassila 2011, 20–1).

Lassila's views are, however, strikingly anthropic and anthropocentric, since for him the forest is merely a human space, a reflection of human mentality. The three works of contemporary Finland-Swedish prose fiction I discuss in this chapter contest Lassila's views. They are works of literature that bring forth existential questions, ideological and even spiritual issues, while pondering on the relationship between "nature" and "culture." It seems that all three texts are also moving away from the anthropocentric perspective and changing the focus to see the human condition side by side with non-human existence. And they elaborate on these questions in connection with Finnish forests. One of the main questions of this chapter is: How do these literary texts problematize anthropocentrism by placing the forest as the focal point of narration?

I argue that in recent Finnish prose fiction written in Swedish, the forest is materialized as a space of and for transformation—and in here I discuss these transformations in detail. Additionally, it seems that by focusing on the depiction of the forest, literary expression can also tackle the question of manifold encounters between human and non-human creatures (such as animals or monsters)—these encounters are filled with various affects. This chapter asks questions such as: How is the forest depicted as an affective space? How do the characters perceive forests? What is the relationship between the characters and the spaces in which they are situated? In order to answer these and other questions I turn to the geophilosophical concepts of Gilles Deleuze and Félix Guattari and then proceed to an analysis of the novels.

Thinking Literary Forests with Deleuze and Guattari

I tackle the transformative nature of the forests in these novels by thinking about literary space using the geophilosophical concepts of Deleuze and Guattari. To start with, the prose fiction by Kaj Korkea-aho, Johanna Holmström, and Henrika Ringbom exceed the limits of the representational regime by creating such forests that cannot be experienced in our everyday reality: they do not invest in re-presenting existing Finnish forests but create new forest lands through imageries of transformation, liminal spaces, and human–non-human encounters. While giving expression to the spatiality of the forest, they thus emphasize the imaginative forces of literature. To use a concept created by Gilles Deleuze alone and in collaboration with Félix Guattari, they explore *fabulation* (see Deleuze 1989, 133), of telling stories of new spaces, creating new spatialities of the forest. These forests can only be imagined; they are the result of literary fabulation. Conceptually, fabulation emphasizes imagination and the creation of something new, which does not stem from reminiscence or fantasy (Deleuze and Guattari 1994, 171). According to Ronald Bogue (2010, 18–20), the concept of fabulation also presents itself as deeply political, since Deleuze connects fabulation with the invention and creation of a social collective. Deleuze calls this collective that authors and other artists fabulate in their works *people to come* (peuple à venir). Deleuze (1989, 216) writes about *a people who are missing*, and therefore it is the task of the artist to invent a people. As Gregory Flaxman (2012, 227) points out, the force of fabulation lies in the affirmation of a people and politics that is yet to come.

The prose fiction of Korkea-aho, Holmström, and Ringbom invents new forests, but they can also be said to enter the area of *the powers of the false* (puissance du faux), another concept coined by Deleuze. Although, as Gregory Flaxman (2012, xvii–iii) has pointed out, Deleuze uses the concept sparingly, it is found throughout Deleuze's philosophical thinking. The powers of the false cover a region of stepping over such thinking that is governed by a division into "the truth," "the real," "the wrong," and "the fictional." Instead of trying to find the truth, the powers of the false celebrate "the false," and by affirming its existence the forces to create the new, to fabulate, are born. As Deleuze (1989, 133) writes:

(…) contrary to the form of the true which is unifying and tends to the identification of a character (his discovery or simply his coherence), the power of the false cannot be separated from an irreducible multiplicity. "I as another" [Je est un autre] has replaced Ego = Ego.

The logic of the powers of the false rests on the movement toward the creation of the new, that is, of fabulation, of telling stories. It gives several forms to the false/unreal, because its foundation is metamorphosis, becoming.

When literature is understood as Deleuzian fabulation and as an expression of the powers of the false, it also engenders a special way of studying literary spaces; unlike, for example, what Bertrand Westphal suggests in his geocritical approach, literary spaces are not discussed as re-presenting "real" spaces or as referential spatialities nor is literature seen as a mimetic art (see Westphal 2011, 3). Instead the emphasis lies on the potentialities of literature to fabulate new kinds of spatialities. In *What is Philosophy?* Deleuze and Guattari (1994, 85) write:

> Subject and object give a poor approximation of thought. Thinking is neither a line drawn between subject and object nor a revolving of one around the other. Rather, thinking takes place in the relationship of territory and the earth. (…) the earth constantly carries out a movement of deterritorialization on the spot, by which it goes beyond any territory: it is deterritorializing and deterritorialized.

Drawing on this citation, thinking or studying literature means forming a spatial relation with the work of art. The book or literature is not considered a separate object of study onto which the subject (i.e., the researcher) reflects his/her perspectives and concepts. Instead, studying literature means thinking with literature. According to Ian Buchanan and Gregg Lambert (2005, 5) in *A Thousand Plateaus*, Deleuze and Guattari configure new ways for spatial fields, which replace the tripartite division of spatial fields normally associated with "mental representations" such as literature: the field of reality (the world), the field of representation (the book), and the field of subjectivity (the author). Instead of these, Deleuze and Guattari think of literature as an assemblage of planes, of lines, and between these, points of variation (becoming)—in another words literature expresses the movements between chaos (*terra*) and socially, linguistically, bioethologically, and so on reframing territories. The earth, *terra*, can be infinitely divided and framed (Grosz 2008, 17) into new territories through the movements of de- and reterritorializations. For Deleuze and Guattari the production of space is much less based on a history of labor and social relations—as is the case with, for example, Henri Lefebvre—than a history of desire and perception (Tynan 2016, 482). "Geography (…) is not merely physical and human but mental, like the landscape," Deleuze and Guattari write (1994, 96).

Spaces are thus affective sensations, but spaces are also born with perception. A body or matter can be perceived and sensed as located in a certain geometrical space, which can be described as a set of relations formed by the body in its location. For Deleuze, however, as Claire Colebrook (2005, 196) insists, space is not constructed from sense, socially and culturally consisted, but spatiality opens sense, since "any location bears the potential to open up new planes, new orientations." Deleuze does not see space as effected from sense, but instead spatiality is an opening to sense. To study spaces in this manner also means acknowledging them as always already different in themselves, constantly changing. It also means focusing on the potential of literature to produce, to fabulate, new spatialities. As Aidan Tynan (2016, 484) has written, the geophilosophy of Deleuze and Guattari "is a means of tracing the relationship between thought, politics and space that have dominated Western consciousness, but it also insists that our concepts and institutions have been geographically conditioned."

In what follows I will discuss Kaj Korkea-aho's, Johanna Holmström's, and Henrika Ringbom's prose with spatial concepts by Deleuze and Guattari.[2] The functions and actualizations of the forest in these texts take different forms, and it is thus necessary to consider them with different concepts. When discussing Korkea-aho's novel, I focus on the ways the forest becomes territorialized as the space of the uncanny—the uncanniness of the forest is shared by all three depictions. The forest in Holmström's prose undergoes a process of transformation effected by the movements of the characters—the concepts of territory, reterritorialization, and deterritorialization are useful in approaching this transformation. Ringbom's novel builds on the juxtaposition of two spaces, the city and the forest, which I discuss with the concepts of the striated and smooth space. I will define these conceptualizations when using them. First, I will discuss Korkea-aho's novel, then Holmström's, and finally Ringbom's prose.

Territorializing the Forest as Uncanny

In the beginning of Kaj Korkea-aho's[3] *Gräset är mörkare på andra sidan* (2012; "The Grass is Darker on the Other Side"), a sudden earthquake makes a peaceful forest tremble, shake, and wave like a stormy ocean. The earthquake lasts only 20 seconds, but afterward the inhabitants of Gränby, a fictional village located in Ostrobothnia in Western Finland, return to discuss the convulsive sensations of "(…) standing on the ground which no longer felt stable" (Korkea-aho 2012, 19).[4]

The earthquake is described in connection with the forest, as the narrator depicts shivering branches, rabbits running aghast, or a rumbling noise traveling fast through the forest resembling an underground freight train. By choosing to concentrate on the effects that the earthquake has on non-human creatures and on nature, the narrator also chooses to move away from an anthropocentric perspective. The scene appears as if the forest, or the whole earth, were at the point of transformation, which can be conceptualized with the concept of *deterritorialization* as proposed by Deleuze and Guattari (see 1988, 310–50). The very beginning of the novel thus points to a forest undergoing deterritorializing movements: the area, the territory of the forest, formerly territorialized as a rigid, solid, and peaceful space, is turning into something else. The forest becomes dispersed through the process of deterritorialization. Situated in the early pages of Korkea-aho's novel, the scene also functions as a premonition of future happenings, which are again centered in the forest. Korkea-aho's novel consists of many storylines, several central characters acting as focalizers, and it covers a multitude of themes. The storyline in which the forest has a special function focuses on Christoffer, a young man who returns to Gränby, where he grew up as a child. Christoffer and his friends gather to spend time together and also to reminisce about their childhood, when they used to play in the forest. The forest now no longer appears as a happy space filled with joy and laughter, but a frightening space of violence and anxiety.

In the course of the novel the forest is depicted, for the most part, like any Finnish forest. The narration functions in terms of familiarity when describing the forest—in other words, the description *reterritorializes* those features of the forest that are known to most Finnish readers into the ways the novel builds the territorial area of the forest. The Finnish legislation with its legal concept of "everyman's right" gives everybody the chance to enjoy outdoor activities and the country's vast forests with few restrictions. This freedom to roam in the forest is also actualized in Korkea-aho's novel. The forest is territorialized as an adventurous playground for the nearby village children. Adults go jogging on the pathways in the forest and yearly a big running competition takes place there. An isolated gravel road runs through the forest, where people pick berries and mushroom. All in all, the forest in Korkea-aho's novel appears to be a typical Finnish forest, filled with activities characteristic of the traditional Finnish forest-centered lifestyle.

At the same time, Korkea-aho's novel also invests in the forces of literary fiction to fabulate and imagine new kinds of spaces. The forest described in the novel is anything but typical, because a huge monster dwells there. The villagers have told stories about the monster for so long that it has become a mythical creature. In a fashion reminiscent of horror or ghost stories, the characters of the novel blame the monster for killing children decades ago as well as for deaths currently taking place.

Interestingly, though, the monster is neither illusory nor real, but something in-between. The villagers are convinced they have seen the monster, but for the most part the novel builds on the suspense created by the thoughts of the main characters as they ponder whether this dark, shadowy creature is a real, an actual material being, or has been born from the imagination. This suspense is heightened by the fact that one of the key figures, Christoffer, is completing his Master's thesis on a mythological figure called Raamt. Raamt belongs to the fictitious folklore oral tradition of the Ostrobothnian region, where it is taken to represent "pure evil," although, according to Christoffer's study, sometimes Raamt is also seen as a kind of guardian angel who protects young children. The monster living in the forest is juxtaposed with Raamt in the course of the novel. The creature is photographed sitting beside a woman in the front seat of a car just seconds before the car mysteriously crashes while she is driving through the forest. The novel hints that the monster causes the woman's death. The central characters of the novel also meet the monster on several occasions. Due to this, the monster becomes a real figure within the reality of the novel's storyworld.

Reading the novel, one becomes puzzled by the monster: How is it possible that a typical forest near a typical village might contain a creature normally reserved for fairy tales and horror stories? The reader experiences a sense of doubt especially because the novel's narration mostly builds on psychological realism and mimetic attitude in terms of reality. Thus, in Korkea-aho's novel, the most natural Finnish space, the forest—according to the Finnish Natural Resources Institute forest or forest land covers 78% of the total area of Finland (see Metla 2015)—is turned into something unnatural or supernatural. In other words, the forest undergoes a process of deterritorialization and enters the area of *the uncanny*.

Korkea-aho's novel departs from "consensus reality" (see Hume 2014, 21) and proposes a world where the laws of our world are integrated with laws uncommon to us—thus his novel can claim to give expression to the powers of the false, which efface the hierarchical oppositions between "right" and "wrong." Following Tzvetan Todorov's (1987, 41–51) definition, Korkea-aho's novel can be placed in a specific genre of fantastic literature: the uncanny. As Todorov points out, the genre manifests itself in many variations ranging from Edgar Allan Poe to Dostoyevsky, but perhaps the one characteristic element common to all of them is that the existence of the supernatural is given a rational explanation. In Korkea-aho's novel the existence of the supernatural monster is linked to the personal psyche of the central character, Christoffer, and the being of the monster is given a rational explanation, but the reader still remains somewhat puzzled. The monster is born from Christoffer's anxiety and distress, which are combined with his knowledge of the mythical figure of Raamt. At the end of the novel Christoffer is finally able to recognize his depression and its manifestation in the monster. After that the monster disappears from the forest, but remains on guard inside Christoffer, ready to come alive again if necessary. Rosi Braidotti (2002, 201), upon writing on the monstrous as a dominant part of the social imaginary, argues that twenty-first-century horror and science-fiction literature and film show an exacerbated version of anxiety in the form of the "otherness within": the monster dwells in the character's embodied self, ready to unfold. Korkea-aho's novel manifests this.

In this chapter I do not, however, concentrate on the figure of the monster or on definitions of the genre of the uncanny. Instead, I focus on the forest, the monster's milieu, by posing the following questions: Why is it that in contemporary Finland-Swedish prose fiction the forest is inhabited by uncanny elements? Why is the forest a space in which the uncanny takes place? Korkea-aho's novel is not the only example of recent prose depicting the Finnish forest as a space to negotiate the relationships between natural and unnatural happenings, since Johanna Holmström's *Camera Obscura* and Henrika Ringbom's *Martina Dagers längtan* are also examples of the uncanny forest, as this discussion will later show.

In his study of the uncanny, Nicholas Royle (2003, 6) argues that the uncanny is a "means of thinking the so-called 'real life', the ordinary, the familiar and everyday." For Royle, the uncanny is not a literary genre, but a critical elaboration bound up with analyzing, questioning, and even transforming what is called "everyday life." Referring to Anthony Vidler, Royle (2003, 6) writes that the uncanny is a metaphor for a fundamentally unlivable modern condition. The uncanny is an expression of estrangement and unhomeliness typical of our times. The uncanny forest per se has a long tradition in Western literature, from Shakespeare's forests to the fairy tales of the Grimm brothers, among others, and the Finland-Swedish prose fiction dealt with in this chapter also reinforces the uncanny forest.

In Korkea-aho's, Holmström's, and Ringbom's prose, the forest becomes a space for questioning the borders of everyday life. As "a strangeness of framing and borders, an experience of liminality" (Royle 2003, 2), the uncanny has an immense affective force, which in the works under scrutiny in this chapter seems to be connected with the problems of defining both the human and the non-human in the contemporary world. The uncanny appears as an affective encounter between humans and non-humans; this encounter is either embodied inside the characters as a form of "otherness within," as in Korkea-aho's and Ringbom's novels, or with non-human creatures, such as the wolf in Holmström's prose. Most significantly, these encounters take place in the forest. Korkea-aho's novel moves away from anthropic attitudes by allowing the unhuman qualities to enter the scene in the figure of the monster. In bringing realistically depicted human characters together with a clearly fictional monster and by claiming that both of these are "real" characters, Korkea-aho's novel exemplifies the uncanny. But at the same time, Korkea-aho's novel follows the logic of the Deleuzian powers of the false, which celebrates the existence of the uncanny and questions the division into (hierarchical) oppositions.

Vanishing Points in the Forest Darkness

In Johanna Holmström's[5] *Camera Obscura*, a group of friends, young adults living in the Finnish capital of Helsinki, discuss their options on how to most effectively oppose the capitalist system and consumer society. The topic of their discussion makes Holmström's prose late modern. One of them, Ida, says that the only way to stop the capitalist apparatus is to destroy it. To her, the destruction of capitalism can only be achieved by abolishing the part that is necessary for the continuation of the machinery: the consumer. Although as a group they cannot stop other people from buying things, they can at least stop themselves from consuming. Another member of the group, Anna asks: "What? What shall we do then? Shall we move into the forest and build a tiny cabin there and live off nature?" (Holmström 2009, 46). Ida's answer to Anna's provocation is an emphatic "no," her own suggestion being that they should "quit existing" and commit suicide, fulfilling her idea by jumping off a balcony. Later, however, Anna, her boyfriend, and another couple move into an isolated forest, since as radical eco-activists they need to escape the police after performing a violent act against fur farmers. They literally live in and off the forest, a place in which to hide from the norms and ideologies of the prevailing society. From the perspective of the society, the group "quits existing" and vanishes into the forest.

To begin with, the forest is thus connected to ideological issues in Holmström's book. In comparison to the long tradition of Finnish forest fiction, which focused on the peaceful bliss of the forest (see Lassila 2011, passim.), Holmström's forest becomes a site to negotiate between various ecological and economic ideas concerning the prevailing world. The forest is territorialized as a space of politics and ethics—the forest is marked by them, since the characters of the novel return to discuss the forest in terms of different ideologies of consumer capitalism and ecological activism. In *A Thousand Plateaus*, Deleuze and Guattari (1988, 314–16) write about how territories are produced by repetitive rhythms; in Holmström's novel the forest is depicted on several occasions as a space where ecoactivists and conservatives fight each other. But at the same time the forest in Holmström's prose is also reterritorializing traditional dimensions of the forest: for Anna and her friends the forest is a space to hide, to be alone, and to rest.

The title of Holmström's book, *Camera Obscura*, can be understood in at least two ways. It refers to a literal "dark room," and many dark and gloomy places are depicted in the course of the happenings, varying from Ida's room in Helsinki to the forest where Anna and her friends hide. Anna, walking alone in the forest, faces an especially dark and gloomy room with elements of the uncanny when she comes across a tiny, rundown, seemingly inhabited cabin. Anna takes a look inside the cabin through a small window and is shocked to see a little baby, sitting alone at the kitchen table. Anna soon realizes that the baby is a doll, skillfully crafted to look lifelike. To meet this spooky figure in the middle of the woods gives birth to an uncanny experience—a strange combination of the mechanical and the natural (see Royle 2003, 2). But the title of the book also refers to the functional optical medium, which, according to Friedrich Kittler (2010, 52) made the revolutionary concept of a perfect perspective painting possible. Camera obscura, starting from the eye of the observer, offered new combinations which involved the eye, pinhole images, paintings, mirrors, and the outside world (Kittler 2010, 57). Camera obscura enabled linear perspective in which the parallel lines of an image seem to converge to a vanishing point.

The functional camera obscura can also be linked to the genre of Holmström's book. The subtitle defines the work as a collection of "short stories," and it is indeed possible to read the book as seven long short stories. The title story "Camera Obscura" also takes up the optical device when the main character, a photographer called Laura, remembers "(…) an artist who believed he could see the world clearer with a camera obscura, the truth in a box, distorted but nevertheless exact" (Holmström 2009, 202). The stories or the chapters are all linked together through their characters. The Laura of the title story, for example, is the half-sister of the above-mentioned Anna; characters function as lines that connect chapters to each other. As the stories progress, they also shed light on the whereabouts and fates of the characters in the other stories. Holmström's work can thus also be seen as a novel in which chapters offer different perspectives, albeit sometimes briefly, on the happenings. As a whole, the composition of Holmström's hybrid work seems to function on the level of constant re- and deterritorialization, since the stories/chapters explain and complete previous happenings in different circumstances, forming a rhizome-like continuation of intersecting lines. Events are reframed in new territories.

More important, the novel seems to put forth an image of thought, which acts upon and fabulates with the various elements connected to camera obscura by thematizing and conceptualizing them. Most of the chapters are narrated by a third-person narrator, though focalized through a main character, which gives this character's perspective on what is narrated. In the chapters minor or major characters literally vanish, either by dying or by disappearing—this infatuation with death and disappearance (see Royle 2003, 2) also enhances the uncanniness of the work. In "The Children of the Dollmaker," at the beginning of the twentieth century in St. Petersburg small children are disappearing; in "Camera Obscura" Laura's girlfriend keeps on disappearing and returning; and in "Blue

Anemone Hill" ("Blåsippsbacken") a skater drowns in the icy sea. It is as if the narration forms a collection of lines, which converges into a hole, a vanishing point in the manner of the camera device itself.

In "The Year of the Wolf" ("Vargens år"), Anna acts as the focalizer on the plane of composition. As such, her perceptions and affects have a strong impact on the ways the forest is expressed. It is as if the description is set on a line creating a kind of beam of light analogous to Anna's affects. When she feels threatened, the forest is depicted as a violent environment, where "stones are sharp and relentless" and "the spruce stand high like spearheads" (Holmström 2009, 58). When walking in the forest and leaving the cabin behind, Anna "feels safe again in the clear-cut area" (Holmström 2009, 62). Sometimes "the forest is a tunnel of a spanning light" (Holmström 2009, 91). These depictions of the forest are thus always connected to the ways that space affects Anna; the literary expression of space cannot be separated from the senses and sensation of the person perceiving them—in one sense Anna herself functions as the mechanical camera obscura: the perspective is restricted only to cover her affective observations. The forest is deterritorialized into an affective space when Anna wanders there alone: the political aspects linked to the forest no longer prevail. In this way the forest is deterritorialized into a regime of subjective signs as Anna's passions and consciousness color the space (see Deleuze and Guattari 1988, 508).

The events of the story take place in the forest, where Anna and her three friends have hired a small cabin with only basic amenities, such as an outdoor toilet. They have no nearby neighbors and the only visitor they meet is their landlord, an elderly man. Their car is parked hidden behind the cabin, because they do not want to leave any signs of themselves living in the cabin. The gravel road or rather the path leading to the cabin has no name, nor has the cabin, and for Anna they are both "pieces of a world that has been forgotten" (Holmström 2009, 54). At the very beginning of the chapter Anna is depicted at a point of becoming something else, at the edge of transformation: she sits alone in the kitchen looking at the ceiling, the walls, and the kitchenware, but slowly she starts to breath heavily, exposing her teeth while sensing a spatial image inside her mind. She imagines the Big Bang taking place at that very moment, and she realizes that the empty space is expanding more and more, and there is no way to escape it. Anna feels small and insignificant.

Right after this scene Anna is depicted as "having the look of an animal"[6] (Holmström 2009, 56). In the totality of "The Year of the Wolf" an animal, namely a wolf, and human beings are intertwined in a complicated manner. The landlord comes to warn Anna and her companions of a pack of wolves that has been seen and heard in the forest, and he is about to form a team to hunt them down. This causes a serious conflict between him and the eco-activists, for whom the wolves have every right to live and wander in the woods. They argue fiercely about the wolves and their rights with dramatic consequences. Lotta and Markus, two of the cabin dwellers, call some other eco-activists, who arrive in the woods with drums and horns to warn the wolves, causing the local hunting group to become very upset and angry.

The wolves also play an important role in the ways the chapter builds the territory of the forest. In *A Thousand Plateaus*, Deleuze and Guattari (1988, 310–50) discuss how a territory is constituted as an area with boundaries separating it from the outer milieu. A *refrain* or *ritornello* (ritournelle) marks the boundaries of the territory. A refrain is not just any borderline, but it draws an expressive relation between the territory and its milieu. The territory itself is an assemblage and its maintenance and cohesion is also regulated by the refrain. The refrain is a rhythmic feature because it keeps on framing the territory again and again. Refrains also mark new territories through de- and reterritorializations. The territory can be transformed into a new or expanded area or be stabilized again. In Holmström's "The Year of the Wolf," a wolf becomes an expressive element delineating the territory of the forest, or rather a more-than-human assemblage, formed by Anna and the wolf, becomes the refrain defining the contours of the forest. The wolf and the pack formed by Anna and the wolf function as a refrain—their assemblage, as Deleuze and Guattari (1988, 232) note, "draws a territory and develops into territorial motifs and landscapes." The encounters between Anna and the wolf are also deterritorializing the forest into the space of the uncanny, since these encounters between them are fabulated in a manner which expands over natural laws and everyday life: wolves and humans rarely intertwine in such friendly ways as Holmström describes them. Producing an eerie atmosphere, these scenes also engender the potentiality of founding a new kind of collective consisting of wild animals and humans interacting with each other in a non-violent way. The uncanny forest opens up a new set of spatial relations that enable the "more-than-human" people to come.

When Anna meets the wolf for the first time, she takes the creature to be a skinny and shaggy German shepherd. The wolf stands at the corner of the cabin's outdoor toilet and stares at her. After realizing it is a wolf Anna is startled. The wolf keeps returning to the cabin yard always when

Anna is alone, and soon she is so used to the she-wolf that she even feeds her. When Anna wanders alone in the forest, the wolf is always near her, making herself both seen and heard:

> Då hon [Anna] når snårskogen och letar efter en väg runt det täta gallret hedjas hon för andra gången den eftermiddagen, då den långa utdragna tonen når henne. Den ensamma vargen vänder nosen mot himlen och ylar. Hon ylar högt, längtande, länge, och i dag får hon svar. (Holmström 2009, 93)

> When she [Anna] reaches the brushwood and looks for a way around the thicket she is stopped for the second time this afternoon when a long, drawn out sound reaches her. The lonesome wolf turns its nose towards the sky and howls. She [the wolf] howls loud, longing, for a long time, and today she gets a reply.

In Holmström's novel the territory of the forest is described as a space where more-than-human encounters are made possible in the manner of "otherness within"—by letting human animosity surface. In the many scenes where Anna undergoes metamorphic changes, the forest is pictured as a manifestation of *affect*. As Deleuze and Guattari (1994, 169) write: "Affects are precisely these nonhuman becomings of man." Slowly, Anna is described as increasingly developing the gestures and appearance of an animal, sometimes feeling a strong urge to "growl and grasp their [her friends'] throats with her teeth" (Holmström 2009, 89). The wolf, on the other hand, is sometimes depicted as a docile pet-like creature. But Anna's friends, Sebbe, Lotta, and Markus, also become juxtaposed with wolves. The narration gives special attention to the fact that the she-wolf forms a pack with three other wolves, just like Anna forms a pack with her three friends. In this way the forest is deterritorialized into a space in which human beings become animals. In the case of Anna her transformation also helps her to escape from the despair and sadness she has felt ever since her best friend Ida committed suicide. Becoming an animal is the vanishing point for Anna.

Just as the human characters are animalized, the she-wolf is humanized. The human and the non-human are set in a flipped, reversed order, which is a means to thematize the ways the camera obscura device functions: the user of the device sees the object upside down. The characterization in the text is thus based on "being double," the duplication of Anna and the wolf enabling the uncanny to be manifest as the ghost-like figuration of these creatures: Anna is doubled in her wolf-like gestures, and the wolf is given a ghostly addition when she is described as resembling a human (see Royle 2003, 16). In many scenes in "The Year of the Wolf" the wolf is an anthropomorphic figure. A flashback takes the reader into Anna's childhood. The narrator recounts how Anna's mother, who suffers from severe mental problems, took her five-year-old daughter to the forest and left her there. Anna waited and waited for her mother to return and take her home, but she never did. After a long time Anna hears steps running toward her and soon sees the face of a furry dog with yellow eyes. Anna realizes that it is not a dog but some other animal, and begins crying and reaching out with her hands as if somebody was there to take her in her arms. Seeing Anna crying, the wolf—for that is what it is—stops its loud noises and begins sniffing Anna. The wolf looks into Anna's eyes, turns and stands close by the girl. Anna, who is no longer crying, takes hold of the wolf's fur and together they walk out of the woods.

In this flashback reminiscence the wolf is a guide or a surrogate mother taking care of the little girl. By narrating this scene from Anna's past, the refrain of the more-than-human assemblage is enhanced in the story. This story of the past also brings new elements to the territorialization of the forest by deterritorializing it to fill it with affects associated with aloneness and abandonment. The refrain of the wolf turns into a *line of flight* (ligne de fuit), a way toward transformation and change—the wolf functions as a positive line of flight (see Deleuze and Guattari 1988, 133), since she enables Anna to literally escape from the loneliness and disappointment of being abandoned in the middle of the forest.

At the very end of the chapter the scene of the wolf leading Anna away from her childhood forest is reterritorialized into another setting, as the past event of Anna's childhood is brought to the present day. Anna is alone in the cabin when she sees the wolf standing outside. Anna is no longer astonished by the wolf; she keeps looking at the wolf, she meets her yellow eyes and nods. Anna steps outside and for a moment it seems that the wolf will run away. But she remains standing still, waiting for Anna, and together side by side they walk deeper and deeper into the forest and vanish there.

The forest in Holmström's prose undergoes several transformations, constantly deterritorializing into new assemblages. Holmström's forests underline the fact that these are indeed places of high biodiversity in which many forms of life—both human and non-human—interact with each other in affective encounters. The forest for Holmström appears as a literal vanishing point, an escape from consumer capitalism and from life itself—

when Anna and the wolf disappear into the dark forest, it becomes a space of absolute deterritorialization, a space of death. Simultaneously, the forest also points to a potential future-to-come; the complicated manner of combining ethical and ecological issues in the encounter between Anna and the wolf also points to a potentially new kind of collective: an assemblage of humans and non-humans inhabiting the same space. In Holmström's book, however, this potential is only partially fulfilled: Anna and the wolf step into the vanishing point.

Disappearing into Smooth Forest

Henrika Ringbom's[7] novel *Martina Dagers längtan* (1998; "Martina Dager's Longing") builds an oppositional spatial imagery between Helsinki and a small forest, reachable by local city buses, situated in the vicinity of the city. The described spaces of the novel do not function as a background to the storylines; instead spatiality comes to the fore, both in terms of happenings and in terms of textual spatiality. As the novel constructs its spatial imagery, it both creates an opposition between the city and the forest, and deconstructs this oppositional positioning. Both spaces are defined in relation to each other. In the course of the novel the city and the forest are both depicted in terms of transformation, but they both also function as spaces that enable the metamorphosis of the main character, Martina.

The first-person narrator of the novel, Martina Dager, is an economist working at the Bank of Finland, the most powerful monetary institution in the nation. The bank is located in downtown Helsinki, in one of the most prestigious quarters of the capital. The building is made of stone, and for Martina the building is "heavy and monolithic" (Ringbom 1998, 11). Martina lives at walking distance from her workplace, and every day she walks to the bank along the streets of Helsinki. When narrating her route, Martina names streets and street corners, buildings, bridges and statues, thus making her walk a literal cartography. She takes notice of buildings that represent the Finnish nation and its institutional power, such as the Presidential Palace or the Evangelical Lutheran Cathedral. When Martina travels by city bus, she carefully gives her starting points and end points according to their coordinates on a map.

The way in which Martina perceives the surrounding city can be regarded as an example of *striated space* (l'espace strié) in the manner of the geophilosophy of Deleuze and Guattari. In striated space one goes from one point to another (Deleuze and Guattari 1988, 478), the way Martina does every morning as she walks from home to her workplace. Striated spaces are highly organized spatial forms, such as the streets of Helsinki, which are structured according to a city plan. Striated spaces are divided into separate sections, like the quarters Martina mentions in her narrations. As Deleuze and Guattari (1988, 149) point out, striated space is one of measures and properties, and while walking in the city Martina's perception of the capital is based on measuring and the measurable visual qualities derived from her vision: striated space is a space that is seen.

Deleuze and Guattari (1988, 478–51) also define striated spaces as hierarchical spaces of institutional power, and the city of Helsinki for Martina seems to be filled with powerful institutions with their grand buildings made of stone. In Ringbom's novel, Martina's job emphasizes capitalist power, for Martina is building a successful career in the Bank of Finland. Inside the building, in the privacy of her working area, she feels safe. The striated spaces with their systematic organization calm Martina. If during her walking routes she is confronted with graffiti on the walls, litter on the ground, or garbage trucks, she becomes startled and distressed.

The Helsinki that Martina describes is recognizably the Finnish capital. But the referentiality of the depiction of the city is mixed with fabulation in the way that the novel enters the area of the powers of the false: real geoplaces are mixed with false and imaginary ones. In the novel a river runs through the city, whereas in the actual capital there is no such thing. On her walking tours in the mornings and gradually in the middle of her working days, Martina takes a walk along the riverside under the "Opera Bridge." Beneath the bridge Martina makes a space of her own: "Here under the bridge there are no sharp contours, colors or light, nothing moves or blinks. Only ice with its rough gray and white, spotty surface and the bridge vault overarching it" (Ringbom 1998, 39). Sitting there, Martina does not perceive the sharp lines and closed forms that are typical of striated spaces. Underneath the bridge Martina sees people different from those she encounters on the streets of Helsinki, such as small boys throwing snowballs or a woman who appears homeless.

The scene where Martina sits under the bridge marks a change in the novel and in its depiction of the city. This change can be conceptualized as the transformation of striated space into *smooth space* (l'espace lisse). Deleuze and Guattari (1988, 474–5, 478) define smooth space as a counterpoint to striated space. Smooth spaces are intensive spaces without borders or limits. Smooth space cannot be divided into separate sections or hierarchical divisions. These two spatial variations, the smooth and the striated, can also reflect each other in such a way that the connection between them becomes a process of metamorphosis. In Ringbom's novel many striated spaces, such as her room in the bank, begin to become something other, for when Martina sits there her thoughts and mind begin to fill up with images of smooth spaces, of the running river and other watery images rather than the previous calculations and statistics. For Deleuze and Guattari (1988, 481) the ocean with its waves and flows is a smooth space par excellence. In the course of the novel Martina feels ever more frequently an urge to live by water. Flowing water in the form of the river or night-time dreams filled with the flow of soft water mark the process of Martina's transformation: she is becoming something other than a highly organized economist. Martina's metamorphosis is given spatial expression in the novel.

In Ringbom's novel a concrete spatial turn takes place when striated space is turned into smooth space, though this turn can also be linked to fabulation and the uncanny. At the beginning of the novel, Martina appears as a literal cartographer who maps a Helsinki which is recognizable to those who know it. The novel is a map; it is easy to follow its trails. But the reader also gets lost in the city, since Martina adds strange elements to the landscape, thus causing the map of the city to change. In Ringbom's novel Helsinki becomes a space of the uncanny, a space of estrangement not only to Martina, but also to a reader who is familiar with the "real" Helsinki. Fabulating the city in this double manner, by bringing the strange and the familiar together, by combining referentiality with the imaginary, points to the potential of Helsinki becoming something other. Tom Conley (2005, 258), writing on Deleuzian spatial concepts, argues that it is the task of the artist to make non-places visible through creative manipulation. Ringbom is doing precisely this by making the non-places at the borders of everyday spaces visible, whether they are imaginary or express the potentiality of referential spaces.

Deleuze and Guattari (1988, 491) define striated space as an optical space, referring to how it is usually perceived through vision and mostly from a distance. Smooth space, on the other hand, is a haptic and tactile space; it is sensed through touch. In Ringbom's novel, Martina's narration of these separate spaces changes accordingly. These differences in the narration of the spaces are connected to the changes taking place in Martina's personality. This points to Eric Prieto's (2011, 23–4) idea of spatial orientation in which spatial narration is connected to themes of personality. In striated spaces Martina orientates on the basis of visual perceptions. The transformation from striated to smooth space is depicted especially through hearing. By the riverside Martina hears noises from afar and close at hand, and this simultaneously distant and close auditory sensation makes Martina one with the riverside.

The novel gives no explanation for the changes that Martina's personality undergoes; they just seem to happen. And this, of course, adds to the uncanny atmosphere of the novel. Slowly, Martina begins to have strange sensations, as if a forest outside Helsinki is calling her. She interrupts her everyday routines to take bus trips to the suburbs, and during one of these trips she steps out of the bus and takes a walk in a small forest. This first trip to the forest takes place by accident, since for no particular reason she decides to hop out of the bus. She begins to walk toward the forest as if it was her original destination, although she has never been there before.

Martina cannot remember the last time she visited a forest, and thus she feels puzzled and a little frightened when she moves deeper into it. She pushes the branches aside, and in the middle of the trees and brushwood sees a meadow in which stands a lonely stump. She touches the stump and senses its moisture when a sudden tapping breaks the silence of the forest. The knock sharpens Martina's senses: "I hear my heart beating in my breast and blood pounding in my temples." (Ringbom 1998, 71) In the middle of the forest Martina can even hear her own blood running, she smells the decomposing soil and the sprouting leaves; sitting on the stump she feels its sharp edge against her thighs. In this scene the meadow in the forest is perceived in haptic and tactile terms, and the forest is narrated not through vision but by hearing, smelling, and touching. In other words, the forest appears as a smooth space.

Martina returns to the forest many times. Every time there she narrates her perceptions and sensations by means of touching and hearing. Along with the changes in Martina's sensations, the depiction of the material spatiality of the forest changes. Once Martina describes herself urinating in the forest, which makes her feel like a little girl again. In the middle of the forest, in the middle of the smell of her urine and the different scents of the forest, Martina is able to lose all the restraints of her age, her sex, and her professional identity. This moment of sensations is also filled with the event of Martina's becoming other. This process of becoming is also made clear on the level of textual spatiality, by the positioning of words and lines. In other words, this scene effectuates a deterritorialization in the totality of the novel's composition as the textual spacing of the lines changes in radical ways:

> Ut glider en kropp på huk bakom en enbuske. Den vädrar
> i den fuktiga, svala luften, stirrar på skogen som badar i
> månsken och ser
>   fält av mörker och ljus
>   och i dem minsta rörelse.
>   Dofterna böljar som moln utan namn (…). (Ringbom 1998, 127)

> Out glides a body crouching behind a juniper bush. It smells
> the moist, cool air, gazes at the forest which bathes in
> the moonlight and sees
>   a field of darkness and light
>   and the tiniest movements in them.
>   Scents flow like clouds without name (…).

In this scene a transformation takes place as Martina's prose narration turns into verse. Martina also becomes other, something else, something uncanny, something moving away from human contours: she becomes a body with no other restraints but an emerging relationship to the surrounding spatiality sensed by smelling, hearing, and seeing. The contours referring to her human body or appearance or to her professional or sexual identity disappear, but the emerging body cannot be categorized as any non-human creature, such as an animal. This scene gives expression to the *movement* between human and non-human entities that is without categorization. The transformation in the textual spatiality of the scene gives expression to *metamorphosis as a spatial event*, enhancing the differences between prose and poetic writing.

After this scene, Martina returns to the forest to encounter a totally different kind of spatiality. The forest is no longer a smooth space, since it is filled with machines and spotlights and workmen about to cut the forest down. The demonstrators gathered there to oppose the decimation play drums and sing, but all in vain. This scene actualizes the beginning of the transformation from smooth forest into a striated space, as if to denote that the capitalist culture Martina has tried to escape is entering the forest, profiting from the cut down trees. Throughout the novel the forest is depicted as an oppositional and distinct space in relation to the urban Helsinki, but this scene actualizes how capitalism invades every space.

At the very end of the novel, Martina stands by the river with the homeless woman. Martina opens her handbag, pulls out her keys and ID card, her wallet, and throws them into the running water as if she is throwing away all the emblems of capitalist society. In this scene Martina herself chooses smooth space rather than remaining in the striated spatiality of the city center, but by choosing it she also chooses to situate herself outside the prevailing society. The small forest, however, marks the beginning of Martina's choice. The forest is depicted as the actual space of her metamorphosis, and the final scene by the riverside appears merely to be the logical ending of her transformation, of getting rid of all strings attached to being a citizen of the city. The forest is the space for opening up Martina's senses—there she begins to turn into a creature with other senses besides vision.

Ringbom's novel actualizes a multitude of spatial perceptions, since it includes both optical and haptic ways of perceiving spaces. The novel also shows how various spaces are defined in relation to each other, as is the case with the urban space of the city and the space of the forest land. The novel also highlights the reciprocity of affective processes and especially the ways they are connected to spaces; spaces, whether the city or the forest, affect Martina's personality but these spaces are also affected by Martina: the fabulative faculty of literature makes it possible to narrate this interrelatedness of affections by means of changes in the narration.

Conclusion: Uncanny Forest as the Expression of Late Modern Estrangement

In this chapter I have discussed the uncanny forest in recent Finland-Swedish prose fiction. All three works describe forests as spaces of transformation and metamorphosis. The forests themselves are set in the middle of transformative processes. By using spatial concepts as proposed by Deleuze and Guattari, such as re- and deterritorialization and smooth and striated spaces, I have captured the spatial changes taking place in the forests. Drawing on Deleuze and Guattari, I have proposed that spatiality, perception, and affectivity are tied together. I have moreover shown how spaces are not merely perceived visually but in a multisensory way by hearing, smelling, and touching.

The three chosen texts—Kaj Korkea-aho's novel, Johanna Holmström's "hybrid" fiction, and Henrika Ringbom's novel—bring forth questions and themes that are linked to notions of human subjectivity. They all describe human and non-human encounters and place them within the forest, which then becomes *the* location of these encounters. If such a space as "a typical Finnish forest" ever existed, these texts neither represent nor recreate it. These texts are filled with ethical, ideological, and spiritual problematics. My reading thus disagrees with Pertti Lassila's view when he defines post-war depictions of Finnish forests and nature as "commercialized." Instead of representing and referring to "real" forests, these novels rely on the fabulative forces of literature and the powers of the false to imagine new spatialities as well as spatialities anew. By bringing together elements from "real" and "imaginary" forests, these texts also point to spaces to come, to the potential of forming new spaces, where non-human and human creatures are imagined as living together in peace. I suggest that these three texts point to a new "people to come" in the Deleuzian sense of the concept, a collective that allows both humans and non-humans to exist side by side. Although this new collective is not achieved in the novels, it nevertheless exists as a potentiality.

I have argued that these three texts participate in the genre of the uncanny. By describing the forests as uncanny spaces, the novels give expression to the experiences of estrangement and unhomeliness pertinent in late modern societies. The forest enables the depiction of uncanny otherness that human subjects often experience. The recent return to the uncanny that seemingly takes place in the forests of Finland-Swedish fiction is perhaps connected with the predominantly urban character of late modern society. Although Finnish people today would appear to have a close relationship with the forest, it still persists as "the other," and very many Finns have a nonchalant relation to the forest and many urbanized Finns are even estranged from it. In the works discussed in this chapter, the uncanny becomes doubled: as works of art they carry on the long tradition of the uncanny forest, which is one way to express the experience of unhomeliness. At the same time, the three novels themselves express the experience of estrangement typical of late modernity by depicting forests as uncanny spaces.

The three works interconnect these experiences in spatial terms, but they do it in different ways. In Korkea-aho's novel the Other is situated within the human subject, since the non-human monster reflects the main character's despair and anxiety. In Holmström's text the uncanny is manifested as an encounter with a literal Other, as Anna and the wolf become so close to each other that the human no longer appears as human and the wolf is no longer just an animal. In Ringbom's novel the uncanny Other actually *is* the human subject, with Martina experiencing a metamorphosis into a bodily creature beyond categorization. The fabulation of the uncanny forest critiques the human condition in late modern capitalism but simultaneously participates in it by reterritorializing its features.

Notes

1. Although the forest has always been an important theme and setting in Finnish literature, there hardly exist any detailed and systematic studies on it in the field of Finnish literary studies besides Lassila's volume. Perhaps this is due to the fact that the forest with its various meanings (economic, national, recreational, sacred) is taken for granted; the meanings have become "shared property," almost stereotypes, and it is only recently, with the development of ecocriticism, environmental studies, and posthumanism, that researchers have begun to question the traditional approaches toward the forest and its meanings.
2. My readings focus mainly on the contents of the storylines, since it is not possible to analyze the linguistic forms and expressions of these texts in this chapter, although they are crucial in shaping the spatialities of literature.
3. Kaj Korkea-aho (b. 1983) is the Finland-Swedish author of three novels. His first novel (*Se till mig som liten* är) was published in 2009 and the latest (*Onda boken*) in 2016. With Ted Forsström Korkea-aho has published two humorous juvenile novels, of which the first *Zoo! Viral Geniuses* (2017) was nominated as a candidate for the Finlandia Junior Prize.
4. All translations from Swedish into English are mine.
5. Finland-Swedish author Johanna Holmström (b. 1981) has published five novels as well as collections of short stories since 2003. In 2009 *Camera Obscura* received a Prize in Literature issued by the Swedish newspaper *Svenska Dagbladet*.
6. The metamorphosis of a woman into a wolf is not a rare theme in Finnish literature and Holmström's text is another variation of it. Perhaps the best-known example of this tradition is *Sudenmorsian* (1928; "The Wolf's Bride") by Aino Kallas. Henrika Ringbom's novel, on which I focus later, can also be linked to this tradition. Ringbom's novel even places a quotation from Kallas' novel with another citation from *Der Steppenwolf* (1927; "Steppenwolf") by Hermann Hesse as mottos for the novel. Within the limited length of this chapter it is unfortunately not possible to discuss the tradition of "werewolves" or she-wolves as part of the depictions of the forest.
7. Henrika Ringbom (b. 1962) is a Finland-Swedish poet and novelist who has published five collections of poetry (since 1988) and two novels. Ringbom also works as a translator.

References

Bogue, Ronald. 2010. *Deleuzian Fabulation and the Scars of History.* Edinburgh: Edinburgh University Press.
Brady, Elizabeth. 2003. *Aesthetics of the Natural Environment.* Edinburgh: Edinburgh University Press.
Braidotti, Rosi. 2002. *Metamorphoses: Towards a Materialist Theory of Becoming.* Cambridge and Oxford: Polity.
Buchanan, Ian, and Gregg Lambert. 2005. Introduction: Deleuze and Space. In *Deleuze and Space*, ed. Ian Buchanan and Gregg Lambert, 1–15. Edinburgh: Edinburgh University Press.
Colebrook, Claire. 2005. The Space of Man: On the Specificity of Affect in Deleuze and Guattari. In *Deleuze and Space*, ed. Ian Buchanan and Gregg Lambert, 189–206. Edinburgh: Edinburgh University Press.
Conley, Tom. 2005. Space. In *The Deleuze Dictionary*, ed. Adrian Parr, 257–259. Edinburgh: Edinburgh University Press.
Deleuze, Gilles. 1989 [1985]. *Cinema 2: The Time-Image.* Translated by Hugh Tomlinson, and Robert Galeta. London: The Athlone Press.
Deleuze, Gilles, and Félix Guattari. 1988 [1980]. *A Thousand Plateaus: Capitalism and Schizophrenia, Volume 2.* 2nd Printing. Translated by Brian Massumi. Minneapolis: University of Minnesota Press.
———. 1994 [1991]. *What Is Philosophy?* Translated by Hugh Tomlinson, and Graham Burchill. London and New York: Verso.
Flaxman, Gregory. 2012. *Gilles Deleuze and the Fabulation of Philosophy: Powers of the False, Volume I.* Minneapolis: University of Minnesota Press.
Grosz, Elizabeth. 2008. *Chaos, Art, Territory: Deleuze and the Framing of the Earth.* New York: Columbia University Press.
Holmström, Johanna. 2009. *Camera Obscura. Noveller.* Helsingfors: Söderströms.
Hume, Kathryn. 2014 [1984]. *Fantasy and Mimesis: Responses to Reality in Western Literature.* 2nd ed. New York and London: Methuen.
Kittler, Friedrich. 2010 [2002]. *Optical Media: Berlin Lectures 1999.* Translated by Anthony Enns. Cambridge and Malden: Polity.
Korkea-aho, Kaj. 2012. *Gräset är mörkare på andra sidan.* Helsingfors: Schildts & Söderströms.
Lähde, Erkki. 2015. *Suomalainen metsäsota. Miten jatkuva kasvatus voitti avohakkuun.* Helsinki: Into.
Lassila, Pertti. 2011. *Metsän autuus. Luonto suomalaisessa kulttuurissa 1700–1950.* Helsinki: SKS.
Lummaa, Karoliina. 2008. Sairaat ja pahat metsät suomalaisessa ympäristörunoudessa. In *Ympäristö täynnä tarinoita. Kirjoituksia ympäristön kuvien ja kertomusten kysymyksistä*, ed. Arto Haapala and Virpi Kaukio, 125–145. Helsinki: UNIpress.

Metla. 2015. Forest Cover in Landscape. www.metla.fi/metinfo/sustainability/c4-forest-cover.htm.
Prieto, Eric. 2011. Geocriticism, Geopoetics, Geophilosophy, and Beyond. In *Geocritical Explorations: Space, Place, and Mapping in Literary and Cultural Studies*, ed. Robert T. Tally Jr., 13–28. New York and Basingstoke: Palgrave Macmillan.
Ringbom, Henrika. 1998. *Martina Dagers längtan*. Helsingfors: Söderströms & C:o Förlags AB.
Roiko-Jokela, Heikki, ed. 1997. *Luonnon ehdoilla vai ihmisen arvoilla? Polemiikkia metsiensuojelusta 1850–1990*. Jyväskylä: Atena Kustannus.
Royle, Nicholas. 2003. *The Uncanny*. Manchester: Manchester University Press.
Sepänmaa, Yrjö, Liisa Heikkilä-Palo, and Virpi Kaukio, eds. 2003. *Metsään mieleni*. Helsinki: Maahenki.
Tarkka, Lotte. 2005. *Rajarahvaan laulu. Tutkimus Vuokkiniemen kalevalamittaisesta runokulttuurista 1821–1921*. Helsinki: SKS.
Todorov, Tzvetan. 1987 [1970]. *The Fantastic: A Structural Approach to a Literary Genre*. 3rd Printing. Translated by Richard Howard. Ithaca: Cornell University Press.
Tynan, Aidan. 2016. Desert Earth: Geophilosophy and the Anthropocene. In *Deleuze and Guattari in the Anthropocene. Deleuze Studies*, ed. Arun Saldanha and Hannah Stark, vol. 10, no. 4, 479–495. Edinburgh: Edinburgh University Press.
Westphal, Bertrand. 2011. *Geocriticism: Real and Fictional Spaces*. Translated by Robert T. Tally Jr. New York and Houndsmill: Palgrave Macmillan.

Open Access This chapter is licensed under the terms of the Creative Commons Attribution 4.0 International License (http://creativecommons.org/licenses/by/4.0/), which permits use, sharing, adaptation, distribution and reproduction in any medium or format, as long as you give appropriate credit to the original author(s) and the source, provide a link to the Creative Commons licence and indicate if changes were made.

The images or other third party material in this chapter are included in the chapter's Creative Commons licence, unless indicated otherwise in a credit line to the material. If material is not included in the chapter's Creative Commons licence and your intended use is not permitted by statutory regulation or exceeds the permitted use, you will need to obtain permission directly from the copyright holder.

CHAPTER 12

"The World in a Small Rectangle": Spatialities in Monika Fagerholm's Novels

Hanna Lahdenperä

A suburban terraced house. Two teenagers in a bedroom, listening to the adults in the living room on the other side of the wall. It is an image so familiar it borders on the pedestrian, and yet it is a utopia:

> **Men välkommen till åren noll i alla fall, här kan allting hända.** För i Leos rum, det riktiga Utopins rum, som snarare är en fysisk plats än någonting i huvudet. Där finns, fortfarande och alltid, två ungar som är eviga. Det är Leo och jag, och vi är eviga. (Fagerholm 1998, 39)[1]
>
> **But welcome to the years zero in any case, anything can happen here.** Because in Leo's room, the real Utopia room, which is a physical place rather than something in one's head. There is, still and forever, two kids who are eternal. It is Leo and I, and we are eternal.

This is Diva, the narrator and protagonist in Finland-Swedish author Monika Fagerholm's novel *Diva. En uppväxts egna alfabet med docklaboratorium (en bonusberättelse ur framtiden)* (1998; "Diva. The Alphabet of an Adolescence with a Doll Laboratory (A Bonus Tale from the Future)").

H. Lahdenperä (✉)
University of Helsinki, Helsinki, Finland

She makes Utopia an actual, real place in the world as opposed to something dreamed, imagined or false, and then immediately goes on to create something broader by claiming that she and her boyfriend Leo are in this Utopia forever and that they are eternal. A similar move takes place in *The American Girl* (2009), where a swimming pool becomes "the world in a small rectangle": A place expands beyond the physical boundaries of the room in a move which is, as I shall show below, typical of Monika Fagerholm (Fagerholm 2009, 261, 266, 269, 274).

As a novelist, Fagerholm has been successful in Finland and Sweden as well as internationally, and her influence can be seen in a new generation of Finland-Swedish and Swedish authors.[2] She made her debut in 1987 with *Sham*, a collection of short stories, and her first novel *Wonderful Women by the Water* was published in 1994 (*Underbara kvinnor vid vatten*, trans. 1997/1998). Since then she has published four critically acclaimed novels, which have been translated into several languages, and she has won prestigious literary awards in both Finland and Sweden. One of Fagerholm's central themes is girls and girlhood: she frequently lets a girl be the one who sees and defines the world, and thus Fagerholm grapples with questions concerning gender, language and agency. She is also a writer of spatiality. She layers real geographical places and their fictional counterparts, or places that vaguely resemble them. Places that may already exist in literature through other authors are given new layers of meaning, and thus our images of them are strengthened and expanded. Just as often Fagerholm dislodges the connection between the fictional place and its referent by creating her own, modified version of a place. These layers are a spatial metaphor in themselves and move the discussion toward ideas concerning mental spatiality. Philosopher and sociologist Henri Lefebvre uses the term *mental space* to denote "the space of philosophers and epistemologists," in other words the result of a theoretical practice concerning knowledge, as opposed to physical and social space (Lefebvre 1991, 6). Here I am simply referring to a spatiality which is expanded from the "real" world, whether that world is real within the novel, outside it or both. Fagerholm's characters frequently go further than merely being in or inhabiting a place, they take possession of a place and use it for their own purposes. While this is not a theoretical practice as such, it is a form of knowledge creation through narrative, and it creates new spatialities which often extend beyond the place itself. It is this conflation of space and place I will discuss through key works and the kinds of places, spaces and spatialities they exhibit. This means reading spatiality on multiple levels, from place as a geographical point to space as a mental construct.

Indistinct Distinctions

Space and place are notoriously nebulous concepts and, as literary scholar Eric Prieto writes about place, "something I seem to understand well enough, provided that nobody asks me to define it" (Prieto 2012, 12).[3] However, the discussion above hints at the kind of concepts at work in this chapter. Simply put, place is a geographical site that someone has developed a relationship to, which means it can be a locality as well as, say, a building or your favorite spot in the forest. It can usually be located on a map, albeit perhaps not a map of the world outside the novel. Space in turn is more abstract and does not lend itself to geographical maps quite as naturally. While place too can be abstract (e.g. having a place on a course, finding one's place in life), I will be using space to refer to a more conceptual spatiality in addition to space as something general and undifferentiated in line with geographer Yi-Fu Tuan, to whom I will return below (Tuan 2001, 6).

Space is frequently seen as a more abstract economic or scientific quantity, while place is connected to personal experiences, values and affiliation. A geographical site becomes a place when it is meaningful to someone—it is an experience which creates signification.[4] This is not only an individual experience, however, but also happens when we participate in the experiences of others, like reading descriptions and experiences of a place, whether the context is factual or fictional. In other words, place can be seen as a way to organize space both individually and collectively, to distinguish a geographical site from everything around it.

Therefore, Prieto notes, poststructuralist scholarship has been more focused on space. Space offers a way to examine power structures, discursive networks and social institutions like language, ideology and political economy rather than the subjective experience of a geographical site (Prieto 2012, 75ff.). As I will discuss further, and as has been pointed out by literary scholars Bertrand Westphal and Jan Hellgren, among others, the line between space and place is unstable at best, and a hard and fast separation of the two is not necessarily productive. Hellgren, for example, notes that "a place always has spatial dimensions and a defined portion of space is always characterized by a specific perspective which marks, defines, and measures" ("en plats alltid har rumsliga dimensioner och ett avgränsat stycke rum alltid är präglat av ett specifikt perspektiv som markerar, definierar och mäter upp") (Hellgren 2014, 26).[5]

For the purposes of this chapter, I will use Tuan's discussion on how space and place relate to each other as a starting point:

> The ideas "space" and "place" require each other for definition. From the security and stability of place we are aware of the openness, freedom and threat of space, and vice versa. Furthermore, if we think of space as that which allows movement, then place is pause; each pause in movement makes it possible for location to be transformed into place. (Tuan 2001, 6)

For Tuan, space and place are very much connected, both on the experience level and on the defining level. What he calls "undifferentiated space" becomes place when someone assigns value to it (Tuan 2001, 6). This also means that space is something uncharted, unfamiliar and even potentially threatening. Tuan's starting point is consciousness: the gaze is directed *from* a place or space rather than *at* either. There is a direction from place which is then expanded in space (and vice versa), rather than two separate but related phenomena.

Tuan frequently works with a geographical concept of space—space may not have paths and signposts but it can still be placed on a map—but he also discusses mythical space and worlds of fantasy, be it spatial aspects of a world view or religion or an unknown area far away (Tuan 2001, 85ff.). While Tuan's analysis of different cultures and their cosmologies certainly differs from the idea of mental spatiality I am outlining in this chapter, he makes a useful observation regarding the possibilities of an extended, abstract space: "[m]ythical space is also a response of feeling and imagination to fundamental human needs. It differs from pragmatic and scientifically conceived spaces in that it ignores the logic of exclusion and contradiction" (Tuan 2001, 99). In a Fagerholmian context this means that awareness of openness, freedom and threat develops, as we have seen, into an expansion of the concrete place into a spatiality that combines characteristics of both space and place, and frequently defies the constraints of physical and geographical spaces and places. Instead, this spatiality allows an emotional or intellectual exploration of central themes like gender and subjectivity or, in a larger context, social positions and discourses.

Time and Timelessness as an Effect of Place

Wonderful Women by the Water (1997) is often seen as Fagerholm's breakthrough novel.[6] It is, on the one hand, a description of children observing and negotiating family tensions and, on the other hand, a story about their mothers and their attempts to be glamorous and modern women in the

1960s. The general tone of the novel reflects this ambition and is thus deliberately breezy, with considerable focus on appearances, objects and celebrity culture. During the winters, Thomas and his parents Bella and Kayus "live in a third-floor city apartment above a square courtyard./In summer they live in a summer paradise" ("På vintrarna bor de i en stadslägenhet på tredje våningen ovanför en gårdskvadrat./På somrarna bor de i ett sommarparadis") (Fagerholm 1997, 7). This summer paradise is also where the majority of the novel takes place, and where Bella and Rosa meet and become close friends. Save for the beach, the summer paradise is described in terms of buildings (the red cottage, the white villa), but not much more: the interior seems more important and is given slightly more detail even though it too is kept fairly general. The summer paradise is not an identifiable place, and yet it is archetypically familiar in Finland: the summer cottage or house is a place which has always looked the same, where you do things the way they have always been done. In practice, it is a place where you store furniture and household items you do not have the heart to throw away but do not want to keep at home. This frequently creates a sense of living outside of time, or of time having stopped: several childhood homes worth of paraphernalia have accumulated and project different decades into the same space.[7]

As a contrast to this timelessness and fixity we have the wonderful women by the water, who are busy performing a specific femininity, which is very much anchored in time and points to 1960s luxe magazine covers and glamorous film stars. Their communication is superficial and seemingly cheerful:

> Men Bella och Rosa då, strandkvinnorna, vad gör de, var finns de? Jo. De är nog där. På stranden, ibland i Rosas vardagsrum på eftermiddagarna också, men mest i vita villan, på verandan, i stora rummet, några timmar någongång på dagarna. Rosa dricker kaffe och pratar. Hon pratar om ett nytt koncept som hon och Tupsu Lindbergh ska vara de första att lansera i det här landet. Deras dröm Tupperware för det moderna perfekta hushållet. För det perfekta moderna hushållet, skrattar Rosa Ängel, men inte ett sådant där skratt som i sig liksom innesluter sin absoluta motsats, skrattet i stunden just innan man slänger sin bystdel i trädgårdsbersån annars bara och inte för att visa sina nakna bröst för någon, skrattet innan man drar stöpseln till en luftkonditioneringsapparat ur väggen och säger att man ju pratar strunt och börjar prata om andra saker, någonting helt annat än Elizabeth Taylors kärleksliv som alla är övertygade om att man håller på och pratar om.

Men ett vanligt skratt. Ett lätt skratt. Ett skratt så att man faktiskt tror eller måste tro att Rosa Ängel menar exakt det hon säger. (Fagerholm 1994, 111)

But Bella and Rosa then, the shore women, what are they doing, where are they? Yes, they are there all right. On the shore, sometimes in Rosa's living room in the afternoons as well, but mostly on the veranda of the white villa, in the big room, for a few hours sometime during the day. Rosa drinks coffee and talks. She is talking about a new idea she and [wealthy neighbor] Tupsu Lindbergh are to be the first to launch in this country. Their dream Tupperware for the perfect modern household. For the perfect modern household, says Rosa Angel with a laugh, but not the kind of laugh that seems to contain the absolute opposite, the laugh of the moment just before you chuck your suntop into the arbour, but not to show your bare breasts to anyone, a laugh before you yank the air-conditioning plug out of the socket and say you are talking nonsense and start talking about something else, something quite different from Elizabeth Taylor's love life everyone's convinced you are talking about.

But an ordinary laugh. A light laugh. A laugh so that you actually believe or have to believe that Rosa Angel means exactly what she says. (Fagerholm 1997, 96–7)

Bella and Rosa want something else, something new and different. This is a life project, meaning that it goes deeper than a general interest in the trends of the day. However, these are not politically aware, well-read women; they do not have a language for their emancipation. Instead, they speak in images and objects and consumption: "Where the explanations of psychological prose should be, there are lines which have been restyled as slogans or clichés, plastic Mickey Mouse measuring cups, cine-film sequences in absurd repetition," as literary critic Pia Ingström (2000, 325, trans. HL) puts it. Much of Bella's and Rosa's speech is similarly stylized, like the idea of the perfect modern household—which characteristically is instantly destabilized by the rest of the quote. Through the different nuances of laughter, the narrator shows how Bella's and Rosa's intellectual pursuits are seen as limited and probably not intellectual at all. The laughter is performative, it is adapted not to different situations but to how they want to *appear* in different situations. This is emphasized by the laugh in the second paragraph, which both reveals that Bella sometimes speaks between the lines and covers up these cracks.

The 1960s serve as a backdrop to Bella's and Rosa's emancipatory efforts, but it is not necessary to read the narrative as an accurate and uncritical reproduction of the decade. While the chapter titles explicitly place the narrative in time ("Gabby's White Angel," 1963 (Gabbes vita ängel, 1963), "Out into the World," 1965 (Ut i världen, 1965)), Fagerholm also uses cultural markers and objects to situate the novel in time. Fredric Jameson calls this pastness, which means to evoke a feeling of nostalgia through stylistic references to historical periods rather than an attempt at rendering "real" and "authentic" history. In this Jameson includes adaptations from one medium to another, for example a screen version of a novel where the viewer's knowledge of the original is part of the pastness of the new version (Jameson 1991, 19–20; Jameson 2015, 106). Rosa's and Bella's performative aesthetic with its nods to Hollywood glamor functions as an intermedial adaptation and an additional evocation of pastness. In other words, the novel does not gain depth through a representation of "real" history.

Pia Ingström notes that the novel emphasizes superficiality both thematically and linguistically and asks if there is an authentic statement behind the clichés in *Wonderful Women by the Water* (Ingström 2014a). The novel itself asks questions in the same vein:

> Men Rosa då, vad tänker hon på, när hon går med raska steg över gården bort och upp till huset på berget för att byta om till boating-kläder och måla läpparna i en rosa nyans och knyta ett vitt band kring håret för att det inte ska blåsa i hennes ansikte ute på det öppna havet? Är det som det ser ut? Tänker hon på Tupperware som hon och Tupsu ska bli de första att lansera i det här landet, för det moderna perfekta hushållet, som hon nyss förklarat för Bella i vita villan? Tänker hon på det moderna perfekta hushållet? På Tupsu Lindberghs djupa vänskap som betyder så mycket för henne som hon också nyss förklarat? Gabbes flygvärdinnor till exempel som börjar komma in i bilden de här åren och för Rosa mest fungerar som en påminnelse om att hon är mark- och inte flyg- *och att det faktiskt är en stor skillnad*? På hur hon ska förhålla sig? Vilket av de få förhållningssätt som är accepterade varav inget intresserar henne hon ska välja; martyrisk duktighet eller sårad stolthet? (Fagerholm 1994, 113)

> But Rosa, then, what is she thinking about as she walks rapidly across the yard and away up to the house on the hill to change into boating clothes, paint her lips a pink shade and tie a white ribbon round her hair so that it will not blow in her face out on the open sea? Are things as they look? Is she thinking about Tupperware she and Tupsu are to be the first to launch in this country, for the perfect modern household, as she has just explained to Bella in the white villa? Is she thinking about the perfect modern household?

About Tupsu Lindbergh's great friendship that means so much to her, which she has also just explained? About all the other things you might think she might be thinking about? Gabby's air hostesses, for instance, who start coming into the picture over these years, to Rosa mostly functioning as a reminder that she is a ground- not an air-hostess and *that actually there is a great difference*? About what attitude she is to take? Which of the few acceptable attitudes, none of which interest her is she to choose? Martyred bravery or hurt pride? (Fagerholm 1997, 98–9)

The subjects of the narrator's questions—what might constitute a perfect household, whether or not Rosa's husband is faithful, how Rosa compares to the women her husband is seeing—do indeed point to depth beneath the surface. But what is being asked is what kind of attention Rosa gives these subjects, whether she has the ability and willingness to reflect. Rosa herself provides a partial answer. First of all, she will not launch Tupperware: "She would rather die." Moreover, "she needs the idea as a façade for things she does not—well, ye gods, how can that be described?" ("hellre dör hon," "hon behöver idén som en fasad för något i sig själv, en fasad för saker hon inte—ja, gudar hur ska man beskriva det?") (Fagerholm 1997, 99). Rosa is literally unable to put her yearning into words but does make the performative aspects explicit. She cannot reach beyond the façade, which illustrates both her lack of language to express herself and the question of what, if anything, lies below the surface. However, the questions highlight the assumption that Ingström too is making: there is something to be found, what we see is indeed a mere surface. If we instead read the characters' experimentation with repetition and performance as attempts to make the clichés themselves into authentic statements, the focus will instead be on the postmodern attributes of the novel.[8]

While the question of surface and depth is spatial in itself, the aim here has been to contrast Rosa's and Bella's image of a new time with the temporal fixity of the summer cottage. Their emancipatory efforts are indicated through temporal as well as spatial markers and movement, like the perfect modern household, air hostesses as opposed to ground hostesses and successful and, in particular, unsuccessful water skiing. As a contrast, the timelessness of the summer paradise, a generic place which is expanded into a string of identical perfect summers, anchor and counterbalance their endeavor to live a more glamorous time.

Spatiality and Narrative Potential

Diva, the narrator in the quote at the beginning of this chapter, is the 13-year-old protagonist of Fagerholm's eponymous novel (1998). She is, in general, concerned with the real and true, as opposed to what she sees in literary tradition and narrative. Leo's and her Utopia room is contrasted with the Utopia house, the living room on the other side of the wall, where "Leo's mum and dad and the friends and acquaintances of Leo's mum and dad talked over each other, quoted right and quoted wrong and corrected each other and called this **we build the utopias** and believed it themselves" ("Leos mamma och pappa och Leos mammas och pappas vänner och bekanta babblade i munnen på varandra, citerade rätt och citerade fel och rättade varandra och kallade detta här **vi bygger utopierna**, och trodde på det själva") (Fagerholm 1998, 38). Here Diva builds a contrast between a perceived cliché or self-consciously bourgeois make-believe and the kind of spatiality so typical of Fagerholm, where the starting point is a concrete place which characters expand into an abstract, mental spatiality.

Diva says that she lives with her mother and her brothers "in an apartment on the third floor in Värtbyhamn and its surroundings which is a suburb in the east" ("i en lägenhet på tredje våningen i Värtbyhamn med omnejd som är en förort österut") (Fagerholm 1998, 34). This suburb can be placed on a map, partly because there is an identifiable street address and partly because it is recognizable: Pia Ingström writes that the Helsinki native recognizes Botby gård (Puotila), but that anyone can see, as the novel puts it, the desert plains around the supermarket (Fagerholm 1998, 321, 323; Ingström 2014a).[9] All of this is to say that it is possible, sometimes with a bit of effort, to identify and locate quite a few of the geographical places in Monika Fagerholm's works. I shall return to the function of identifiable geographical places below and just note here that identifying Botby gård emphasizes the importance of the suburb itself in *Diva*. At the time of the novel's present, the 1970s, the suburb is relatively recent: the oldest apartment buildings are from the early 1960s. Thirteen-year-old Diva is both a regular teenager and a feminist experiment: her first person narrative is a postmodern medley of intertextuality, metafictionality and transgressions of various norms, both literary and otherwise.[10] She is a new kind of girl in a new kind of landscape, and the suburb becomes an empty stage or canvas for her to fill.[11]

Diva creates and recreates places by giving them her own names: the Utopia room, the Island of Happiness, the laboratory of dolls, the Hobohobo kiosk (named after a fictional sweet). If something is important enough to be given a new name, it is part of her creating—narrating—herself as a new kind of subject. She does this by building a specific mental environment and even giving herself a new name. The geographical site itself is more or less of an age with Diva, so recent that the narrating Diva can construct her own version and fill it with significance. It becomes an inquiry into discourse, gender and language. In a move typical of the novel, Diva gives the reader an interpretation of what she is doing:

> Men i Östra läroverket, jag går genom rummen, före skoldagen, under skoldagen och när skoldagen är slut. Jag har **min allnyckel**; med allnyckeln tar jag min in på olika ställen i Östra läroverkets inre delar. Går långt ut i Östra läroverkets **inre arkitektur**, och det som händer där, det är mitt eget, det är privat.
> Vad är det jag håller på med?
> **Jag inlöser med mitt eget liv vad jag tror på.** (Fagerholm 1998, 41)
>
> But in Östra läroverket [Diva's school], I walk through the rooms, before the school day, during the school day and when the school day is over. I have my **master key**; with the master key I enter different places in the inner parts of Östra läroverket. I walk far into the **inner architecture** of Östra läroverket, and what happens there, it is my own, it is private.
> What is it that I am doing?
> **With my own life I redeem what I believe in.**

Diva uses the school building to create different versions of herself and her stories, and other characters in Diva's narrative use the school for similar purposes. Prosaic and out of the way places like the audiovisual library, the map room and the theater storage closet start as repositories and dumps but develop into sites of narrative potential, that is sites where stories expand a place beyond its natural limits. All of these rooms hold larger worlds even before characters take possession of them: the audiovisual library is storage for knowledge, the map room literally contains the world and the theater storage closet contains more or less fanciful detritus for creating different lives.[12] Yet they are put to decidedly different use and the traditional stories the rooms contain are warped.[13]

If Diva and other characters create mental spatialities through renaming and repurposing, Fagerholm's next novel, *The American Girl* (2004/2009), is a clear example of how mental spatiality is contingent on narratives. Again the novel, a murder mystery and coming of age story, is set in an identifiable geographical place which has been renamed in the novel, and again the real-world geography is less relevant for the moment. Instead I will focus on a scene in which a swimming pool becomes an entire universe.

In the beginning of the novel we see a little girl, Sandra Wärn, running back and forth in an empty swimming pool, swinging her arms like a swimmer and pretending to use the pool like it was meant to be used. This is a solitary scene, tinged with sadness, and seen through the eyes of a boy looking through the window (Fagerholm 2009, 43). The swimming pool comes to life only when Sandra makes it her own place by hauling some of her things there and playing in it. When the audacious Doris Flinkenberg turns up—she breaks in and Sandra finds her in the swimming pool—and empties her backpack full of treasures, the girls' things are mixed up into new, unexpected combinations:

> Och det var Doris med kappsäck och Sandra med kappsäck: två kappsäcksflickor som tömde ut innehållen i sina väskor på simbassängsbottnens gröna kakel så att allt blandades ihop. Så att det uppstod intressanta nya sammanhang och nya, oväntade kombinationer. Det ena med det andra, idéer, hugskott, smått och stort.
> (...)
> Den ena kappsäcken och den andra kappsäcken och allt som fanns däri; av detta uppstod lekar och berättelser, berättelser och lekar, lekar som var berättelser, som skulle sysselsätta Doris och Sandra i många, många år. Och föras upp, småningom i en annan verklighet.
> Och vidare, nästan upp i vuxenhet. (Fagerholm 2004, 107–8)

> And it was Doris with a backpack and Sandra with a backpack: two back packgirls who emptied out the contents of their bags on the green-tiled bottom of the swimming pool so that everything mixed together. So that new connections arose and new, unexpected combinations. The one with the other, ideas, whims, big and small.
> (...)
> The one backpack and the other backpack and everything inside them, games and stories, stories and games, games that were stories, would occupy Doris and Sandra for many, many years. And would be elevated, little by little, into another reality.
> And beyond, almost into adulthood. (Fagerholm 2009, 106–7)

The girls build worlds, they tell each other stories, play complicated games and recreate, among other things, the mystery of the American girl.[14] The mixed treasures form an intertextual universe, made up of a variety of popular culture phenomena: actors Jayne Mansfield and Lupe Vélez, Swedish easy-listening pop ("*Lasting Love Songs for Moonstruck Lovers* (Doris's intolerable music)") ("'slitstarka bugg för kärlekskranka' (Doris olidliga favoritmusik)"), magazines about dreadful crimes and accidents, Nancy Drew novels (Fagerholm 2009, 106–7). The world grows in the swimming pool as a result of stories, intertextual as well as the ones Sandra and Doris make up, but at the same time it shrinks as they disregard and even reject the rest of the world. This is underscored as the greenery outside the window grows and thickens until the visibility is next to zero. The swimming pool becomes "a world in a small rectangle" ("världen i en fyrkant minimal"), and Sandra and Doris exclude everything else in favor of focusing on each other, first through childhood play and later through love and sexuality (Fagerholm 2009, 261–76). The pool changes from something half-finished to something more than a concrete square in the basement floor and finally to a world full of potential. It is endless, but also very much anchored in the girls' personal and emotional space.

Eventually Doris's and Sandra's relationship changes, and Doris's suicide brings it to an abrupt end. In the midst of all this the pool is filled with water, but it is used mostly as a bin: no-one swims in it, and the surface is littered with cigarette ends and paper scraps. Thus, when the pool is as it is "supposed" to be, i.e. full of water, it is a dead container of revulsion rather than "the world in a small rectangle" and a site of endless narrative potential. Later Sandra's stepmother attempts to lay out a tropical garden in the pool, but it too fails—the plants cannot thrive in the damp and the dimness, and everything dies. The potential dies with Doris, and Sandra's and her symbiotic language universe cannot exist anymore. The pool has become a place again, and the more or less endless abstract room that Sandra and Doris created is gone.

The Real and the Imaginary Place

> The text no longer comes before the virgin land and uncharted seas: the text comes before a text, which in turn comes before another text, and so on in an endless chain in which the layers of paper pile upon one another with the beautiful regularity of geological and archaeological data. (Westphal 2011, 155)

As we have seen, geography is present in Fagerholm's novels even though it tends to be obfuscated and even though the places are relatively unknown even by Finnish standards. So why would it be interesting or relevant to identify the referents, what would this knowledge add to an analysis? Bertrand Westphal sees three types of connections between text and referent: text which influences the view of space, places which become text through overdetermination, and a complete conflation of text and place. He also discusses places through the texts that precede them: many travelers to Paris, for example, have a connection to the city through various artistic representations. This turns Paris into a mix of immediate sensory experience and "the intertextual construction that makes up their separate personal encyclopedias" (Westphal 2011, 152, 158).

Westphal's main subject is cities which have appeared in literature time and time again, but what are we to make of a place which, as in Fagerholm's works, is not already a text? Her versions of small and even obscure Finnish places certainly do not have the same effect as the nth version of Rome or Dublin. However, Fagerholm often uses places and spaces which are evocative, like a recently built suburb or the ubiquitous summer cottage, so generally described that they function as an icon—or a Soviet leasehold:

> I begynnelsen var kriget, och kriget, det förlorades.
> Segrande makt, det väldiga landet i öster, fick upp ögonen för vissa områden som man gärna ville ha för vidare militärbasverksamhet och övrigt; och landet fick behålla sin självständighet i alla fall.
> Ett område gavs över till segrande makt, för en tid. På just det området fanns Trakten. Befolkningen evakuerades med raska tag, alla tvingades att flytta alltså, och sedan under de följande åren var området som stängt för yttervärlden. (Fagerholm 2004, 17)
>
> In the beginning was the war, and the war, it was lost.
> Certain areas caught the eye of the victorious nation, the great land in the east, areas that were highly desirable for future military exploits and just in general, and the country could keep its independence regardless.
> One area was handed over to the victorious nation, for a time. The District was located in just that area. Consequently, the people were evacuated and everyone was forced to move, and later during the years that followed it was as though the area was closed off from the outside world. (Fagerholm 2009, 11)

To a Finnish reader this quote from the beginning of *The American Girl* obviously refers to Porkala (Porkkala), a peninsula and the surrounding areas which were leased to the Soviet Union 1944–1956. However, whether or not the reader is familiar with Finnish history the passage describes something dramatic and out of the ordinary, underscored by the fact that large parts of the fictional area changed ownership through a fateful game of poker. "[A]lmost all of the Second Cape and a significant portion of the woods and so on" ("nästan hela Andra Udden och en betydande del av skogen och så vidare") are no longer owned by Baron von B., but by the considerably less distinguished cousin's papa and the Dancer (Fagerholm 2004, 17, 2009, 11–2). Now, the fact that the District used to belong to "the victorious nation" and that people were forced to move is of little consequence to the present and the plot of *The American Girl* and its sequel, *The Glitter Scene*. Land ownership and lucrative land deals certainly do affect how the cousin's papa, a generally disagreeable and passive man, is read, and the fact that he has secured ownership of previously inaccessible land even more so. In other words, the geographical particularities are interpretive aids rather than key plot components or spatial markers.

If the geographical referent was present but more or less concealed in *Diva, The American Girl* and *The Glitter Scene*, Fagerholm's latest novel *Lola uppochner* (2012; "Lola upside down") brings it closer to the surface. The novel takes place on two different temporal levels. In the present, Jana Marton reluctantly returns to her home town Flatnäs ("Flat Cape") after receiving a puzzling invitation to an "autumn dinner party for the girls" ("höstmiddag för flickorna"), which turns out to provide answers for a series of events that took place some 25 years earlier (Fagerholm 2012, 12). Jana Marton is also the one who found the murdered Flemming Pettersson in 1994, the main temporal level of the novel.

Lola uppochner is labeled a thriller—it has a murder, investigating police officers and suspects—but Fagerholm is, as is her wont, not overly concerned with genre conventions.[15] There is a wealth of characters who slide in and out of focus, and it is not easy to determine which of them, if any, is the protagonist. In her review of the novel, literary scholar and critic Mia Österlund notes that "[t]he real main character is the small town. If you choose that perspective, the novel's glimpse-like and kaleidoscopic essence is easier to discern and finds its meaning" ("Den egentliga huvudpersonen är småstaden. Väljer man det perspektivet urskiljs romanens glimtvisa kalejdoskopiska väsen lättare och finner sin mening") (Österlund 2012). The novel is set in Flatnäs, a town at least somewhat reminiscent of

Ekenäs (Tammisaari), a small town west of Helsinki, and Fagerholm herself writes that Ekenäs and the surrounding area "really *is* not the Flatnäs in this novel, but someone who has been here will surely recognize a little bit" ("det *är* ju inte den här romanens Flatnäs, men lite kan den som varit här säkert känna igen sig") (Fagerholm 2012, 460). Some aspects of Flatnäs are so closely parallel with Ekenäs that the reader is convinced of its actual location, others so different that the reader is jolted out of the image of an Ekenäs they are familiar with. The reader experiences Flatnäs through its inhabitants and joins their creation of meaning in their making of place. However, it becomes a different Flatnäs, especially for those with Ekenäs at the back of their minds, since the reader's Flatnäs is a conglomeration of the characters' versions as well as the narrator's. A partially transformed referent, when it is as identifiable as Ekenäs in *Lola uppochner*, has the reader teetering on the border between the real and the imagined place. A recognized or suspected referent reminds the reader that the fiction is indeed fiction, and some readers may even be yanked out of the fiction entirely when Flatnäs suddenly diverges from a familiar Ekenäs.

What, then, are we to make of Ekenäs, a perfectly nice and perfectly ordinary small town, as a referent? Or any of Fagerholm's referents as geographical points? They certainly are not what Westphal might call overdetermined, and text and place are not completely conflated. The novels can influence the view of these places, as far as the reader recognizes them, but more importantly, the basic definition of place as a site which is meaningful to someone comes into play here: for a reader not familiar with, say, a particular suburb in eastern Helsinki, the referents are created as places through the text.

Potential Subjectivities

In the beginning of this chapter I called Monika Fagerholm an author of place and space. The former refers to portrayals of geographical sites—whether they have equivalents in the world outside the novel or not—which acquire meaning both through the characters who experience them and through the experience of the reader. However, it is not necessarily a specific geographic location which carries meaning in the novels. Instead referents, when they exist, constitute one layer among many in the literary space Fagerholm builds. Fagerholm as an author of space in turn refers to different types of abstract spatiality, what Tuan described as expansion and movement made possible by place.

Literary scholar Maria Margareta Österholm calls the swimming pool a girl's room of their own for Sandra and Doris. She sees a trope of the girl's room in contemporary literature, where girls are both cloistered and free to create their own worlds with their own rules, and she calls the swimming pool "[Doris's and Sandra's] own world, a place where they play with femininity and make up stories based on their own experiences" (Österholm 2016, 104ff.). Building on this, my claim is that this "world of their own" is not only a turn of phrase but a mental spatiality at work in several of Monika Fagerholm's works: a swimming pool or a closet is transformed into a whole universe, a bedroom becomes an eternal utopia.

These are neither meaning-carrying places nor undifferentiated, uncharted space, but rather a combination of the two—space and place meet or even coincide. This mental spatiality opens up an exploration of norms and transgressions, of potential subjectivities: as Yi-Fu Tuan notes, "[c]ompared to space, place is a calm center of established values" (Tuan 2001, 54). Fagerholm explores the lives of women who look for a different life but are caught at the crossroads between fixity and future; the 13-year-old who charts new ways of being a girl in a new suburb, the girls who lose themselves in each other and the private universe they construct.

Notes

1. All quotes from *Diva* and *Lola uppochner* (2012) trans. HL, emphases in originals.
2. While borders based on nationality and language are problematic at best, historically Finland-Swedish literature has been written by Swedish-speaking Finns and has usually been published in Finland. For further information on Finland-Swedish literature and Fagerholm in a minority literature context as well as Fagerholm's influence, see Malmio and Österlund 2016, 9–11.
3. Prieto is paraphrasing Leman Stefanovic 2004.
4. I am aware of the anthropocentrism of this definition, but it is apt in this context. As a baseline, all the characters in Fagerholm's novels are human, even if some transformations take place in *Diva*. See for example, Kurikka 2016; Lahdenperä 2016.
5. For further discussion and definitions of space and/or place, see Prieto 2012; Westphal 2011; Cresswell 2004.
6. Published in the US under the title *Wonderful Women by the Sea* (The New Press, New York, 1998).
7. Merete Mazzarella (1999, 134–5) notes that the summer paradise in *Wonderful Women by the Water* does not quite conform to the cliché, as

Bella and Kayus rent their house and have to renegotiate the lease every year, while the Angel family are arrivistes who have built their house. For the summer cottage as heterotopia in *Wonderful Women by the Water*, see Cosslett 2007. See also Ekman (1995, 214–8) on the trope of the summer cottage as a contrast to city life, and Ingström (2014b, 117–219) on Finland-Swedish summer cottages in general.

8. See also Lahdenperä and Malmio 2017, 158ff., 175ff.
9. Place names are given in Swedish with the Finnish name in parenthesis.
10. For more on Diva as a figure of resistance, see Lahdenperä 2016.
11. See also Ingström 2000.
12. For an analysis of Diva's foil Kari, her sister SannaMaria and their use of the theater storage closet, see Österholm 2009.
13. See for example, pp. 426–7: "Jag tar mig in i kartrummet, jag lägger mig på mage på en av de allra äldsta kartorna. En karta över gamla Mesopotamien, den är stilig, min favorit. Gnider magen mot det sköra underlaget så att det söndras av min gnidning, gnider ännu hårdare, **lilla döden lilla döden** (…) i det här ögonblicket av **totalnjutning** vet jag något som jag inte kan förklara. **Det kommer att gå bra.** Det finns överhuvudtaget ingen möjlighet att det inte kommer att gå bra." ("I enter the map room, I lay down on my stomach on one of the very oldest maps. A map of Old Mesopotamia, it is grand, my favorite. Rub my stomach on the fragile material so that it breaks from my rubbing, rub even harder, **the little death the little death**. (…) in this moment of **total pleasure,** I know something I cannot explain. **It will be alright.** There is absolutely no way it will not be alright.") See also p. 362: "Kari är ett hus av glömska. Kari är ett hus av ord. Kari är en skrubb, **den dolda läroplanen**. Kari är det samlade bråtet som ska lämnas i en skrubb därifrån fjärilen ska flyga." ("Kari is a house of forgetfulness. Kari is a house of words. Kari is a closet, **the hidden curriculum**. Kari is the collected debris which will be left in a closet from which the butterfly will fly.")
14. The mystery of the American girl refers to Eddie de Wire, a young American girl who came to stay with relatives in the area and drowned under mysterious circumstances. The mystery is explained in the following novel, *The Glitter Scene*.
15. For more on *Lola uppochner* and genre, see Österlund 2016.

References

Cosslett, Tess. 2007. The Summer Cottage in Finland-Swedish Literature: Tove Jansson, Solveig von Schoultz and Monika Fagerholm. In *Tove Jansson Rediscovered*, ed. Kate McLoughlin and Malin Lidström Brock, 209–221. Newcastle upon Tyne: Cambridge Scholars Publishing.

Cresswell, Tim. 2004. *Place: A Short Introduction*. Malden: Blackwell Publishing.
Ekman, Michel. 1995. I novembers tröstlösa nätter – om Helsingforsskildringen hos några yngre finlandssvenska prosaister. In *Rudan, vanten och gangstern. Essäer om samtida finlandssvensk litteratur*, ed. Michel Ekman and Peter Mickwitz, 209–231. Helsingfors: Söderströms.
Fagerholm, Monika. 1994. *Underbara kvinnor vid vatten*. Helsingfors: Söderströms.
———. 1997. *Wonderful Women by the Water*. Translated by Joan Tate. London: The Harvill Press.
———. 1998. *Diva. En uppväxts egna alfabet med docklaboratorium (en bonusberättelse ur framtiden)*. Helsingfors: Söderströms.
———. 2004. *Den amerikanska flickan*. Helsingfors: Söderströms.
———. 2009. *The American Girl*. Translated by Katarina E. Tucker. New York: Other Press.
———. 2012. *Lola uppochner*. Helsingfors: Schildts & Söderströms.
Hellgren, Jan. 2014. *Bo Carpelan. Rummets diktare*. Skrifter utgivna av Svenska litteratursällskapet i Finland, nr 792. Helsingfors: SLS.
Ingström, Pia. 2000. Den nyaste prosan. In *Finlands svenska litteraturhistoria II*, ed. Clas Zilliacus, 318–326. Helsingfors: SLS.
———. 2014a. Play and Dreadful Seriousness in the Writings of Monika Fagerholm. *The History of Nordic Women's Literature*, November 28. https://nordicwomensliterature.net/2014/11/28/play-and-dreadful-seriousness-in-the-writings-of-monika-fagerholm/.
———. 2014b. *Känslor äger rum. Liv i hem, stuga och villa*. Helsingfors: Schildts & Söderströms.
Jameson, Fredric. 1991. *Postmodernism, or, the Cultural Logic of Late Capitalism*. 7th Printing. Durham: Duke University Press.
———. 2015. The Aesthetics of Singularity. *New Left Review* 92 (Mar–Apr 2015): 101–132.
Kurikka, Kaisa. 2016. Becoming-Girl of Writing: Monika Fagerholm's DIVA as Minor Literature. In *Novel Districts: Critical Readings of Monika Fagerholm*, Studia Fennica Litteraria 9, ed. Kristina Malmio and Mia Österlund, 38–52. Helsinki: SKS. https://doi.org/10.21435/sflit.9.
Lahdenperä, Hanna. 2016. Reading Fiction and/as Theory: Monika Fagerholm's *Diva* as a Barthesian Text and Feminist Theory. In *Novel Districts: Critical Readings of Monika Fagerholm*, Studia Fennica Litteraria 9, ed. Kristina Malmio and Mia Österlund, 53–65. Helsinki: SKS. https://doi.org/10.21435/sflit.9.
Lahdenperä, Hanna, and Kristina Malmio. 2017. 'Ett brunetternas hjärtlösa skratt.' Postmodernism och parodi i Monika Fagerholms *Underbara kvinnor vid vatten* (1994) och *Diva* (1998). *Historiska och litteraturhistoriska studier* 92: 151–177. https://hls.journal.fi/article/view/65646. Helsingfors: SLS.

Lefebvre, Henri. 1991 [1974]. *The Production of Space*. Translated by Donald Nicholson-Smith. Oxford, UK and Cambridge, MA: Blackwell.
Leman Stefanovic, Ingrid. 2004. Speaking of Place: In Dialogue with Malpas. *Environmental & Architectural Phenomenology Newsletter* 15 (2): 6–8. https://newprairiepress.org/cgi/viewcontent.cgi?article=1035&context=eap.
Malmio, Kristina, and Mia Österlund. 2016. Introduction. In *Novel Districts: Critical Readings of Monika Fagerholm*, Studia Fennica Litteraria 9, ed. Kristina Malmio and Mia Österlund, 8–21. Helsinki: SKS. https://doi.org/10.21435/sflit.9.
Mazzarella, Merete. 1999. Idyllens kronotop. Kjell Westös novell 'Moster Elsie'. *Historiska och litteraturhistoriska studier* 74: 133–140. Skrifter utgivna av Svenska litteratursällskapet i Finland nr. 618. Helsingfors: SLS.
Österholm, Maria Margareta. 2009. Docklaboratoriet. Vårt alternativa laboratorium som i Frihet Utvecklas där Frihet Finns. Om systrarna SannaMaria och Kari i Monika Fagerholms *Diva*. *Tidskrift för Litteraturvetenskap* 1: 49–60.
———. 2016. The Song of the Marsh Queen: Gurlesque and Queer Desire in Monika Fagerholm's Novels *The American Girl* and *The Glitter Scene*. In *Novel Districts: Critical Readings of Monika Fagerholm*, Studia Fennica Litteraria 9, ed. Kristina Malmio and Mia Österlund, 99–116. Helsinki: SKS. https://doi.org/10.21435/sflit.9.
Österlund, Mia. 2012. På återbesök i docklaboratoriet (en småstads egna alfabet om flatheten, en bonusberättelse ur dåtiden). *Lysmasken*, October 12. http://www.kiiltomato.net/monika-fagerholm-lola-uppochner/.
———. 2016. 'A Work You Cannot Explain, Only Experience.' The Struggle with Readability in the Reception of Monika Fagerholm's Novel *Lola uppochner*. In *Novel Districts: Critical Readings of Monika Fagerholm*, Studia Fennica Litteraria 9, ed. Kristina Malmio and Mia Österlund, 134–154. Helsinki: SKS. https://doi.org/10.21435/sflit.9.
Prieto, Eric. 2012. *Literature, Geography, and the Postmodern Poetics of Place*. New York: Palgrave Macmillan.
Tuan, Yi-Fu. 2001. *Space and Place: The Perspective of Experience*. 8th Printing. London and Minneapolis: University of Minnesota Press.
Westphal, Bertrand. 2011. *Geocriticism: Real and Fictional Spaces*. Translated by Robert T. Tally Jr. New York: Palgrave Macmillan.

Open Access   This chapter is licensed under the terms of the Creative Commons Attribution 4.0 International License (http://creativecommons.org/licenses/by/4.0/), which permits use, sharing, adaptation, distribution and reproduction in any medium or format, as long as you give appropriate credit to the original author(s) and the source, provide a link to the Creative Commons licence and indicate if changes were made.

The images or other third party material in this chapter are included in the chapter's Creative Commons licence, unless indicated otherwise in a credit line to the material. If material is not included in the chapter's Creative Commons licence and your intended use is not permitted by statutory regulation or exceeds the permitted use, you will need to obtain permission directly from the copyright holder.

CHAPTER 13

The Miracle of the Mesh: Global Imaginary and Ecological Thinking in Ralf Andtbacka's *Wunderkammer*

Kristina Malmio

In 2008 Finland-Swedish author Ralf Andtbacka, known for his postmodernist collections of poetry, published his fifth book entitled *Wunderkammer*. It is a book characterized by excess and heterogeneity. It includes poems which have the form of inventories and catalogues, poetry written in dialect, or created by using a search engine or poems generator, assemblages of objects, words, ways of speech and forms of language, sentences, fragments, genres, and styles. It experiments with the materiality of text, practices word-construction, word-destruction, and word-deconstruction and makes use of literary strategies typical of modernist and postmodernist poetry as well as procedural writing. It even incorporates and parodies theoretical discussions put forward by Karl Marx, Sigmund Freud, and Charles Darwin, and depicts the developments of the modern technology of reproduction. The reviewers defined *Wunderkammer* as a "sensual language bath" (Ekman 2008), and characterized it as "entertaining and humorous" (Hertzberg 2008). The overall topic, which combines the various poems

K. Malmio (✉)
University of Helsinki, Helsinki, Finland

© The Author(s) 2020
K. Malmio, K. Kurikka (eds.), *Contemporary Nordic Literature and Spatiality*, Geocriticism and Spatial Literary Studies,
https://doi.org/10.1007/978-3-030-23353-2_13

written according to various poetic conventions and practices, is that of objects and their relations to each other, and to the collector, the ways objects "behave" in collections, and the psychology and identity of the collector. Many of the poems consist of lists of various things, both real and invented.

Andtbacka not only experiments with language and objects; the book even includes an exhaustive variety and abundance of spatial forms, often described in a playful and self-reflexive manner. Already the title, *Wunderkammer*, signals an explicitly spatial form of art and science as it refers to an art historical tradition which evolved and flourished during the sixteenth, seventeenth, and eighteenth centuries. Cabinets of curiosities were rooms or cabinets filled with objects that the collector had gathered according to a special logic, the principle of pertinence (Ingvarsson 2015, 54–6). The title refers to this tradition of putting objects on display and makes the book a textual representation of the tradition. Moreover, the book contains the poems' visual and material play with the spatiality of the pages of the physical book, references to real geographical places from all over the world, descriptions of local milieus experienced by the writer, and depictions of general and abstract social, linguistic, cultural, and economic spaces as well as utopian and imaginary ones. It even depicts objects and technological, historical developments that have created connections between people far from each other, such as cables that unite continents, and objects that restore sound and knowledge, which can then be moved from one place to another.

The many objects and spatialities depicted in *Wunderkammer* are curious and striking, and raise questions: How is one to grasp the listed objects and the spatial heterogeneity and excess in it? From which (theoretical) perspective, then? What kind of spatial politics does it express? In order to answer these questions, I will concentrate on two recurrent forms of spatiality in Andtbacka's collection of poems: (1) "Wunderkammer" and (2) "Chinese box." "Wunderkammer," as mentioned above, goes back to a concrete, physical, and material form of spatiality, that of the closet, and to an art historical tradition. "Chinese box" is the term used of a set of boxes of graduated size, each fitting inside the next larger one. "Wunderkammer" and "Chinese box" have two traits in common: first, they propose a (traditional) form or pattern of how to organize objects in space, and, second, they refer on a semantic level to a limited space, a "container." These traits raise even more questions: How is one to understand Andtbacka's use of these forms which both suggest a bounded, physical-material, traditional form of space? Why now, in the twenty-first century?

Traditionally, the difference between space and place has been defined as follows: space is an abstract entity which can be depicted in terms of volume, distance, and proportions, while place is a site loaded with (human) meaning, emotions, and attitudes—that is, space made meaningful by someone (see e.g., Cresswell 2004, 7–10; Prieto 2012, 12–14). However, during the last decades, earlier apprehensions of space have been profoundly questioned, problematized, and replaced by more complex views. The spatial turn has given birth to new ways to describe and understand space, including a growing awareness of space and its complexity, and the problems attached to it; there is a need for new spatial thinking connected to science, politics, and existence (Tygstrup 2015, 303).

One of the scholars who has been of seminal importance for a novel approach to space is geographer Doreen Massey. As she points out, space is not static, but is "constructed out of interrelations, as the simultaneous coexistence of social interrelations and interactions at all spatial scales, from the most local level to the most global" (Massey 1992, 80). Space is the product of relations-between, the possibility of existence of multiplicity, and always under construction. The relational constructedness of everything includes even such "things" as identities and political subjectivities. Spatiality is also integral to the constitution of such identities in themselves, which in turn poses questions connected to geography (Massey 2005, 9–10). Thus, we need a geography of relations, and a fuller recognition of heterogeneity and multiplicity on a global scale, as she argues in *For Space* (Massey 2005, 9-15).

The idea of interrelatedness is pushed even further by Timothy Morton in *The Ecological Thought* (2010). What for Massey is (in particular social) inter*relation*, is inter*dependency* in Morton's thinking, and includes not only human beings but everything: the ecological thought imagines the interconnectedness of all living and non-living things, *the mesh* (Morton 2010, 15). The mesh, which usually designates one of the openings between the threads of a net, is here used in a manner that bears similarities with posthumanism and materialistic thinking.[1] It consists of "infinite connections and infinitesimal differences" as "exchange and interdependence occur at all levels" (Morton 2010, 30, 36).[2] A mesh has no absolute center, nor is there any distinction between background and foreground, inside or outside. It is shot through with uncanniness, gaps, and absent presences, made of insubstantial things, and populated by "strange strangers"—that is, by "something or someone whose existence we cannot anticipate" (Morton 2010, 42). The strange strangers might be animal, or us, or the environment (Morton 2010, 40–2). We live in the mesh because "we are the world" (Morton 2010, 119).

Ecological thought is, then, about thinking interconnectedness and totality, and "(...) a practice and a process of becoming fully aware of how human beings are connected with other beings—animal, vegetable, or mineral" (Morton 2010, 7). The mesh includes all things and embraces an ethical attitude of profound coexistence. It is a new tool to think (and act) with, and strives to "(...) enable us to accommodate the strangeness-in-intimacy and zooming shifts of scale required to more adequately re-imagine the 'environment' and our relations with and within it" (Clark 2013, 99). It is a perspective based on "connectionist" models of mind (Morton 2010, 115) and affects our ideas of spatiality in a far-reaching way. Namely, "the essence of the local isn't familiarity but the uncanny," as Morton declares (2010, 50). Morton is highly critical of Western thinking concerned with place, localism, and earth, and traditional ecological thinking of "nature" as something clearly defined, place-bound, limited, and based on a distinction between humans and non-humans. (Even) the environment should be thought of as a form of the "strange stranger," as something we cannot predict, something at the limit of our understanding (Morton 2010, 15–17), and the ecological thought needs to think of place as "anywhere," and extend our sense of location to include "anywheres" (Morton 2010, 55).

Morton's definition of "mesh" is, I think, highly inclusive, heterogeneous, and oppositional. He aligns far-flung fields, strives for an alliance between the humanities and the sciences (Watson 2013, 2), freely mixes ideas from Freud, Marx, Darwin, Derrida, and Levinas, just to mention a couple of his sources of inspiration, and criticizes polemically but at times on loose grounds earlier ecological or phenomenological thinking (Clark 2013). He constantly opposes his ideas to earlier research; what ecological thought is *not* becomes as important for his definition as his all-inclusive definition of what it is. It strikes me that "mesh" is not only a term created to describe a new way of thinking ecological interconnectedness but is also a description of the way in which Morton combines, mixes, and uses various theoretical, scientific, and artistic perspectives. Thus, rather than using "mesh" as an ordinary "tool" to analyze spatiality in *Wunderkammer*, I will read Morton's mesh and Andtbacka's spatial structures side by side in order to point out some similar features in their way of thinking about spatiality. The interconnectedness performed in Andtbacka's book is of the kind which reveals the uncanny "nature" of familiar things, places, and surroundings—*Wunderkammer* both produces uncanny space and makes room for the uncanny. But from the spatial perspective that focuses on the mesh, it also follows that a distinction between place and space comes to an end and gives room to something new.

In the following, I will argue that ecological thought is exactly what Andtbacka is up to in *Wunderkammer*. Curiously, probably the only themes that the book *does not* explicitly discuss are those of ecology and nature. That *Wunderkammer*'s spatial politics is that of ecological thought becomes visible only after a careful scrutiny of it. Therefore, I will take a closer look at some examples of "Wunderkammer" and the Chinese box structure in a couple of poems, and, paraphrasing Morton (2010, 15), ask "Who or what is interconnected with what or with whom" in *Wunderkammer*.

Collecting and Mapping the Old and the New World

Ralf Andtbacka is known as a language materialist, using letters, words, and language as material to be transformed, circulated, put together in new ways, according to various systematics, by accident or by a machine. American language poetry and in particular the work of poet John Ashbery (1927–2017) have been mentioned as important forerunners of Andtbacka's writing. It is from Ashbery that Andtbacka imports the postmodern long poem, which deliberately strives to avoid traditional poetical depth, a hidden meaning below the surface of the text produced by using symbols or other rhetorical figures (see, e.g., Gäddnäs 2009). *Wunderkammer* includes poems from various poetical traditions: modernist poems, procedural writing, postmodern poetry, and catalogue poems, an ancient poetical form which combines entertainment and knowledge (Hertzberg 2008), and so on. Many of the various features, which according to Brian McHale are recurrent in the postmodernist long poem and in Ashbery's works, are found in the book (McHale 2004, 142, 251–61).

The central theme of the book is collecting and writing about it, and the dominant milieus in which this activity takes place are the flea markets and shops in Vasa, a city on the West coast of Finland, and an old factory where the author has his working room. However, the objects depicted and enlisted enlarge the "narrated world" in a radical way; they create connections to far away geographical sites as they "float in" from everywhere in the world.

Wunderkammer consists of six subdivisions, which have descriptive and at times enigmatic titles. The first part, called "Winks to collectors," focuses on the collector and his collections, and the second one, entitled "The spirit in the machine," depicts various forms of media, ways, and forms of how to store image, sound, and text. The third, "Persons and objects," the fourth, "The great chain of being," and the fifth called "Sweet Sistah Lockjaw," list names, languages, words, and objects. These more or less distorted objects are natural as well as produced by machines. The next part, "The new world," opens with the poem "Imago mundi" in which even the space surrounding the planet is included as the poem maps, among other things, even flying phenomena in the skies. In the poems of this part the reader comes across the Russian astronaut Yuri Gagarin, the voyages of discovery, dialogues on the internet and email messages, objects from around the globe, and poems about the West Atlantic Ocean as the author strives to find words to depict "the new world," which is so huge that it cannot be mapped with human measures. The last part of the book is entitled "Votivoffer" ("Votive gifts"), and it ends with the poem "12 assemblage (Svalbard)." After that, a couple of end poems are included.

Wunderkammer begins with descriptions of small, limited spatialities like boxes, caskets, and tiny rooms, but soon vast spaces like the universe enter the sphere of the book. The scale of the objects and phenomena depicted varies widely. In the poem "Jupiter" for example, the planet is mentioned side by side with the flea market named "Jupiter" in Vasa, the author's home town. The planet Earth also exists as a miniature object in the collection. The time span is immense: the poet imagines himself back in time to 1500 BC, but is also present in 2005, the temporal dimension in the collection as a whole being as prevalent as that of spatiality (see e.g., Tally 2017, 1–2).

Postmodern spatiality and temporality are characterized by polytopy, "the composition of different spatialities," "space understood in its plurality," and by isotropy, "systemic indeterminacy" (Westphal 2011, 43, 37). In *Wunderkammer* both polytopy and isotropy occur. First, it is filled with spaces, and places of all kinds and on various levels, and second, the spaces and places depicted in it transgress all kinds of boundaries, mixing inside and outside, real and invented, material and symbolical, local and global. Thus, also the distinction between space and place comes to an end and ceases to be relevant. But having said that, the starting point is often an enclosed space, a room, or a box.

"Wunderkammer," Cabinets of Curiosities, and (The Ironic) Revival of Global Imaginary

Repetition and the uncanny are the two defining features of the endless interconnections that make up what Morton calls the mesh. Repetition and the uncanny, "the strangely familiar and the familiarly strange" (Morton 2010, 50), also characterize the many occurrences of "Wunderkammer" in Andtbacka's book. *Wunderkammer* is not only the title of the book; it even includes several poems entitled "Wunderkammer," and the word "Wunderkammer" occurs in some of the poems. The repeated use of the word creates a semantic, thematic, material, and visual connectedness and brings together a geographical here and there. A closer look at the occurrences of "Wunderkammer" reveals its meshed features.

Despite the fact that Andtbacka's book is written in Swedish, the word "Wunderkammer" mostly appears in its German form, at times also in Italian and French.[3] Thus, it is made strange in its Swedish linguistic context, but simultaneously the interconnectedness of the word to its other linguistic and geographical forms and existence in various European languages and areas is made explicit. The poems in which the word "Wunderkammer" occurs also take place in various geographical milieus, like Vasa, Svalbard, and Knaresborough in Yorkshire, to mention only a few. Moreover, "Wunderkammer" is even an email domain (wunderkammer.fi), a virtual "container" which resides in the "universe" of networks created by interconnected computers (Andtbacka 2008, 118).

At the beginning of the book, the word "Wunderkammer" enters into one of the eight paratexts, and offers an explanation of the content as well as the main structuring principle of the book. According to the paratext:

> Det här verket … är avsett att fungera som en … Wunderkammer—ett kuriosakabinett—både till sin uppbyggnad och till sitt innehåll. Såsom är fallet med alla Wunderkammern, är det dess öde att fortsätta växa och förändras. Jag ser redan lakuner i min samling—och hela områden av nytt vetande som bör införlivas i framtiden. (Andtbacka 2008, 7)

> This literary work … is intended to function as a … Wunderkammer—a cabinet of curiosities—when it comes to its structure and its content. As is the case with all Wunderkammers, its fate is to continue to grow and transform. I already see lacunas in my collections—whole areas of new knowledge that must be included in the future. (Trans. KM)

Andtbacka's cabinet of curiosities is here openly connected to its art historical predecessors, both in terms of the objects included, and concerning the structure and logic of the way in which the objects are organized. It is also described as an organism; it grows and transforms.

The paratext declares that *Wunderkammer* imitates/simulates a tradition of collecting. In order to figure out if this really is the case, we must go back to the historical cabinets of curiosities. Horst Bredekamp in his study of cabinets of curiosities from the sixteenth to eighteenth centuries has described how these great collections of natural and human objects consisted of four categories. The first category, *naturalia*, included natural objects, such as minerals, and products made of minerals (like ancient sculptures), as well as specimens of vegetable and animal life. The second, *artificialia*, involved arts and crafts, refined objects made from organic and inorganic materials, giving the impression of dissolving the boundary between natural and human creations. The third category, *scientifica*, contained globes, watches, and other instruments for measuring and weighing, and the fourth, *exotica*, consisted of odd objects that could even be placed in every other category (Bredekamp 1995, 34–5). The collections and the various categories of the objects included served explicitly spatial aims. According to Bredekamp, Kunstkammers demonstrated a wish to understand "the earth in its horizontal, spatial entirety." He concludes:

> Thus the *Kunstkammer* combined the three vertical stages of development—from *naturalia* to *artificialia* to *scientifica*—with a horizontal plane that represented efforts to research the entire globe. In a certain sense, then, the *Kunstkammer* were at one and the same time like time-lapse photography *and* microcosms of the world. (Bredekamp 1995, 36)

The closet represents/imitates/symbolizes the world and its development, and strives at the same time to copy and understand reality. A similar kind of world-mapping dimension is also obvious in Andtbacka's *Wunderkammer* as I will show later.

What or whom, then, are connected to who or what in *Wunderkammer*? In one of the opening poems, "Ting" ("Objects"), the poetic "I" lists objects and describes the significance of the things as they come together in a collection. Here the reader finds souvenirs ("arc de triomphe, big ben, den lille havfrue"),[4] scrapbooks, mail order catalogues, spiral galaxies, and specks of dust, horns of unicorns, screws of certain kinds, "odds and ends." Moreover, fossils, various extinct groups of marine mollusks, "monsters of the imagination," as well as "an armful of stuffed birds" occur side by side with scrap, litter, remainders, flanges, feathers, "rotten mattresses," and odd machines that no longer work. All these objects are those that "you would take with you to a deserted island/bring back home from the deserted island" (Andtbacka 2008, 12).

Each poem in the first part of the book can also be seen as a "Wunderkammer" as they, like "Ting," consist of collections of objects. And indeed, as Jonas Ingvarsson observes in an article in which he studies *Wunderkammer* as an example of "digital epistemology" in literature (Ingvarsson 2015, 54),[5] Andtbacka's book relates to the original cabinets of curiosities what comes to its associative logics and view of knowledge. What Ingvarsson does not pay attention to, however, is the fact that the relation of Andtbacka's *Wunderkammer* to cabinets of curiosities from the sixteenth, seventeenth, and eighteenth centuries is ironic. All the objects listed in "Ting" have one thing in common: they have no value/are not valuable in an ordinary sense. The objects are either rubbish, useless parts of things, unknown objects that can have no use or value, or things that do not exist. Thus, "Ting" is a collection of objects that you cannot own, or have no value or are impossible to value. Some of the objects found in the poem can be classified according to the categories of European cabinets of curiosities, but most of them are in opposition to the valuable objects in the collections of early modern times, at least those owned by princes and aristocrats, the rich and powerful (see Impey and MacGregor 2001, xix–xx).

Usually, you are supposed to take with you to a desert island only one or two things. By giving us the long list of objects, the poem depicts how humans surround themselves with objects and connect emotionally to objects. Obviously, the project of this cabinet of curiosities is similar to that of its predecessor, namely to research the entire globe, but now the global space is full of litter and strange objects, which are beyond the normal or expected. In reading the poem, the reader is confronted with and made aware of the simultaneous coexistence of strange strangers, all kinds of non-living things and beings that cannot be anticipated. The reader, moreover, is connected to them, and they are made meaningful to the reader: you are only supposed to list things that are especially valuable to you to take to a desert island.

In an interview from the time of the publication, Andtbacka explains his aims with *Wunderkammer*:

We try to organize and arrange our living-space in a reality consisting of a chaotic overflow of objects/signifiers, but these spaces continuously leak, are undermined, vary. (...) To go through the garbage, the rubbish, the rest, the shit, is maybe a way to search for an alternative to, or maybe at least an opening in, the suffocating loss of alternatives characteristic to our time, in the middle of its supposed polyphony and pluralism. (Gäddnäs 2009; Trans. KM)

Morton uses the term "junkspace" to describe how in contemporary culture even space becomes junk, part of a throwaway culture (Morton 2010, 51). The presence of waste in "Ting" is not only an ironic comment upon the historical tradition of cabinets of curiosities, but also a depiction of "junkspace" produced by industry and automation (Morton 2010, 53). And obviously, in the interview Andtbacka expresses a longing for a space that would be the opposite of junkspace.

On the final pages of the collection, the word and phenomenon of "Wunderkammer" is once again clarified. First, there is a short, historical explanation of how cabinets of curiosities arose in the sixteenth century during the era of voyages of discovery, due to the radical expansion of human knowledge connected to these voyages. The collections were ways to represent a macrocosm through a miniature cosmos, and strove to combine magic, knowledge, and aesthetics. Andtbacka's use of the tradition of the cabinets of curiosities suggests the similarity of our late modern era and that of the voyages of discovery. Then and now, cabinets of curiosities are used as tools for knowledge organization and interpretations of the world made through a spatial arrangement and a mapping of the objects included.

In the second part of the poem, Andtbacka connects historical cabinets of curiosities even more explicitly to his own time and place, that of the little room in which he writes in Vasa in the year 2005. During the process of writing, he explains, the room turned into an extension of the manuscript. It became filled with his findings from the seashore, various objects that the ocean had brought, and "thus partly connected to the cabinet of curiosities of the present age" (Andtbacka 2008, 144). For the author, *Wunderkammer* is a way to examine the phenomenon of collecting, and to study "objects as language, and language as object" (Andtbacka 2008, 144). He ends the last "Wunderkammer" poem by pointing out, paradoxically, that "to collect is to approach, object by object, what one is not" (Andtbacka 2008, 144). The page contains not only historical cabinets of curiosities, the room in which the author writes and the objects included in it, but it also connects to other contemporary cabinets of curiosities. All the various rooms and historical levels are interconnected as they occur (materially) on the same page. The examination of the world becomes an examination of oneself and of knowledge. The place and the text are connected to each other without any barriers as the author notices that "the room was soon transformed into an extension of the manuscript" (Andtbacka 2008, 144).

The occurrence of cabinets of curiosities, here revived in contemporary Nordic literature, is not as exceptional as one might at first think.[6] Art historians and scholars of museology have lately noticed an enhanced interest in cabinets of curiosities in contemporary art as well as in museum exhibitions. Recently, cabinets of curiosities started to reappear in museums across the United States (Lasser 2015, 225–6). According to Ethan W. Lasser, the new popularity of this way of displaying objects is due to the fact that it invites the visitor to assume an active position as an examiner and interpreter of history, a position which "points to the deep relationships between today's cabinets and their Renaissance antecedents" (Lasser 2015, 236–7). In the case of Andtbacka, I would rather argue that the traditional cabinets of curiosities have been adopted due to the way in which they illustrated a new view of nature. As Anthony T. Grafton (1995, xii) writes in his introduction to Bredekamp's book, cabinets of curiosities "emphasized the radical changes that nature underwent over time as its powers and resources were exploited in new ways." Here we witness a similar awareness of the exploitation of nature, but now combined with the endless amounts of waste, and a room which grows full of objects of various kinds and in which all limits between humans and non-humans collapse. In traditional cabinets of curiosities as well as in Andtbacka's book, the microcosm is the picture of the macrocosm. The new view on nature put forward here is then that there is no nature.

But cabinets of curiosities had even further functions. The existence of cabinets of curiosities both in the past and in the present emphasizes the global circulation of knowledge, imaginary, objects, images, and ways of thought. Already during the era between 1400 and 1800, called "the first global age" by historians, a wide range of goods circulated across continents and global markets (Gerritsen and Riello 2015, 111). As Anne Gerritsen and Giorgio Riello argue:

> The spatial dimension of the so-called "first global age," however, should not be solely interpreted through the categories of physical geography. (...) it was also because people had the capacity to imagine and make sense of worlds beyond their own, something we call a "global imaginary." Artefacts and especially popular commodities had a significant role to play in the creation of this global imaginary. (Gerritsen and Riello 2015, 117)[7]

Obviously, following the tradition of cabinets of curiosities, *Wunderkammer* also functions as a global imaginary. Objects connect faraway places and people, and give access to "imaginative geographies" (Brosseau 2017, 13–14). Countless combinations of uncanny objects connect various places in the world, making here and there coincide. Thus, the meshed "nature" of *Wunderkammer* appears. This becomes even more obvious in the poem "Ask," which exemplifies the second spatial form to be studied here, the Chinese box.

The Chinese Box: Meshing Together Objects Within Objects

The Chinese box is a recursive structure which is produced when you carry out the same operation over and over again, each time operating on the product of the previous operation. As an inherently spatial form and a recurring feature in postmodern literature, it is not surprising that the Chinese box structure also occurs in Andtbacka's collection (see McHale 1987, 112–30). The poems entitled "Wunderkammer" in the *Wunderkammer* collection are of course the most obvious examples of the structure. Chinese boxes make us aware of the strange logic of meshing on a structural and logical level, illustrating the endless interconnectedness of mesh and the way in which large and small, inside and outside, near and far lose their meanings as relative terms (Morton 2010, 39; Clark 2013, 103).

The poem "Ask" ("The box"), written according to the principle of "nesting or embedding" typical of a Chinese box, illustrates these ideas. The poem opens with a citation by Margaret Cavendish, Duchess of Newcastle (1623–1673), from a poem entitled "Of many worlds in this world," which in itself is an example of the structure of Chinese boxes.

In "Ask," we have a list of objects included within each other. On the opening line a spatial paradox immediately arises: Andtbacka's poem titled after a small defined space ("ask" in Swedish means "box," but is also the name of a tree, the ash) begins with "The universe," designating a limitless space or world:

UNIVERSUM är en grön onyxsköldpadda.
Inuti sköldpaddan finns en mindre sköldpadda.
Inuti den lilla sköldpaddan finns en balinesisk danserska skuren i trä.
Inuti danserskan finns en leksakssnurra av fabrikatet Lorenz Bolz.
Inuti snurran finns ännu en träfigur, med en guldfärgad klisteretikett:
Kwakiutl medicine man. Made in Canada. Thorn Arts, Nanaimo, B.C.
Inuti indianen finns en lätt bucklad tennask köpt på en loppis i Storuman.
Inuti tennasken finns en japansk munk, i rödlera, som visar pitten.
Inuti munken finns ett reklamfat (diameter: tio centimeter):
Björns Glas • Porslin AB. Solna centrum 30.11.1962.
Inuti fatet finns en ödla i täljsten.
Inuti ödlan finns nästa ask.

Den är snidad av Elis, Elis Ask.
... (Andtbacka 2008, 9)

THE UNIVERSE is a green turtle made of onyx.
Within that turtle there is a smaller turtle.
Within the little turtle there is a wooden carved dancer from Bali.
Within the dancer there is a pinwheel manufactured by Lorenz Bolz.[8]
Within the pin wheel there is one more wooden figure, with a golden label on it:
Kwakiutl medicine man. Made in Canada. Thorn Arts, Nanaimo, B.C.
Within the Indian there is a slightly buckled tin box bought at the flea market in Storuman.[9]
Within the tin box there is a Japanese monk in clay showing his prick.
Within the monk there is an advertising dish (diameter: ten centimeters):
Björns Glas • Porslin AB. Solna centrum 30.11.1962.[10]
Within the dish there is a lizard made of soapstone.
Within the lizard there is the next box.

Which is carved by Elis, Elis Ask. /
... (Trans. KM)

Within the small box, an enormous universe is included, a row of structures within structures strangely closed by the surname of the Swedish carver. "Ask" is a closed space, which at the end "returns" to its origin, the creator Elis Ask, humorously also the name of a Finnish boxer (1926–2003). The closed structure contains, however, phenomena that are basically impossible to grasp or limit. Also the three periods at the end of the poem indicate its openness. Further on in the collection, the closed spaces depicted become more and more porous, as objects and phenomena flow across all limits and barriers. Thus, the meshed features of the spatiality depicted become more and more obvious. But here, still, the Chinese box, a repetitive spatial structure, is left untouched, and its uncanny, artificial features are visible.

Between the opening and the end of the poem, a catalogue of embedded objects of various kinds occur: valuable things, toys, souvenirs, kitsch, curious objects, and all man-made. During the Renaissance in Italy, cabinets of curiosities were single rooms, extravagant, fanciful spaces displaying the rare and unusual artifacts that belonged to elites (Lasser 2015, 226). Hence "Ask" like "Ting" provides an ironic response to traditional cabinets of curiosities, as the objects in it are, again, mostly rubbish, souvenirs, and kitsch. Instead of a room, we have here a box; instead of treasures and valuables, Andtbacka lists souvenirs of cheap materials, objects of everyday mass production from all over the globe for the "masses" of the world.

The depicted objects refer to various parts of the world. As a form of mapping, *Wunderkammer* connects places with vast geographical distances, spaces and places from far away and near. And here again, as in "Ting," the journeys these objects make and their relations to each other create interconnections between different parts of the globe, in a similar way as the objects in the early cabinets of curiosities did. The objects circulate globally, a movement described by Andtbacka especially in Part 1 "Hints for collectors." Through the movements of these obviously useless objects manufactured in various parts of the world, the reader is invited to imagine and reflect upon global market capitalism (see also Malmio 2017). *Wunderkammer* is, then, not only a means of understanding the world and expanding knowledge, but also an archive of global commerce. And simultaneously it shows how utterly strange the objects produced and circulating are as well as the interconnectedness of "us" to everything else, living and dead, in the mesh.

But, even more important, "Ask" reveals a meshed form of knowledge and logic related to spatiality. A Chinese box is an uncanny form of spatiality (see McHale 1987, 126), raising a question: How it is possible that the objects listed might be contained within each other? As Ingvarsson suggests, Andtbacka's book follows the logic of early modern cabinets of curiosities, which were created according to a playful, associative logic, the "principle of pertinence" (Ingvarsson 2015, 53–4). *Wunderkammer*, the tradition of cabinets of curiosities as well as Chinese boxes are spatial arrangements that question the principle of provenance, and that of origin and development (Ingvarsson 2015, 54). But they also resist and question a Western scientific understanding of sizes and dimensions of objects in space. Thus, the Chinese box structure offers a similar kind of alternative to the modern project as the cabinet of curiosities.

The space created in "Ask" is characterized by a high degree of interconnectedness of both the objects and the structure; they are all included within each other. The way in which the objects are linked to each other and the repetition connected to the Chinese box together strengthen the uncanny features of the poem. "Ask" is a strange box indeed, a paradoxical form of spatiality which can include both very huge and very small things and phenomena, all included within each other along repetitive lines. Thus it overthrows the relation of inside-outside in a manner characteristic of mesh. Similarly, another "Wunderkammer" poem shows the uncanny "unnatural" and threatening floating together of subject and object, human being and thing (Andtbacka 2008, 135). The radical interconnectedness of ecological thought means that exchange and interdependency occur at all levels (Morton 2010, 36). The way in which Andtbacka uses the Chinese box structure demonstrates this with an almost pedagogical clarity.

Wunderkammer thus performs "enmeshed" thinking. In it, the traditional spatial markers of up-down, out-in, exterior-interior, center-periphery, near-far, national-international, familiar-strange, subject-object have expired, or at least are questioned, as I will show in yet another "Wunderkammer" poem.

The Wonder of the Wunderkammer: The Uncanny Oddness of the Ordinary and the Extraordinary

In the next poem entitled "Wunderkammer" (Andtbacka 2008, 50–1), the miracle of the cabinet of curiosities is finally explained when the author describes what happens in artistic creation. "Even I sometimes get the question what makes me write. Let me explain," he states at the beginning of the poem. The writer/narrator in the poem then starts to depict the view from his work room desk of a gym in another part of the old factory building where he works. What he sees is strange: he has a partial view of people doing their exercises at various apparatuses; what he sees are merely their legs. Legs running on running carpets, using exercise bikes, training the muscles of the inner thighs in chairs looking like those a gynecologist would use—all this is described as a "concert of anonymous movement" (Andtbacka 2008, 50). He comments upon the activities he sees: "it might not be preposterous to imagine that such a collective muscle energy must not be lost, but gives force to alchemical generators." He then describes how the power produced by the exercisers at the gym is connected to various kinds of cables, both old-fashioned and new, which force their way through the walls of the building, and continue all the way through the earth's crust to the earth's core. There, they make a U-turn to return, making their way up to his part of the factory, through the corridor on the third level, and opening up a door on which "Wunderkammer" is written in white letters against a black background. Having forced their way into the room, the cables sneak up to the author where he sits by his table facing his computer, and connect to his brain. "This is roughly how I imagine it all," he closes the poem (Andtbacka 2008, 51).

The poem consists of ten verses of three lines each, plus a final closing line. The depiction of the flow of energy from beginning to end, combined with the narrative form of the poem, gives the impression of movement from one verse to the next. The lines of the poem also "flood" from one verse to the next, as the lines do not end with a full stop but with a semicolon or period. A natural law, namely that energy can never be destroyed but can only change form, is here transformed into a strange and humorous psychological-mechanical-material-technological-artistic process in which the energy from the machines in the gym enters the brain of the poet and makes him write. The text created is the product of a compilation of human and machine energy. In a mysterious and odd manner, this energy makes its way through all kinds of walls and surfaces, no matter whether they are buildings, earth crust, or a skull.

This is, I think, a fine description of the interconnectedness of an author and artistic creation, between near and far, inner and outer, machines and bodies, technology and nature, performed here and now, in the poem. Once again, the spatial form is that of a box within a box, as the poem "Wunderkammer" includes a room entitled "Wunderkammer." The gym, which also has the form of a box, now includes living physical bodies. The poem, moreover, makes ordinary, familiar practices like exercising, viewing, working, and writing strange and defamiliarized. As in traditional cabinets of curiosities the interconnectedness of objects is emphasized by displaying objects side by side in the same "room" in combinations that resist ordinary logic. The oddness of the way energy moves in the poem enhances the strangeness of the ordinary objects on display, thus questioning the commonplace way of seeing, combining, comparing, classifying—the scientifically based reasonable way of making sense of the world around us. The uncanny, unnatural character of the mesh appears as the poem imagines the interconnectedness of alchemy, technology, the planet, and the individual. Alchemy is a historical form of producing miracles, technology the current one, art still another form. Here "Wunderkammer" becomes a space where miracles take place.

In a similar uncanny manner, the connections between the author, language, identity, and place are deconstructed. Vasa in the region of Ostrobothnia is the central milieu of the collection, the place where Andtbacka and his family live and belong. The region is also the home of several other important Finland-Swedish authors. In a procedural poem, this local spatial dimension is interconnected to digital technology, algorithms producing the author's text. The introductory poem that opens the "Suite Ostrobothnienne (un cabinet de curiosités)" (Andtbacka 2008, 78), is created by putting the name of the author Ralf Andtbacka into a poetic generator. This results in two pages of variations and repetitions of letters and syllables based on the word "ralf" combined with random chosen words in alphabetic order from a dictionary, and ending with the comment "Word meld" (Andtbacka 2008, 80). Automation, machine, repetition, and the author come together and produce—again—interconnectedness, on several levels at the same time. If repetition and automation are the central features of the uncanny, we have here a poem which is truly uncanny. Not only is it throughout structured by a machine/algorithm based on breaking down and repetition, but also the way it breaks into pieces the author's identity marker, his name, is a prime example of destruction and deconstruction. It comments on the unique status of an author as a creating individual, with his name as an artistic "trade mark" or guarantee of style and quality of writing. Altogether, the word mix produces not only a form of erasure at the level of both language and projected world, but is also an example of aleatory and mechanical procedures typical of postmodernist poetry (see McHale 2004, 253).

After having erased the name of the author himself, the Ostrobothnian cabinet of curiosities continues by listing "I Poètes ostrobothniens," including names of more or less known national and international people, among them Darwin, Frankenstein, and "Lasr Hrulldén," a corrupted form of the name of another Finland-Swedish Ostrobothnian author Lars Huldén (1926–2016). By including Kafka, Mayakovski, and John Ashbery among Ostrobothnian authors, Andtbacka turns inside out the relation between center and periphery, local and global. In the following parts, "II Dialectes suédois en Ostrobothie," "III Fétisches ostrobothniens," and "IV Essences ostrobothniennes," absurd combinations of adjectives, objects, and forms of grammar are included and described as essential to the area depicted. Uncanny, strange, and foreign too are the collections put together under the title "Ostrobothian," an area that is familiar and local for Andtbacka. This of course comes close to the ecological thought that aims to defamiliarize what we usually perceive to be familiar and local surroundings.

Finally, the word "Wunderkammer" is part of the language material manipulated by the author. The word and the collection turn at the end of the book into material objects, which during reading become more and more fragmented, as if they were pieces of nature in a process of decay. This is evident in the last poem of the collection, "12 assemblage (Svalbard)," which also includes a commentary upon the ideas of Darwin as well as a parody of our thoughts of development as progress. The poem includes a metaliterary statement on the process of the collection, as it states that "this. book" is about to reach its "qlrhfqöu" as it has not achieved "öwjhöowhqewäivjew3vjqevp" for several weeks. The poem simulates an organic and/or digital development taking place, using fragments of words that are only partly possible to identify: "wrundrkammer. hålle.rr på/att. Gjyttra in i. ett murkr. av lqiurujthester./utan inbördes/ hjord./ning" ("wrundrkammer. is abou.tt./to. Chlusster together. into a rotte.n. lqiurujthester./without an inner/hjord./er") (Andtbacka 2008, 138; Trans. KM). The word "Wunderkammer" turns into a muddle or something rotten. This development erases the differences between digital and organic, machines and nature, text and world.

The basis of ecological thought is Darwin's theory of evolution (Morton 2010, 30). According to Morton (2010, 8), it is not surprising that we come across "unnatural" beings in ecological thinking. After all, "(…) what we call 'nature' is a 'denatured,' unnatural, uncanny sequence of mutations and catastrophic events: just read Darwin" (Morton 2010, 8). In evolution things do not disappear, they become vestigial or mutate. Morton then draws parallels between Darwin's ideas of evolution and art. Uncertainty, variety, and continuity are characteristic features of both evolution and language and stand for continuity and change, he argues (Morton 2010, 65–6). These ideas find their counterpart in Andtbacka's mutations of words. The seemingly organic process that takes place in the poem illustrates how art and nature are similar things which develop side by side. The poem makes the falling apart of the world it has created obvious, and the artificiality of both art and nature evident.

CONCLUSION

There are many forms of "Wunderkammer" in Ralf Andtbacka's collection of poetry, as I have shown above. "Wunderkammer" is a (material) word, collections of different kinds, a historical genre, the name of the working room of the author, a digital domain, a word and a collection that is about to become rotten. Both cabinets of curiosities and Chinese boxes are limited spatial forms, but what characterizes Andtbacka's use of them in *Wunderkammer* are the various ways in which the spatial structures "flow" over their limits. When one studies the various forms of spatiality in *Wunderkammer*, it becomes obvious that (one of) the miracles that takes place here is the transformation of all kinds of containers and boxes into open and porous spaces, and finally into a textual representation of mesh. Both the "Wunderkammer" and the Chinese box structures illustrate the radical interconnectedness of the objects and phenomena depicted. Thus *Wunderkammer* shows many similar features to the notion of mesh as put forward by Timothy Morton.

Even the uncanny nature of mesh is demonstrated in *Wunderkammer*. The repetition of words and absurd chains of fragments and objects end in a representation of the depicted phenomena in "decay," as something which is becoming rotten, something organic and chaotic, and beyond reason. The order of no-order and the interconnectedness of everything are the result of the "progress" of this book. The ideas of "evolution" and "development," thought of as being something logical and progressive and leading to better and more rational forms of existence, are destroyed and at times even deconstructed. This repetition, produced for example by poetry engines, presents an uncanny portrayal of signification beyond signification.

I have focused in this chapter on two spatial forms in this postmodernist collection of poems, and interpreted them as ways of thinking "enmeshed," as ecological thought. I have argued that mesh is found especially by focusing on its spatial forms. *Wunderkammer* is literally saturated with all forms of spatiality and "strange strangers," and the interconnectedness of everything living and dead, organic and not organic is demonstrated on various levels. Morton (2010, 55) points out: "The idea of authentic place is a powerful Western myth." Obviously, the cabinets of curiosities are already such rooms, which were highly artificial, and in the eyes of us now, "enmeshed," as they included very rare objects and combined them according to a logic which has long been lost in Western scientific and aesthetic thinking. Therefore, the tradition of cabinets of curiosities offers a kind of model for the interconnectedness of all things. This tradition from the first global era is updated to the twenty-first century by Andtbacka and pushed even further—the spaces and places *Wunderkammer* constructs are all artificial. The project of the book is partly that of deconstructing Western ideas concerning the authenticity of place.

"In the future, people might see what we now call postmodern art and culture as the emergence of global environmental culture," Morton (2010, 19) states. In *Wunderkammer*, at least, ecological thought is already fully present. The way in which spatiality is created in *Wunderkammer* points toward an awareness of the spatial turn, a development of the late twentieth century, but it is even pushed further. The global space that has been under construction since journeys of exploration began is here depicted as "junkspace," full of rubbish and waste. Thus, I argue that *Wunderkammer* shows an awareness of spatiality which goes beyond a merely artistic or "global" perspective. The way in which the collection proposes spatiality as a form of heightened interconnectedness refers to a recent development within spatiality, namely a planetary turn. In this approach, research turns away from the *globe*, apprehended as a financial-technocratic system, toward the world ecology of the *planet*, building on a relationality model and a return to ethics (Elias and Moraru 2015, xvi–vii). In this re-orientation, our planet becomes increasingly the conceptual and political dimension in which twenty-first-century writers and artists situate themselves and their work. It sees "*the planet as a living organism, as a shared ecology, and as an incrementally integrated system both embracing and rechanneling the currents of modernity*" (Elias and Moraru 2015, xii; italics original). After all, the spatial forms of *Wunderkammer* not only comment upon globalization, but also perform ecological thinking by showing the enmeshed interrelatedness of all things and spaces.

Notes

1. Despite the obvious similarities between ecological thinking and posthumanism, Morton argues that ecological thinking escapes posthuman "ideological barriers" (Morton 2010, 113).
2. Morton writes that he prefers "mesh" instead of "web" because web is "a little bit too vitalist and a little bit Internet-ish" (Morton 2010, 28).
3. The Swedish word for cabinet of curiosities is "kuriosakabinett."
4. The little mermaid, which here probably refers to the statue in Copenhagen of the protagonist from the fairy tale by Danish author H.C. Andersen.

5. Jonas Ingvarsson analyzes Andtbacka's collection as an example of "digital epistemology," a critical discourse analytic and media archeological concept that strives to open up new perspectives on the present aesthetic and cultural world and history. He argues that digital archeology and the aesthetics of the cabinets of curiosities have several traits in common, namely the combination of a manifest materiality, and an associative and aesthetic practice, a playful science in which knowledge is created through free associations rather than systematic logic (Ingvarsson 2015, 47–8).
6. I would like to thank Thomas Mohnike, who called my attention to this at a research seminar at Humboldt-Universität zu Berlin, Nordeuropa-Institut, May 2017, when I presented my paper on Andtbacka.
7. This description of the way in which objects link various places to each other differs from the "imaginative geographies" discussed by Marc Brosseau (2017, 13–14). Being a concept originally put forward by Edward Said, "imaginative geographies" refer to a complex web of power relations connected to colonialism and imperialism which can be studied in literary texts.
8. A German toy factory.
9. A municipality in Northern Sweden.
10. The name of a Swedish manufacturer of items made in glass and porcelain.

References

Andtbacka, Ralf. 2008. *Wunderkammer. Dikter.* Helsingfors: Söderströms.
Bredekamp, Horst. 1995. *The Lure of Antiquity and the Cult of the Machine: The Kunstkammer and the Evolution of Nature, Art and Technology.* Translated by Allison Brown. Princeton: Markus Wiener Publishers.
Brosseau, Marc. 2017. In, of, out, with, and through. New Perspectives in Literary Geography. In *The Routledge Handbook of Literature and Space*, ed. Robert T. Tally Jr., 9–27. London and New York: Routledge.
Clark, Samantha. 2013. Strange Strangers and Uncanny Hammers: Morton's *The Ecological Thought* and the Phenomenological Tradition. *Green Letters: Studies in Ecocriticism* 17 (2): 98–108. https://doi.org/10.1080/14688417.2013.800339.
Cresswell, Tim. 2004. *Place: A Short Introduction.* Oxford: Blackwell Publishing.
Ekman, Michel. 2008. Sensuella språkbad. *Hufvudstadsbladet*, September 23.
Elias, Amy J., and Christian Moraru. 2015. Introduction: The Planetary Condition. In *The Planetary Turn: Relationality and Geoaesthetics in the Twenty-First Century*, ed. Amy J. Elias and Christian Moraru, xi–xxxvii. Evanston, IL: Northwestern University Press.
Gäddnäs, Katarina. 2009. Poesin utanför marknaden. *Nytid*, October 22.

Gerritsen, Anne, and Giorgio Riello. 2015. Spaces of Global Interactions: The Material Landscapes of Global History. In *Writing Material Culture History*, ed. Anne Gerritsen and Giorgio Riello, 111–133. London, Oxford, New York, New Delhi, Sydney: Bloomsbury Academic.

Grafton, Anthony T. 1995. Introduction. In *The Lure of Antiquity and the Cult of the Machine*, ed. Horst Bredekamp, xi–xiii. Princeton: Markus Wiener Publishers.

Hertzberg, Fredrik. 2008. Lika kuriöst som kompromisslöst. *Svenska Dagbladet*, November 21.

Impey, Oliver, and Arthur MacGregor. 2001. Introduction. In *The Origins of Museums: The Cabinet of Curiosities in Sixteenth- and Seventeenth-Century Europe*, ed. Oliver Impey and Arthur MacGregor, xvii–xx. Oxford: Clarendon Press.

Ingvarsson, Jonas. 2015. BBB vs WWW. Digital epistemologi och litterär text från Göran Printz Påhlsson till Ralf Andtbacka. *Tidskrift för litteraturvetenskap* 1: 45–60.

Lasser, Ethan W. 2015. The Return of the Wunderkammer: Material Culture in the Museum. In *Writing Material Culture History*, ed. Anne Gerritsen and Giorgio Riello, 225–239. London, Oxford, New York, New Delhi, Sydney: Bloomsbury Academic.

Malmio, Kristina. 2017. De tings must be in order. Den de coustumers buy better. Kapitalismkritik i Ralf Andtbackas diktsamling *Wunderkammer*. In *Modernitetens uttryck och avtryck: Litteraturvetenskapliga studier tillägnade professor Claes Ahlund*, ed. Anna Möller-Sibelius and Freja Rudels, 138–148. Åbo: Föreningen Granskaren.

Massey, Doreen. 1992. Politics and Space/Time. *New Left Review* 1 (196): 65–84.

———. 2005. *For Space*. London: Sage.

McHale, Brian. 1987. *Postmodernist Fiction*. London and New York: Routledge.

———. 2004. *The Obligation Toward the Difficult Whole: Postmodernist Long Poems*. Tuscaloosa and London: University of Alabama Press.

Morton, Timothy. 2010. *The Ecological Thought*. Cambridge, MA: Harvard University Press.

Prieto, Eric. 2012. *Literature, Geography, and the Postmodern Poetics of Place*. New York: Palgrave Macmillan.

Tally, Robert T., Jr. 2017. Introduction: The Reassertion of Space in Literary Studies. In *The Routledge Handbook of Literature and Space*, ed. Robert T. Tally Jr., 1–6. London and New York: Routledge.

Tygstrup, Frederik. 2015. Plats. In *Litteratur: Introduktion till teori och analys*, ed. Lasse Horne Kjælgaard, Lis Møller, Dan Ringgaard, Lilian Munk Rösing, Peter Simonsen, and Mads Rosendahl Thomsen, 301–310. Lund: Studentlitteratur.

Watson, Matthew C. 2013. Ecological Thought (Review). *Interstitial Journal* (May): 1–5.

Westphal, Bertrand. 2011. *Geocriticism: Real and Fictional Spaces*. Translated by Robert T. Tally Jr. New York: Palgrave Macmillan.

Open Access This chapter is licensed under the terms of the Creative Commons Attribution 4.0 International License (http://creativecommons.org/licenses/by/4.0/), which permits use, sharing, adaptation, distribution and reproduction in any medium or format, as long as you give appropriate credit to the original author(s) and the source, provide a link to the Creative Commons licence and indicate if changes were made.

The images or other third party material in this chapter are included in the chapter's Creative Commons licence, unless indicated otherwise in a credit line to the material. If material is not included in the chapter's Creative Commons licence and your intended use is not permitted by statutory regulation or exceeds the permitted use, you will need to obtain permission directly from the copyright holder.

Index[1]

A

Affect, 2, 3, 6, 11, 16, 57, 59, 107, 119n6, 124, 130, 166, 186, 188, 233, 243, 245, 246, 252, 270, 280
Affective turn, 11, 12
Agamben, Giorgio, 14, 104–107, 110, 160, 161
Agape, 161, 162
Ahmed, Sara, 89, 106, 124, 125, 140n4
Alchemy, 292, 293
American language poetry, 281
Andersson, Lena, 103–118
Andtbacka, Ralf, 18, 277–296
Anthropocentrism, 233, 272n4
Apostrophe, 33
Apparatus, 14, 104–106, 109–112, 116, 117, 118n2, 240, 291
Aristotle, 160, 161, 167n4
Art history, v, 18, 112
Articulation, 31, 47
Ashbery, John, 281, 293

Assemblage, 235, 244, 246, 247, 277, 282, 294
Associative logics, 285, 290
Avant-garde, 121

B

Bachelard, Gaston, 172
Bank-note poem, 123, 134, 138, 141n17, 141–142n18
Barthes, Roland, 107, 115, 119n6
Bauman, Zygmunt, 80, 86, 106, 107
Beck, Ulrich, 80, 87
Bergman, Kerstin, 6
Berkeley, George, 225
Berlant, Lauren, 106
Beyer, Absalon Pederssøn, 152
Biodiversity, 28, 29, 40, 46, 48, 246
Blank space, 16, 169–181
Born translated (literature), 196, 197
Braidotti, Rosi, 49n16, 239

[1] Note: Page numbers followed by 'n' refer to notes.

Bredekamp, Horst, 284, 287
Bunch, Mads, 6, 7

C
Cabinet of curiosities, 18, 283–286, 290, 291, 293, 296n3
Cage, John, 125
Capitalism, 3, 13, 14, 29, 33, 81, 105, 124, 133–139, 141n17, 142n19, 142n20, 231, 240, 241, 246, 251, 254, 290
Cartographic novel, 68–70, 74
Catalogue poems, 281
Caucus-race, 36, 37, 45
Certeau, Michel de, 1
Chinese box, 18, 278, 288–291, 295
Christensen, Inger, 180
Class, 19n3, 56, 60, 61, 81, 92, 132, 133, 141n16
Cognitive mapping, 13, 57, 63, 67, 69, 70
Cohabitation, 80, 85–91
Collage, 125
(The) Commons, 13, 25–48
Community, 5, 6, 13, 19n2, 29, 43, 46, 47, 69, 71, 74, 75, 81–85, 89–91, 96, 97, 132, 226
Conceptual poetry, 128
Conte, Joseph, 123
Contemporary poetry, 139
Continental North, 5, 18
Cox, Steve, 162
Culler, Jonathan, 33
Cultural appropriation, 59, 60, 68

D
Danish literature, 13, 25, 30, 31, 46, 47, 48n2
Darwin, Charles, 277, 280, 293, 294
Dass, Peter, 153
Defamiliarization, 294
Deleuze, Gilles, 10, 13, 17, 18, 26, 30, 35–38, 49n15, 124, 127, 188, 196, 212–215, 228, 233–237, 241, 243–249, 252
Depression, 123, 125–130, 139, 239
Derrida, Jacques, 10, 50n22, 187, 280
Desubjectification, 14, 104, 106, 115, 117
Detective story, 86
Deterritorialization, 26, 35, 188, 235–237, 239, 242, 247, 250, 252
Dispositive, 104
Diversity, 19n3, 29, 80, 91, 225
Documentary, 128, 133, 139, 179
Dramatic monologue, 126, 131, 132, 157
Druker, Elina, 85, 86, 90
DuBois, Thomas A., 9
Dystopian space, 13, 56, 57, 62, 64

E
Ecological thought, 18, 279–281, 291, 294–296
Ekelöf, Gunnar, 178
Eliot, T. S., 123
Emotion, 14, 15, 105, 107, 110, 121–140, 228n3, 279
Entre-deux, 4, 64
Environment, 3, 7, 11, 13, 30, 34, 37, 40, 42, 45, 48n8, 58, 63, 67, 80, 85, 89, 92, 96, 112, 166, 176, 177, 211–213, 216, 217, 219–221, 223–225, 227, 231, 243, 266, 280
Epiphany, 175, 223, 224
Epistolography, 150
Estrangement, 189, 240, 249, 252–254
Event, 30, 33, 43, 47, 81, 91, 96, 126, 178, 211, 212, 216, 217, 221, 222, 224, 229n8, 242, 243, 246, 250, 251, 270, 294

Evolution, 47, 294, 295
Experimental poetry, 14, 15, 121–140

F
Fabulation, 231–254
Fagerholm, Monika, 16, 18, 185–201, 257–272
Falk Jensby, Niels Henning, 39–43, 50n21
Fatness, 132, 133
Federici, Silvia, 39, 48n6, 50n17
Feeling, 14, 41, 43, 58, 68, 79, 109, 124, 125, 127, 132, 133, 137, 140n5, 158, 172, 221, 223, 245, 260, 263
Feminist criticism, 179
Finance capitalism, 14, 122, 133–138, 142n20
Finland-Swedish literature, 188, 189, 198, 272n2
Finnish literature, 15, 122, 202n6, 231–233, 254n1, 254n6
Flaxman, Gregory, 234
Flea markets, 18, 281, 282, 289
Flickering effect, 17, 212, 213
Fold, 212–221, 227, 228
Forest, 8, 17, 18, 85, 180, 231–254, 259
Foucault, Michel, 10, 86, 104, 105, 118n2, 171
Found material, 15, 123, 125, 139
Freud, Sigmund, 277, 280

G
Gender, 18, 19n3, 81, 82, 91, 114, 127, 141n8, 258, 260, 266
Geoaesthetics, 10
Geocriticism, v, vi, viii, 3, 13, 26, 57, 188, 213
Geophilosophy, v, 236, 247
Geopoetics, v, 10

Gerritsen, Anne, 287, 288
Glissant, Édouard, 36, 49n15
Global imaginary, 277–296
Globalization, vi, 6, 7, 10, 11, 57, 200, 296
Godard, Jean-Luc, 125
Goldsmith, Kenneth, 129, 130
Grafton, Anthony T., 287
Gregg, Melissa, 11, 124
Guattari, Félix, 13, 18, 26, 30, 35, 38, 49n15, 127, 188, 196, 233–237, 241, 243–249, 252

H
Hagalund, 13, 56–59, 64, 68–74
Hansen, K.T., 6
Haraway, Donna, 2
Heiberg, Luise, 26, 27
Heidegger, Martin, 104, 118n1
Heikkinen, Tytti, 121–123, 130–132, 134, 139, 140n1
Hellgren, Jan, 259
Helsinki, vii, 17, 140n7, 211, 215–221, 225–227, 240, 241, 247–251, 265, 271
Heterotopic interference, 17, 212, 215, 216, 220, 227
Hjorth, Vigdis, 109–112, 116
Holmström, Johanna, 17, 232, 234, 236, 239–247, 252, 253, 254n5, 254n6
Homiletics, 150
Homotopic consensus, 215, 216, 219, 220, 227
Hoover, Paul, 123, 140n3
Hutcheon, Linda, 129

I
Iconotext, 82, 87
Imaginative geographies, 1, 8, 288, 297n7

Imaginative space, 171
Imago mundi, 225
In-betweenness, 4, 5
Individualism, 80, 89, 91
Inequality, 6, 64, 75, 93, 94
Ingström, Pia, 262–265, 273n7
Ingvarsson, Jonas, 277, 285, 290, 297n5
Inscription, 154, 169, 173, 179
Insecurity, 166
Interconnectedness, 2, 10–12, 14, 17, 18, 33, 34, 279, 280, 283, 288, 290–293, 295, 296
Intermediality, 187, 192, 201n2, 202n5
Interpellation, 89, 111
Intersectional, 19n3, 81
Interstitial place, 64
Irony, 80, 87, 90, 129, 130
Iser, Wolfgang, 171
Isotropy, 282

J

Jameson, Fredric, 10, 13, 15, 57, 63, 69, 70, 124, 125, 140n5, 263
Jasiensko, Jean-Michel, 162
Joensuu, Juri, 126, 132
Johannesen, Georg, 150
Joyce, Laura, 133

K

Keen, Suzanne, 124, 140n4
Kilmartin, Joanna, 162
Kittler, Friedrich, 109, 116, 242
Knausgård, Karl Ove, 7
Kokko, Karri, 121, 123, 125–131, 133, 134, 139, 141n7, 141n11
Korkea-aho, Kaj, 17, 232, 234, 236–240, 252, 253, 254n3

L

La banlieue, 56
Lacuna, 169, 171, 172, 174, 283
Landscape of memory, 175
Language ideology, 187, 259
Lasser, Ethan W., 287, 290
Lassila, Pertti, 232, 233, 241, 253, 254n1
Late capitalist society, 46, 57, 226
Late modern society, 98n1, 124, 221, 253
Layout, 16, 169, 172, 173, 177, 181n2
Lefebvre, Henri, 10, 81, 96, 236, 258
Leibniz, Gottfried Wilhelm, 213–215, 225
Lem, Stanislav, 159, 162
Lethem, Jonathan, 211
Lidegaard, Liv Sejrbo, 30, 31, 43–46, 50n24
Lidman, Sara, 179
Lindholm, Audun, 159, 167n3
Linear orientation, 176
Literary multilingualism, 16, 186, 187, 198
Longing, 14, 45, 103–118, 176, 245, 286
Long poem, 15, 31, 150, 151, 153, 281
Løppenthin, Lea, 35–40, 43, 45, 49n14
Love, 14, 27, 39, 49n12, 82, 103–118, 134–139, 161, 162, 170, 189, 190, 195, 262, 268
Lyotard, Jean-François, 10

M

Magnus, Olaus, 152
Manghani, Sunil, 106
Marginalization, 37, 56, 63, 94
Martinson, Harry, 179
Marx, Karl, 29, 106, 277, 280

Massey, Doreen, vii, 5, 9, 10, 13, 81, 82, 84, 89, 91, 97, 279
Material language, 173, 178
Material turn, 11
McHale, Brian, 17, 122, 140n3, 212–215, 227, 281, 288, 290, 293
Mental space, 114, 117, 258
Mesh, 18, 277–296, 296n2
Metamorphosis, 191, 235, 247, 249, 251–253, 254n6
Migration, 55, 59, 60, 64
Million Housing Programme, 13, 55, 56, 71–74
Modernist poetry, 123
Moretti, Franco, 12
Morton, Timothy, 3, 18, 48n8, 49n13, 279–281, 283, 286, 288, 291, 294–296, 296n1, 296n2
Multicultural society, 60, 64
Multifocality, 70
Multilingualism, 15, 16, 186–189, 192, 197–199
Munch, Edward, 140n5
Music, vi, 59, 61, 64–70, 75, 84, 185–187, 190, 191, 193, 198, 199, 201n2, 202n3, 202n4, 203n14, 214, 268

N
Nationalism, 5, 19n1, 187, 197
Natureculture, 2
Nemo, 57–60, 62–65, 67–71, 73, 75
Nestingen, Andrew, 6
New Sentence, 15, 126, 140n6
Nikolajeva, Maria, 79, 83, 87, 88, 90
Niremburg, Boris, 162
Node, 9, 10
Nomadic distribution, 26, 36–38, 45
Non-human, 3, 11, 17, 18, 232–234, 237, 240, 245–247, 251, 253, 280, 287

Nordenhof, Asta Olivia, 31–34, 38, 40, 43, 44
Nordic Noir, 6, 8
(The) North, vii, 4, 5, 8, 9, 13, 18, 19n1, 56, 126, 152
Norwegian literature, 1, 150

O
Olsson Hagalund, Olle, 71, 74, 75
Ørstavik, Hanne, 112, 113, 115, 116
Österholm, Maria Margareta, 186, 193, 195, 203n13, 203n17, 272
Österlund, Mia, 186, 270

P
Pastness, 263
Picturebooks, 18, 79–98
Place effect, 75
Planetary turn, 11, 18, 296
Poetic form predating Romanticism, 149, 155, 158
Poetics generator, 277, 293
Poetics of boredom, 129
Poetic topology, 180
Pohjavirta, Tatu, 141n18
Pollari, Niina, 131, 132
Polytopy, 4, 282
Portal figure, 170
Post-apocalyptic, 218–220, 228n5
Postcolonial experience, 70
Post-industrial, 125
Postmodern, 3, 4, 6, 10, 11, 15, 18, 55–75, 86, 122–126, 129, 149–166, 179, 186
  literature, 17, 151, 212, 213, 227, 228, 288
  space, 3, 18, 69, 212
  storyworld, 17, 212
Postmodernism, 6, 7, 10, 122–124, 151

Postmodernist
  long poem, 281
  poetry, 123, 277, 293
Post-structuralist theories, 121
Powers of the false, 234, 235, 239, 240, 248, 253
Prendergast, Christopher, 223
Prieto, Eric, 4, 13, 18, 56, 57, 63, 64, 70, 74, 75, 76n7, 76n8, 249, 259, 272n3, 279
Procedural poetry, 126
Prose poetry, 126
Public space, 12, 15, 83, 122–125, 128, 131, 134, 139
Pynchon, Thomas, 125

R
Reassertion of space, 10
Repetition, 113, 116, 186, 189, 190, 196, 200, 201, 202n3, 202n4, 203n18, 204n24, 262, 264, 283, 291, 293, 295
Reterritorialization, 26, 188, 236, 244
Rhetorics, 6, 150, 152, 153, 157, 158
Riello, Giorgio, 287, 288
Rimbereid, Øyvind, 15, 16, 149–166
Rimminen, Mikko, 17, 211–228
Ringbom, Henrika, 17, 216, 232, 234, 236, 239, 240, 247–253, 254n6, 254n7
Ringgaard, Dan, 9
Rougemont, Denis de, 107, 116
Royle, Nicholas, 240, 242, 246
Rynell, Elisabeth, 16, 169–181

S
Saarikoski, Pentti, 136
Safka, Melanie, 186, 192–196, 199, 201, 202n11, 203n13, 203n16, 203n19
Salmenniemi, Harry, 141n9

Sandberg, Mark B., 4, 5, 8, 9
Santanen, Eino, 121, 123, 124, 133–140, 141n17, 141n18
Sattarvandi, Hassan Loo, 13, 55–75
Schriftraum, 16, 172, 173
Seigworth, Gregory J., 11
Sentiment, 34, 124, 132, 140n4, 217
Shelley, Mary, 220
Sibelius, Jean, 126
Silliman, Ron, 140n6
Smartphone, 14, 103–118
Smooth space, 30, 236, 248–252
Social relations, 13, 79–98, 236
Soderbergh, Steven, 162
Södergran, Edith, 179
Soja, Edward, 10
Solidarity, 33, 47
Sondrup, Steven P., 4, 5, 8, 9
Sonnevi, Göran, 150
Space of readers response, 171
Space of transformation, 231–254
Spatial politics, 278, 281
Spatial turn, vii, 8–12, 249, 279, 296
Spatiotextual boundary, 177
Stavanger, 149–166
Storied spaces, vii, 1–18
Strange strangers, 279, 280, 285, 295
Stratigraphy, 70
Striated space, 26, 30, 247–252
Structure of feeling, 15
Subjectification, 14, 104, 105, 115, 117
Suburb, 55–75, 250, 265, 269, 271, 272
Sullivan, Gary, 130, 131, 141n12
Swedish literature, 188, 189, 198, 272n2

T
Tally, Robert T. Jr., 5, 10, 187, 282
Tarkovsky, Andrei, 159, 162
Technique of gaps, 169
Territorialization, 26, 31, 35, 36, 49n15, 246

Text-as-building, 171–178
Textual interlinkage, 174
Textual space, 8, 177
Textus, 172, 178
Throwntogetherness, 13, 81, 84, 89, 91, 97
Topographic literature, 149, 150, 152, 164
Topographic verse, 15, 16, 149–166
Topos, 68, 73, 116
Translation, 16, 32, 33, 48n1, 49n14, 50n21, 50n24, 119n5, 130, 141n13, 155, 161, 162, 181n1, 181n3, 186–192, 194, 196–201, 202n5, 203n16, 228n1, 254n4
Tuan, Yi-Fu, 18, 259, 260, 271, 272
Typographical landscape, 16, 180

U
Ulven, Tor, 154
(The) uncanny, 17, 221, 231–254, 280, 281, 283, 288–295
Unhomeliness, 240, 253
Utopian space, 73

V
Vanitas, 154, 177
Verne, Jules, 62
Visual construction, 13, 79
Voyages of discovery, 282, 286

W
Waade, A.M., 6
Walkowitz, Rebecca L., 16, 196, 197, 201, 204n25, 204n28
Warhol, Andy, 125
Waste Land, 123
Westphal, Bertrand, 3, 4, 13, 16–18, 25, 26, 30, 57, 70, 188, 212–216, 220, 227, 235, 259, 268, 269, 271, 272n5, 282
Williams, Raymond, 15, 125
Wunderkammer, 278, 281, 283–288, 291–295

Y
Yildiz, Yasemin, 187, 198

The manufacturer's authorised representative in the EU is Springer Nature Customer Service Centre GmbH, Europaplatz 3, 69115 Heidelberg, Germany. If you have any concerns regarding our products, please contact ProductSafety@springernature.com

Printed and bound by CPI Group (UK) Ltd, Croydon, CR0 4YY
23/03/2026
02076670-0005